The Sciences of Homosexuality in Early Modern Europe

The Sciences of Homosexuality in Early Modern Europe investigates early modern scientific accounts of same-sex desires and the shapes they assumed in everyday life. It explores the significance of those representations and interpretations from around 1450 to 1750, long before the term homosexuality was coined and accrued its current range of cultural meanings.

This collection establishes that efforts to produce scientific explanations for same-sex desires and sexual behaviors are not a modern invention, but have long been characteristic of European thought. The sciences of antiquity had posited various types of same-sexual affinities rooted in singular natures. These concepts were renewed, elaborated, and reassessed from the late medieval scientific revival to the early Enlightenment. The deviance of such persons seemed outwardly inscribed upon their bodies, to be documented in treatises and case studies. It was attributed to diverse inborn causes such as distinctive anatomies or physiologies, and embryological, astrological, or temperamental factors.

This original book freshly illuminates many of the questions that are current today about the nature of homosexual activity and reveals how the early modern period and its scientific interpretations of same-sex relationships are fundamental to understanding the conceptual development of contemporary sexuality.

Kenneth Borris is Professor of English at McGill University and is a recipient of the MacCaffrey Award and a Canada Research Fellowship. His previous books are *Same-Sex Desire in the English Renaissance* (Routledge, 2004), *Allegory and Epic in English Renaissance Literature: Heroic Form in Sidney, Spenser, and Milton* (Cambridge, 2001), *Spenser's Poetics of Prophecy* (University of Victoria, 1991), and a co-edited collection, *The Affectionate Shepherd: Celebrating Richard Barnfield* (Associated University Presses, 2001).

George Rousseau is Co-Director of the Centre for the History of Childhood at Oxford University. His previous publications include *Nervous Acts: Essays on Literature, Culture and Sensibility* (Palgrave Macmillan, 2004), *Framing and Imagining Disease in Cultural History* (Palgrave Macmillan, 2003); (with Roy Porter) *Gout: The Patrician Malady* (Yale, 1998), *Pre- and Post-Modern Discourses: Medical, Scientific, Anthropological* (Manchester, 1991).

The Sciences of Homosexuality in Early Modern Europe

**Edited by
Kenneth Borris and
George Rousseau**

Routledge
Taylor & Francis Group

LONDON AND NEW YORK

First published 2008
by Routledge
2 Park Square, Milton Park, Abingdon, Oxon OX14 4RN

Simultaneously published in the USA and Canada
by Routledge
270 Madison Ave, New York, NY 10016

Routledge is an imprint of the Taylor & Francis Group, an informa business

© 2008 Kenneth Borris and George Rousseau

Typeset in Baskerville by
HWA Text and Data Management, Tunbridge Wells
Printed and bound in Great Britain by
Antony Rowe Ltd, Chippenham, Wiltshire

British Library Cataloguing in Publication Data
A catalogue record for this book is available from the British Library

Library of Congress Cataloging-in-Publication Data
The sciences of homosexuality in early modern Europe / edited by
Kenneth Borris and George Rousseau.
  p. cm.
  Includes index.
  1. Homosexuality–Europe–History. 2. Gays–Identity. 3. Gays–Europe–
History. 4. Homosexuality in literature. I. Borris, Kenneth.
  II. Rousseau, G. S. (George Sebastian)
HQ76.2.E9S35 2008
306.76'60940903–dc22   2007017384

ISBN10: 0–415–40321–9 (hbk)
ISBN10: 0–415–44692–9 (pbk)

ISBN13: 978–0–415–40321–4 (hbk)
ISBN13: 978–0–415–44692–1 (pbk)

Contents

PART II
Divinatory, speculative and other sciences

PART III
Science and sapphisms

Figures

Contributors

Harriette Andreadis is Professor of English at Texas A & M University. Her books include *Sappho in Early Modern England* (2001), awarded the 2002 Roland Bainton Prize for Literature. Having recently published a new essay on Katherine Philips and homoerotic desire in *SEL*, she is investigating the early modern afterlife of Ovidian erotics in Dryden's *Heroides*.

Cristian Berco, Assistant Professor of History at Bishop's University, has authored *Sexual Hierarchies, Public Status: Men, Sodomy, and Society in Spain's Golden Age* (2007). His essays have appeared in various serials and collections including *Sixteenth Century Journal, Medieval Encounters, Confraternitas*, and *Power and Gender in Renaissance Spain*. He is currently researching the social history of venereal disease in early modern Toledo.

Kenneth Borris, Professor of English at McGill University and a former Canada Research Fellow, has authored *Allegory and Epic in English Renaissance Literature* (2000) and *Spenser's Poetics of Prophecy* (1991); edited *Same-Sex Desire in the English Renaissance: A Sourcebook of Texts, 1470-1650* (2004); and co-edited *The Affectionate Shepherd: Celebrating Richard Barnfield* (2001). His current research deals with Spenser's Platonism, allegory, and early modern engagements with the varieties of unbelief.

Guido Giglioni is the Cassamarca Lecturer in Neo-Latin Cultural and Intellectual History at the Warburg Institute, University of London. He has authored *Immaginazione e malattia* (2000), on Jean Baptiste van Helmont, and edited Francis Glisson's manuscripts relating to *De natura substantiae energetica* (1996). Currently he is working on Girolamo Cardano.

Allison B. Kavey is Assistant Professor of History at CUNY John Jay College. Her *Books of Secrets in England, 1550-1600*, is forthcoming from the University of Illinois Press in 2007. She is co-editing a collection on the natural philosophy and cultural currency of J. M. Barrie's *Peter Pan*, forthcoming from Rutgers University Press.

Derek Neal is Assistant Professor of History at Nipissing University. Having completed *The Masculine Self: Men in Late Medieval England*, forthcoming from the University of Chicago Press, he is now studying gender in social relations among the English clergy, 1460-1560.

P. G. Maxwell-Stuart is a lecturer in History at the University of St. Andrews. His books include *The Occult in Early Modern Europe* (1999); Martin Del Rio's *Investigations into Magic*, an edited translation (2001); *Satan's Conspiracy: Magic and Witchcraft in Sixteenth Century Scotland* (2001); and *The Occult in Mediaeval Europe* (2005). Forthcoming are a new edited translation of the *Malleus Maleficarum* (2007) and a history of alchemy.

George Rousseau is Co-Director of the Centre for the History of Childhood at Oxford University. His books include *This Long Disease, My Life: Alexander Pope and the Sciences* (1968), with Marjorie Hope Nicolson; *The Languages of Psyche: Mind and Body in Enlightenment Thought* (1990); the trilogy *Pre- and Post-Modern Discourses: Medical, Scientific, Anthropological* (1991); *Gout: The Patrician Malady* (1998), with Roy Porter; *Framing and Imagining Disease in Cultural History* (2003), *Nervous Acts: Essays on Literature, Culture, and Sensibility* (2004), and *Children and Sexuality: The Greeks to the Great War* (2007).

H. Darrel Rutkin, Visiting Assistant Professor of the History of Science at the University of Oklahoma, has authored *Reframing the Scientific Revolution: Astrology, Natural Philosophy and the History of Science* (forthcoming from Kluwer, 2008), and co-edited *Horoscopes and Public Spheres* (2005). His essays have appeared in *Galileana* and *The Cambridge History of Science*, Vol 3: *Early Modern Science*.

Winfried Schleiner is Professor of English at the University of California, Davis. His books include *Melancholy, Genius, and Utopia in the Renaissance* (1991) and *Medical Ethics in the Renaissance* (1995). His articles range widely through the early modern history of medicine, gender, sexuality, and sport.

Kevin Siena is Associate Professor of History at Trent University. He has authored *Venereal Disease, Hospitals and the Urban Poor: London's "Foul Wards"1600–1800* (2004); and edited *Sins of the Flesh: Responding to Sexual Disease in Early Modern Europe* (2005).

Faith Wallis is Associate Professor of History and the Social Studies of Medicine at McGill University. Her various edited volumes include *Medieval Science, Technology and Medicine: An Encyclopedia* (2005), co-edited with Steven Livesay and Thomas Glick. Her essays on the transmission of medieval medical learning and on medieval time-reckoning have appeared in *Traditio, Social History of Medicine, Journal of the History of Medicine and Allied Sciences*, and numerous scholarly collections.

Preface and acknowledgments

Though we ordinarily work in different periods, we were brought together by a shared perception of sexual history. To both of us it appeared that the scientific aspects of early modern (and indeed premodern) European same-sexual history had as yet received insufficient attention. And yet they have much importance for understanding the prehistory and history of so-called homosexuality, because it has been conceptually a scientific development. To what extent and in what ways, for example, did the early modern sciences anticipate or support conceptions of constitutional sexual deviance and same-sexual identities, and prefigure or precondition the later emergence of the "homosexual"? While a single collection cannot resolve such large and complex questions that our book's subject entails, its survey of related disciplines, texts, and issues expedites the further research and historiographical debate that are necessary, and that was our aim in launching this venture.

The science of sex differences–which have become conceptualized as "sexualities"–was an emergent intellectual concern long before the later nineteenth century. The remains of Greco-Roman antiquity show it was already then a developing subject. It underwent further development in the Latin West, and our authors demonstrate how a remarkable range of resources for exploring its possibilities were available in the former sciences from around 1450 to 1750. Those who participated in same-sexual relations could thus be subdivided into various categories and subcategories; assigned distinctive constitutions, deviant anatomies, and physiologies; demarcated by a range of publicized morphologies; and attributed to embryological, astral, and complexional etiologies. They could be treated to surgical, punitive, and other therapeutic regimes, while parents could obtain advice on how not to conceive sexually suspect fey sons and viragos. Physicians could inspect male anuses for forensic assessment of the degree of their conversion to sodomitical pleasures, whereas venereological writers meanwhile long ignored the possibilities of same-sexual transmission in their treatises on the pox. Though haunted by studied silences and profound repressions, the former sciences richly enhance knowledge of the social, cultural, and conceptual history of male and female same-sexual relations, and the exploration of this forgotten archive has only just begun.

Although not all those with whom we have had related conversations over the years can be thanked here, Meredith Donaldson Clark, Konrad Eisenbichler, David Halperin, Guido Giglioni, Anthony Grafton, Nancy Partner, H. Darrel Rutkin, Stephen Vanden Broecke, Faith Wallis, Kendall Wallis, and Joseph Ziegler provided particularly valuable advice, encouragement, or referrals. After much consideration of how best to proceed, the editors collaborated on the initial proposal and identification of contributors, and then also, through the project's various stages, from that conception to its execution. George Rousseau handled the contractual negotiations with Routledge in England, read and commented on each draft of the manuscript, and made numerous suggestions for its improvement; while Kenneth Borris sought the contributors, thoroughly assessed and reassessed the drafts, performed the editing of the several successive versions in consultation with the contributors, and prepared the final manuscript. Both the editors thank the contributors for their most cooperative engagement in the editorial process. We the editors have also been blessed with a team at the press who supported this project and ensured its swift publication.

Borris' goldpanning operations for identifying many primary astrological, physiognomical, legal, and medical sources for chapters one to four and seven to nine, and for selecting this book's illustrations (except Figures 11.1, 11.2, and 13.1, supplied by Allison Kavey and Harriette Andreadis), were undertaken at the British Library, Harvard University's Houghton Library, the New York Public Library, the Library of the New York Academy of Medicine, the University of Toronto's Thomas Fisher Rare Books Library, McGill University's Osler Library for the History of Science and Medicine, and also, via interlibrary microfilm loans, the National Library of Medicine. George Rousseau worked with the successive drafts in the British Library and Bodleian Library in Oxford. This project would not have been possible without these libraries' marvelous collections and the generosity of their staff. Meredith Donaldson Clark provided invaluable research assistance throughout. McGill University furnished essential funding through a McGill Humanities Research Grant and an Arts Legacy Grant.

Kenneth Borris, Montreal
George Rousseau, Oxford

Note on ancient sources

Citations and quotations of ancient Latin and Greek texts refer to the Loeb series, unless the context states otherwise.

1 Introduction

The prehistory of homosexuality in the early modern sciences

Kenneth Borris

The Western scientific antecedents of homosexuality date from antiquity, and yet much of that sexual archaeology remains unknown. The early modern period has particular interest for the recovery of this occluded history. While the Renaissance[1] furthered the recovery of the ancients' resources of natural knowledge that had begun c.1100 through Arabic and Byzantine transmissions and Latin translations, Gutenberg's invention of movable type in the mid-fifteenth century enabled hitherto impossible disseminations of texts. Both humanism and print made ancient views of same-sexual relations[2] that clashed with Christian moral orthodoxy more accessible. The procedures, disciplines, and disciplinary boundaries of natural inquiry were being redefined, and innovations in medical understanding were proceeding apace. This volume enhances knowledge of the genealogies of homosexuality by exploring representations of same-sexual desires and behaviors in the diverse intellectual disciplines that sought to study and interpret natural phenomena and the order of nature, from c.1450 to 1750. As the characteristics of homosexuality's prehistory before the seventeenth century are currently most controversial, so my introduction will focus on the relevance of those disciplines prior to 1600.

Only in limited senses did "the sciences of homosexuality in early modern Europe" exist. The modern connotations of both "science" and "homosexuality" are precisely what must be placed in question to assess the interaction of their precursors and its historical effects. Thus restricted, the adjective "homosexual," for example, becomes refocused on its root meaning of "same-sexual," while marking the difference between that significance and the term's accumulated connotations in the nineteenth century and beyond. But differences do not necessarily preclude correlations and continuities, and the recent scientific transformation of same-sexual relations into so-called "homosexuality" was not without precedents and a long prehistory. As homosexuality remains to some extent conceptually inhabited by former notions of sex and gender deviance, so it continues to subsume, amongst its instabilities and contradictions,[3] some residues of the premodern sciences.

Although "science" acquired its current meaning in the nineteenth century, by historiographical convention it subsumes the congeries of medieval and early modern disciplines that variously sought natural knowledge as formerly conceived. "Science" and *scientia* broadly meant "knowledge" then, and their specialized applications were not congruent with modern "science" either.[4] Ideas of nature, and of serious, disciplined study of its order and phenomena, radically differed from ours. Nature ordinarily appeared to reflect God, its presumed Creator and "first cause," so that creation constituted a divinely informative "book of nature" infused with normative moral standards.[5] The status and definition of that created nature's "secondary causes" or operations varied. From Aristotelian natural philosophical viewpoints, for example, nature appeared to have intrinsic developmental principles, processes, flux, and teleology, yet sixteenth-century Lutheran and Calvinist nature passively reflected God's will, and seventeenth-century mechanist nature followed the immaterial mathematical laws of its Creator.[6]

The former definitions, categorizations, and boundaries of disciplines concerned with natural inquiry now seem strangely incoherent, for they accorded with a perceived world that has been lost.[7] Our current scientific disciplines were nascent, with some overlappings, in various early modern intellectual and technical domains, including medicine, natural philosophy (*scientia naturalis*), natural history, and "mixed mathematics" (*scientiae mediae*). The latter category incorporated disciplines using quantity to study material things, in mathematically "mixed" rather than "pure" considerations, such as astronomy and astrology (terms that were long interchangeable), mechanics, optics, and music theory. Natural philosophy, mathematics, and medicine had higher epistemological status than the others.

Former quests for natural knowledge and hence the origins of modern science were often involved with what now appear to be occult pursuits, for these too sought nature's secrets. In his early works, Giovanni Pico della Mirandola (1463–94) considered natural magic the consummation of natural philosophy.[8] Though fundamental to much occult philosophy and divination, astrology was as much one of the *scientiae mediae* as astronomy, founded on Aristotelian natural philosophical principles, and included in university curricula for centuries, partly for medical training.[9] Classification of premodern physiognomics and alchemy entails similar complexities. Now widely presumed forefathers of modern science, Nicolaus Copernicus (1473–1543), Johannes Kepler (1571–1630), and Galileo Galilei (1564–1642) all practiced astrology, and Sir Isaac Newton alchemy (1642–1727). Girolamo Cardano (1501–76) and Giambattista della Porta (1535?–1615), leading proponents of occult philosophy, contributed significantly to mathematics and optics. Learned divinatory and other occult pursuits cannot even be defined as nonacademic early modern modes of scientific inquiry, for many of their enthusiasts held academic appointments, such as Cardano. The development of the presently forceful distinction between those endeavors and science was a long, complex, and contentious process extending beyond the seventeenth century.

The early modern "sciences" as they pertain to the archaeology of homosexuality thus subsume diverse learned approaches to seeking natural and preternatural knowledge. These may be naturally philosophical, addressing the material world as it can be sensed; or may seek to probe and manipulate nature's hidden (and in that sense "occult") influences for divinatory or other ends. Both modes of inquiry engaged the varieties of human sexual potential, and did so at some interpretively significant removes from the discursive domain of theology and its preferred explanatory strategies.

Besides natural philosophy and medicine (with such subdisciplines now familiar as anatomy, physiology, embryology, gynecology, and venereology), the relevant former sciences thus include astrology, alchemy, and physiognomics (with its main subdisciplines of physiognomy, evaluation of the human body's range of parts, aspects, and mannerisms; chiromancy, study of the hands; and metoposcopy, assessment of the forehead). The disciplinary divisions between them and medicine were porous. Though medicine's interactions with astrology and alchemy are now well known, physiognomics partook of so much medical and natural philosophical knowledge that many of its leading authorities were medical practitioners. While astrology, physiognomics, and alchemy were not universally accepted or beyond criticism, neither were any of the antecedents of modern science; nor do many former medical orthodoxies now appear any less strange than the most fabulous pronouncements of occult philosophy. Insofar as broad swathes of early modern European society in all strata took astrology, physiognomics, and alchemy seriously, so must historians of that culture, as meaningful reflections of its mentalities, assumptions, attitudes, desires, and preoccupations.

So defined, the medieval and early modern sciences afford much altogether new evidence about same-sexual history. Such research will most affect understandings of the former cultural circumstances and possibilities of sexual relations between males, because prior explorations of that subject have rarely addressed the sciences of those times.[10] Yet medical accounts of tribades have been fundamental for recent study of lesbianism's precursors.[11] Nevertheless, premodern complexional physiology, embryology, astrology, and physiognomy, for example, still have much to reveal about the relation of apparent viragos to lesbian prehistory. Also, accounts of early modern sapphism (a term warranted by Sappho's Renaissance resurgence[12]) and its prospects for female same-sexual identities have been to some extent mapped onto the putative coordinates of its male counterpart.[13] Any significant shift in prevalent conceptions of the latter according to study of the former sciences would also require some reformulation of sapphic sexual history, to define its parallels and contrasts to the changed masculine model.

Although the premodern sciences have manifold implications for the study of the prehistory and history of homosexuality, they have particular relevance to the ongoing "intense debate"[14] about whether perceived same-sexual identities existed before so-called homosexuality's late nineteenth-century advent, and if so, what configurations they assumed. In sexual historiographies, much depends upon the possibilities of same-sexual identification, self-awareness, and agency assigned to any given period and cultural situation. Those assumptions or conclusions determine not only the extent to which individuals who engaged in same-sexual behaviors could formerly appear to have corresponding dispositions, but also their potential capacities of resistance and dissent, options of sexual contacts and relationships, and access to like-minded sexual undergrounds, fellowships, and subcultures.

According to the "acts paradigm" of much prior historiography of homosexuality, the useful distinction between same-sexual acts and identities further defines an absolute chronological dichotomy in Western sexual history. "Before the modern era," in that view, "sexual deviance could be predicated only of acts, not of persons or identities," and this "bogus theoretical doctrine" is often erroneously advanced on Michel Foucault's authority.[15] Exponents of the acts paradigm typically assume that same-sexual acts begat corresponding sexual identities and subcultures at some point such as (depending on the hypothesis) 1650, 1700, or 1875, thereupon inaugurating the modern sexual regime.[16] Before that point, in effect, same-sexual relations could only be experienced and understood as random disconnected acts somehow undertaken without any consciousness of particular, corresponding, and personally distinctive desires, tastes, and dispositions. As Eve Sedgwick indicates, this paradigm entails "narratives of supersession" that obscure the genealogical accretions of disparate and conflicting notions within concepts of homosexuality.[17] It also requires us to believe that same-sexual and social history are utterly simple, as if there can be just two significant phases, without meaningful variations or fluctuations in the first according to time, place, personalities, upbringing, innate factors, individual experience, education, or class.

The acts paradigm further assumes that, prior to the modern sexual regime's advent in 1650 or later, same-sexual relations were in principle simply universalized.[18] If they were only conceivable as acts, then everyone had a notionally equivalent potential to commit them. That is an essential premise for the acts paradigm, because any allowance for former recognition of individualized same-sexual inclinations entails some correlative acknowledgment of distinctive sexual natures and hence identities. Universalizing perspectives were indeed current, but only in contradictory cultural interplay with minoritizing perspectives most obviously evinced in former "othering" terminology such as "sodomite," "cinaedus," "tribade," and so forth.[19] That cultural logic of denigration, disqualification, and exclusion had more subtle and complex corollaries, such as the promulgation of sexually deviant constitutions in the sciences. The premodern era already prefigured the "internal incoherence and mutual contradiction" that Sedgwick discerns in modern homosexuality, "inherited from the architects of our present culture." The current conceptualization and cultural role of that perceived sexuality, she observes, reflect both "universalizing" and "minoritizing" views of sexual definition.[20]

A major paradigm shift in the conceptualization of premodern same-sexual history has been under way for some time, motivated by theoretical revaluations and newly discovered historical evidence. Many scholars now concur that same-sexual characters, dispositions, subjectivities, and modes of identity existed in the sixteenth and much earlier centuries.[21] Yet the acts paradigm and its absolutely universalizing premises have been so broadly current that they still too often predetermine interpretive assumptions and hence readings of historical evidence. Study of the premodern sciences newly clarifies the former minoritizing linkages of same-sexual acts with apparently distinctive sexual affinities, affiliations, classifications, morphologies, and physiologies. The diverse discourses that sought natural knowledge provide ample evidence that, beginning in the Middle Ages if not earlier, such acts could appear expressions of distinctive constitutional factors that characterized certain sexually defined types of individual. While that does not amount to the advent of the male or female homosexual in Western culture, nor did those beings and the associated conceptualizations somehow arise *ex nihilo*, without important precedents and precursors in premodern thought.

Unless defined otherwise in context, the formerly complex word "sodomy" in this introduction refers inclusively to sex between males and between females and, to register oppression, its cultural proscription. Although that provisional and pragmatic usage accords with some major premodern conventions following St Thomas Aquinas (1224/5–74), "sodomy" most commonly applied to sex between males in early modern culture.[22] I address former scientific hypotheses of constitutional bases for same-sexual relations not because of any investment in either side of the nature/nurture debate about the personal origins of homosexuality,[23] but because these hypotheses have much historical importance for early modern concepts and etiologies of sex differences, and have subversive implications for orthodox sexual morality in late medieval and early modern Europe. Much of that history infuses current notions of homosexuality and the related culture wars.

The early modern sciences and the historiography of homosexuality

Long before 1600 it was possible within the sciences to consider the medical and forensic implications of anal intercourse; the anatomical, mental, or physiological causes of same-sexual relations; whether such persons had outwardly identifiable characteristics enabling the construction of sexual morphologies; their classification into subtypes; the prospects of reclamation through medical therapies; and even whether, through appropriate management of conception and pregnancy, parents could avoid having children with certain same-sexual affinities and, as we would now say, gender dysphoria. Yet Anglo-American historiographies of male homosexuality have addressed the former sciences so little that many readers will be surprised that such a range of inquiries and concerns was even conceivable before modernity.

In defining early modern same-sex cultural contexts, conceptualizations, and experience, the nascent historiographies of the 1980s tended to over-emphasize law and theology.[24] They discounted the sciences and insufficiently allowed for the interchanges of ideas about sex and sexual mores across Europe through travel, commerce, and the circulation of texts in both Latin, the former international language, and the vernacular languages.[25] Yet the inaugural models of same-sexual history still influence common assumptions about the sexual past.

A copy of the Neoplatonic *Dialoghi d'amore* by Leone Ebreo (fl. 1460–1521) bears the signature of Sir John Cheke (1514–57), tutor of England's Edward VI, and it contains discussions of males astrologically inclined to pursue *amor masculino*, loving those of their own sex, or to be metaphorically "hermaphroditic" by exchanging insertive and receptive sex roles with each other.[26] Until homosexuality's conceptual advent in the late 1800s, it is nonetheless said, male same-sexual relations were experienced in such fixed and polarized hierarchical patterns ("active/passive, insertive/receptive, masculine/feminine, or man/boy") as to preclude bonding of both partners "on the basis of their sameness," and "companionate, romantic, and mutual" love.[27] But Leone took for granted that some male lovers freely exchange sex roles.[28] Until modern homosexuality, it is often repeated, same-sexual object choice could not in itself appear a decisive "marker of sexual difference."[29] But there is now ample evidence that, from at least the mid-fifteenth to late seventeenth centuries throughout Europe, a discursive tradition flourished that recognized male same-sexual relations as a distinctive amorous phenomenon: "*amor masculino*" as Leone says, or "masculine love."[30] This model radically differs from and cuts across the standard historiographical models of prehomosexual male deviance in sex and gender: effeminacy, pederastic sodomy, passivity or inversion, male amorous friendship.[31] Since masculine love, unlike them, both avoids polarizing sexual roles or status and focuses on same-sex sexual object choice, it prefigures male homosexuality in significant ways unanticipated in many recent accounts of sexual history.[32] Not later than the fifteenth century, other evidence confirms, the sexual preferences of males could already be understood according to a nascent same-sex/opposite-sex model that assumed male sodomites were disinclined or averse to sex with females.[33]

Whereas theology and law typically engaged same-sexual relations only as a topic of condemnation and restricted the parameters of discussion accordingly, the sciences, though influenced by those views, nonetheless provided alternate modes of thought, inquiry, and explanation that promoted curiosity about the causes, purposes, analysis, and classification of natural phenomena and any apparent anomalies. Resultant scientific modes of accounting for same-sex divagations from the putatively procreative norms of nature in turn affected some moral philosophical and theological thought. Though still condemning sodomy, the Roman Catholic theologian and ethicist Martin Le Maistre (1432–81) nonetheless conceded that "sodomitic inclinations may be due to sickness or to defective physical qualities."[34] Such ideas had already long been circulating in commentaries on Aristotle's *Nicomachean Ethics*, even that of Aquinas. Desires conducing unnatural behaviors, including sex between males, he declares, arise either from engrained habit or from the particular "nature of a corporeal complexion."[35]

But in order to focus on purposes of condemnation, legal and theological discourses routinely excluded the former sciences' implications of that kind. Or if they were acknowledged, the commentator would insist on the primacy of free will, so that an individual would remain responsible for choosing to act in accord with any allegedly sinful inclinations. Yet if some intrinsic and distinctive characteristics of mind or flesh conduce same-sexual relations, as the premodern sciences could variously allow, particular same-sex variants of humanity come into being, and the extent of their alleged legal and theological culpability becomes debatable. The norms of nature thus appear ambiguously variable, and the choice to have such amorous and sexual relations becomes much less simply a matter of individual volition, for a complicating inborn inclination or even determination is at play. Same-sexual desires and behaviors would accord with the distinctive natures of these persons: sexually defined species of humanity mandated as such by the resources of natural knowledge. Although their condemnation would still accord with Calvinist double predestination, whereby God preordains some individuals to be damned (and may thus appear to cause evil while withholding any meaningful prospect of grace from many), such a fate would be awkward to reconcile with other early modern conceptions of divine providence.[36]

While remaining implicit in scientific contexts, both to avoid controversy and because theological and legal concerns were beyond the scope of natural inquiry, these challenges to sexual orthodoxy were obvious enough. When commenting on the *Problemata* ascribed to Aristotle, the physician Ludovico Settala (1552–1633) refused to discuss the section that argues that some males seek receptive anal sex on account of particular constitutional traits, lest he thus assist such persons' self-justifications, which would undermine doctrines of moral responsibility.[37] The magus and natural philosopher Heinrich Cornelius Agrippa (1486?–1535) observed that astrology "maintaineth [i.e. upholds] vices, excusing them as though they did descend upon us from above."[38] Devoting considerable attention to human sexual variations, including a range of same-sexual affinities, the astrological authorities ascribed them to imprints of the heavens upon an individual's constitution or temperament at birth or later. Partly to protect moral orthodoxy, Sixtus V formally condemned the divinatory sciences in 1586, including interpretation of "people's birth horoscopes with a view to foretelling . . . actions dependent on human will."[39] As we will see, that ruling, renewed by Urban VIII in 1631, climaxed a series of restrictions upon those former sciences. Much medieval and Renaissance science that impinged upon same-sexual relations derived from pagan antiquity, which had a sex/gender system contrary to the "sodomophobic"[40] regime of Christianity.

Hence the relationship between scientific discourses on one hand and legal and theological discourses on the other was fraught with potential contradiction. Historiographies of homosexuality that privilege the latter disciplines in their representations of former cultural and conceptual possibilities are bound to underestimate the range and complexity of premodern views. Whereas the literary and visual arts could imaginatively realize explorations of alternatives to sexual orthodoxy as well as efforts to promote or confirm it, the sciences had to account for same-sexual phenomena according to their rationalized models of the natural order. And whereas theology, seconded by legal enforcement, appointed procreation the divinely ordained purpose of sex, within scientific discourses the nature of "nature" could appear much more complicated as they sought to explain the manifest existence of sexual types contrary to that ostensibly essential and unproblematic sexual function. Although we lack much biographical evidence about same-sexually desirous premodern individuals, the verbal and visual arts have revealed something of the complicated encounters between, on one hand, their humanity (their desires, loves, and lives) and, on the other, the official mandate and social diffusion of sodomophobia.[41] Study of the former sciences can supplement our inferences and deductions by clarifying the early modern conceptual opportunities of sexual dissidence, while revealing the conceptual fault lines, the logical incoherencies, in that culture's anathemas of sex, and in all that ensuing sexual regimes derived from them and perpetuate.

The procedures of Arnold I. Davidson's *Emergence of Sexuality* (2001) demonstrate the importance of premodern science for assessment of the history of homosexuality. Though seeking to define sexuality's emergence and its implications according to the history of science, he uses theology and law to define Western culture before the later 1800s and discounts premodern science.[42] His argument fundamentally assumes that sexuality's conceptual emergence depended on the prior conceptual advent of sexual perversion, and that such perversion became conceivable only in the nineteenth century. Before then, Davidson claims, there was *only* a concept of sexual "perversity," in the sense of generalized vice in which individuals culpably involved themselves by *choice*. In his view, nineteenth-century science radically transformed understandings of sex so that "the etiology of perversion was thought to be *constitutional*," not volitional, and then, as never before, "the distinction between perversity and perversion was in principle easily drawn."[43]

That argument reiterates the acts paradigm and depends upon an oversimplified chronological dichotomy between nineteenth-century "homosexuality" and prior "sodomy," as if the latter, understood by Davidson as a legal and moral category or criminal vice,[44] exhausts all possibilities of former same-sexual experience, conceptions, and definitions. Before sexuality's emergence in the late 1800s, he assumes, same-sexual lovers could only appear types of sinner who just differed from the rest of the population in the mode of temptation to which they willfully and momentarily succumbed through a "deficiency of the will." Their behavior was a vice, they themselves "merely evil or wicked."[45] They were not conceivable as types of persons characterized by some putatively intrinsic differences of mind or body relative to others. Since moral theology and law are the sole bases of Davidson's notions of what could be conceived about same-sexual desires and behaviors prior to 1800, in his view those human realities could only be understood according to sodomy as "a legal category, defined in terms of certain specifiable behavior," and as "a vice, a problem for morality and law." "All we find before the nineteenth century are descriptions of sodomy. . . . Perversion is a thoroughly modern phenomenon."[46]

Nineteenth-century scientific conceptualizations of sex thus appear strikingly new in Davidson's representation, but at the cost of argumentative circularity: the parameters of inquiry are so restricted that the hypothesis is bound to appear confirmed. That methodological problem afflicts many efforts to assign to sexual history some specific turning point corresponding to the distinction between sexual acts and identities. They focus on legal and theological evidence, or cite prior such studies, and conclude that only same-sexual acts or sins were conceivable prior to some historical moment. But legal and theological standpoints were necessarily acts-based anyway, for they were concerned to hold the sexual sinner or offender responsible for *a specific sex act*, so that his or her attendant interiorities and personal traits were irrelevant and even dangerous distractions from the purposes of conviction and exemplary humiliation. Evidence drawn from those disciplines proves nothing about the conceptual limits of premodern sexual thought unless we assume it could *only* operate *within those* disciplinary domains. Since the biographical evidence of same-sexual pursuits in the past is scant due to oppression, insofar as we are interested in perceived sexual interiorities, dispositions, and predispositions we had best turn to the former visual arts, imaginative literature, and sciences. In any case, we cannot confidently assess the extent to which nineteenth-century science was doing anything new with sexual topics, and in what ways, without thorough investigation of those topics *in preceding science*. That will require much research by many scholars over several decades.

It is nonetheless already clear that scientific notions of constitutionally based sexual perversions far antedate the nineteenth century.[47] This is not to say that the concepts of sexuality and homosexuality advanced in the late 1800s were nothing new. But definition of the degree, nature, and implications of their novelty requires historically informed and nuanced approaches. In view of medieval comments that attribute "to the Sodomite many of the kinds of features that Foucault finds only in the nineteenth-century definition" of the homosexual, such as a "Sodomitic anatomy and physiology, personal history, and secret community," Mark D. Jordan observes that "the invention of the homosexual may well have relied on the already familiar category of the Sodomite. The idea that same-sex pleasure constitutes an identity of some kind is clearly the work of medieval theology."[48] Whether same-sexual relations were attributable to willful vice or to constitutional traits of certain individuals, and to what extents, had been questionable from scientific standpoints in the postclassical West since probably the twelfth century. Various theories of innate same-sexual affinities had circulated in ancient Greek and Roman medicine, astrology, and physiognomy, and in their Arabic developments. In the later Middle Ages, texts incorporating or reflecting some of those ideas became newly accessible in the West and began gaining cultural influence. In 1277, shortly after the apparent expulsion of many reputedly sodomitical theologians and theological students from Paris, Étienne Tempier (d. 1279), the bishop of Paris, condemned the proposition that "the sin against nature, . . . although it is against the nature of the species, is not, however, against the nature of the individual."[49] Particular, constitutionally based sexual perversions had come to be conceivable in the West no later than 1277 – not 1875. Moreover, the doctrine of free will had incurred astrological and other challenges that opened up questions of moral responsibility, volition, and possible determinisms.[50] In any case, same-sexual relations could not only be conceived as sodomy before the late 1800s, but also according to a variety of possible models with considerable currency, including, from c.1450 to c.1650, that of "masculine love" for males.[51]

Same-sexual phenomena in the early modern sciences

Through such medieval or ancient texts as Avicenna's medically comprehensive *Liber canonis*, the natural philosophical *Problemata* attributed to Aristotle, and the astrological manuals of Ptolemy, pseudo-Ptolemy, and Firmicus Maternus, scientific assessments of the etiologies and expressions of same-sexual relations had a manifest presence in premodern European culture from at least the later twelfth century onward. Yet apparent absence paradoxically infuses that presence. Not only does much remain to be discovered, but such topics were presumed unspeakable in many circles due to the former abomination of sodomy, the sin "not to be named."[52]

Insofar as nature seemed replete with divine inscriptions, the status of sexual relations and relationships theologically and legally considered *contra naturam* was bound to be paradoxical at best within the domains of natural inquiry. The scope of that investigative territory included nature's apparent vagaries such as deviant individual natures and even same-sexual ones, whose infractions were thus perceived to "originate *in* nature, albeit a nature burdened by particularity and contingency."[53] In general, the former sciences' relations with religion ranged from mutual cooperation, through neutral coexistence, to open conflict.[54] While various scientific propositions, authors, and publications were condemned by religious authorities, the communities of natural inquiry would have accommodated private heterodoxies and heterodox exchanges. Yet even proponents of new readings of nature's book that proved to excite religious opposition, such as Copernicus and Galileo, would not necessarily have conceived their theories in any conscious opposition to scripture or the Church's authority.[55] Sodomy's profound cultural odium combined religious, legal, social, and professional pressures to discourage scientific inquiries into questions of same-sexual behaviors and affinities, so that such comments when recorded are usually brief. Writers who proceeded otherwise could risk their professional status and reputations, as the eminent barber-surgeon Ambroise Paré (c.1510–90) discovered.[56] Beginning c.1500 and especially after 1550, growing prospects of censorship and inquisitorial anathemas tended further to restrain authors' adventures in print.

When medieval and Renaissance scientific writers addressed this sexual subject, then, they usually did so according to an authoritative pretext, rarely went further than that except in a commentary, genuflected to orthodox sexual morality (sincerely or not), and either avoided acknowledging any challenges to orthodoxy implied in the pretext, or tried to neutralize them. These discussions were often restricted to Latin to exclude vernacular readerships who were supposedly more impressionable.[57] A group of fourteenth- and fifteenth-century Latin manuscripts relating to the supposed Aristotle's survey of coital matters in book 4 of the *Problemata* epitomizes some possible responses to sexual inquiry in premodern natural philosophical communities. Sometimes resorting to outright suppression, they evince "a general climate of uncertainty and disagreement about what may appropriately be said concerning human sexual organs and their uses," and the male same-sexual content of *Problemata* 4.26 tended to have "particular" sensitivity. Yet at that time, the bounds of science on "sexual subjects were . . . negotiated, marked out, and patrolled – all in a fairly unsettled manner – by the writers and readers of natural philosophy themselves."[58] During the sixteenth century, virulent syphilis, the Reformation, and the Counter-Reformation stimulated rigorous official efforts to regulate sex throughout Europe, and institutionalize inquisitorial and other controls upon authors, print, and readers. However, even the self-censorship evoked by same-sexual subject matter expresses the writers' awareness of its potential to subvert orthodox Christian morality, their anxiety about the social or personal effects, and the possibilities of private dissent. Early modern scientific inquiries into same-sexual relations are most likely to appear in treatises composed in Latin, and to disappear in vernacular translations and adaptations.

Bound up with the former sciences' portrayals of sex and gender deviance, then, are their significant silences, evasions, repressions, and obfuscations evident throughout this volume. Insofar as the premodern sciences were almost a male preserve,[59] their androcentrism further distorts their sapphic engagements. In Chapter 13 Harriette Andreadis explores how appropriate inferences about love between women may be teased from the texts of the tribadic era, when medical texts epitomized that love in a peculiarly minoritized anatomy. Yet as Winfried Schleiner indicates in Chapter 12, the sciences could also stimulate representations of same-sexual desires in early modern erotica. If Cardano had any, as certain aspects of his life, love of music, and interest in boys could suggest, Guido Giglioni's survey of that scholar's voluminous scientific, musical, and other writings in Chapter 10 shows he repressed them at least in his authorial persona. If writers appeared to address sodomy too much or too flexibly, we find in Chapter 7, they risked provoking verbal sanctions within their own disciplines, like the barber-surgeon and leading physiognomer Bartolommeo della Rocca or Cocles (1467–1504). Despite the devastations wrought by the virulent pox's advent in the late fifteenth century, venereological treatises long ignored possibilities of same-sexual transmission, and as Cristian Berco explains in Chapter 5, that practice seems to have been deliberate, for it continued even in the midst of notorious Valencian sodomy scandals.[60] This medical silence remained predominant into the eighteenth century, as we find in Kevin Siena's Chapter 6.

Professional self-censorship was indeed so prevalent that early modern medical expertise in the physical implications and detection of anal sex, whatever the biological sex of the recipient, seems to survive almost only in legal documents. Florentine, Venetian, and Luccan legal records show that sexual penetration of the anus had long occasioned various kinds of medical interventions. That body of diagnostic and therapeutic knowledge, and reportage of such patient consultations, could figure in legal proceedings. Anal intercourse could possibly entail venereal infections or excrescences, and injuries from over-exuberant or forcible intercourse. Though these afflictions would have arisen throughout Europe,[61] they are best documented by some detailed Italian records that are still extant. Injurious anal intercourse occurred often enough that Florence enacted a law specifically ensuring its rigorous prosecution in 1449, and Venice required barber-surgeons to report all such cases in 1467.[62] Fifteenth- and sixteenth-century Florentine legal records show that "numerous boys . . . suffered anal injuries from sodomy," and would thus have required medical treatment.[63] As continental jurisdictions could and did use torture to investigate alleged sex crimes, there would usually have been little practical need for medical forensic testimony.[64] It seems most likely to have been used in cases involving minors.[65] But Lucca had institutionalized medical testimony in prosecution of anal intercourse by c.1550 if not earlier, partly because the Luccan authorities associated sodomy in that sense with transmission of the pox.[66] Between the years 1551 and 1647 (those covered by the extant Luccan records), "enlargement and inflammation of the rectal sphincter was frequently offered as evidence of anal sex," and so were any perceived anal injuries or manifestations of venereal disease.[67] These were described with specific detail and terminology. As in the Florentine and Venetian documentation, medical practitioners of various types would have encountered all this before 1550.

Despite the accumulation of expertise about various signs and possible ill effects of anal intercourse, medical writers were chary of recording it, so that it was presumably communicated through oral exchanges and collegial demonstrations of particular cases. Passages of ancient medical treatises, as yet unidentified, may have provided some textual guidelines. But Amato Lusitano (1511–68) is the only sixteenth-century physician currently known to have commented on such "abominable (*nephandus*)" coital matters in print, and he did so briefly in Latin.[68]

Otherwise, a legal context seems to have been required to make early modern medical knowledge of anal sex fit for print, yet again only in Latin. The Roman physician Paolo Zacchia (1584–1659) included medical-legal investigation of sex crimes in his magisterial compendium of forensic medicine first published in 1630. Including anal intercourse in that survey, and particularly focusing on violated boys and habitual cinaedi (defined n.75 here), he advises how to evaluate the condition of the anus to determine whether sexual penetration had occurred, and how often, so as to detect and convict offenders. The mental or constitutional factors that could affect these sexual behaviors are thus beyond his discussion's specific discursive mandate, whatever he himself might have thought about such questions, or had assimilated from his copious learned readings and professional interactions. Though Zacchia's text cannot enlighten us on these points, George Rousseau shows in Chapter 4 that it is a central document for inquiry into early modern medical engagements with the physical effects and traces of anal intercourse, and the potential juridical applications. The Florentine, Venetian, and Luccan legal records indicate that Zacchia's forensic disquisition seeks to codify long-standing legal uses of medical knowledge in such cases. Since Lusitano is Zacchia's sole medical reference here and he habitually multiplies citations, it may have been the only one he knew in print. Yet when Zacchia mentions sphincter-relaxing emollients favored by this "nefarious" pleasure's receptive devotees, he discloses something of their early modern sexual underground and the possibilities of transgressive medical or pharmacological collaborations.[69]

Despite the anathemas and anxieties restricting researches on same-sexual topics within the premodern disciplines of natural and preternatural inquiry, the remains of the former sciences still reveal much association of same-sexual behaviors with particular constitutional causes, and establish the currency of such assumptions in late medieval and early modern Western thought. Among the premodern scientific domains, learned medicine's role in the archaeology of homosexuality has been most investigated to date, chiefly in connection with genital anatomy.[70] Hence my following review of constitutionally significant medical theories focuses instead on their relatively unfamiliar therapeutic, prophylactic, embryological, and physiological implications.

Some ancient Greco-Roman and medieval Arabic sources associated tribadic interests in penetrating other women with pseudophallic labial or clitoral hypertrophy. Those views appear to have had some currency in Europe after the twelfth century, and explicitly appear in various Renaissance medical treatises.[71] In that connection, Valerie Traub has aptly termed the underlying explanatory approach "an anatomical essentialism – the riveting of body part to behavior – that continues to underpin modern discourses of sexuality" and "construction of the homo/hetero divide."[72] Yet premodern medicine institutionalized female same-sexual relations in that midwives digitally stimulated the genitalia of female clients who apparently suffered from spoilage of feminine seed caused by sexual abstinence.[73] The medical accounts of hermaphrodites relate to those of tribadism and have now been much canvassed.[74]

Likewise, anatomically essentialist accounts of cinaedi, males who desire receptive intercourse with males,[75] circulated in Europe from at least the later Middle Ages, as in the supposed Aristotle's *Problemata*; the major commentary on it by Pietro d'Abano (1257–1315/16); the medically magisterial *Liber canonis* of Avicenna (980–1037); and the general reference work *Lectionum antiquarum*, by Lodovico Ricchieri (1469–1525).[76] Some authorities, Avicenna reports, believed these males have a particular pattern of genital nerves requiring sexually receptive stimulation. But the supposed Aristotle says they have a unique pattern of sperm ducts producing the same result. In Chapters 2 and 3, Derek Neal and Faith Wallis elucidate the complex early modern reception of these Avicennan and pseudo-Aristotelian texts, and the ongoing attempts to reconcile their insights with Christian moral orthodoxy. Just as these essentialist conceptions of tribades and cinaedi date from antiquity, both had long been conceivable as same-sexual types constitutionally distinct from other individuals.

Further such means of accounting for cinaedi, again inherited from antiquity, had also been available to late medieval and Renaissance medical discourse. Caelius Aurelianus (c.400 CE) reports various alternatives in *On Chronic Diseases*, a treatise not unknown in the Middle Ages, that had four sixteenth-century printings. This condition arises from the particular circumstances of conception, whereby the parental male and female seeds do not aptly merge in producing the infant. Or it is inherited, passed on by the seed through successive generations. Or it is a particular affliction or aberration of the mind, for which there is no physical treatment.[77] Avicenna's *Canon* similarly emphasizes "the cause of their illness lies in their imagination (*meditatiuum*)," and yet allows for some physical as well as mental aspects, such as "a womanly constitution" marked by feebleness of heart or timidity, and by weak erectile capacity when attempting conventional masculine sex roles.[78]

Inversions of the sexual roles deemed apt for each gender as well as other variances from gendered behavioral expectations occasioned theories and practices of prophylactic and curative intervention. Renaissance authorities such as Paré and André du Laurens (1558–1609) recycled ancient Greco-Roman and medieval Arabic advice to amputate the female genital hypertrophies supposedly conducive to tribadism.[79] Particular surgical procedures were devised, presumably tested, and publicized by Rodrigo de Castro (1546–1623/9), Fabricius ab Aquapendente (c.1533–1619), and his student Johann Schultes (1595–1645; see Figure 12.1).[80] Both Caelius Aurelianus and Avicenna dismissed the ongoing medical attempts to "cure" cinaedi. Since "the cause of their illness" is imaginative, "not natural," the latter objects, their desire must be broken punitively.[81] A physician could otherwise prescribe a regimen of diet, exercise, and drugs to increase the supposedly masculine constitutional qualities of heat and dryness in a cinaedus, or the contrarily feminine ones of cold and moisture in a virago. According to formerly standard Hippocratic–Galenic principles of sex difference, gendered temperament, and curative prescription,[82] these would have been obvious procedures, possibly of interest to anxious parents, or to a sodomite fearful of social, legal, and religious sanctions.

Though the extent to which such interventions entered medical print is as yet unclear, Pietro d'Abano's commentary on the *Problemata* mentions use of "diet and drugs of a drying nature" to normalize cinaedi, and the natural philosopher and magus Porta published another therapy c.1600:

> cinaedi who wish to become tough, and to change their phlegmatic [i.e. cold and wet, hence effeminate] constitution for a warm [i.e. masculine] one, should live in hot, harsh, windy places. They should eat hot, rustic foods, and devote themselves to exercise; so shall they emerge strong and tough, and lose their feminine demeanor.

Just as Porta's counsel combines Hippocrates' *Airs, Waters, and Places* with age-old medical assumptions about gendered temperaments and prescriptive regimens, it would have been readily conceivable many centuries before Porta.[83]

Some theories of generation and embryology allowed for congenital production of differing degrees of masculinity and femininity, and hence also inversions of sex roles.[84] The Hippocratic–Galenic model of generation, predominant in the early Middle Ages and newly topical in the Renaissance, allowed for "a spectrum of intermediate sexual possibilities" that potentially challenged "the male–female dichotomy, and . . . the whole social and sexual order." After c.1550, moreover, "new interpretation of the hermaphrodite as a being of intermediate sex" had the effect of showcasing issues of "sodomy and other sexual crimes, and the proper relationship and boundaries between men and women."[85] Using the Galenic two-seed theory, whereby both male and female contribute seed to generation, the physician Levinus Lemnius (1505–68) explains that predominant male seed falling on the womb's right side produces males "by reason of heat," whereas female seed on the left produces females "by reason of cold and moisture."[86] But male semen falling on the left makes a "half man (*semivirile*), . . . fairer, and whiter or smoother and less hairy [and softer (*mollitiem*) of body] than is convenient for a man to be, or the voice will be small, and sharp, or the chin . . . bald, and the courage will be lesse." Conversely, female semen on the right makes a woman "more viraginous than ordinary women [beyond what the nature of the sex permits]."[87] Though not directly applied to same-sexual relations in this account, such theories suggested cinaedi and masculine tribades could have embryonic causes. Although the Aristotelian model assumed that males and females are opposites lacking prospects of mediation except for some possible overlapping of warmth or coolness,[88] it still assigned embryonic etiologies to nonmenstruating viragos and infertile effeminate men.[89]

In *Examen de ingenios para las sciencias*, the Spanish physician Juan Huarte (1529?–1588) drew on Hippocratic, Galenic, and Aristotelian resources of embryology, anatomy, and physiology to help couples produce "properly" male children of superior mental capacities. Frequently published throughout Europe between 1575 and 1734 in several languages, Huarte's eugenic program promoted the Galenic theory whereby male and female genitals are structurally homologous, but appear externally in males and internally in females. The genitals and gender assignment were thus potentially convertible, at least female to male and also, Huarte maintained with some others, male to female.[90] So powerful was this theory that the great advances of mid-sixteenth-century anatomical research at first appeared to confirm it. Perceiving and dissecting female reproductive organs according to Galenic expectations, Andreas Vesalius (1514–64) splendidly published the pseudo-phallic findings, and these became paradigmatic for many subsequent sixteenth-century representations of female genitalia.[91] The widely used anatomical handbook of Juan Valverde de Amusco (c.1525–c.1588) closely follows Vesalius (Figure 1.1).

To Huarte, effeminacy in males and masculinity in females appeared so personally engrained or congenital that they seemed accountable only as effects of an intra-uteral sex-change understood according to the Galenic genital homology. An individual thus comes to have genitals the reverse of those corresponding to his or her initial gender, yet retains some of its characteristics and usually its sexual affinities:

> diuers times nature hath made a female child and she hath so remained in her mothers belly for the space of one or two months: and afterwards, plentie of heat growing in the genitall members, upon some occasion they have issued forth, and she become a male. To whom this transformation hath befallen in the mothers womb, is afterwards plainly discovered, by certain motions which they retaine, unfitting for the masculin sex, being altogether womanish, and their voice shrill and sweet. And such persons are enclined to perform womens actions, and fall ordinarily into uncouth offences. Contrariwise, nature hath sundrie times made a male with his genetories outward, and cold growing on, they have turned inward, and it became female. This is knowen after she is borne, for she retaineth a mannish fashion, as well in her words, as in all her motions and workings. (p. 269)

"Uncouth offences" is the translator's euphemism, for Huarte declares these male effeminates fall "ordinariamente en el pecado nefando," into the abominable sin, by which he would mean sodomitical relations with other males here.[92] Their

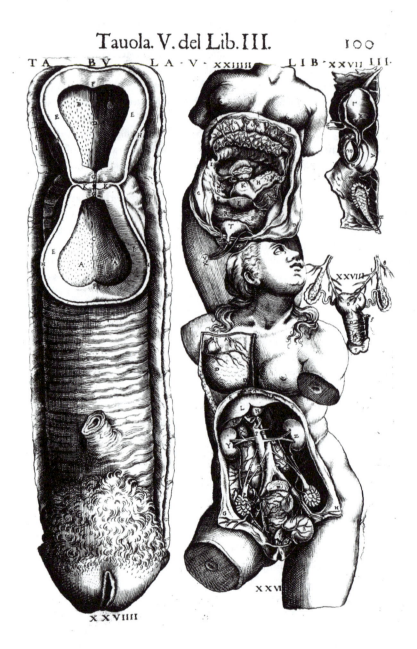

Figure 1.1 Feminine reproductive organs according to the Galenic "one-sex" genital homology, from Juan Valverde de Amusco, *La anatomia del corpo umano*, Venice: Nella stamperia de Giunti, 1586, p. 100. First published 1556. By permission of the Osler Library for the History of Science and Medicine, McGill University. Biblioteca Osleriana 576.

sexually receptive rather than penetrative affinities result from initial embryonic femininity, and the corresponding viragos would logically tend toward tribadism.

"It is a conclusion of all Philosophers and Phisitions," Huarte adds, "that if the seed be cold and moist, a woman is begotten, and not a man; and if the same be hot and dry, a man" (p. 270).[93] According to the Galenic homology, masculine heat ensures genital protrusion, feminine cold retraction. Yet males could still be cold and moist relative to masculine norms, and females vice versa. Men of such a temperament, Huarte observes, "are no great friends to women, nor women unto them" (p. 282). His eugenic program seeks to optimize the proportion of hot, dry, cold, and moist principles in prospective parents and in the paternal and maternal "seeds" during conception and pregnancy. This involves dietary prescriptions, exercise, and techniques to ensure that both parental seeds fall on the right side of the womb and that the conception stays there, because the right side's greater heat engenders males, whereas the left produces females (pp. 289, 298).

The complexional physiology[94] that dominated Western medical thought throughout most of the premodern era profoundly influenced medical and cultural understandings of masculinity, femininity, sex, and any perceived anomalies. Despite its importance for investigation of homosexuality's archaeology, it has only just begun to be researched in that connection. Everyone was thus supposed to have a unique temperament resulting from the particular balance of hot, cold, wet, and dry qualities produced by the distinctive mix of the four elements composing his or her body.[95] This complexion is innate, Nancy Siraisi explains: "an essential identifying characteristic acquired at the moment of conception and in some way persisting throughout life." Someone could have, for example, "a hot complexion relative to other human beings, and this characteristic would apply to him or her throughout life."[96] However, complexion nonetheless varies according to age, so that youth in general is relatively hot and wet, old age cold and dry. Innate complexion would remain normative for an individual because, in a hot case, both youth and age would be hotter than usual. Normative complexion varies also by gender according to most authorities: as Huarte assumes, males are thus relatively hot and dry, females cold and wet. Climate produces further regional norms. Even particular organs have distinct complexional norms producing further possibilities of differentiation. The brain is normatively cooler than the heart, for example. Balance of the four qualities constitutes the temperate complexional ideal from which everyone, or almost everyone, more or less departs in various ways.

Complexional physiology thus afforded scientific means to envision and explain the full range of human traits and personalities in a quasi-essentialist way.[97] While allowing for many variables including age, personal habits, and environment, it nonetheless stressed innate factors. Medicine thus sought to enhance or restore health by adjusting the conditions of life to make complexions more temperate or balanced – hence the conceptual possibility of "normalizing" cinaedi and viragos by adjusting relative coldness or warmth. Nevertheless, the complexional account of personal differences tended toward constitutional determinism: people are substantially the way they are because they are born that way. In *The Optick Glasse of Humors* first published c.1607, Thomas Walkington (1580?–1621) stresses, like

Galen, "the soule followes the temper of the body."[98] The temperaments themselves "were at once somatic and psychic."[99] Hence premodern medicine could again appear at odds with Christian moral theology. If mental, emotional, and behavioral phenomena are expressions of material factors – the particular somatic mix of the qualities corresponding to the four elements – free will and moral responsibility for alleged sins become questionable. And as the soul becomes materialized, so its ostensible immortality is compromised. Although medical writers avoided discussing those issues in the premodern West, such possible implications of Galenic and complexional thought were obvious enough, just as various religious writers noted and condemned them.[100] Huarte's book incurred difficulties with the Inquisition.

Relative to later times up to the 1800s, the era of complexional physiology's Western scientific prestige – from before 1200 to c.1650[101] – may have been especially well equipped to perceive particular sex differences and gender anomalies as functions of individuals' distinctive constitutions or natures. Various widely influential historiographies of homosexuality have instead advocated straightforward narratives of "evolution" based on a single, relatively late turning point, without significant fluctuations and discontinuities. But the complexional model afforded: (1) an account of normative male/female differentiation in biological sex and gender conformation according to the relative proportion of the four qualities; (2) an account of male and female variances from that norm according to atypical proportions and mixtures; (3) a theoretical contextualization assuming that these variances are largely inborn. Hence complexional physiology was widely applied to explain the range of human deviations from perceived norms of biological sex, gender, and sex roles, including male effeminates, viragos, and various same-sexual behaviors. These phenomena appeared scientifically accountable as effects of variant human physiologies and hence of individual natures within the total scope of nature, as distinct from supposedly normative nature. In Aquinas' commentary on Aristotelian ethics, sodomitical and other allegedly unnatural desires arise from habituation or, in other cases, some "corporeal complexion."[102] Astrology similarly posited astral imprints that natally establish particular human constitutions and hence temperaments.[103]

Male effeminacy, which had various perceived types,[104] was commonly attributed to complexions too cold and wet for normative masculinity, despite phallic endowment. Though there currently seems to have been little explicit discussion of complexional factors in female same-sexual relations, the virago had long been a common medical topic, and considered too hot and dry, again to varying extents, for normative femininity. That logic readily encompassed females perceived to appropriate masculine sex roles. "In some women," the anatomist Du Laurens observed in 1593, the clitoris "expands so untowardly that it hangs down . . . like a penis, and the women called tribades or 'rubbers' (*fricatrices*) rub each other on that part." Women with a clitoris that "may feign the male penis" are "*very hot* from the outset (*a primo ortu*) and are so formed by Nature," so that they are complexionally semi-masculine.[105]

However, these classifications of effeminates, viragos, and tribades are only basic, for the complexional explanatory repertoire enabled many distinctions and subtleties. Cocles allows for a second type of cinaedus aside from the constitutionally feminine one, who has a more complex interplay of qualities including more heat and sanguine humor (Ch. 7). Complexional physiology theoretically enabled much finer classifications of sexual subtypes, for the complexions of individuals' bodily organs were also thought to vary, and the conditions of the genitals and liver, an organ thought to affect sexual desire, could thus be relevant. Whether any authority sought to record such finer classifications is currently unknown, but they were readily conceivable. As Cocles's reception indicates (Ch. 7), dissemination of this kind of thinking would have been constrained by the cultural opprobrium of sodomy, enforced by law and religion, and writers' fears for their reputation. Also as yet unknown are any complexional discussions of "femme" women, sapphists who appeared conventionally feminine. Perhaps, as in the extant medical sources of antiquity, they did not seem sufficiently alien to the sex/gender system, or socially obvious enough, to appear to demand recourse to embryological, genitally anatomical, or physiological rationales.

Similarly, unlike males who enjoyed being sexually penetrated, their insertive counterparts did not occasion any extant medical explanation in antiquity, nor even from Avicenna, apparently because their sexual behaviors could at least be reconciled with conventional masculine insertive norms. However, as Jordan points out, their Christian transformation into sodomites rendered them, as well as their receptive partners, an abominably atypical category of sexually defined person.[106] Thus appearing specially prone to a particular and extremely transgressive type of amorous desire or lust, insertive male sodomites came to seem complexionally characterized by factors conducive to inordinate sexual desire, and to some extent sex with males in particular, and by corresponding physical traits. In the common scheme allowing for nine complexions, two especially tended to amorous excesses: the "simple" hot temperament, dominated by heat, and the "compound" sanguine, ruled by joint heat and moisture, or blood.[107]

According to Lemnius' complexional manual *De habitu et constitutione corporis*, those who "abound with Bloud, and be sanguine complexioned," are particularly inclined to "riot, wantonnesse, . . . filthy and detestable loues (*obscenos nefandosque amores*)," "horrible lustes, incest, and buggerie (*probrosas libidines, incestus, foedosque concubitus*)."[108] As for those with simply hot complexions (whereas sanguine is compound), "their loynes be verye hoate," so "they are . . . greatlye geeuen to leacherie . . . and thrall to all other pleasures of the body" (fol. 45b). Like other complexional theorists, Lemnius takes for granted that both these types of temperament (simply hot, and sanguine) have further subcategories produced by different degrees of heat and proportions of qualities, which accounts for differences of appearance and behavior within each of these two general groups (fol. 39a–b). For example, "a hoate and moyste quality incident to bloude, produceth in men diuerse natures, . . . according to the more or lesse mixture of other humours" (fol. 96a). Although sanguine "heate and abundance of bloude" tend to conduce pursuit of "all sensuall lustes and unbrydled affections" (fol. 101b), complexional theory allows for characteristic variations in them, just as it allows for different sanguine personalities and affinities.

Unfortunately the easily scandalized Lemnius, prone to moralistic rants and misogynies, shrinks from such enormities (from his viewpoint) as buggery, so that he can never bring himself to discuss what might physiologically explain why some men with hot or sanguine temperaments evinced those particular sexual desires and behaviors, whereas others pursued different ones. Other commentators, such as Cocles, sought to classify distinctive sexual types and study their various constitutions and signifiers (Ch. 7). But even Lemnius indicates how complexional theory enabled such inquiries to be conceived and pursued, and what basic temperamental profiles would have been most often associated with insertive sodomites. Since they were complexionally either hotter or both hotter and moister than males with other complexions, they were oversexed by nature. If simply hotter, they were hypermasculine, since heat was definitively masculine and, in Galenic reproductive theory, crucially differentiated males from females by causing genital extrusion. Or if their constitutions emphasized masculine heat together with a degree of moisture beyond what appeared normatively male, the latter trait could have seemed somewhat relatively feminine in a paradoxically hot conjunction. For the physician-astrologer Antoine Mizauld (1510–78) the feminine sex is emphatically moist, hence lunar, while for Cardano it differs from masculinity "more in moistness than in coldness."[109] Yet temperamentally hot or sanguine males were the complexional elite. Aside from the theoretical but practically elusive ideal of perfect balance, these complexions are the best, Lemnius stresses, though intemperancies would cause further qualitative imbalances impairing health (fols. 38a, 46a, 87b–89a). Sodomitical arousals and acts would presumably exacerbate constitutional heat, and heighten an individual's sexually transgressive temperament, so that habituation would be reciprocally psychic and somatic. In Walkington's quadripartite temperamental scheme that assumes that only compound complexions practically exist, their "paragon" is the sanguine, blessed with "rare qualities and admirable vertues" despite its "naturall fault" of being "too prone to venery."[110]

During the long ascendancy of complexional physiology, medicine interpenetrated with physiognomics, for both disciplines, like Galen himself, assumed that a person's appearance, personality, and behaviors were functions and signifiers of her or his particular complexion.[111] Physicians analysed patients' complexions and humoral imbalances accordingly, and so complexional manuals inventoried the outward signs and personal traits of each main temperature, with advice on subcategories. After c.1200, Western physiognomics was a confluence of complexional physiology, natural philosophy, ancient physiognomical treatises, postclassical developments in the discipline,[112] and astrology. Leading physiognomical writers were often also medical practitioners, astrologers, or both. As long as complexional physiology appeared scientifically viable, so too did physiognomics, for they shared many assumptions, analytic procedures, and perceived indicators. The title-page of the much-reprinted treatise *Of Phisionomie* emphasizes its basis in the Galenic dictum, "the maners of the mynde do folow the temperature of the bodye": hence the importance of bodily signs.[113]

To assess complexional physiology's implications for same-sexual history, then, we must study not only medical but also physiognomical texts. Whereas medicine was not centrally concerned with the extent to which individuals conformed to normative models of gender and sexual affiliation, that was a main focus of physiognomics according to its foundational ancient authorities.[114] Yet sexual historiography has hardly begun to reckon with the resources and implications of physiognomics, despite its detailed morphologies of sexual types, its deterministic potential, and hence its importance for former perceptions of sexual identities.[115] I will use "physiognomics" inclusively to denote the full range of early modern endeavors to interpret bodily features as signs of personal characteristics, conditions of life and death, good or ill fortune, and future prospects. Judging by the number of treatises published on chiromancy, physiognomy, and metoposcopy (the main subdisciplines of early modern physiognomics), the size and elaboration of the texts, and the number of printings, chiromancy (now called palmistry, study of the hands) was the most influential among not only the general public but also the social and intellectual elites between at least 1475 and 1675, followed by physiognomy (study of the human body's range of parts, aspects, and mannerisms). Metoposcopy, evaluation of the forehead, ran a distant third.

From physiognomical standpoints (based partly on ancient precedents, astrology, and complexional theory), sexual inclinations and characteristics are functions of the distinctive constitutions and living conditions of individuals. As in complexional medicine, those change over time in accord with personal circumstances and age, and yet there is a continuity of innate factors, so that physiognomical understandings of sexual affinities are quasi-essentialist. The inner conditions that conduce them also leave physical traces legibly inscribed upon the body. According to an anonymous seventeenth-century French chiromantic treatise, various marks on the palm indicate a man is "principally tainted with the sin of Sodomy," or has "some inclination to the Italian vice," or "a great aptitude for indecent vices and particularly Sodomy." In the latter case the sign and its signified sexual tendencies reflect a melancholic temperament involving "too much coldness mixed with excessive dryness."[116]

Ancient physiognomics assumed that cinaedi can be identified through various outwardly discernible departures from conventional masculine norms. Supposedly at least quasi-essential, these signifiers also appeared transhistorically definitive. Early modern treatises on physiognomy largely tend to follow their ancient precursors on the traits of cinaedi, and routinely include ancient personalities in case studies.[117] Although insertive male sodomites are sometimes said to have typically lacked apparent sexual, constitutional, or other abnormalities, physiognomics had already began to codify their alleged traits by 1300.[118] But this thoroughly androcentric discipline had little interest in females except insofar as they were to be evaluated as prostitutes, mistresses, prospective wives, vessels of motherhood, and objects of titillating gossip. While physiognomics acknowledged viragos and some texts inventoried their characteristics, it strongly tended to ignore female same-sexual interactions,[119] even though those became increasingly topical in anatomical and gynecological treatises after the mid-sixteenth century. Following Cocles but adding shock ("your virgin ears stop us here"), the chiromancer Antonio Piccioli (fl. 1587) mentions Sappho and elliptically acknowledges sapphic

Mais celuy qui eſt marqué de celles-cy , ſera
vn ſodomite.

Celuy qui eſt marqué en la ſitüation gauche de la
Balance , ſera vicieux , luxurieux , Sodomite & homicide , lequel mourra au ſupplice.
    Mais la femme ſera paillarde , laquelle expoſera ſes
enfans
    R A P P O R T. Ce ſeing teſmoigne à l'homme,
qu'il a vn autre ſeing caché ſous les teſticules, lequel luy
• predit des priſons , & en fin vne mort en public : & à la
femme ſous les parties honteuſes, qui lui prognoſtique
des maladies incurables , & enfin la mort par pauureté.

Mais cette ligne , auec vn ſeing poſé entre les
yeux ; marque vn ſodomite , qui corrompra auſſi
ſes ſœurs , & lequel finalement periſra par le
glaiue.

Figure 1.2 Sodomitical faces, from Girolamo Cardano, *La metoposcopie*, tr. Sieur Claude
Martin de Laurendière, Paris: T. Jolly, 1658, pp. 141, 188, 211. By permission of the Osler
Library for the History of Science and Medicine, McGill University. Biblioteca Osleriana
2242.

pleasures.[120] Jean Taxil (fl. 1602–14) catalogues bodily signs that a woman has a
big clitoris or mons Veneris (physiognomers assessed penises likewise), and notes a
strong voice in a woman indicates a virago with abundant heat.[121]

    Whereas some influential sexual historiographies subsume same-sexual relations
in undifferentiated debauchery before c.1650, or even later, the more frank and
substantial early modern commentators on physiognomics who address sexual
issues proceed according to specific classifications.[122] They sensibly recognize a
wide variety of possibly discrete sexual affinities *as well as* possible combinations
thereof. One or more would be attributed to a given subject according to her or
his particular ensemble of signs.

    Like the metoposcopic treatise associated with Ciro Spontoni (c.1552–1610),
Cardano's includes a category of the sodomite, distinguished by certain marks upon
his forehead (Figure 1.2).[123] Since the most common legal and social application of

"sodomite" was a male who sought same-sexual relations, that would have been the expected interpretation of the term when not otherwise defined by context. Cardano means to be specific because other illustrations address and categorize other types of sexual transgressors. Jean Taisnier (1508–c.1562) provides a chapter on the chiromantic signs of the diverse species of lust, with 74 illustrations. Drawn from Cocles, one group deals specifically with types of "sodomite," another with cinaedi (Figures 1.3–5): the former insertive and the latter receptive.

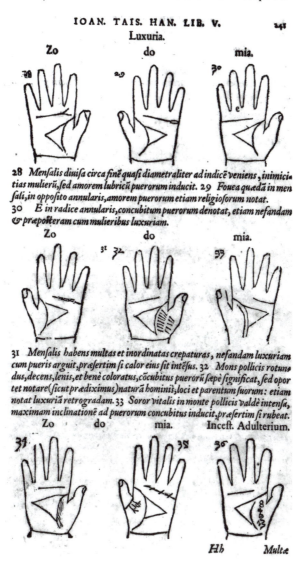

Figure 1.3 The hands of sodomites, from Jean Taisnier, *Opus mathematicum octo libros complectens*, Cologne: Apud Theodorum Baumium, 1583, p. 241. By permission of Houghton Library, Harvard University.

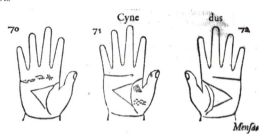

Figure 1.4 The hands of cinaedi, from Jean Taisnier, *Opus mathematicum octo libros complectens*, Cologne: Apud Theodorum Baumium, 1583, p. 247. By permission of Houghton Library, Harvard University.

248   ABSOLVTIS. CHYROMAN.
Luxuria.

70 *Menſalis eſt radix,ſignificans virtutem genitiuam.Ideo prudentes eam vocant linam generationis, ſi fuerit fracta, diſcontinua,aut pallida,aut à varijs punctis, foſſulis, aut ſemicirculis obſeſſa,debilitatē coitus denotat,&̃ for taſsis gignituam impotentiam, ſi in medio ſpatio inter lineas trianguli non ſit planities, & malè coloretur defectum caloris arguit, & per côſequens,defectum coitus. Notandum,quòd multoties impotentia coitus eſt qualitatiuæ, aliquando quantitatiuæ: igitur conſiderare oportet annexiones ſignorum atq; que concordantiam, aut contrà operantiam, aliter inditium poteſt eſſe inane. Homo ante 20. annum eſt effœminatus ex parte complexionis, cuius ſignum apparet in mollicie carnis, atq; in moribus appetitibuſque, & in eorum vocibus, & poſt hoc tempus adoleſcentiæ cum hominis creſcentia omnia mutantur:quia naturalis calor præualet ſuper humidum incongruum:igitur propter ætatem iſtam adhuc ſunt effœminati,quod patet per ſigna in manibus eorum reperta.*

71 *Tuberculum Veneris tumefactum,coloratum, atque lineatum,aut conglomeratum multum lineis,Cynedi ſignum eſt.*

72 *Soror vitalis protenſa in monte Veneris & rubra, Cynedorum ſignum eſt.*

73 *Via lactea,continua cum ſua proportione, cynedos eſſe indicabit.*
74 *Complexio effœminata,compoſitio & lineamenta,cynedi amabilis,& placabilis maximum eſt inditium.*

Color candidus atque perſpicuus cum venis apparentibus, non eſt dubium, quin Cynedum denunciet,in fœminis ſi ſit, meretrices ,præcipuè quando corpus carnoſum exiſtit:quia talem colorem facit Venus,& extenditur quaſi in complexione ſanguinea:quia parum differt à natura Iouis.

Notandum, quòd ea omnia,quæ compræhenduntur ſub documento caliditatis & humiditatis in habitudinibus & lineamentis hîc poſſunt accommodari,vt in primis radicibus dictum fuit, tamen hîc accidit magna diſtinctio: quia propriè coitus in actu eſt calificatus ex calido & humido, vt dictum eſt: alia diſtinctio eſt quoad appetitum, & non in re, prout ſunt Melancholici propter materiam ventoſam,euaporatiuam incitantem coitum. Errant illi, qui leguminibus cæpis,allijs diuerſiſque alijs cibis veſcuntur,dicentes eiuſmo
di le•

Figure 1.5 The hands of cinaedi, from Jean Taisnier, *Opus mathematicum octo libros complectens*, Cologne: Apud Theodorum Baumium, 1583, p. 248. By permission of Houghton Library, Harvard University.

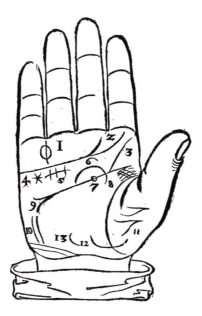

Figure 1.6. Chiromantic sign no. 11: visible capillaries indicating a same-sexually "versatile" pedicator. Patricio Tricasso, *Enarratio pulcherrima principiorum chyromantiae*, Nurnberg: Apud I. Montanum & U. Neuberum, 1560, sig. 2B1b. By permission of Houghton Library, Harvard University.

Patricio Tricasso (1491–c.1530) surveys diverse sexual types including the pederastic sodomite who assumes both insertive and receptive sex roles. Rogue capillaries appear on his chiromantic Mount of Venus, and they would have appeared to indicate that his sexual nature is constitutionally most sanguine and overheated (Figure 1.6).

This sexually classificatory animus of physiognomics also appears in some widely circulating reference works, miscellanies, and encyclopedias from c.1500 onward, but had much earlier precedents such as Aquinas' analysis of the species of lust, and ancient astrology.[124] Physiognomics represented and reified particular sexual types according to the body's perceived expression of the constitutional factors producing those inclinations. Having originated in antiquity, such researches and commentaries rapidly expanded in the later Middle Ages and Renaissance.

Astrology too had sexually analytic, classificatory, and potentially deterministic implications complementing those of complexional physiology and physiognomics.[125] Hippocratic–Galenic medicine entailed assessment of subjects' bodies to determine their complexions and personal inclinations; chiromancy and metoposcopy were founded partly on astrological principles; and astrology could be used for medically diagnostic and curative purposes, as could chiromancy. The complexional scheme of corresponding temperaments, elements, humors, and ages could be given a further astrological development, with corresponding planets and signs, and diagrammatic representations appeared in medical as well as astrological handbooks (Figure 1.7).[126]

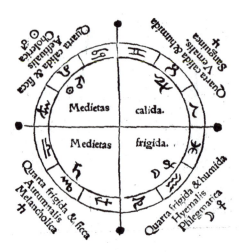

Figure 1.7 The correlations of complexions, qualities, seasons, and astrological signs, from Johann Schöner, *Opusculum astrologicum*, Nurnberg: Apud Jo. Petreium, 1539, sig. D4a. Rare Books Division, The New York Public Library, Astor, Lenox, and Tilden Foundations. By permission.

Some physicians would presumably have insisted with Lemnius that the causation of "diuers sorts and sondry differences of Natures and maners" that astrologers attributed to planetary and stellar influences was primarily complexional in origin (fols. 100b–101a). Yet the physician Johannes Rothmann (fl. 1592–5) published research claiming to demonstrate, through studies of nineteen individuals' hands in relation to their horoscopes, the full accordance of chiromantic, astrological, and biographical data, and Rudolph Goclenius Jr. (1572–1621) followed suit.[127]

A reproductive handbook that had wide European currency far into the seventeenth century, *De conceptu et generatione hominis* (1544), demonstrates the former astrological appearances of personal formation. Not only the seed produces an infant, its author Jakob Rüff (1500–58) advises, but also "the motion of the Starres is supposed to prevaile some thing."[128] The portrayal of birth in a sixteenth-century edition includes astrologers, whom the parents would have commissioned. As the infant is being drawn from the mother's womb, astral prognostications of its nature and future prospects have already begun (see Figure 8.1).

Like medicine and physiognomics, astrology provided various theories and rationales that would have facilitated the recognition and development of specific types of sexual disposition, predisposition, and deviance, and their justification through sexual dissidence. The chief ancient sources of Renaissance astrology, Ptolemy's *Tetrabiblos* and Firmicus Maternus' *Mathesis*, both identified specific celestial arrays that each produce a certain type of natal same-sexual affiliation.[129] In Ptolemy, these include "men who have relations with both males and females, but no more than moderately inclined to either"; men who are "pathics"; men pursuing "only . . . love of boys"; and men who love "males of any age" (4.5; tr. F. E. Robbins). Likewise he identifies horoscopes that produce various kinds of tribades. The variety of human temperaments could be explained according to the constitutional imprints of astral influences at conception or birth. Astrology afforded a scientific basis for recognition and conceptualization of persons characterized by various types of same-sexual inclination, hence with distinctive sexual subjectivities. At least for those whose horoscopes included apparent astral causes of same-sexual desires, those tendencies could appear to originate in the natural circumstances of their nativities. The extent to which they could control and suppress those inclinations was diversely interpreted.

In Chapter 8, P. G. Maxwell-Stuart surveys representations of same-sexual love in early modern astrology, and clarifies their contemporary status by reviewing the varied reactions to the discipline. In Chapter 9, H. Darrel Rutkin compares Cardano's practical analyses of celebrity horoscopes to his comments on same-sexual topics in his astrological treatises. As a theorist, Cardano insists on the importance of a subject's personal and cultural circumstances for interpreting the sexual implications of astrological data. Yet in Cardano's published analyses of particular horoscopes, he writes as if their sexual signs determine each subject's affinities and behaviors in later life. His exploration of causal factors and influences thus somewhat prefigures much later nature/nurture debates about particular sexual affiliations, and the related controversies about the extent to which they are essential or culturally constructed.

As Rutkin observes, this discrepancy between Cardano's theory and his practice epitomizes a fundamental contradiction inherent in premodern astrology (paralleled, we have seen, in complexional physiology and physiognomics). The stars, many astrologers appeared to insist, impart inclinations not compulsions, in accord with theological doctrines of free will and hence moral responsibility for alleged sins. Yet their diction and attitudes often appear so deterministic, Maxwell-Stuart argues, that same-sexual relations seem effects of astrally instilled determinations (Ch. 8). Free will and choice in sexual and other spheres could thus be questioned, hence also much of orthodox moral theology, including claims that certain kinds of sex are "against nature."[130] According to the title-page of a widely published astrological text's English version, its science enables us "to fynd the *fatal desteny*, constellation, complexion, and natural inclination of euery man and childe by his byrth."[131]

Such challenges to Christian moral orthodoxy could not go unanswered. To some religious authorities the divinatory sciences' attempts to disavow determinism too often seemed insincere or unheeded, and they had long been suspect. Counter-Reformation efforts to control the dissemination of ideas through restrictions upon authors, books, and hence readers came to target those sciences. The Venetian Index of Prohibited Books issued in 1554 includes Cocles, for example, and this trend culminated in the more broadly condemnatory papal Indexes of 1557, 1559, and 1564. The 1559 Index bans divinatory texts in general, including physiognomics and astrology, while naming a range of such authors, and the 1564 version maintains the general ban.[132] These sciences received their consummate anathema in the papal bull of 1586 that, as we have seen, partly aimed to protect orthodox conceptions of human will.

Although, unlike the other sciences reviewed so far, alchemy could offer no same-sexual exculpations, morphologies, typologies, or constitutional rationales, it conceptualized chemical research through metaphoric transmutations of sex and gender. As Allison Kavey explains in Chapter 11, these could involve couplings between metallic males, mercurial sex-changes, production of chemical hermaphrodites, and anxieties about sodomy. Some practitioners could have pursued both alchemical and physically same-sexual interests. The production of a medieval alchemical translation has been linked to the apparent spousal relationship, sharing the same bed and bedroom, of the learned couple Robert of Ketton (fl. 1141–57) and Hermann of Carinthia (fl. 1138–43).[133] Early modern alchemical texts are often reprints or developments of medieval documents, and thus reflect earlier ideas about sex and gender while renewing their dissemination. Comparison of alchemical texts originating in different periods can clarify historical shifts in the meanings and uses of sex and gender at this juncture of natural and occult philosophies. Their alchemically expressive function derives from contemporary cultural norms that imbue these metaphors with presumed communicative value. Yet the figurative transpositions of sex and gender into the chemical world modify their conventional significances and expose them to new interrogation. Study of alchemy enhances knowledge of their varied roles in sexual history, for the alchemical quest for the philosopher's stone proceeds, Kavey shows, through myriad sexually represented transformations and combinations.[134]

The sexual arcana and the inquisitors of nature

Replete with continuities and discontinuities, subsumptions, and prolepses, same-sexual history requires flexible approaches for the exploration and definition of its chronologies and genealogies. As Caelius Aurelianus reported c.400 CE, Parmenides pondered c.450 BCE how "pathics come into being as a result of a circumstance at conception."[135] Central to the postclassical history of the sciences' engagement with same-sexual relations has been the emancipation of thought about sexual questions from religious influence and intimidation, and its increasing emergence into unrestricted public discourse. But even that aspect of sexual history evinces some temporal irregularities. Some premodern scientific writers were exceptionally candid and loquacious about the etiologies and manifestations of forbidden sex, such as the once-prestigious authorities Pietro d'Abano and Cocles, even though their discussions still to some extent reflect the adverse judgments of moral theology.

The discontinuities in Western culture's sexual history include the invention of sodomy as a terrible sin and various others such as those mentioned at this chapter's outset, and yet the assumptions of conventional morality founded on Christian proscriptions continued to infuse the nineteenth-century emergence of so-called sexuality in science. Sexually significant paradigm shifts in the sciences themselves are not merely recent. The demises of complexional physiology and of astrology as a legitimate natural discipline ended their power to make departures from normative sexual roles and gender models appear scientifically intelligible and thus naturalized to some extent within European culture. That former accountability of these phenomena then had to be reinvented. The Western sciences became increasingly dissociated from the scientific paradigms and authorities of antiquity during the seventeenth century. This entailed the sciences' further alienation from the residues of the Greek and Roman sex/gender system infusing the remains of ancient medicine, astrology, and physiognomics, where various same-sexual desires and dispositions had been acknowledged and explicated in ways uncompromised by conceptions of sodomy.

These explanations would only have first developed in the speculative milieu of the ancient sciences because in many cases same-sexual behaviors already seemed to entail engrained commitments anyway, so that rationalizations that had essentialist and quasi-essentialist implications appeared to make sense and were invented accordingly. Ancient astrology documents these processes of thought most extensively, but they appear also in genital anatomy, physiology, embryology, and physiognomics. The sciences of antiquity and their medieval Arabic inheritors prestigiously mediated these theories of differing sexual expressions and affinities to medieval and Renaissance Europe.

Already by 1277, we have seen, these rationales afforded means to question the sexual nature of nature and hence disturbed orthodox sexual morality. When human sexual natures themselves may appear so diverse, and even intrinsically so, from posited natural causes, what is "natural" and "unnatural" in biological sex, sexual relations, and gender conformation? Some scientifically possible standpoints and modes of inquiry thus differed from central tenets of Christian moral theology. While that dissonance usually remained unacknowledged or latent in written scientific discourse, due to felt social pressure, intimidations, and culturally assimilated aversions, it still had many expressions within and beyond the sciences. Since relatively relaxed views of at least sex between males seem to have been most current in Renaissance Italy (though France seems to have been competitive on sapphism), it seems the most promising regional locus for further researches into scientific reflections upon same-sexual relations at that time. Currently known writers who pursued such inquiries and published the results at some length are predominantly Italian, such as Pietro d'Abano, Cocles, Cardano, Porta, Zacchia. The first four all had some divinatory and other occult interests, and difficulties with religious authorities (Cocles posthumously). Lemnius, Du Laurens, and Huarte are all relatively brief, while Taisnier's same-sexual material derives from Cocles. Yet, as Taisnier shows, the Italians' Latin publications had considerable influence in European learned communities.

As always in the study of same-sexual history beyond the recent past, we must allow for much that is hidden or lost, for we are dealing in part with an "archive of repression"[136] to be deciphered, where much was censured, censored, or never recorded. As the medieval and early modern sciences' extant documents cannot fully represent the former scope of thought on such topics, so our knowledge of it remains provisional and heuristic. Often when scientific texts of those times engage or represent theories that could challenge morally orthodox views of same-sexual relations, particularly by supporting recognition of persons characterized by such dispositions and predispositions, we find studied silence on the possibly subversive implications, or awkward attempts to reconcile those views with moral orthodoxy. We should not take the written prevalence of those gestures within the sciences at face value, as if less obedient manipulations of those explanatory paradigms were unthinkable. For Antonio Vignali (1500–59), writing c.1525, the very notion that "buggery is against nature is beyond Nature's comprehension. If she had not wanted man to bugger, she would not have made it such a sweet thing, and would have made the anus so it could not take a cock. . . . The anus can take a penis as comfortably as the vagina can."[137] Reconstruction of the potential heterodoxies of sex encouraged or enabled by the premodern sciences requires re-enaction, in effect, of the sixteenth- and seventeenth-century hermeneutics of heresy bred by a culture of censorship. Texts suspected of encoded deviance from orthodoxy were inquisitorially decoded, or those and other texts were interpreted heretically, to develop heterodox arguments and ideas.[138] Even Aquinas could be mined in this way, for in condemning the species of lust including sodomy, he lists a range of libertinous arguments before stating his own contrary case.[139] One of these is natural philosophical: "a seminal discharge is, according to Aristotle, from a surplus to nourishment. No sin is present in the discharge of other superfluities, consequently not in that of sexual activity."[140]

The resources of the premodern sciences could be appropriated in diverse sexually interested ways, both to support moral orthodoxy, like Guastavino in Chapter 3, or to contest it. In various early modern discourses beyond the sciences, especially literary or erotic, there are quite numerous assertions and evident assumptions that some males and females are naturally characterized by same-sex attraction, so that such ideas clearly had a cultural presence.[141] Advocating intergenerational sex between males, Antonio Rocco (1586–1652) assumes that some individuals have same-sexual affinities by nature. And as each clock runs according to the design of its maker, he argues, "inclinations (*inclinazioni*) are counterweights given us by nature and God; whoever follows these does not depart from his own first principles (*propri principii*)," nor "go against the maker."[142] Such interpretations of sexual nature, I have shown, were condemned and hence already circulating in 1277. The accounts of sex in Avicenna's *Liber canonis* and the *Problemata*, Pietro d'Abano's commentary on the latter, Ptolemy's *Tetrabiblos*, Cocles's *Anastasis*, and similar texts would have had some sodomitical readers capable of conceiving sexual heterodoxies and disseminating them in friendly or desirable ears. Such medieval and early modern scientific resources introduce us not only to a history of repression which sought to mask or defuse their subversive implications, but also to its inversion adumbrated in part by the very demonstration of that concern: a history of deviant awareness, agency, and advocacy.

Notes

1. Both "Renaissance" and "early modern" assist same-sexual historiography. The former e.g. contextually evokes the humanist project of reviving antiquity, which publicized the ancients' different sexual mores and endued them with new authority. "Premodern" in my usage includes "early modern": also before modern.
2. My usage of "same-sexual relations" does not exclude homoeroticism nor relationships nor love. Circumstances varied in particular cases.
3. Cf. Eve Kosofsky Sedgwick, *Epistemology of the Closet*, Berkeley and Los Angeles: University of California Press, 1990, pp. 10, 45–8.
4. See e.g. Michael N. McMorris, "Science as *Scientia*," *Physis*, 23 (1981), 171–95. See further Charles B. Schmitt *et al.* (eds), *The Cambridge History of Renaissance Philosophy*, Cambridge: Cambridge University Press, 1988; Norman Kretzmann *et al.* (eds), *The Cambridge History of Later Medieval Philosophy*, Cambridge: Cambridge University Press, 1982.
5. Peter Harrison e.g. discusses the notion of nature's book in *The Bible, Protestantism, and the Rise of Natural Science*, Cambridge: Cambridge University Press, 1998, pp. 44–63. On nature's perceived normative force, see Lorraine Daston and Fernando Vidal (eds), *The Moral Authority of Nature*, Chicago: University of Chicago Press, 2004. Andrew Cunningham and Edward Grant debate natural philosophy's interactions with theology in "Open Forum: The Nature of 'Natural Philosophy'," *Early Science and Medicine*, 5 (2000), 258–300.
6. Cf. Gary B. Deason, "Reformation Theology and the Mechanistic Conception of Nature," in David C. Lindberg and Ronald L. Numbers (eds), *God and Nature: Historical Essays on the Encounter between Christianity and Science*, Berkeley: University of California Press, 1986, pp. 167–91; John Hedley Brooke, *Science and Religion: Some Historical Perspectives*, Cambridge: Cambridge University Press, 1991, ch. 4.
7. See Katharine Park and Lorraine Daston (eds), *Early Modern Science*, vol. 3 of *The Cambridge History of Science*, Cambridge: Cambridge University Press, 2006; esp. their "Introduction: The Age of the New," pp. 1–17. Hereafter cited as *EMS*. Also Peter Dear, *Revolutionizing the Sciences: European Knowledge and its Ambitions, 1500–1700*, Houndmills: Palgrave, 2001.
8. Brian P. Copenhaver, "Astrology and Magic," in Charles B. Schmitt *et al.* (eds), *The Cambridge History of Renaissance Philosophy*, Cambridge: Cambridge University Press, 1988, p. 268.
9. See H. Darrel Rutkin, "Astrology," in *EMS*, pp. 541–61.
10. I provide an overview of relevant former sciences in Kenneth Borris (ed.), *Same-Sex Desire in the English Renaissance: A Sourcebook of Texts, 1470–1650*, New York and London: Routledge, 2004. On males, see further Joan Cadden, *Meanings of Sex Difference in the Middle Ages: Medicine, Science, and Culture*, Cambridge: Cambridge University Press, 1993, pp. 209–27; her "'Nothing Natural is Shameful': Vestiges of a Debate about Sex and Science in a Group of Late-Medieval Manuscripts," *Speculum*, 76 (2001), 66–89; her "Sciences/Silences: The Natures and Languages of 'Sodomy' in Peter of Abano's *Problemata* Commentary," in Karma Lochrie *et al.* (eds), *Constructing Medieval Sexuality*, Minneapolis: University of Minnesota Press, 1997, pp. 40–57; Mark D. Jordan, *The Invention of Sodomy in Christian Theology*, Chicago: University of Chicago Press, 1997, ch. 6   Katherine Crawford's *European Sexualities, 1400–1800* considers former science only insofar as it was medical and concerned with male–female sex (ch.3). Cambridge: Cambridge University Press, 2007.
11. E.g. Katharine Park, "The Rediscovery of the Clitoris: French Medicine and the Tribade, 1570–1620," in David Hillman and Carla Mazzio (eds), *The Body in Parts: Fantasies of Corporeality in Early Modern Europe*, New York and London: Routledge, 1997, pp. 171–93; Valerie Traub, *The Renaissance of Lesbianism in Early Modern England*, Cambridge: Cambridge University Press, 2002; Harriette Andreadis, *Sappho in Early*

Modern England: Female Same-Sex Literary Erotics, 1550–1714, Chicago: University of Chicago Press, 2001. On medieval medical notions of female same-sex transgression and viragos, see Karma Lochrie, *Heterosyncrasies: Female Sexuality When Normal Wasn't*, Minneapolis: University of Minnesota Press, 2005, ch. 4.

12. See Borris (ed.), *Same-Sex Desire*, pp. 19–20, ch. 9.

13. E.g. Andreadis accepts Alan Bray's widely influential but very belated date of 1650 for the putative dawn of male same-sexual identities, and applies it to women. *Sappho*, pp. 16, 51–2, 96–8.

14. Carla Freccero's phrase, *Queer/Early/Modern*, Durham, NC: Duke University Press, 2006, p. 33.

15. Halperin, *How to Do the History of Homosexuality*, Chicago: University of Chicago Press, 2002, pp. 29, 46, 167. Compare Sedgwick's *Epistemology of the Closet*, introduction, and Freccero's *Queer/Early/Modern*, ch. 3. I discuss the early modern implications in *Same-Sex Desire*, general introduction.

16. Cf. e.g. Alan Bray, *Homosexuality in Renaissance England*, 2nd edn, New York: Columbia University Press, 1995 (first published 1982); Randolph Trumbach, in a series of essays summarized and referenced in his *Sex and the Gender Revolution*, vol. 1, *Heterosexuality and the Third Gender in Enlightenment London*, Chicago: University of Chicago Press, 1998, pp. 1–9, 18–22, 432–3; Arnold I. Davidson, *The Emergence of Sexuality: Historical Epistemology and the Formation of Concepts*, Cambridge, MA: Harvard University Press, 2001; Jeffrey Weeks, *Sex, Politics, and Society: The Regulation of Sexuality since 1800*, London: Longman, 1981.

17. Sedgwick, *Epistemology of the Closet*, pp. 46–8.

18. See e.g. Alan Bray, *The Friend*, Chicago: University of Chicago Press, 2003, pp. 183–4. His references tell only the universalizing half of a much more complex history. For a critique of such approaches, see Borris (ed.), *Same-Sex Desire*, general introduction.

19. It is now widely accepted that "sodomy," hence "sodomite," most often referred to sex between males in early modern culture (see n. 22). Hence it could readily function as a term of such targeted abuse. Benvenuto Cellini e.g. takes for granted that being publicly called a sodomite – contextually a male who has sex with male youths, as Cellini's reply makes clear – is a horrible infuriating injury. *La vita*, in *Opere*, ed. Bruno Maier, Milan: Rizzoli, 1968, book II, lxxi (pp. 530–2). Likewise Brantôme (Pierre de Bourdeille), in Borris (ed.), *Same-Sex Desire*, p. 310. On "cinaedus," see n.75.

20. Sedgwick, *Epistemology of the Closet*, pp. 1–2, 9.

21. For Freccero e.g. "identities can be said to be made by acts." *Queer/Early/Modern*, p. 33. Halperin urges sexual historians to "inquire into the construction of sexual identities before the emergence of sexual orientations." *History of Homosexuality*, pp. 42–4. Compare Freccero, ch. 3. For additional bibliography, see Borris (ed.), *Same-Sex Desire*, pp. 4–6. See further Crawford, *European Sexualities, 1400–1800*, pp. 6–7; David M. Robinson, *Closeted Writing and Lesbian and Gay Literature: Classical, Early Modern, Eighteenth-Century*, Aldershot, UK: Ashgate, 2006, ch. 1; Jonathan Goldberg and Madhavi Menon, "Queering History," *PMLA*, 120 (2005), 1608–17; Sarah Salih, "Sexual Identities: A Medieval Perspective," in Tom Betteridge (ed.), *Sodomy in Early Modern Europe*, Manchester: Manchester University Press, 2002, pp. 112–30; Helmut Puff, *Sodomy in Reformation Germany and Switzerland, 1400–1600*, Chicago: University of Chicago Press, 2003, introduction. Ruth Mazzo Karras surveys recent medieval scholarship in *Sexuality in Medieval Europe: Doing unto Others*, New York: Routledge, 2005, pp. 160–81.

22. For the term's premodern currency in Aquinas' sense, and in its application to sex between males, see Chs. 5, 7 (end of their introductions), this volume. For broader discussion of "sodomy," see Borris (ed.), *Same-Sex Desire*, pp. 18–20, 23–35, 73–86, 204; Puff, *Sodomy*, pp. 7–9, 12–13. See also Karras, *Sexuality*, pp. 134–5; William Naphy, "Sodomy in Early Modern Geneva: Various Definitions, Diverse Verdicts," in Tom

Betteridge (ed.), *Sodomy in Early Modern Europe*, Manchester: Manchester University Press, 2002, pp. 96–7, 106–7; George Rousseau, "The Pursuit of Homosexuality in the Eighteenth Century: 'Utterly Confused Category' and/or Rich Repository?," in Robert Parks Maccubbin, *'Tis Nature's Fault: Unnatural Sexuality During the Enlightenment*, Cambridge: Cambridge University Press, 1985, pp. 132–68.

23. Homosexual acts are justified by an individual's moral right to have free and consensual choice in such a personal and private matter. Compare Sedgwick, *Epistemology of the Closet*, pp. 41–4.

24. E.g. Bray's very influential *Homosexuality in Renaissance England*, first published 1982.

25. Cf. Borris (ed.), *Same-Sex Desire*, pp. 1–18; Freccero, *Queer/Early/Modern*, pp. 34, 41.

26. Leone Ebreo, *Dialoghi d'amore*, Venice: Domenico Giglio, 1558. Copy at Thomas Fisher Rare Books Library, University of Toronto. See Borris (ed.), *Same-Sex Desire*, pp. 176–7.

27. E.g. Halperin, *History of Homosexuality*, pp. 133–4.

28. Compare Aristotle's and Cicero's observations of the equalizing impulses and mutualities at play in male–male relationships, *Nicomachean Ethics*, 8.7.2, 8.8.5; *On Friendship*, 19.69, 20.71–3. As that could happen in hierarchical ancient culture, so too in the Renaissance. Compare also Michael Rocke's argument that early modern Florentine youths orally penetrated their anally penetrative older partners. *Forbidden Friendships: Homosexuality and Male Culture in Renaissance Florence*, Oxford: Oxford University Press, 1996, pp. 91–4. He also documents cases of mutual sexual pleasures and attachments, pp. 94, 129, 167, 172, 190. Cf. Bruce Smith, *Homosexual Desire in Shakespeare's England: A Cultural Poetics*, Chicago: University of Chicago Press, 1991, pp. 75–6.

29. E.g. Halperin, *History of Homosexuality*, pp. 17 (quoted), 131–2. Compare Sedgwick, *Epistemology of the Closet*, pp. 2, 8.

30. Joseph Cady discovered the early modern model of "masculine love" and defined it in a series of essays beginning in 1992. Some found his evidence insufficient. I present ample new evidence for the model in *Same-Sex Desire*, pp. 6–9, with a redefinition and bibliography.

31. Halperin provisionally offers this four-part taxonomy informed by previous scholars in *History of Homosexuality*, pp. 108–30, and lists its precursors, pp. 186–7 n. 6.

32. For further explanation, see Borris (ed.), *Same-Sex Desire*, pp. 6–9.

33. See Rocke, *Forbidden Friendships*, pp. 40–1, 119, 123–4, 131–2. Compare Cocles's account of pedicators in Ch. 7, this volume. Questions pertaining to aversion to sex with females could figure in legal defences and prosecutions of alleged male sodomites. Cardano advises on how to deal with such legal and social issues; see Ch. 10, this volume. In Reformation Geneva, William Naphy observes, "everyone seems to have expected" that a male who had opposite-sexual relations "was very unlikely to have committed sodomy." "Sodomy in Early Modern Geneva," pp. 105–6. Correlative assumptions also figure in literary fictions. See e.g. Borris (ed.), *Same-Sex Desire*, pp. 35–43, 356–7.

34 John T. Noonan, Jr., *Contraception: A History of Its Treatment by the Catholic Theologians and Canonists*, enl. edn, Cambridge, MA: Harvard University Press, 1986, p. 357 n. 34.

35. Tr. Joan Cadden. See her "Trouble in the Earthly Paradise: The Regime of Nature in Late Medieval Christian Culture," in Lorraine Daston and Fernando Vidal (eds), *The Moral Authority of Nature*, Chicago: University of Chicago Press, 2004, pp. 224–31.

36. Cf. Richard A. Muller, "Predestination," in Hans J. Hillerbrand *et al.* (eds), *The Oxford Encyclopedia of the Reformation*, 4 vols, Oxford: Oxford University Press, 1996, vol. 3, pp. 332–8.

37. See Ch. 3, this volume.

38. Agrippa, *Of the Vanity and Uncertainty of Arts and Sciences*, ed. Catherine M. Dunn, tr. James Sanford, Northridge, CA: California State University Press, 1974, p. 106; a translation first published in 1569.

39. P. G. Maxwell-Smith (ed. and tr.), *The Occult in Early Modern Europe: A Documentary History*, London: Macmillan, 1999, p. 112.
40. A term reflecting the importance of Sodom's destruction in late medieval and early modern aversion to same-sexual relations (especially between males). See Borris (ed.), *Same-Sex Desire*, p. 20.
41. Cf. Freccero, *Queer/Early/Modern*, chs. 1–3; Borris (ed.), *Same-Sex Desire*, pp. 11–17.
42. Davidson discusses only one premodern scientific text (written 1629 or 1639) and allows that "much more historical detail would be needed to produce an unequivocally convincing argument that proves the conceptual shift from perverse choice [i.e. volition] to the pervert [i.e. constitution]." That shift is crucial to Davidson's historiography of sexuality, first articulated in a series of essays subsumed in his book. *Emergence of Sexuality*, pp. 54–65 (quoting p. 64).
43. Ibid., chs 1–3, quoting p. 25 (emphasis mine). See esp. pp. 22–5, 57, 61–5, 137–41.
44. Ibid., pp. 22–5.
45. Ibid., quoting pp. 140, 23. Cf. pp. 22–3, 57, 61, 137, 140.
46. Ibid., quoting pp. 22–3, 25. Via Aquinas, Davidson represents former moral theology as if it assumes "we are all subject to all the kinds of lust, and the principle by which we distinguish lusts from one another does not permit us to distinguish different types of people from one another" (p. 61). But individuals were not theologically considered *equally* subject to *all* the kinds of lust or other vices, for they were perceived to have distinctive inclinations. See Borris (ed.), *Same-Sex Desire*, ch. 1, and compare e.g. pp. 130–40 on Pietro d'Abano.
47. Moral theology had long established some basic preconditions for conceptions of sexual perversion by designating procreative sexual behaviors "natural" and nonprocreative ones "unnatural." These thoughts of Richard von Krafft-Ebing, *c.*1900, could have been expressed e.g. in the thirteenth century: "with opportunity for the natural satisfaction of the sexual instinct, every expression of it that does not correspond with the purpose of nature – i.e., procreation – must be regarded as perverse" (cit. Davidson, *Sexuality*, p. 74). Ancient sources may present comparable perspectives: e.g. Ovid, *Metamorphoses*, 9.727–63; Ptolemy, *Tetrabiblos*, 3.14. While moral theology stressed perverse *volition*, hence sexual "perversity," premodern sciences variously hypothesized *constitutional* causes, hence allowed for sexual "perversion" in Davidson's sense.
48. Jordan, *Invention of Sodomy*, pp. 163–4. Similarly Carolyn Dinshaw, *Getting Medieval: Sexualities and Communities, Pre- and Postmodern*, Durham, NC: Duke University Press, 1999, p. 195. Compare Christopher A. Jones, "Monastic Identity and Sodomitic Danger in the *Occupatio* by Odo of Cluny," *Speculum*, 82 (2007), 1–53.
49. Cit. Cadden, "Vestiges of a Debate," 72–3. See further J. M. M. H. Thijssen, "What Really Happened on 7 March 1277: Bishop Tempier's Condemnation and its Institutional Context," in Edith Sylla and Michael McVaugh (eds), *Texts and Contexts in Ancient and Medieval Science*, Leiden: Brill, 1997, pp. 84–114.
50. E.g., drawing on mathematical concepts, Robert Holkot (d. 1349) argued that either human free will was limited or God could not always be able to reward merits and punish sins in afterlife. See Edward Grant, "Science and Theology in the Middle Ages," in David C. Lindberg and Ronald L. Numbers (eds), *God and Nature: Historical Essays on the Encounter between Christianity and Science*, Berkeley: University of California Press, 1986, pp. 60–1.
51. Halperin provisionally proposes four such models for males in *History of Homosexuality*, ch. 4. For three further ones, and a survey of proposals for females, see Borris (ed.), *Same-Sex Desire*, pp. 6–9, 12–13, 17–19.
52. Cf. e.g. Cadden, "Sciences/Silences," pp. 40–57; Winfried Schleiner, "'That Matter Which Ought Not to Be Heard Of': Homophobic Slurs in Renaissance Cultural Politics," *Journal of Homosexuality*, 26 (1994), 41–75.
53. Cadden, "Regime of Nature," p. 228.

54. Cf. Rivka Feldhay, "Religion," in *EMS*, pp. 727–55; Gary B. Ferngren (ed.), *Science and Religion: A Historical Introduction*, Baltimore: Johns Hopkins University Press, 2002; Brooke, *Science and Religion*.

55. Cf. Ian Maclean, "Introduction," in John Brooke and Ian Maclean (eds), *Heterodoxy in Early Modern Science and Religion*, Oxford: Oxford University Press, 2005, pp. x–xxi.

56. See Jean Céard, "Introduction," in Ambroise Paré, *Des monstres et prodiges*, ed. Céard, Geneva: Droz, 1971, pp. xiv–xix. Summarized in Borris (ed.), *Same-Sex Desire*, pp. 234–5.

57. In *The Anatomy of Melancholy* (a prototypical study in psychology), e.g., Robert Burton (1577–1640) shifts from English into Latin when discussing same-sexual relations. See Borris (ed.), *Same-Sex Desire*, pp. 310–16.

58. Cadden, "Vestiges of a Debate," quoting pp. 66, 89.

59. Cf. Judith P. Zinsser (ed.), *Men, Women, and the Birthing of Modern Science*, DeKalb, IL: Northern Illinois University Press, 2005; Londa Schiebinger, *The Mind Has No Sex? Women in the Origins of Modern Science*, Cambridge, MA: Harvard University Press, 1989.

60. Also, whereas venereological print was long silent on same-sexual transmission, legal investigations of sodomy in Lucca after c.1550 (and perhaps earlier) contrarily assumed that anal intercourse could readily transmit the pox. Cf. Mary Hewlett, "The French Connection: Syphilis and Sodomy in Late-Renaissance Lucca," in Kevin Siena (ed.), *Sins of the Flesh: Responding to Sexual Disease in Early Modern Europe*, Toronto: Centre for Reformation and Renaissance Studies, 2005, pp. 239–60.

61. In London e.g. Humphrey Stafford was executed in 1607 for anal rape of two male youths who thus needed medical care. See Borris (ed.), *Same-Sex Desire*, pp. 99–101.

62. Rocke, *Forbidden Friendships*, p. 54; Ruggiero, *Boundaries of Eros*, p. 117.

63. E.g. depositions confirm that in 1461 a boy thus "had to have his ass medicated," and in 1500 another's recovery required bed-rest "for two months." Rocke, *Forbidden Friendships*, pp. 66, 162–3.

64. On torture and European sodomy law, see Borris (ed.), *Same-Sex Desire*, pp. 73–86.

65. After c.1550 if not earlier, Genevan courts "heard a report from the medical authorities" in cases of alleged sexual assault involving someone under 16. I thank William Naphy for this information. For early modern Italian legal authorities who report similar norms, see Ch. 4, this volume.

66. Hewlett, "Syphilis and Sodomy," pp. 239–60. She informs me that the relevant Luccan records prior to 1550 are lost.

67. Ibid., pp. 244–58; quoting p. 248.

68. Lusitano, *Curationum medicinalium centuria secunda*, Venice: Ex officina Erasmiana Vincentij Valgrisij, 1552, s. 87 (1st edn 1551?). See Ch. 4, this volume.

69. On use of saliva, oil, and ointments in anal sex c.1525, see Antonio Vignali, *La Cazzaria: The Book of the Prick*, New York: Routledge, 2003, pp. 82, 87.

70. For an overview with bibliography, see Borris (ed.), *Same-Sex Desire*, ch. 3. For general context, see Cadden, *Sex Difference*; Danielle Jacquart and Claude Thomasset, *Sexuality and Medicine in the Middle Ages*, tr. Matthew Adamson, Cambridge: Polity, 1988; Ian Maclean, *The Renaissance Notion of Woman*, Cambridge: Cambridge University Press, 1980, ch. 3; Nancy G. Siraisi, *Medieval and Early Renaissance Medicine: An Introduction to Knowledge and Practice*, Chicago: University of Chicago Press, 1990; Thomas Glick *et al.* (eds), *Medieval Science, Technology, and Medicine: An Encyclopedia*, New York: Routledge, 2005; Lawrence I. Conrad *et al.*, *The Western Medical Tradition, 800 BC to AD 1800*, Cambridge: Cambridge University Press, 1995.

71. E.g. Ambroise Paré, *Deux livres de chirurgie*, Paris: André Wechel, 1573, pp. 416–17; and *Œuvres*, Paris: Gabriel Buon, 1575, pp. 813–14. See Borris (ed.), *Same-Sex Desire*, pp. 234–8, 402 n. 45. Bernadette J. Brooten surveys ancient and Arabic sources in *Love between Women: Early Christian Responses to Female Homoeroticism*, Chicago: University

of Chicago Press, 1996, pp. 162–71. On medieval European diffusion, see Lochrie, *Heterosyncrasies*, ch. 4.

72. Traub, *Renaissance of Lesbianism*, pp. 208, 218, 220.

73. See Rachel P. Maines, *The Technology of Orgasm: "Hysteria," the Vibrator, and Women's Sexual Satisfaction*, Baltimore: Johns Hopkins University Press, 1999, ch. 2; Winfried Schleiner, *Medical Ethics in the Renaissance*, Washington, DC: Georgetown University Press, 1995, pp. 107–29.

74. For bibliography, see Borris (ed.), *Same-Sex Desire*, p. 401.

75. Though "cinaedus" had been anciently a more complex word, by the Renaissance it had come to focus on the meanings "catamite" and "pathic." Renaissance cinaedi were by definition males distinguished by a perceivedly deviant commitment to having receptive sex with males, and to varying extents by apparent effeminacy. Not all of them would necessarily have altogether eschewed active sex roles, nor sex with females. Some say that in antiquity the cinaedus primarily instanced gender deviance and secondarily sexual deviance. In any case, the conceptual invention of sodomy ensured that the cinaedus became clearly a type of *sexual* deviant. On controversies about the term's ancient implications, see Halperin, *History of Homosexuality*, index, s.v. "kinaidos." Its functions within Renaissance culture are different.

76. Cf. Borris (ed.), *Same-Sex Desire*, pp. 122–4, 127–40, 144, 205–7. Contrast Jacquart and Thomasset, *Sexuality and Medicine*, p. 156: "homosexual behavior" was simply considered "a corruption in the soul and doctors found no physical basis for it."

77. For text, see Borris (ed.), *Same-Sex Desire*, pp. 125–7.

78. Ibid., p. 129, tr. Faith Wallis.

79. Paré, *Deux livres*, pp. 416–17; *Œuvres*, pp. 813–14. Cf. Brooten, *Love between Women*, pp. 162–71.

80. Cf. James V. Ricci, *The Development of Gynaecological Surgery and Instruments*, Philadelphia: Blakiston, 1949, pp. 113–68.

81. See Borris (ed.), *Same-Sex Desire*, p. 129.

82. Cf. Andrew Wear, "Galen in the Renaissance," in Vivian Nutton (ed.), *Galen: Problems and Prospects*, n.pl.: Wellcome Institute, 1981, pp. 229–62; Owsei Temkin, *Galenism: Rise and Decline of a Medical Philosophy*, Ithaca, NY: Cornell University Press, 1973; Siraisi, *Medieval and Early Renaissance Medicine*, chs. 4–5.

83. Quoting Pietro from Borris (ed.), *Same-Sex Desire*, p. 137; tr. Faith Wallis. Porta, *De humana physiognomonia li. vi*, Naples: apud Tarquinium Longum, 1602, book VI, ch. 10; tr. Wallis (1st 6-book edn 1599?). Cf. Borris (ed.), *Same-Sex Desire*, pp. 191–5. Galen documented prophylactic regimens to ensure young males aptly masculinized. See Dale B. Martin, *The Corinthian Body*, New Haven: Yale University Press, 1995, pp. 27–9. For the medieval Arabic treatise by Rhazes (as he was known in the West) on male passives and curing them, a text apparently unknown in Europe, see Frank Rosenthal, "Ar-Râzî on the Hidden Illness," *Bulletin of the History of Medicine*, 52 (1978), 45–60.

84. Cf. Jacquart and Thomasset, *Sexuality and Medicine*, pp. 141–2; Cadden, *Sex Difference*, pp. 201–9.

85. Lorraine Daston and Katharine Park, "The Hermaphrodite and the Orders of Nature," in Louise Fradenburg and Carla Freccero (eds), *Premodern Sexualities*, New York and London: Routledge, 1996, quoting pp. 120–1, 129. Compare Traub, *Renaissance of Lesbianism*, index, s.v. "hermaphrodite."

86. Lemnius, *The Secret Miracles of Nature*, London, 1658, Wing L1044, pp. 10–11. His source is the Patristic writer Lactantius (c.240–c.320), *De opificio mundi*, ch. 12 (in e.g. his *Minor Works*, tr. Sister Mary Francis McDonald, Washington, DC: Catholic University of America Press, 1965, p. 40).

87. I interpolate significant Latin terms and missing phrases from Lemnius, *De miraculis occultis naturae*, Antwerp: Christoph Plantin, 1581. The mother's imagination also has great influence, Lemnius insists.

88. Cf. Cadden, *Sex Difference*, pp. 24–5.

89. Aristotle, *Generation of Animals*, 746b–747a. Book 4 reviews various theories of human generation.

90. Early modern medical writers focus on cases of females becoming males through apparent genital extrusion. Though Maclean observes, "what is perfect [i.e., male] is unlikely to change into that which is less so [i.e., female]," Huarte shows conversions of males to females were conceivable. *Examen de Ingenios: The Examination of Mens Wits*, tr. Richard Carew, London, 1594, pp. 269–70. Cited parenthetically within my text hereafter. Cf. *Renaissance Notion of Women*, pp. 38–9. Also Sherry Velasco, *Male Delivery: Reproduction, Effeminacy, and Pregnant Men in Early Modern Spain*, Nashville: Vanderbilt University Press, 2006.

91. Traub, *Renaissance of Lesbianism*, pp. 90–3; Katharine Park, *Secrets of Women: Gender, Generation, and the Origins of Human Dissection*, New York: Zone, 2006, pp. 186–7, 194, 219, 255.

92. Huarte, *Examen de ingenios para las sciencias*, ed. Guillermo Serés, Madrid: Catedra, 1989, p. 609.

93. Compare Maclean, *Renaissance Notion of Woman*, pp. 31–7; Cadden, *Sex Difference*, pp. 171–7.

94. I avoid calling complexional theory "Galenic" because the actual and perceived extent and manner of its Galenism varied at different times in the premodern West, and it always involved extensive mediations and modifications of Galen. He himself appeared Hippocratic in the Renaissance (Wear, "Galen," 231–2).

95. Cf. Siraisi, *Medieval and Early Renaissance Medicine*, ch. 4; Temkin, *Galenism*. See further Rudolph E. Siegel, *Galen's System of Physiology and Medicine*, Basel: Karger, 1968, ch. 4; his *Galen on Psychology, Psychopathology, and Function and Diseases of the Nervous System*, Basel: Karger, 1973, pp. 173–219; Raymond Klibansky *et al.*, *Saturn and Melancholy*, London: Nelson, 1964.

96. Siraisi, *Medieval and Early Renaissance Medicine*, pp. 101–3. Followed subsequently in this paragraph.

97. Cf. Siegel, *Galen on Psychology*, ch. 3; Klibansky *et al.*, *Saturn and Melancholy*, pp. 12–13, 55–66, 98–123, 302–3.

98. Thomas Walkington, *The Optick Glasse of Humors*, Oxford, 1631–3?, STC 24968, p. 32.

99. Temkin, *Galenism*, p. 103.

100. Cf. ibid., pp. 44–5, 82–4, 171–2; Temkin's "Medicine and the Problem of Moral Responsibility," *Bulletin of the History of Medicine*, 23 (1949), 1–20; Siraisi, *Medieval and Early Renaissance Medicine*, p. 106; Siegel, *Galen on Psychology*, pp. 202–19.

101. Western complexional physiology was redeveloped in the twelfth century through Byzantine and Arab contacts and sources, and again through Renaissance efforts to recover Galenic texts. Sixteenth-century Paracelsian medicine provided an alternative to that physiology and its Galenic bases. But despite advances in anatomy, complexional theory could not appear demonstrably invalid until William Harvey (1578–1657) propounded the blood's circulation in 1628. That discovery took further decades to gain acceptance, and the theory of temperaments with its somatic account of human behaviors remained influential into the 1800s. See Klibansky *et al.*, *Saturn and Melancholy*; Temkin, *Galenism*, chs. 3–4; Siraisi, *Medieval and Early Renaissance Medicine*, pp. 192–3.

102. Tr. Cadden. See her "Regime of Nature," pp. 227–8.

103. Cf. Siraisi, *Medieval and Early Renaissance Medicine*, pp. 111, 189.

104. Calling a male "effeminate" could mean he was (1) "lascivious" with the opposite sex; *or* (2) a cinaedus. These usually functioned as different meanings, the latter far more pejorative. Cf. Halperin, *History of Homosexuality*, pp. 111–12.

105. Du Laurens, *Opera anatomica*, Lyon: Sumptibus Ioannis Baptistae Buysson, 1593, vol. 2, ch. 12; quest. 7, pp. 259, 264 (emphasis mine). According to Lochrie, medieval

medicine also associated sex between females with clitoral hypertrophy and viragos with complexional masculinity. *Heterosyncrasies*, ch. 4.

106. Jordan, *Sodomy*, pp. 163–4.
107. Melancholic temperaments could also be considered "usually lustful," as in the supposed Aristotle's *Problemata*, 30.1 (953b). Cf. Klibansky *et al.*, *Saturn and Melancholy*, pp. 22, 120, 302–3; Jacquart and Thomasset, *Sexuality and Medicine*, p. 143.
108. Levinus Lemnius, *The Touchstone of Complexions*, tr. Thomas Newton, London, 1576, STC 15456, fol. 23b. Cited parenthetically within my text hereafter. Compare Lemnius, *De habitu et constitutione corporis*, Frankfurt: Sumptibus haeredum Jacobi Fischeri, 1619, p. 27 (1st edn no later than 1561).
109. Mizauld, *Les Secrets de la lune*, Paris: Frederic Morel, 1571, ch. 2. Cardano, *Contradicentium medicorum libri*, II, Tract. 6, Cont. XVIII, in *Opera omnia*, vol. 6, Lyon: Sumptibus Ioannis Antonii Huguetan and Marci Antonii Ravaud, 1663, pp. 651b–652a.
110. Walkington, *Glasse of Humors*, pp. 111, 117.
111. Cf. Joseph Ziegler, "Médecine et physiognomie du XIVe au début du XVIe siècle," *Médiévales*, 46 (2004), 89–108; Valentin Groebner, "*Complexio/*Complexion: Categorizing Individual Natures, 1250–1600," in Lorraine Daston and Fernando Vidal (eds), *The Moral Authority of Nature*, Chicago: University of Chicago Press, 2004, pp. 361–83; Siegel, *Galen on Psychology*, pp. 173–202; Klibansky *et al.*, *Saturn and Melancholy*, pp. 55–66, 88–123.
112. Cf. Charles S. F. Burnett, "The Earliest Chiromancy in the West," *Journal of the Warburg and Courtauld Institutes*, 50 (1987), 189–95; Joseph Ziegler, "Text and Context: On the Rise of Physiognomic Thought in the Later Middle Ages," in Yitzhak Hen (ed.), *De Sion exibit lex et verbum domini de Hierusalem: Essays on Medieval Law, Liturgy, and Literature in Honour of Amnon Linder*, Turnhout: Brepols, 2001, pp. 159–82.
113. Anonymous, *Of Phisionomie*, tr. William Warde, in Richard Roussat, *Booke of the Famous Doctor and Expert Astrologian Arcandam*, London, 1562, STC 724.
114. Cf. Borris (ed.), *Same-Sex Desire*, pp. 181–2; Jacquart and Thomasset, *Sexuality and Medicine*, pp. 143–8.
115. For an overview and bibliography of physiognomics in relation to same-sexual history, see Borris (ed.), *Same-Sex Desire*, ch. 5. See also Joseph Ziegler, "Sexuality and the Sexual Organs in Latin Physiognomy 1200–1500," *Studies in Medieval and Renaissance History*, 3rd ser. 2 (2005), 83–108; Maud W. Gleason, *Making Men: Sophists and Self-Presentation in Ancient Rome*, Princeton: Princeton University Press, 1995, chs 2–5.
116. Anonymous, *La science curieuse, ou traité de la chyromance*, Paris: François Clousier, 1665 (sometimes falsely attributed to Jean Taisnier). For the latter sign (a little pit or trench in the mensal line), see Figures 7.4-5. On melancholic lust, see n.107.
117. The terminology varies, for in some physiognomical treatises the vocabulary of "effeminate" and "womanly," etc., can mean "libidinous" without any same-sexual implication, while in others it is discreet code for "sexually passive with males." The usage can be clarified by checking what diction a treatise uses for the cinaedus's major ancient signs, such as the knock knees of his stereotypically somewhat waggling gait. See e.g. the anonymous *Of Phisionomie*, sig. R8a.
118. For Halperin e.g. the "active" male sodomite often or typically appeared "conventionally masculine," and so that sexual type seemed unattached to any unique or abnormal constitution. *History of Homosexuality*, pp. 113–16; compare p. 169 n. 44. But see Ziegler, "Sexuality," on medieval physiognomical typologies of insertive male sodomites; and Ch. 7, this volume, on Renaissance developments. Early modern exponents of physiognomics who comment on one or more male same-sexual types in some detail include Cocles, Porta, Cardano, Jean Taisnier, Thomas Hill, Guglielmo Gratarolo, Michelangelo Biondo, and Antonio Piccioli, while brief comment appears in Patricio Tricasso, Andreas Corvo, and Honorat Nicquet (all mentioned, discussed, or referenced in this chapter or in Ch. 7 below). Further mentions appear e.g. in Antioco Tiberto, *Chiromantia*, Bologna: Benedictus Hectoris, 1494; Jean Belot *Traicté de*

la chiromence, in *Les œuvres*, Lyons: C. la Rivière, 1649, pp. 120–3; Gaspar Schott, *Magia universalis*, 4 vols, Würzburg: Joannis Godefridi Schönwetteri, 1657–9, vol. 3, p. 653.

119. Partly to maintain perceived proprieties, it seems. For exceptions, see Borris (ed.), *Same-Sex Desire*, pp. 182, 185–6. Compare Tricasso's shocked reaction to Cocles, Ch. 7, this volume.

120. Piccioli, *De manus inspectione libri tres*, Bergamo: J. B. Ciotti, 1587, p. 29. Compare Cocles, in Borris (ed.), *Same-Sex Desire*, pp. 85–6.

121. Taxil, *L'astrologie et physiognomie en leur splendeur*, Tournon: R. Reynaud, 1614, pp. 62–3. For more on viragos, see Giovanni Ingegneri, *Fisonomia naturale*, Padua: Pietro Paolo Tozzi, 1626.

122. Many physiognomical texts, most often those in vernacular languages, are relatively vague or silent on same-sexual matters. But insofar as the authors knew physiognomics reasonably well, they themselves would have known its rich traditions of commentary on sexual diversity.

123. On Spontoni's, possibly by Giovanni Antonio Magini, see Borris (ed.), *Same-Sex Desire*, pp. 195–9. A mark signifying *turpes libidines* appears in Thaddeus Hagecius ab Hayek, *Aphorismorum metoposcopicorum libellus unus*, Frankfurt: A Wecheli, 1584, p. 59. For *nefando vitio* (presumably sodomy), see Filippo Finella, *De metrosposcopia*, 3 vols, false imprint Antwerp, actually Naples: Jacob Gaffarus, 1648, vol. 2, p. 57. See also Christianus Moldenarius, *Exercitationes physiognomicae*, Wittenberg?: Zacharia Schurer, 1616, book 3, pp. 221, 232–4.

124. See Borris, "Encyclopedias and Reference Works," in Borris (ed.), *Same-Sex Desire*, pp. 201–23.

125. For overviews and bibliographies of astrology in relation to same-sexual history, see Borris (ed.), *Same-Sex Desire*, ch. 4; and see Ch. 8, this volume. On early modern astrology in general, see Steven Vanden Broecke, *The Limits of Influence: Pico, Louvain, and the Crisis of Renaissance Astrology*, Leiden: Brill, 2003; and H. Darrel Rutkin's forthcoming monograph.

126. Cf. S. K. Heninger, *The Cosmographical Glass: Renaissance Diagrams of the Universe*, San Marino: Huntington Library, 1977, ch. 4.

127. Rothmann, *Chiromantiae theorica practica concordantia genethliaca*, Erfurt: Ioannes Pistorius, 1595. Goclenius, Jr., *Uranoscopia, chiroscopia & metascopia*, Lich: Wolfgang Kezel, 1603.

128. Jakob Rüff, *The Expert Midwife*, London, 1637, STC 21442, p. 66 (1st publ. 1544).

129. For debate about the implications for sexual history, see Bernadette J. Brooten and David Halperin in "The *GLQ* Forum: Lesbian Historiography Before the Name?," *GLQ*, 4 (1998), 564–6, 617–18, 625.

130. Compare Borris (ed.), *Same-Sex Desire*, pp. 162–75.

131. Richard Roussat, *Booke of the Famous Doctor and Expert Astrologian Arcandam*, London, 1562, STC 724 (my emphasis). This treatise has little content on same-sexual relations. Its title-page usefully epitomizes one common former view of astrology's significance.

132. See J. M. de Bujanda *et al.* (eds), *Index des livres interdits*, 10 vols, Sherbrooke: Centre d'études de la Renaissance, 1984–96, vol. 3, p. 226, vol. 8, pp. 126–7, 140, 144, 291–2, 818.

133. Richard Lemay, "L'authenticité de la Préface de Robert de Chester à sa traduction du *Morienus*," *Chrysopoeia*, 4 (1990–1), 3–32.

134. I thank Allison Kavey for advice on this paragraph.

135. Caelius, *On Acute Diseases and On Chronic Diseases*, ed. and tr. I. E. Drabkin, Chicago: University of Chicago Press, 1950, pp. 902–5.

136. Appropriating Carlo Ginzburg's phrase, from *The Cheese and the Worms: The Cosmos of a Sixteenth-Century Miller*, tr. John and Anne Tedeschi, Baltimore: Johns Hopkins University Press, 1980, p. xxi.

137. Vignali, *La cazzaria*, ed. Pasquale Stoppelli, Roma: Edizioni dell'elefante, 1984, pp. 67–8.

138. Cf. John Brooke and Ian Maclean (eds), *Heterodoxy in Early Modern Science and Religion*, Oxford: Oxford University Press, 2005.
139. Cf. Borris (ed.), *Same-Sex Desire*, p. 33.
140. Aquinas, *Summa theologiae*, 61 vols, Cambridge: Blackfriars, 1963–81, 2a2a3.153, articles 3, 12; tr. Gilby.
141. See e.g. Borris (ed.), *Same-Sex Desire*, pp. 7–18, 35–43, 268, 274–9, 329–36, 356–7. Authors include Leone Ebreo, Marsilio Ficino, Lodovico Ricchieri, Agnolo Firenzuola, Matteo Bandello, Pietro Aretino, Pontus de Tyard, Pierre de Ronsard, Ètienne Jodelle, Antonio Rocco.
142. Rocco, *L'Alcibiade fanciullo a scola*, Rome: Salerno, 1988, p. 59.

Part I
Medicine

Figure 2.1 Inception of Avicenna's "De alubuati" with surrounding commentary, from *Liber canonis*, in *Praesens maximus codex est totius scientie medicine principis Aboali Abinsene cum expositionibus omnium*, 3 vols, Venice: A Philippo Pincio Mantuano impresse, sumptibus Luceantonii de Gionta, 1523, book 3, fen 20, tr. 1, ch. 36. By permission of the Osler Library for the History of Science and Medicine, McGill University. Biblioteca Osleriana 470.

2 Disorder of body, mind or soul

Male sexual deviance in Jacques Despars's commentary on Avicenna

Derek Neal

The *magnum opus* of Jacques Despars (?1380–1458), *magister regens* of medicine in Paris and occasional physician to the court of Burgundy, was his commentary on one of the age's most important medical texts: Avicenna's *Canon of Medicine*. Despars took more than 30 years to write his commentary, finished in 1453 and first printed at Lyons in 1498; that edition, combining Avicenna's *Canon* with Despars's text, ran to 2667 pages.[1] Measured against this monumental length, the 1200 words Despars wrote about same-sex desire and sexual intercourse between men are barely a footnote. Yet the tantalizing multivalence of these brief passages, in all their linguistic complexity, offers a challenge to the modern historian of sexuality.[2] Their Latin often most resists translation precisely at the points where they promise to say the most about exactly the issues that interest us: in other words, how medically literate people classified and categorized the possibility of same-sexual activity. In part, they confirm some recent scholarship that has clarified the meaning of sodomy in late medieval discourse, making us realize how much could be comprehended by this term and how far it went beyond the simple assumptions we may now make about polarities such as "active–passive," "insertive–receptive," and "masculine–feminine." Less reassuringly, they also suggest that a full understanding of premodern belief about sexuality remains just out of our grasp.

The portions of Despars's text I discuss here comment on two distinct and non-contiguous chapters in Avicenna's *Canon*. Since Despars's edition of Avicenna was the twelfth-century Latin translation of Gerard of Cremona, my references to Avicenna mean Gerard's Avicenna, unless otherwise qualified. The earlier, shorter section addresses sexual contact between men and children; the other, entitled "De alubuati," sexual desire and intercourse between males more generally (Figure 2.1).[3] Predictably for a late medieval physician, Despars writes censoriously about both sexual patterns. So did Avicenna in the *Canon*. But Avicenna originally wrote in the eleventh century in Arabic, without a Western concept of "sodomy," and even in translation, his text does not in itself argue for any causative or categorical relationship between the two forms of same-sexual activity. The mere fact that they are discussed in two completely different parts of the *Canon* suggests that Avicenna saw no reason to connect them.

Despars's commentary, in contrast, elides the one pattern into the other. In well-established medical fashion, Despars grounds some of his remarks in physiology and natural philosophy. He also, however, draws on personal experience and what might be called "heteronormative common sense." For Despars, sexual truth was provable not only by reference to ancient authorities, but also by appealing to the assumed common experience of male author and male reader.

"Cum infantibus"

Despars's comments on men's sexual use of children add a thick moralistic varnish to Avicenna's terse, dry and rather pragmatic treatment of the phenomenon. They also shift the subject. A careful reading of both Avicenna and Despars leaves room for doubt whether the two writers really describe the same thing.

To be sure, Avicenna declares that many nations consider sex between adults and children foul and outlaw it. Yet what kind of children did Avicenna have in mind? Gerard must have had a reason for preferring the nonspecific *infantibus* ("children") to the specific *pueris* ("boys"). Faith Wallis's recent English translation of this passage specifies "boy" as the man's sexual target, and Bartolommeo della Rocca or Cocles applied it that way c.1500.[4] Yet Gerard's Latin does not exclude girls, suggesting that what Avicenna censured here was sex across generational boundaries, possibly involving quite young children (*infans* in classical Latin referred to those still lacking the power of speech). Moreover, the moral turpitude of the practice concerned Avicenna less than did its effects – on the *man*. Avicenna discussed it simply as one among several examples of "harmful intercourse," akin to sex after eating the wrong foods (ch. 6).

For Despars, in contrast, copulation with children, rejected by any civilized people, immediately recalls the example of Sodom. His references to bestiality and masturbation show that he finds this practice comparable to other kinds of coitus deemed sinful and nonprocreative. Most of all, however, he associates it with sexual activity between male individuals, as the language he uses in his subsequent comments indicates. Like Avicenna, Despars does not comment specifically on sex with underage girls. Yet he chooses to elucidate Avicenna's text with reference to the body parts of the chosen sexual objects, specifying the natural one as female ("the pleasing and lovely object that helps and excites men") and the unnatural one as very likely not ("the dung-hole"). Despars appeals to his reader's normative masculine sense of sexual attractiveness.

Avicenna had asserted a seeming paradox: coitus with children could be both more and less harmful to men than coitus with women. Ejaculation with children, he claimed, produced less semen and therefore expended less of a man's essential substance, but it also required more effort, because in such a situation "Nature lacks the powerful movement required to draw out the sperm."[5] Despars, in contrast, attributed both effects on ejaculation to the same cause:

> he says that this detestable coitus is less harmful than natural coitus in this way: that less sperm is emitted than in the natural way with women. And it

follows that less pleasure accompanies this sexual practice than that with the vulva if we take into consideration the power of the beloved object. Even touching the vulva and breasts of a female person, and kissing them, causes much more pleasure, and makes much more sperm flow out, than touching a foul dung-hole. (ch. 6)

There are several important things to note in these references. First, the "object" in this unnatural coitus with children is primarily the anus, as opposed to the "pleasing and lovely" female genital orifice. Further, Despars seems to consider the anus in question a boy's. His reference to the "breast and vulva" of a *femina*, a "female person," rather than of a *mulier*, a "woman," suggests that he does not see a sharp distinction between women and girls as sexual objects, and this makes sense given the early age at which girls in late medieval Europe might be married to older men. The kind of intercourse he is describing sounds like "paedophilia" in its quite literal sense: love of boys.[6]

Despars clearly assumes his reader will accept, without any need of proof, his assertion that *of course* normal (male–female) intercourse takes less effort and elicits more semen; it is more pleasurable, because the sexual object, supposedly more beautiful, generates greater sexual arousal. Even masturbation, of either male or female genitals, however far from the perfection of natural intercourse, produces greater excitement in his view than sexual contact with the anus. This is the rhetorical pose of one sexually knowledgeable man to another, as Despars's desirous reference to the charms of breasts and vulva suggests.

I say "sexual contact," somewhat vaguely, because Despars does not specify actual penile penetration of the anus. Although that imprecision may be deliberately decorous, the precise deployment of the penis seems less important in this passage than the general focus of the man's sexual attention. Note that Despars draws a comparison between the delights of "touching" or "kissing" the breast or vulva and "touching" the anus. Penetration is not the main point. Rather, what makes the difference between greater and lesser ejaculations for Despars here is the power of foreplay and non-penetrative acts in stimulating sexual pleasure, something Avicenna had himself recommended as an aid to female pleasure and therefore conception.[7] And this raises the question of how Despars conceptualizes male attraction to these possible sexual objects.

Most significantly, Despars does not seem able to conceive of a man who would derive the same pleasure from copulation with a child (especially a boy) that another man would experience in copulation with a female (especially a woman). If this is true, we might wish to ask Despars, why then would any man bother with pederasty? Despars does not inquire into the reasons for the behavior. His silence implies that, to him, it is either a poor substitute (much, one suspects, like bestiality), or a product of the individual's perverse and sinful choice, with the latter the more probable reason given his prior insistence that the pleasure involved is somehow inferior. I will return to this point about pleasure later.

Despars refuses, on the grounds of prudence, to elaborate further about other kinds of sodomitical coitus ("in order not to put human nature, which is subject to evil and to sexual sins, up to new ones"), but thereby declares his awareness of them (ch. 6). Adult sexual use of children appears for Despars to be one among an array of unnatural sexual acts in which both men and women are known to indulge, all of them reprehensible. Yet we are bound to notice his apparent assimilation of child–adult sex to male–male sex, and to suspect that the transgression of the boundary between the sexes, rather than between the generations, seems even more loathsome to him than other kinds. Indeed, by this point in the commentary, the reader could easily forget that Despars was addressing a text specifically about sex with children.

Alubuati: corruption of the mind?

Modern classifications of sexual activity encounter yet greater difficulties in engaging Despars's comments on the sexual pattern that Avicenna called *al-ûbnah*. Despars did not attempt to find a native Latin equivalent for this Arabic term, instead adopting the Latinization of Gerard of Cremona, *alubuati* (or, in some versions, *aluminati* or *alguagi*). I have deliberately used Gerard's term here, resisting the temptation to render it as "sodomy," because in thinking about Avicenna's text, Despars was working with a concept that differed from the theological definitions implicit in "sodomy." What Avicenna described was a medical condition, in effect, rather than a category of sin (compare Figure 2.1). That did not mean that the condition of *alubuati* had no moral implications, and Despars was quick to point them out. As he did with the earlier section, the French physician explicated Avicenna's text according to his own society's moral system. Yet he did this while retaining the original concept of *alubuati* as a disease. I have used *alubuati* to refer both to the disease and to the subject(s) exhibiting this kind of same-sex erotic behavior. For the sake of euphony, I have used the same word for both singular and plural.

What exactly was *alubuati*? Let us consider first the physical or behavioral symptoms, so to speak. Avicenna had commented simply that it was "a disease which befalls a man who is accustomed to have other men lie upon him."[8] Wallis parenthetically glosses this phrase "i.e., who takes a receptive or 'passive' sexual role," which corresponds roughly to the Arabic understanding of *al-ûbnah*, a pathological desire to be anally penetrated.[9] Yet we cannot assume that notions of receptivity or passivity are equally important to Avicenna and Despars.

In the very first sentence of his commentary, Despars significantly qualifies Avicenna's vague definition. *Alubuati* befalls "those who are accustomed to have men lie on them as if copulating [with them], one man's genitals placed against another man's genitals" (fol. 402r). Despite some modern associations of "receptive" or "passive," this does not sound like a description of anal intercourse.[10] Despars's next comments, perhaps the most surprising and intriguing in this section, confirm that it is indeed something else instead:

> When I was a *submonitor* [junior prefect] in a school, I knew someone like this, who got some pupils to lie on his abdomen, now one and now another,

rubbing himself against the penis of the pupil until he ejaculated. And when one of the pupils informed me about it, I immediately made it known to the headmaster of the school, so that he could guard against having such a detestable and base sodomite in his house. (fol. 402r)

Despars expresses no doubt that this is an example of *alubuati* and even sodomitical, though the subject in question achieved orgasm by "rubbing himself" against the penis of a schoolboy who was lying "on his [that is, the *alubuati*'s] abdomen." In other words, the partners were face to face, and no one was sexually penetrated. So the episode does not necessarily assign easily identifiable dominant and submissive roles. We should also note that, despite modern associations with paedophilia possibly raised by the school context, Despars does not identify the *alubuati* as a teacher or even as an adult. The anecdote could describe the kind of sexual activity between boys of adolescent or near-adolescent age, well documented in boarding schools up to very recent times. Despars seems chiefly concerned with the fact that the activity was same-sexual, not with the status of the two partners.

After his initial definition, Avicenna proceeds to describe some characteristic features of *alubuati*, some of which sound like symptoms and others possible causes of the condition. Despars chose to organize these as "the seven conditions or properties of those suffering from *alubuati*" (fol. 402r), with a typical aim of medieval medical commentary: "If the logical shape of the text could not be exposed, it had to be invented, for the ideal was to reduce the author's arguments to syllogisms."[11] In this pursuit Despars followed Avicenna quite closely, with a generous sprinkling of condemnatory phrases, producing a complex portrait of a sexual type that deviated from European physiological and sexual norms of masculinity.[12] Thus, the *alubuati* greatly desires intercourse, lusts after it excessively. The intercourse he wants is "not with women in the natural fashion, but in a foul, base and dishonorable way with men and boys," a comment that again groups together male–male intercourse with paedophilia. Such a man is, moreover, not equipped for procreation, "which is the most natural occupation among living things, as Aristotle says" (fol. 402r). These disapproving comments tend, as we might expect, to assimilate *alubuati* to European understandings of unnatural and sodomitical sex.

Despars's arguably more important contribution was to buttress and elucidate Avicenna's own attribution of *alubuati* to psychological causes. Even before explicitly addressing this mental origin of the condition, Despars repeatedly alludes to it. Thus the *alubuati*'s great sexual desire is motivated by "corrupt thoughts" that make same-sex intercourse an irresistible obsession. Those same "evil, dishonourable thoughts" account for his imperfect erection, which Avicenna had defined somewhat vaguely as "weak at the root" (fol. 402r). Despars's interpretation suggests that such evil thoughts fail to generate the degree of arousal required for "true natural coitus." This is logical enough in medieval terms, given the unnatural, non-procreative and therefore imperfect aim of such desire.

But the *alubuati*'s desire for other males is not the only aspect of his sexual makeup to be grounded in the mind. Both Avicenna and Despars feel that his sexual powers themselves may be based in the imagination. Both authors are rather obscure, and to initial appearances self-contradictory, on the subject. In a close paraphrase of Avicenna, Despars comments that the *alubuati* "does not have the power for natural coitus" (fol. 402r). This makes sense if we assume that "power for natural coitus" means erection permitting (vaginal) sexual penetration; Avicenna had already stated that the *alubuati*'s erectile function was in some way defective. Yet Despars continues, "if he can copulate, the power for this is imaginary, that is, originating in his shameful thoughts about the foul coitus" (fol. 402r). The modern reader wonders what difference it makes where the "power to copulate" originates, if the *alubuati* may, in fact, possess that power. But to Despars, it does matter. Apparently, to achieve erection, the *alubuati* requires some additional stimulus: "he desires to see coitus going on between two others" (fol. 402r). So for Despars, the *alubuati*'s desire cannot be equivalent, even in strength (its power to direct the subject toward its unnatural object), to the desire experienced by men for female objects. It is fundamentally a condition of insufficiency.

For both Avicenna and Despars, moreover, the coitus the *alubuati* "desires to see" occurs between males. The masculine pronouns in their comments indicate that this voyeuristic *alubuati* is watching two men. However, in both texts the Latin phrase is still obscure, because the pronouns do not make clear which partner they refer to. Despars's sentence is difficult enough, reading literally "And because he who is with him is more akin to him, therefore his desire moves greatly to the sexual act and ejaculation" (fol. 402r).[13] A more intelligible paraphrase, building on contextual and linguistic clues, might be: "And because that man who is having sex with the other man is very much akin to him [the *alubuati*], he experiences powerful desire for intercourse and orgasm." Here Despars has apparently tried to clarify Avicenna in supplying *quoniam*, "because," to create a relationship between what the *alubuati* sees and the sexual arousal he experiences. Yet what is this affinity the doctors are referring to? Which partner, and which sexual role, is so alluring to the subject? Despars's failure to identify sexual positions is irritating to the modern reader who believes that we need to label one partner "active" or "insertive." (Even the grammar refuses to reveal it; the one man only "is with" the other, with no clear direct object or even any sense of one doing something "to" the other.) This is, however, consistent with the typology of the *alubuati*, not necessarily dependent on anal penetration, as already apparent in the commentary.[14]

It is also consistent with Despars's emphasis on psychological causes. What most excites the *alubuati*, it seems, is recognizing and fully feeling the similarity between himself and a man he watches. The parallels between this explanation, and modern psychological concepts of identification and projection, are impossible to ignore. Despars, it seems, understands the power of fantasy in its modern sense, not only to generate a physical reaction of sexual excitement, but to do so by creating an identification: by compelling the subject to say "That is who I am. That, there, is me, and what he feels, I feel also." Despars's vagueness about which man the subject recognizes as like himself therefore makes psychological sense: either partner's actions could sustain the voyeur's sexual sense of self.

The subject is aroused by seeing intercourse of his own kind, of the kind that is already known to him. Yet Despars evaluates the *alubuati*'s experience by a heteroerotic standard. If *opus coitus* refers, as seems likely, to penetrative sex, there is a self-defeating quality to this sexual preference. In watching others, the *alubuati* can be aroused enough to attain the erection necessary for "natural" intercourse – yet, because he is *alubuati*, he will not perform it. Therefore he will miss out on the supreme pleasure of normal sexual relations. One senses a certain satisfaction in Despars's creation of this slightly illogical scheme: the *alubuati* is doomed to an all-consuming desire for a sexual pleasure he cannot achieve, because the acts to which he submits necessarily yield only an inferior experience.

For Despars, because *alubuati* was a psychological disorder, it was not amenable to medical treatment, as he made clear when he elaborated on Avicenna's dismissal of attempts at such treatment as "foolish" (fol. 402r). Despars specifies that the foolish ones are "doctors of the body," and remarks with scornful detachment that such doctors "have their hands full [trying] to cure them through medicines" (fol. 402r). As Danielle Jacquart has pointed out, Despars "repeatedly stressed that physicians had to be concerned only with bodily causes, through which primary causes act."[15] Only "contrary thoughts," for Despars, can lure the *alubuati* away from his atypical sexual needs (fol. 402r). Treatment of *alubuati* was therefore not the proper province of a physician.

It was, however, the prerogative of a commentator to comment on it, and Despars took an evident rhetorical pleasure in building on Avicenna's recommended regime of aversion therapy, a list of five punishments that would break the *alubuati*'s desire. He expanded Avicenna's five words ("sadness, hunger, sleeplessness, imprisonment, and flogging") to a sequence of five sentences of escalating tension:

> The first [method] is sadness brought upon them by severely scolding and censuring them and detesting their most base imaginings and acts. The second is to torment them through strong and persistent hunger. The third is to tire them out through many tasks. The fourth is to thrust them into prison. The fifth is to subject them often, all naked, to whips and rods until the blood flows. (fol. 402v)

Jacquart recognized in 1980 that the tone of this passage is sadistic.[16] From the first to fifth sentences the authorial voice becomes unmistakably more excited, as the imagined punitive authority moves ever closer to the bodies of the punished: first verbal censure with a purely mental effect, then corporal but distanced punishments, and finally the exposure of the naked, bleeding flesh. The excess in the fifth sentence cannot be explained away through reference to conventions of commentary. Jacquart deemed this verbal aggression possible evidence that what Despars considered the "problem" of homosexuality was fairly common.[17] A quarter-century of subsequent scholarship on the history of sexuality makes this originally probing conclusion more difficult to defend.

I think Despars's passage points us toward a more complex, nebulous group of relationships between Despars, in different aspects of his authorial persona, and his audience: medical authority to other medical doctors; male teacher to male student; literate man to other literate men. Roger French has underscored the use of Avicenna in the classroom instruction of medicine, adding, "Of the techniques of teaching, the most inclusive was commentary."[18] Given the status and prestige conferred by the homosocial environment of a university medical education, wherein not only literacy but literate skill was a marker of masculine specialness and difference from women, it is hardly surprising that words would carry an erotic charge – a charge grounded in authority, privilege, and access to dangerous knowledge. Learned writing about the body, in all its fleshly mysteries, rendered it orderly and intelligible for a cadre of educated men, whose authority then followed from their knowledge. The desire to understand Avicenna was therefore a desire for masculine mastery. We would be more surprised if writing about sensitive sexual topics did *not* generate excitement under such conditions. What we can only call Despars's enjoyment here mirrors his enjoyment, noted above, in contrasting alluring female anatomy to the supposedly disgusting (male) anus. The comments both on the attractiveness of sexual objects and on the punishment of *alubuati* call to mind Jacquart and Thomasset's remarks about the author of the medieval *Breviarum practice*, for whom "virginity and ways of quickly patching up virginity constituted an opportunity for a sexually repressed cleric to refer with precision to the female organs, while at the same time reaffirming the perversity of the other sex."[19] It is a form of authorial pleasure grounded in a normative masculinity defined through the author's relationship to his male reader. French comments that "the ultimate aim of medical education was, by the devices of commentary and disputed question, to make the ancients so clearly understood it was as if they were in the same room, speaking."[20] As intermediary between Avicenna's authority and the contemporary learner, Despars reaches across the hierarchical gap between teacher and student, drawing the reader in by defining a space of shared masculine desire.

Corrupt bodies?

Just as Despars emphasizes psychological causes of *alubuati*, he is quick to discount possible physiological or anatomical explanations. Like Avicenna, he does this most explicitly in refuting a specific anatomical scheme suggested by "some others," in which a neural abnormality requires "vigorous rubbing of the penis" to generate any sexual sensation (fol. 402v). Despars and Avicenna were not referring to the anatomical rationale of the classical author now known as Pseudo-Aristotle, because that depends on an atypical structure of sperm ducts, not on the genital nerves.[21]

Yet Avicenna's text did seem to imply that the bodies of *alubuati* were sexually (and not just constitutionally) different from those of normal men. While a feeble erection, feeble at least for male–female intercourse, might have any number of causes, Avicenna had also written that one kind of *alubuati* had genitals whose "power of endurance is greater than those of men's organs."[22] If "power of endurance" refers to maintaining erection, or perhaps postponing orgasm, this implies that the genitals of *alubuati* might be considered sexually superior to those of "true" males, or at least comparable to them. Despars, however, related this mention of distinctive genitals more specifically to a certain subset of *alubuati* in Avicenna's account: those who "do not ejaculate when someone has sex with them," apparently saving up their sexual energies to allow for a greater variety and frequency of partners ("they stoop to this so that they can have sex like this again"; fol. 402r). These men receive Despars's most severe opprobrium for their willful perversion of God-given male sexual capacities: "indeed, these ones are worthless, and debased in their base and mean soul, of malign nature and evil habits, because they are men both of bad morals and of a constitution that is more womanly than manly" (fol. 402r). In fact they are the only men he thus describes as "womanly" (as did Avicenna before him).

Leaving no room for doubt about the moral status of these bodies, Despars wrote that "their genitals sometimes sustain more base, unlawful sexual acts than [those of] manly and honorable men do lawful ones" (fol. 402r).[23] His choice here of the verb *sustinent* is significant: with both active and passive connotations, like the English "sustain," it implies both "to support or help" and "to endure or undergo." For Despars, the bodies of these *alubuati* are special only in the degree of unnatural abuse they perform, and to which they are subjected. They serve as an index of these men's depravity, not of their physical distinctiveness.

Despars followed Avicenna, then, in dismissing an organic etiology of this condition – though, as we shall see, his attitude was not perfectly consistent. At any rate, in considering other possible factors, non-physical but extra-psychic, he went somewhat beyond the Arab physician. Avicenna had claimed, "apart from this, everything which is said [concerning these men] is without foundation," but had not specified what "everything" was (fol. 402r).[24] Despars was more explicit, rejecting the idea "that they are overseen by evil spirits, or ensnared by sorcerers, or endowed with these forms by some heavenly figure and [its] evil influence" (fol. 402r). Such a comment was quite in keeping with Despars's overt skepticism about astrological influences on the body, his disbelief in healer saints, and his opposition to magicians, sorcerers and mendicant preachers who spread beliefs in supernatural factors.[25] The French physician evenly reports of Avicenna:

> he says that he has heard from certain men who have a certain degree of knowledge and who have been initiated or instructed in the malign arts – i.e. magic or necromancy – that (one should add, sometimes) an *alubuati* is made by means of spells and magical arts. (fol. 402v)

That parenthetical remark ("one should add, sometimes") endows the Arab master with as much of Despars's own skepticism as the Frenchman could get away with, suggesting that Avicenna could not possibly have meant to endorse magical explanations.

Despars's closing comments on the matter of *alubuati* may at first seem somewhat anomalous, comprising a curious anecdote:

> I knew a certain count that said to a newly married soldier, "Do you see this cord?" And the soldier said yes. The count said to him, "I shall knot it, and until you untie it, you will not be able to carry out sex perfectly with your wife." This is what happened, even though, as the soldier swore both to me and to others, he was very sexually potent, and his wife was beautiful and vivacious and aged 20. (fol. 402v)

What does this have to do with sexual relations between men? Jacquart's original suggestion in 1980 – that Despars felt it represented an impotence grounded in homosexuality – now seems insufficiently argued. [26] We might note, first, that Despars does not actually endorse or analyze the story, merely relating it as something told to him, straight from the man involved. Jacquart pointed out that this motif, the knotting of a cord producing male impotence, is a story found in literature with increasing frequency in the sixteenth century, and has been subject to varied modern scholarly interpretations. [27] Despars might intend it to exemplify the kind of outlandish tale that people who believe in sorcery and magic (unlike himself) are likely to accept. It might also be an example of his idiosyncratic use of anecdote. [28]

But we cannot ignore the parallels with Despars's concept of *alubuati*: a psychogenic sexual insufficiency manifesting itself in the inability to carry out "natural" intercourse and the pursuit of same-sexual substitutes. The anecdote illustrates the power of states of mind over sexual phenomena. The count, after all, is the soldier's social superior in a hierarchy. His claim of control over the soldier's sexual function plausibly represents the soldier's fantasized extension of the other controls (for example, juridical, financial, and social) he might very easily exercise over other aspects of the soldier's life. It dramatizes quite credible concerns about the masculinity of subordinate men. By alluding to them here Despars seems to suggest, not that this particular soldier was "really" an *alubuati*, but that the emasculation he experienced was psychological, similar in origin to the allegedly more aberrant condition. Anxiety, not magic, had unmanned the man.

Desire, pleasure, disease?

Both Avicenna and Despars defined *alubuati* not only on the basis of the specific sexual acts that the men were willing to perform, but also according to inner factors, envisioning a discrete sexual type displaying certain variations. We have already noted that Despars, whatever Avicenna's original seemed to suggest, gathered acts that did not conform to a simple active–passive polarity under this rubric. In Despars's personal memory from his school days, did it matter that, while the boy was positioned above the *alubuati*, the latter actually exerted the force that generated an ejaculation? The opposition of genitals to genitals, with partners facing each other, in fact more nearly mirrored the heterosexual coital position considered most normal in Despars's society. In addition, he did not assign sexual penetration any particular part in the definition, suggesting that "insertive" and "receptive" may be misleading terms for us to use in describing what he believed. His emphasis on rubbing, or "friction," rather than penetration, echoes Pietro d'Abano's more detailed treatment of the same subject. Even when speaking of genital–anal contact, Pietro repeatedly refers to rubbing: certain men may "desire to be rubbed vigorously about the anus," or "to rub and to be rubbed on both their parts, for they desire to rub others with their penis, and to be rubbed on the anus by another's penis."[29] This vocabulary surely indicates that anal penetration was not the chief criterion in which either author was interested to classify or explain same-sexual acts. Unsurprisingly, "acts" are basic in Despars's account of *alubuati*, for they are the objective phenomena indicating the condition in question, and thus evoking the mental and constitutional explanations of their occurrence.

Hence the modern concept of a sexual identity defined by what the subject wants, by desire, is not irrelevant to our discussion. For Despars, desire has an important part in defining *alubuati*. First, the *alubuati* is distinguished by the degree of his sexual desire as much as by its object, both of which set him apart from normal men. Avicenna's statement that the *alubuati* had an excess of sperm was too plain to be differed with, and Despars turns it into an explanation for the *alubuati*'s excessive lust. As we have seen, though, that immoderate desire is nevertheless insufficient to generate an erection for "natural" copulation and thereby "true" pleasure. In fact, Despars's thinking stands most apart from modern concepts of sexuality in the connection, or lack thereof, which he conceives between desire and pleasure. The role of desire in Despars's commentary is somewhat ambiguous, reflecting Avicenna's own lack of precision about it, even at the most basic physical level. Despars claims, for example, that "if [the *alubuati*'s] penis becomes erect and emits sperm while somebody is having sex with him, then he can fulfill his desire to finish off the coitus that he seeks" – in other words, he is able to experience sexual pleasure. Why did Despars need to specify, in this backward-seeming way, that erection and ejaculation would be accompanied by pleasure? Indeed, erection and ejaculation here sound like unreliable processes quite independent of sexual desire. Despars seems unable to conceptualize a man whose body responds in an anticipatory fashion to the prospect of same-sexual intercourse (as would that of a man in penetrative heterosexual intercourse); the *alubuati*'s desire must be different not only in degree but in kind.

For Avicenna and Despars, however, who had already defined the *alubuati* as lacking the power for natural intercourse, such a conception was logical. In a worldview where erection and ejaculation were, in effect, unnatural (and not, therefore, to be expected) unless they contributed to natural, procreative sex that suited God's intended purpose for sexual pleasure, how could the rubbing together of male genitals possibly supply a sufficient motivation for them? How, indeed, could a man expect true sexual pleasure from a sex act defined a priori as imperfect? The *alubuati*'s reasons for letting other men lie on him "as if copulating" simply were not comprehensible by these standards. Despars could therefore unproblematically follow Avicenna in claiming that some *alubuati*, though they do experience orgasm, do not desire coitus "except at the time they are being copulated with" (fol. 402r), while others, as discussed above, are capable of willfully avoiding ejaculation altogether in order to have more sex later. He was not concerned to deal with all the logical implications. We are bound to wonder how, for example, the men so described end up in bed with other men in the first place, when they do not feel desire until they get there. Although he seemed to understand that in one sense the *alubuati* was powerfully motivated by a desire for pleasure, Despars could not comprehend either that desire or that pleasure (inasmuch as he actually tried to comprehend either) as fully commensurate to those associated with heteronormative sexual relations. Despars did not envision a sexual repertoire that is normal *to the subject* and encompasses all he wants.

We might think this unsurprising, since a subjectively defined sexuality is a modern, not medieval, concept. And yet the medical discourse in which Despars was immersed was far from antithetical to the idea of individually variable norms. In the logic of humorology and complexion, after all, health and normality consisted not in one unvarying and universal standard but in the balance of humors normal to a particular person. Conceivably, then, a man with an excess of sperm would not be as much harmed by more frequent ejaculation as would one with less sperm, and so possibly the *alubuati*'s sexual voracity expressed a normalcy for him. Similarly, his genital's greater staying power might conceivably arise from his particular humoral complement. But while medical discourse might admit this possibility, moral and religious discourse did not. Despars was, we are told, "even more careful than some of his contemporaries not to introduce any piety into medical practice."[30] Yet even he felt unable, or unwilling, to contradict the dictates of a divinely ordered procreative sexuality.

We have also seen that Despars, following Avicenna, was adamant in rejecting physical causes of *alubuati*. And yet here, too, there is a certain logical ambiguity. Despars was writing within a tradition that attributed aspects of character and personality to physiological factors. His treatment of Avicenna sometimes actually magnifies this effect. For example, where Avicenna had written simply "his heart is feeble," Despars asserted "his heart is weak and worthless, not manly and brave, nor strong nor ready to beget his own kind" (fol. 402r). Feebleness of the heart for Despars went far beyond physical weakness to imply, through all the conventional metaphors, a deep inferiority and difference of character. The moral weakness and tendency to corrupt thoughts, which Despars insisted underlay *alubuati*, thus logically corresponds at least partly to the individual's physical constitution.

Indeed, in both Avicenna and Despars, we are left to wonder where the boundary lies between conscious behavior, the product of deliberate choice, and "disease," whose results we would consider unconscious or involuntary. Both writers initially state that *alubuati* "befalls" men who "are accustomed to" certain sexual practices. If the men have already become accustomed to sexual activity with other men, what then is the "disease" that befalls them? For Despars, perhaps *alubuati* signifies male same-sexual desire that has become naturalized in men who were previously subjected to same-sexual acts. (Both pseudo-Aristotle and Pietro d'Abano allow for this as a possibility in some cases, aside from others produced by atypical genital anatomy.[31]) Despars's blurry distinction between active and passive positions diminishes the possibility that one sexual role is less blameworthy, less corrupt, than the other. In that case, the disease consists of the desire for other men; the wish to keep on performing deviant sex, regardless of how one originally experienced it. Yet, on the other hand, neither Avicenna's nor Despars's accounts, despite themselves, completely exclude intrinsic physical causes.

As Jacquart has pointed out, the "natural explanation of male homosexual practices . . . in Pseudo-Aristotle's *Problems* iv.26 found almost no echo" among medieval physicians, who "did not contradict Christian moral teaching on homosexuality."[32] That same "moral teaching" may account for perhaps the greatest difference between Despars's thinking and ours: a difference in the conception not so much of sexuality, but of disease. For him and for Avicenna, *alubuati* may well have originated in the mind. But where the prevailing model of the mind did not include the Freudian unconscious, there was not *necessarily* any exculpatory assumption that mental disorder excluded either conscious control, or responsibility for the results. (The idea that a natural condition *might* mitigate moral responsibility had grave theological and philosophical implications that did not go unnoticed in the Middle Ages and afterward.[33]) The mind and the will – the inner person – were both diseased in such a condition, and that meant moral corruption. For Despars and his contemporaries, men had sex with each other because they were in some way ill, but that did not, apparently, entitle them to any medical compassion. And perhaps that was, in part, because however inferior the pleasures of same-sex intercourse, they were still pleasures. Such a patient did not suffer enough from his disease.

Notes

1. Danielle Jacquart, "Theory, Everyday Practice, and Three Fifteenth-Century Physicians," *Osiris*, 2nd ser. 6 (1990), 141; Danielle Jacquart, *La médécine médiévale dans le cadre parisien: XIVe-XVe siècle*, Paris: Fayard, 2003, pp. 11, 204.
2. I am grateful for the assistance of Faith Wallis and Nancy Partner, and particularly that of Mark Crane, with various aspects of the Latin source texts for this article, and for Ken Borris's editorial rigour.
3. These sections, in book 3, fen 20, tr. 1, are conventionally numbered 11 and 42–4 respectively. I use Avicenna, *Liber canonis*, tr. Gerard of Cremona (Venice: Giunta, 1523), where they appear as chs 6 and 36–8. In this edition, Despars's commentary is printed alongside the Avicenna text to which it refers. I cite this source parenthetically in my text hereafter.
4. Wallis, in Kenneth Borris (ed.), *Same-Sex Desire in the English Renaissance: A Sourcebook of Texts, 1470–1650*, New York and London: Routledge, 2004, p. 129. For Cocles, see Ch. 7, this volume.
5. Ibid., p. 129.
6. Cocles similarly applied this passage in Avicenna c.1500. See Ch. 7, this volume.
7. Danielle Jacquart and Claude Thomasset, *Sexuality and Medicine in the Middle Ages*, tr. M. Adamson, Princeton: Princeton University Press, 1988, p. 131.
8. Borris (ed.), *Same-Sex Desire*, p. 129.

9. Khaled El-Rouayheb, *Before Homosexuality in the Arab-Islamic World, 1500–1800*, Chicago and London: University of Chicago Press, 2005, pp. 19–20.

10. Yet for Cocles c.1500, Avicenna's category of *alubuati* or *aluminati* is equivalent to the cinaedus, a male sexually typified most of all by being anally penetrable. See Ch. 7, this volume.

11. Roger French, *Canonical Medicine: Gentile da Foligno and Scholasticism*, Leiden: Brill, 2001, p. 54.

12. Jacquart and Thomasset, *Sexuality and Medicine in the Middle Ages*, p. 158.

13. Despars: "Et quoniam sibi proximior est ille qui sit cum ipsomet, tunc magis movet eius desiderium ad opus coitus et sperma emittendum." Avicenna: "propinquior est ille qui est cum eo."

14. Again contrast Cocles to Despars. For the former, Avicenna on *alubuati* or *aluminati* is dealing with cinaedi (understood as males who enjoy being sexually penetrated by males). See Ch. 7, this volume.

15. Jacquart, "Fifteenth-Century Physicians," p. 148.

16. Danielle Jacquart, "Le regard d'un médecin sur son temps: Jacques Despars (1380–1458)," *Bibliothèque de l'Ecole des Chartes*, 188 (1980), 63–4.

17. Ibid.

18. French, *Canonical Medicine*, pp. 11–13.

19. Jacquart and Thomasset, *Sexuality and Medicine*, p. 153.

20. Roger French, *Medicine Before Science: The Rational and Learned Doctor from the Middle Ages to the Enlightenment*, Cambridge: Cambridge University Press, 2003, p. 98.

21. See Borris (ed.), *Same-Sex Desire*, pp. 138–9.

22. Faith Wallis agrees that this more accurately renders Avicenna than "Sometimes their sexual organs are larger than those of males," her translation appearing in Borris (ed.), *Same-Sex Desire*, p. 129.

23. "Veru[m] membra sua plus interdum sustinent de actibus coitus vilibus illicitis quam viriles homines honesti de licitis."

24. Cf. Borris (ed.), *Same-Sex Desire*, p. 129.

25. Cf. Danielle Jacquart, "Moses, Galen and Jacques Despars: Religious Orthodoxy as a Path to Unorthodox Medical Views," in Peter Biller and Joseph Ziegler (eds), *Religion and Medicine in the Middle Ages*, Woodbridge and Rochester: York Medieval Press, 2001, p. 35; Jacquart, "Fifteenth-Century Physicians," pp. 148 (with n. 29), 152–3.

26. Jacquart, "Le regard d'un médecin," 63 n. 5.

27. Ibid.

28. Jacquart remarks that Despars often uses personal anecdotes or descriptions without an obvious connection to the passage on which he is commenting. Ibid., p. 43.

29. Borris (ed.), *Same-Sex Desire*, p. 139.

30. Jacquart, "Moses, Galen and Jacques Despars," p. 35.

31. Cf. Borris (ed.), *Same-Sex Desire*, pp. 122–4, 130–40.

32. Jacquart, "Moses, Galen and Jacques Despars," p. 40. However, Pietro d'Abano provided a full commentary on *Problems*, 4.26. For text and comment, see Borris (ed.), *Same-Sex Desire*, pp. 122–4, 130–40.

33. Joan Cadden, "'Nothing Natural is Shameful': Vestiges of a Debate About Sex and Science in a Group of Late Medieval Manuscripts," *Speculum*, 76 (2001), 72–3; Borris (ed.), *Same-Sex Desire*, chs 1, 3–5. In this volume, see Chs. 1, 3, 7–9.

3 Giulio Guastavini's commentary on Pseudo-Aristotle's account of male same-sexual coitus, *Problemata* 4.26

Faith Wallis

Introduction

Early modern medicine and natural philosophy afford very few discussions of male same-sexual relations as extensive as Guastavini's in his commentary on the first ten books of the pseudo-Aristotelian *Problemata*. Book 4 focuses on sexual issues, and its twenty-sixth question or "problem" considers why some males enjoy receptive anal coitus; thus Guastavini was drawn into providing an explication such as he thought his contemporary natural philosophical readership would find credible and edifying. An annotated translation of this section of Guastavini's commentary is provided below.

As ancient medical or natural philosophical treatments of this topic rarely survived to influence later attitudes and beliefs, so this part of the *Problemata* has central importance for same-sexual history. Along with Pietro d'Abano (1257–1315/16), Guastavini appears as the major figure in its documented reception in the early modern period. By proposing constitutional causes and complicating perceptions of sexual natures and how they are established, *Problemata* 4.26 challenged medieval and early modern sexual orthodoxy. Guastavini responds defensively by insisting that those who engage in such sexual relations retain free will, and hence full moral responsibility, whatever innate or constitutional factors may be involved.

A Genoese physician, scholar, and poet, Guastavini was the author of diverse texts including, aside from his *Problemata* commentary, a miscellany of medical excerpts entitled *Locorum de medicina selectorum liber* and an influential commentary on Torquato Tasso's epic romance, the *Gierusalemme liberata*.[1] The title-page of his *Problemata* commentary states he taught medicine in Pisa (Figure 3.1), and he apparently practiced in Genoa until his death in c.1638.

The *Problemata* have been aptly described as "a sprawling collection of natural questions, or 'problems,' accompanied by sketchy suggestions for scientific answers."[2] Each problem poses a causal question about a phenomenon in the natural world, followed by one or more solutions. Though usually more suggestive and speculative than rigorously reasoned or magisterial, the answers tend to confirm the rationality of the universe and the essential principles of Aristotelian philosophy and science. The subject matter can be medical, biological, or

IVLII
GVASTAVINII
PATRICII GENVENSIS,
ET MEDICINAM, QVAM
PRACTICAM APPELLANT,
PRIMO LOCO IN PISANO
Gymnasio profitentis,

COMMENTARII
IN PRIORES DECEM ARISTOTELIS
PROBLEMATVM SECTIONES:

Nunquam antehac visi, nec in lucem dati, adiecto insuper INDICE *tam rerum, quàm verborum copiosissimo.*

Ad Serenissimum Principem COSMVM Magni Ducis Etruriæ FERDINANDI filium.

LVGDVNI,
Sumptibus Horatij Cardon.

M. DCVIII.

Figure 3.1 Title-page, Giulio Guastavini, *Commentarii in priores decem Aristotelis Problematum sectiones*, Lugduni: Sumptibus Horatii Cardon, 1608. National Library of Medicine. By permission.

meteorological, but the phenomena are always assumed to be real, and matters of common experience.[3] The *Problemata* and its medieval and Renaissance imitators constituted an important genre of scientific and medical reflection. It exerted a formative influence on the scholastic genre of the *quaestio disputata*, and further spawned a number of popular collections of problems ascribed to Aristotle or other ancient figures, apparently intended to entertain and delight.[4]

The Middle Ages produced only a few comprehensive commentaries on the pseudo-Aristotelian *Problemata*, notably that by Pietro d'Abano (finished in 1310),[5] but the revival of interest in classical antiquity and its literature stimulated a Renaissance *problemata* "industry." Enthusiasm for the text crested in Italy in the early seventeenth century; indeed, Guastavini's partial commentary encountered competition from Ludovico Settala's full exegesis in two volumes (1602 and 1607; reprinted 1632), and the rival enterprise of Giovanni Manelfi (1630).[6] However, Settala refuses to comment on the problem relevant here (4.26), and Manelfi deals only with book 1. Based on the Greek text, Guastavini's exegesis makes a considerable display of philological criticism. He especially assails the standard Latin translation of the *Problemata* by the Byzantine humanist Theodore of Gaza (c.1415–75), even though Guastavini himself, like most Renaissance scholars, used it extensively.[7]

The particular problem under review here (no. 26 of book 4) ostensibly addresses the question why some men enjoy taking the "passive" role in sex, and some prefer the "active" role, but actually deals with the former. The Aristotelian author proposed three explanations: anatomical deformity combined with a lustful nature; constitutional effeminacy; and habit. A male can suffer an anatomical deformity, either congenital or induced (as in the case of eunuchs), so that the semen does not flow into its normal receptacle, the penis, but into the nearby fundament; if these men are exceptionally lustful, the semen which collects there will trigger the usual desire for friction, though spirit alone will be emitted when the fundament is rubbed. Alternately, a man can be of an effeminate constitution, secreting little in the way of semen. Such men are "maimed" not only in the almost mechanical manner envisaged in the first example, but in their essential makeup. It is the form of masculinity in them which has been damaged, and in consequence damage has been done to their reproductive organs (which the author somewhat elliptically calls "this part of them"). The form of masculinity is not destroyed, since they are still men, but the type has deviated or been perverted. If semen settles into both the penis and the fundament, then such a man's sexual desires are proportionally both active and passive. Finally, pseudo-Aristotle considers the case of those who become catamites through habit. This is not likely to happen to children, but will happen to young men who are thus initiated into sexual life at puberty, when they can experience the pleasure of ejaculation. Such men will continue to indulge in the type of sexual activity which their memory associates with this pleasure. Habit will become second nature, especially if the man is lustful (as in the first example) or effeminate (as in the second).

In the first case, that of the anatomically deformed, Guastavini's commentary is fairly straightforward, but his religious orientation is apparent in his digression on those who "make themselves eunuchs for the kingdom of Heaven" (i.e. practice sexual continence for religious ends), mentioned in Matthew 19.12. Though Guastavini is ostensibly interested in Matthew's equation of the term εὐνοῦχος("eunuch") with εὐνουχίας ("like a eunuch" – an assimilation he has just denounced in Guillaume Budé), this digression signals his tendency to stress the moral issues surrounding sexuality in a way acceptable to contemporary religious orthodoxy.

This moral intention emerges into slightly sharper focus in the next lemma. Aristotle states that if anatomically deformed males indulge excessively in *sexual intercourse* (λαγνεία), semen collects in the fundament. Guastavini insists on translating λαγνεία as "semen," instead, so that the males whose semen is diverted to the fundament are those who have a lot of it. Conversely those with little semen will not be so affected, for the semen will simply disperse somehow. Indeed (he continues) it takes a considerable amount of semen to force open the unnatural passage to the rear end – a point of view which seems to be contradicted by the Aristotelian author himself, who stresses the ease with which semen can be so diverted.

This curious maneuver on Guastavini's part is difficult, and perhaps impossible to explain. But the effect would seem to be to downplay the importance of lustful propensities, and blame deviant behavior more on the natural abundance of sperm in some males. Guastavini appears to regard pseudo-Aristotle's three types of catamite as a potentially ascending scale of moral responsibility: from the relatively blameless fact of anatomical deformity (though of course, regimen and imagination play a role in arousing desire), through the borderland case of defective sexual constitution, to the clearly ethical realm of habit. Yet when Guastavini discusses the latter, we shall see that he seeks to uphold the orthodox sexual morality of his time by insisting that habit is the main causal factor that makes anyone a cinaedus.

Turning to the second category of the "naturally effeminate," we find that Guastavini likewise seems to avoid the Aristotelian argument of the text, namely that the form or type of masculinity has been damaged. Here he is, to some degree, abetted by Theodore's translation, which renders "this part of them [which is damaged]" explicitly as *virilem partem* – "the male member." More strikingly, Guastavini revises Theodore's translation of this passage in a manner which locates the perversion in the people, rather than the type. Hett's Loeb translation renders the crucial passage as follows: "such maiming produces either complete destruction or a distortion of type. The former is impossible in their case [*i.e.* that of such males] for it would imply their being female. So it must involve distortion and an impulse in some direction other than the discharge of semen" (p. 129). Guastavini's translation, however, ascribes distortion or perversion to the men, not to the type; it is they (the adjective is masculine, and plural) who must of necessity be perverted or perverse (*Necesse igitur peruersos fuisse* . . .). This is reinforced by the commentary he appends to this lemma.

Guastavini thus differs from Theodore, whose translation, reproduced in Guastavini's commentary, follows the Greek quite closely. For Theodore it is the *genus* or type of masculinity which would be destroyed if such males were women rather than men, and as this is not the case, of necessity it (the *genus*) must *peruerti* ("be deviated") and summoned away (*citarique*) in a direction other than that which nature wishes to take for seminal elimination: "At genus illud corrumpens, vt in his sit fieri non potest: ita enim mulieres, non viri crearentur. Ergo peruerti, citarique aliorsum, quam secernendum natura voluit, necesse est." Guastavini's closing reference to those whose *natura* or *generatio* is perverse and depraved might seem to relieve the individual of responsibility. But in the context of what precedes it, this seems less to excuse the sexually penetrable male than to make his alleged moral turpitude innate and ineradicable.

Finally we come to the third pseudo-Aristotelian category of catamite, the one who becomes so out of habit. Some, *Problemata* 4.26 advises, do so without having any anatomical or constitutional predisposition. Of all the causes adduced there, this one seems to be the most serious to the Christian commentator, because it is totally under the control of the will. In that sense Guastavini distinguishes this type quite sharply from the first two. But to the extent that males in the other two categories actually have receptive sex rather than eschew it, they reinscribe themselves into the category of bad habit in Guastavini's view. Even if a man is deformed in his body or constitution, "even with the channels blocked and semen flowing towards the fundament," the commentator argues, such a man can always resist vice, just as not all eunuchs are pathics, and some are most chaste. This is not the argument of *Problemata* 4.26, but rather Guastavini's attempt to appropriate it as reinforcement for current moral orthodoxy. He piles on the condemnatory terminology: the habit is "evil" (*mala*) and the act a "wicked infamy" (*scelata illa foeditate*).

That Guastivini tackles this problem at all, unlike his contemporary Settala, and in such detail, is to some degree the legacy of the first Latin commentator on the *Problemata*, Pietro d'Abano.[8] Pietro boldly chose to deal with this chapter in a full and straightforward manner, rather than pass over it in silence, as had the late Greek commentary which was his source. However, Guastavini never refers to Pietro, and may not have been familiar with his commentary, though it was included in some printed editions of Theodore of Gaza's translation. Overall, Guastavini maps out arguments which are broadly similar to Pietro's, but he is more concerned with philological and textual matters, and less engaged with philosophical and medical authorities, than is Pietro. In this respect, he is typical of the late Renaissance tradition of *Problemata* commentary. Above all, he does not focus as sharply on the issue of the "naturalness" of male receptive sex as Pietro. The latter's moral outrage at those who fall into the habit of sodomy is, superficially at least, every bit as strident as Guastavini's, but Pietro softens the attack by turning his attention to how habit becomes a "second nature." While Guastavini follows Aristotle in asserting that a boy has to be pubescent to pick up the habit, because only then will he experience the pleasure of emission, Pietro takes a slightly different approach. He argues that the naturally soft and impressionable nature of boys makes it easier to entrench the habit; hence it becomes truly "second nature," to all intents and purposes as established as an anatomical defect. Nature, in sum, has a psychological and ethical dimension.[9] Pietro's commentary actually closes by citing Ptolemy's *Centiloquium* on the astrological determination of sexual deviance; Guastavini's, by contrast, ends by asserting the reality of free will and the malign power of pleasure.

But Guastavini's commentary, regardless of its limitations, at least permits same-sexual matters to enter current natural philosophical discourse in print. Though Settala furnishes the Greek text of *Problemata* 4.26 and a Latin translation, he refuses to provide any comment. "Many obscenities" would be encountered, he observes, and any remarks could play into the hands of ingenious degenerates, for those who are "depraved" in this way seek to "contrive for themselves an excuse for this obscene vice."[10] The more it could be ascribed to natural causes and personal inadvertencies, the less moral responsibility could be attached to it, and same-sex lovers could exploit such opportunities. Hence Guastavini's maneuverings and Settala's silence. But as the latter fears, readers could still appropriate this text for their own quite possibly dissident ends.

Translation

Giulio Guastavini, *Commentarii in priores decem Aristotelis Problematum sectiones . . .* , pp. 200–5

Problems 4.26:[11] Why do some men enjoy sexual intercourse when they play an active part and some when they do not? Is it because for each waste product there is a place into which it naturally secretes, and, when energy is employed, the breath [πνεῦμα, Latin *spiritus*], as it passes out, causes swelling, and expels the waste product; for instance urine passes into the bladder, and dessicated food into the stomach, tears into the eyes, mucus into the nostrils, and blood into the veins? Just in the same way semen passes into the testicles and the privates. In those whose passages are not in a natural condition, but either because those leading to the testicles are blocked, as occurs in eunuchs and other impotent [literally "eunuch-like"] persons, or for some other reasons, such moisture flows into the fundament; for it passes in this direction. This is proved by the contraction of this part in intercourse and the wasting of the parts around the fundament. If then a man indulges in sexual intercourse to excess, the semen collects in these parts, so that when desire comes, then that part desires friction in which it is collected. The desire arises partly from food and partly from imagination. For when he is excited by anything, the breath races to that part and such waste product flows into its natural place. If, then, it is light or full of breath, when this passes out, the tension ceases without the emission of moisture, as it does sometimes both with boys and young men. [But] when the moisture [ought to be quenched],[12] if, however, neither of these results occurs, desire continues until one of them happens. But the naturally soft and effeminate are so constituted that little or no secretion occurs in the place in which it occurs with normal persons, but it is secreted in this region. The reason is that such persons are unnaturally constituted; for though they are male this part of them has become maimed. Such maiming produces either complete destruction (*corruptionem*) or perversion (*perversionem*). The former is impossible in their case for it would imply their being female. So they must be perverted, and exercise an impulse to emit semen in another way. So they are unsatisfied, like women; for the moisture is slight and does not force an exit as it is quickly chilled. Those with whom the semen travels to the fundament desire to be passive, and those with whom it settles in both places desire to be both active and passive in sexual intercourse; in whichever direction it inclines the more, so do their desires. In some cases this is the result of habit. For men are accustomed to enjoy what they normally do, and to emit semen accordingly. So they desire to do that by which this may occur and so habit tends to become second nature. For this reason those who have not been accustomed to submit to sexual intercourse before puberty but at about that time, because they have recollection of their enjoyment and pleasure is associated with the recollection, because of their habit desire the passive state, as if it were natural, numerous occasions and habit having the same effect as nature. If a man happens to be both lustful and effeminate, this is all the more likely to occur.

Theodore [of Gaza]'s translation expresses less perfectly the meaning of the whole matter into which Aristotle proposes to inquire, unless we change *vel* [either, or] into *simul* [at once] to correspond to the Greek particle ἅμα, like this: *et alii simul ipsi agere cupiant* [and some at once themselves desire to take the active role]. That is, of those who are subject to sensual pleasure, some indeed at once strongly desire to take the active role, while others desire to take a passive role only.

Aristotle resolves this question with a rather lengthy disquisition, setting forth other matters at the same time, some for the sake of proof, and others for the sake of clarification. We will set forth the summary of the argument before we proceed to explain the meaning of the individual parts.

So this is the summary. Even though, in accordance with Nature's plan, specific places are set aside in the body for each residue,[13] towards which the [residues] are carried, and in which they reside (and if they do not, pain and discomfort arise), there are nonetheless some men whose form deviates so much from Nature (*ita a Natura efformati sunt*) that the vessels which ought to be open are closed, and the residues cannot be carried off to their assigned places. Thus it happens that in some men, the vessels which carry semen to the penis are stopped up; the semen collects in the rear end (*sedem*)[14] and the buttocks. When it is there, and when desire is aroused, it causes that part to want to be rubbed. If all the fluid goes to the rear end, these men only want to take the passive role; but if it is dispersed to both parts [i.e. penis and anus] they desire to take both the active and passive role.

κατὰ φύσιν, *"naturally."* We find in many passages by Galen – notably in *The Preservation of Health* book 1, ch. 12,[15] in which Galen also brings up other things pertaining to the same subject – that for each residue, a specific location has been constituted by Nature in which it is collected from the various parts of the body, for the purpose which Nature intends. I did not think it necessary to quote the words of this chapter at this point, given that it is not pertinent to our primary intention; I have been content to cite the reference. Thus urine descends into the bladder, and food passes into the bowels when the moisture has been drawn out of it and it has been drained (for this is what Aristotle means by ἐξικμασμένη, and Theodore by *consumptus*) of its nutritious humor.

Tears go to the eyes, for tears are termed a residue by Aristotle, and in Problem 35 [*recte* 37] of section 5, they are said to be a kind of sweat, and sweat is a residue.[16] Anatomists teach that tears flow from two small glands in the eyes, for that is where the substance of tears is collected. There is no uniform explanation for the evacuation of all these residues, but each one has a different explanation. I would not think that a healthy brain would produce tears. On the other hand, Galen's opinion expressed in *On the Prognostic of Hippocrates* commentary 1, text 10,[17] is that a person will shed tears because of a flux running down from the brain; and also in *On Purgatives* (which is ascribed to Galen[18]) it is said that the eyes are purged by tears. There is a different reason, I think, for the tears which flow from those affected by grief.

To these residues, Aristotle adds blood, whose destined place is the veins. He calls the blood found in the veins "residue" because it is not generated there, but transmitted from the heart and propelled into the veins: for the heart is the initial source and spring of blood, according to the opinion of Aristotle in *The Parts of Animals* book 3, ch. 4.[19] In Galen's view, blood can be called a "residue" in this manner, for it is produced from the flesh of the liver, and it flows from there, as it were from its primal instrument, into the veins. So when the term ["residue"] is taken in a broader sense, as Aristotle does, [venous blood] can be said to be the "residue" of those primal parts from which it is propelled to other [parts]. But we can say that Aristotle here did not mean all blood found in all veins, but only some which is truly waste product (*excrementum*), or rather, excrementitious blood; for example, the [blood] which flows out of the veins into the anus through hemorrhoids, or menstrual purgations from the veins which end in the uterus.

When these residues are dispersed in other locations, they produce internal pain and discomfort. But at the very time when they are produced, there is already spirit, and this spirit flows out with them.[20] For spirit is Nature's particular instrument; it produces a swelling when it is mingled with flowing residue, and both are conveyed to their specific place. It happens, in like manner, to the seminal residue, which is sent off to the testes and to the genitals.

If the vessels through which the semen is transported are not as Nature would have them, but blocked, as is the case with eunuchs, or if this happens for another reason, then the semen is carried off to the fundament. For this place is close by, and the semen passes through it on its way, with the result that it can be easily turned aside and carried off, as we have seen above at the end of Problem [4.]2. For [Aristotle] demonstrates the transit of semen through those parts of the body from the fact that they contract, or even waste away.[21]

It should be noted that in Problem [4.]2, which we have just adduced, emaciation is proven by the transit of the sperm through those places; here, on the other hand, the transit of the sperm is proven by emaciation; this is not an absurdity, particularly in this type of scientific discourse (*doctrina*).

Διὰ τὸ ἐπιτυφλωθῆναι. *"either because they are blocked."* We have expunged the particle of negation,[22] which was in the printed (*excusis*) Greek exemplars, and which the Latin copies, the old translator,[23] and Theodore followed, and which is even found in Justinian,[24] who marked this [particle] with a point for deletion, notably because the sense required it; for when it is included, it completely contradicts [the sense], unless something is changed. Nor, in my view, is the place where the mistake occurs suspiciously blank. For either that ἄλλα (*sic*) either has nothing on which it depends, or else it depends on the verb συρρεῖ ("flows"), and in either case the sentence is imperfect, or else I do not follow its construction.

εὐνούχοις καὶ εὐνουχίαις. *"eunuchs, and those like eunuchs."* Budé notes that εὐνοῦχος [eunuch] is the same as εὐνουχίας [like a eunuch].[25] However, this is what Aristotle wrote here, implying that there is a distinction, and indeed, since they really are different, [Budé] adds nothing.

I conclude from Theodore's translation *spadonibus, hisque similibus* ("eunuchs, and those like them") that this translator perhaps wishes to understand by these words of Aristotle's all categories of these people, [that is,] those who are without testicles, and those who are impotent. Nonetheless there is a third category mentioned in Matthew 19, the words of which are thus translated by St Jerome, *Sunt eunuchi qui de utero matris ita nati sunt, et sunt eunuchi, qui ab hominibus eunuchizati sunt, et sunt eunuchi, qui se castrauerunt propter regnum dei.* ("For there are eunuchs who have been so from birth, and there are eunuchs who have been made eunuchs by men, and there are eunuchs who have made themselves eunuchs for the sake of the kingdom of God."[26]) However, [Matthew] always uses the word εὐνοῦχος [eunuch] and never the word εὐνουχίας [one who is like a eunuch]; in spite of this, we thought the matter worth mentioning.

ἐὰς οὖν ὑπερβάλλῃ τις τῇ λαγνείᾳ. *"These men, if they abound greatly in genital semen . . . ."* I think it would be better to translate it as *Si igitur aliquis semine genitali admodum abundat* ("If therefore one abounds greatly in genital semen . . ."), for Aristotle begins a new sentence, and the Greek words express this. Indeed it is marvelous how much little words of this kind illuminate a sentence and reveal its meaning, as I have observed on many occasions hitherto. The manner in which λαγνεία is taken here to signify genital semen is made plain by Galen in his commentary on the words of Hippocrates,[27] who in many places uses this word in this sense.

Aristotle, at the outset of his statement, contradicts somewhat the text [which follows], for he relates that semen in the aforementioned men is not collected in this place in all cases; it only happens in those in whom semen is abundant. Theodore adds, on his own authority, "to a great extent," and not without detriment to the meaning, for he implies that in others [semen] is collected, but *not* "to a great extent," which is certainly not what Aristotle says.[28] For in those men who have only a small quantity of semen, [the semen] perhaps might not, even were the vessels blocked, be conveyed to the fundament. The matter might be dispersed; indeed, the pathway is not as easy for a small amount of semen as for a copious amount, especially to the fundament (which is what is principally under discussion here) because the path of the semen does not naturally lead to this place.

Therefore it is conveyed to this place in those in whom [semen] abounds. And if desire is aroused by any of those things to which one is exposed by circumstances, an itch is inflamed there, where [the semen] is, and the part, whether pudenda or fundament, desires friction to allay the itching. It can also happen that desire is strongly aroused without those circumstances, but nonetheless it is moved more readily and more strongly by these [circumstances].

ἡ δ' ἐπιθυμία καὶ ἀπὸ σιτίον. *"Desire arises from food . . .."* What follows these words, up to the phrase, καὶ ὅσοισ μὲν ἐπι τὴν ἕδραν, "those with whom the moisture [i.e. semen] travels completely to the fundament" introduces the conclusion of the problem, and much is said along the way. For when desire is roused, this part ([Aristotle] said) longs to be rubbed, and he shows by what means desire is aroused, and when arousal has taken place, what motions should follow, and what excretions would bring on release. Now in some people, these excretions take place according to nature, easily and in the proper fashion; but in others, this is not the case. Hence it happens that some people readily find release, but others do not, for in these people excretion cannot take place according to nature because they are defective or maimed. In these people, the moisture goes to the fundament, and they wish to take the passive role. But when these things have been explained one by one, everything will be much clearer.

He says that desire is aroused sometimes by food, sometimes by imagination or thought, which is well conveyed by the word διανοία. For it is the opinion of medical men that flatulent foods, of which the principal kinds are onions, turnips, radishes, and bulbs of all kinds, stimulate the desire for sexual intercourse. Hence, as Martial says:

> Since your wife is a crone and your member is lifeless
> The only thing that will get it up is onions![29]

It is not necessary here to bring up what Aristotle says about imagination or cognition in chapter 6 of the book on the common motion of animals, when he proposes [imagination] as the principle of motion in the animal, along with appetite.[30] If anyone has not found out on his own that desire is aroused by [imagination], then let him learn this from those delightful verses of Lucretius, found in book 4 of *The Nature of Things*, which go as follows:

> For his yearning is a presentiment of bliss:
> This is what Venus is for us: this is what we call love:
> That drop of Venus' sweetness that first
> Drips into our heart, to be followed by cold care.

Though the object of your love be absent, images of it are present
And the beloved's name chimes sweetly in your ears.[31]

When agitation has been generated by one cause or another, the spirit, together with the residue, moves to the place to which nature directs it, and by the path which is natural for it – to the pudendum, to be sure, as [Aristotle] said a little earlier, for that is the route that semen takes by nature. But it could be understood that this convergence of spirit and residue in this place [i.e. the fundament] is novel and different from the former [type of convergence], and therefore it is generated. In point of fact, it is irrelevant whether Aristotle understood one thing or two [i.e. spirit or residue alone, or together]: the cause is the same, and it is the same mode of accident. When this residue is thinner and of a more inspirited nature, as it occurs, for instance, in boys and youths, lust will actually cease without the excretion of humor; it does so by the excretion of spirit, through the rubbing of those parts. We have this from Aristotle himself, in book 1, ch. 20 of *Generation of Animals*, as follows:

> The pleasure which accompanies copulation is due to the fact that not only semen, but also spirit is emitted: it is from this spirit as it collects together that the emission of semen results. This is plain in the case of boys who cannot yet emit semen, though they are not far from the age for it, and in infertile men, because all of them derive pleasure from attrition.[32]

And also in the first problem of section 30, thus:

> Even before they can emit semen boys, when they are near to the age of puberty, derive pleasure through lust by rubbing the privates; this pleasure is clearly due to the spirit passing through the channels through which the moisture is afterwards conveyed.[33]

But sometimes the humor is thicker, and not sufficiently inspirited to be discharged. If this does come to pass, the tension is released; but if neither of these is discharged, the appetite endures and the ardor does not cease, until one of these comes to pass.

But at this point Theodore adds much on his own initiative; he does not distort the meaning, but he does, in my opinion, overstep the authority of a good translator. What follows agrees virtually word for word with the Greek:

> If, then, it is light or full of breath, when it passes out, the tension ceases without the emission of moisture, as it does sometimes both with boys and young men. [But] when the moisture [ought to be quenched], should neither of these results occur, desire continues until one of them happens.[34]

I think that Aristotle was very careful to say "to be quenched" in order to signify better the preceding ardor of sexual desire; Theodore turns this into "extruded."

What we render as "and young men," and Theodore, "in young men," in Greek is τοῖς ἐς ἡλικίᾳ ["in those in the prime of life, adults"].[35] For in the passage which we referred to in the first book of *Generation of Animals* Aristotle says ἐγγὺς τῆς ἡλικίας, that is, *prope aetate sunt* ["they are close to the age (for sex)"], as we propose the passage in Latin, following Theodorus; but this might better be rendered "nearing puberty" (just as Aristotle states explicitly in the first problem of section 30) or else "adolescents," as in Theodore's translation of this passage. It is evident that Aristotle means the same age in both passages. It is worth considering why Aristotle would refer here to those who have not yet reached puberty as οἱ ἐς ἡλικία ["those in the prime of life; adults"] – unless we were to say that Aristotle says that people who, in comparison with the boys which he just mentioned, were somewhat more grown up, even though they had not emitted semen, "had come of age," or "were of age." Or else the passage is to be corrected in accordance with *Generation*, and we should write ἐγγὺς τῆς ἡλικίας, which I think is preferable; it is an easy mistake to make.

οἱ δὲ φύσει θηλυδρίαι. *"the naturally soft and effeminate."* Who these people are is shown by the modes of conduct in which their sexual proclivity appears. For because the ardor of libido ceases thanks to the excretions which take place according to the natural and proper channels, it happens that if some so deviate from nature, or rather, who are so damaged that no semen, or very little semen is collected in the proper place, which happens in some men who are held to be of a soft or effeminate nature, in these people it withdraws to another place – the fundament, evidently. But there are some who so deviate from the laws and customs of nature that they have a virile member (*virilem partem*) which is maimed and damaged – not, to be sure, to such an extent that manly nature is totally corrupted, for then they would be women (who likewise are called damaged and imperfect men),[36] but so that the genital semen itself is diverted in a manner other than is found in men.

But like women, they are insatiable, and (it is to be thought) for a similar reason. For the humor which induces libido is small, nor does it possess an impetus capable of making an exit, and it is quickly chilled. For they are colder by nature, and therefore are not [cooled] as much by appeased ardor.

Furthermore, I consider that I would not have fulfilled my duty did I not provide a literal translation of this part of the text. For Theodore departs to a considerable extent from the meaning of the words, and even sometimes omits things which are necessary.

> But the naturally soft and effeminate are so constituted that little or no secretion occurs in the place in which it occurs with normal persons, but it is secreted in this region. The reason is that such persons are unnaturally constituted; for though they are male this part of them has become maimed. Such maiming produces either complete destruction (*corruptionem*) or perversion (*perversionem*). The former is impossible in their case for it would imply their being female.

So they must be perverted, and exercise an impulse to emit semen in another way.[37]

In the passage which we cited above from chapter 20 of book 1 of *Generation of Animals*, Aristotle speaks, as one who is well acquainted with the subject, about people whose nature or conception is perverted or depraved in this manner; and he relates that in these people the bowels are sometimes loose because the residue which descends thither cannot be concocted and made into semen.[38]

καὶ ὅσοις μὲς ἐπι τῆς ἕδραν. *"those in whom the semen travels completely to the fundament."* Justinian reads περὶ [around] for ἐπὶ, and *completely* (*ex toto*) was added by Theodore on his own account.

Be that as it may, Aristotle reaches a conclusion, and briefly treats the principal subject of the problem: why some men desire only to take the passive role, and others desire to take both the active and the passive role, and of these, why some prefer one and others the other.

Moreover, in the text of Justinian we have added all those [words] from ὅσοις up to ἐπιθυμοῦσιν, and which were wanting in the printed versions. They are also found in the old translation and in Theodore. Nevertheless Theodore either misread these final words ἐφ᾿ ὁπότερα δὲ πλεῖος, τούτου μᾶλλον ἐπιθυμοῦσιν, or made a mistake in translating them, for they should be rendered *Whichever part most of that moisture settles into, is where they most feel desire.* For Aristotle is of the opinion that if more moisture is carried to the front part of the body, people desire to take the active role more than to take the passive role, and if more goes to the back parts, they desire to take the passive rather than the active role, and if an equal amount goes to both [parts] they desire in equal measure to take the active and the passive role.

ἐνίοις δὲ γίνεται καὶ ἐξ ἔθους τὸ πάθος τοῦτο. *"But there are those in whom this condition results from habit."* To the aforementioned cause, which arises from the vitiation of nature or from bodily deformity, he adds another, which arises from bad habit. And this indeed should be considered the most potent [cause]; for even with the channels blocked and semen flowing towards the fundament, if a man flees from turpitude and wickedness, and does not become accustomed to it, he will take no pleasure in [receptive sex]. This is the case with many eunuchs (whom, it would seem, Aristotle puts in this category) who preserve and guard their chastity with great obstinacy. Therefore, according to Aristotle, there are those who, because of evil habit, would take pleasure in this wicked infamy.

Now before I propose other things for the sake of explanation, I think it necessary to propose the following translation which actually accords with the words, because throughout this passage Theodore seems to depart rather significantly from the meaning of the words, and on the other hand, to have interposed a passage other than that found in the printed Greek exemplars:

In some cases this is the result of habit. For men are accustomed to take pleasure when they do this, and to emit semen accordingly. So they desire to do that by which this may occur and so habit tends to become second nature. For this reason those who have not been accustomed to submit to sexual intercourse before puberty but at about that time, because they have recollection of their enjoyment at this time and pleasure is associated with the recollection, because of their habit desire the passive state, as if it were natural, numerous occasions and habit having the same effect in them as nature. If a man happens to be both lustful and effeminate, this is all the more likely to occur.[39]

Driven, then, by habit, there are those who would enjoy submitting to sex, and when they have sex – namely, when they take the passive role (for thus I take to be the meaning of ποιῶσι in this passage) – they feel pleasure. Indeed, those who would emit semen in the manner in which they experienced it, desire to have sex in the passive role, as I have just explained.

But Theodore does not take this passage in this sense. Perhaps he reads ὡς ποιῶσι [i.e. "however they do it"], or he takes ὅσα φορ ὡς [i.e. "whatever things they do"], in this sense: There are those who when they submit to sex, take pleasure in it out of habit, for in this way they emit semen just as they would if they were taking the active role. In fact, it is utterly necessary to take what follows this same ποιεῖν, that is, "to do," in the manner which I said: therefore they desire to do it, that is, to submit to sex, and when such things happen to these people, habit changes in them into something like nature.[40]

Book 3, fen 20, tractate 1, chapter 42 of [the *Canon* of] Avicenna also speaks of this condition, which affects not a few people, and proposes the cause of this phenomenon.[41] What follows at this point, Theodore joins to the preceding matter, and makes only one clause out of all, as appears from his translation. But in the Greek exemplars there are two distinct clauses, as appears in our [translation].

Whichever way one reads it, it seems that this is a corollary to what was said before. It is evident that in those who become accustomed to submitting to sex at or about the time of puberty (and not before puberty), because they have already emitted semen, habit is more readily transformed into nature by reason of the memory of something delectable that occurred recently. Such a memory, which assumes experience, and the onslaught of desire, is not generated in this way in those who are accustomed [to submit to sex] before puberty, because at this time [of life] semen is not emitted, nor can they sense this delectation. Up to this point, I think I have reflected Aristotle's argument.

Notes

1. Mario Cosenza, *Biographical and Bibliographical Dictionary of the Italian Humanists*, 2nd edn, New York: G. K. Hall, 1962–7, *s.v.* "Guastavini."
2. Joan Cadden, "Sciences/Silences: The Natures and Languages of 'Sodomy' in Peter of Abano's *Problemata* Commentary," in Karma Lochrie, Peggy McCrachen and James

A. Schultz (eds), *Constructing Medieval Sexuality*, Minneapolis: University of Minnesota Press, 1997, p. 43.

3. Ann Blair, "The *Problemata* as a Natural Philosophical Genre," in Anthony Grafton and Nancy Siraisi (eds), *Natural Particulars: Nature and the Disciplines in Renaissance Europe*, Cambridge, MA: MIT Press, 1999, pp. 171–5. Even the textual history is complex: see E. S. Forster, "The Pseudo-Aristotelian *Problems*: Their Nature and Composition," *Classical Quarterly*, 22 (1928), 163–5.

4. See Blair, "*Problemata*," esp. bibliographical note, pp. 189–90; and Iolanda Ventura, "*Quaestiones* and Encyclopedias: Some Aspects of the Late Medieval Reception of the Pseudo-Aristotelian *Problemata* in Encyclopedic and Scientific Literature," in Alasdair A. MacDonald and Michael W. Twomey (eds), *Schooling and Society: The Ordering and Reordering of Knowledge in the Western Middle Ages*, Leuven: Peeters, 2004, pp. 23–42.

5. See Nancy Siraisi, "The *Expositio Problematum Aristotelis* of Peter of Abano," *Isis*, 61 (1970), 321–39; Cadden, "Sciences/Silences," *passim*; Ventura, "*Quaestiones*," pp. 27–8.

6. Ludovico Settala, *Ludovico Septalii . . . in Aristotelis Problemata commentaria ab eo Latine facta*, Lyons: Claude Landry, 1632; Giovanni Manelfi, *Urbanae disputationes in primam problematum Aristotelis sectionem*, Rome: Guglielmo Facciotto, 1630. Cf. Blair, "*Problemata*," p. 186.

7. Theodore's Latin *Problemata*, dedicated to Pope Nicholas V, was first printed in Mantua in 1473, and went through numerous edns thereafter. It is still considered valuable for establishing the text's meaning, though in many places it is a free and conjectural paraphrase. See W. S. Hett's introduction to the Loeb *Problemata*, pp. vii–viii; John Monfasani, "The Pseudo-Aristotelian *Problemata* and Aristotle's *De animalibus* in the Renaissance," in Anthony Grafton and Nancy Siraisi (eds), *Natural Particulars: Nature and the Disciplines in Renaissance Europe*, Cambridge, MA: MIT Press, 1999, pp. 204–47.

8. English tr. by Faith Wallis, in Kenneth Borris (ed.), *Same-Sex Desire in the English Renaissance: A Sourcebook of Texts, 1470–1650*, New York and London: Routledge, 2004, pp. 132–40.

9. Cadden, "Sciences/Silences," pp. 48–9.

10. "Quoniam si quis quaestionum hanc explicare voluerit, in multa obscoena incidat necesse erit, multique, qui ex mala consuetudine deprauati, ad naturalem defectum recurrentes, obscoeni vitii excusationem sibi parent, propterea nihil hac de re a me agendum esse putaui." That is Settala's full comment. *Problemata commentaria*, p. 289.

11. In Guastavini's commentary (p. 200), this chapter is numbered 27, due to the interpolation of a chapter earlier in book 4. The translation used here is W. S. Hett's in the Loeb edn, modified slightly where required to conform to Theodore of Gaza's translation or Guastavini's reading.

12. This modification to Hett's translation reproduces Guastavini's solution to the problem of a lacuna in the text; see below, n. 34.

13. "Residue" or "waste product" here translate the Latin *excrementum*. In the premodern medical system, *excrementum* connoted all solid, semi-solid or liquid residues of digestion which exited naturally from the orifices of body as waste: urine, stool, sputum, tears, sweat, ear-wax, and menstrual blood, but also semen, which was also the product of the decoction of nutriment. Much of the art of medicine, preventive and therapeutic, revolved around regulating, promoting, and interpreting these evacuations.

14. *Sedes*, literally "seat," and here translated "fundament," can also mean "anus," but since Gaustavini uses the term *anus* elsewhere, I translate *sedes* as "rear end" or "fundament." The more precise connotations of the term should be borne in mind.

15. *Galeni de sanitate tuenda* 1.12, 16–28, ed. Konrad Koch, Corpus medicorum graecorum, 5/4.2, Leipzig and Berlin: Teubner, 1923, pp. 29.31–31.8. For edns available in Guastavini's day, see Richard Durling, "A Chronological Census of Renaissance Editions and Translations of Galen," *Journal of the Warburg and Courtauld Institutes*, 24 (1961), 283, no. 24; "Corrigenda and Addenda to Diel's Galenica. I. Codices Vaticani,"

Traditio, 23 (1969), 470, no. 103a; "Corrigenda and Addenda to Diel's Galenica. II. Codices Miscellanei," *Traditio*, 37 (1981), 379, n. 103a.

16. Aristotle, *Problems* 5.37.

17. Kühn 18, B, 1, pp. 1–317. Critical edn by J. Heeg, *Galeni in Hippocratis prognosticum commentaria III*, 1.10, Corpus medicorum graecorum, 5/9.2, Leipzig and Berlin: Teubner, 1915, pp. 221–5.

18. This work is listed as pseudonymous in Gerhard Fichtner, *Corpus Galenicum: Verzeichnis der galenischen und pseudogalenischen Schriften*, Tübingen: Institut für Geschichte der Medizin, 1985, p. 98, no. 162. On the history and transmission of this text, see Johann Christian Gottlieb Ackermann, *Historia literaris Claudii Galeni*, in *Claudii Galeni Opera omnia*, ed. C.G. Kühn, Leipzig: Cnobloch 1821, vol. 1, p. clxxii, 143; Hermann Alexander Diels, *Die Handschriften der antiken Ärzte*, Berlin: Königliche Akademie der Wissenschaften, 1905–7, p. 138. For Renaissance edns, see Durling, "A Chronological Census," p. 283, no. 24; "Corrigenda and Addenda II," p. 374, no. 24. In the edn by Agostino Ricchi and Vittore Tricavella, Venice: ex officina Farrea, 1541–5, vol. 2, p. 559, the Latin text reads: "Caeterum oculi purgantur per lach<r>ymas, per nares, per mucos." See also Giovanni Sacino, "Il libro 'De catharticis' attribuito a Galeno," *Rivista di storia medica*, 12 (1968), 217–29.

19. Aristotle, *Parts of Animals* 3.4, 665b.

20. *Spiritus*, glossing the Greek *pneuma*, stands for many things in ancient and medieval physiology, depending on the writer's philosophical assumptions. Broadly, it refers to an interior form of air which sustains life in the organism. This *spiritus* is derived from the air one breathes in, but is endowed with special soul-like properties. In this case, *spiritus* is one of the two component elements of sperm, the other being moisture or *humor*. Cf. Aristotle, *Generation of Animals* 2.2 (735a–736a).

21. *Problems* 4.2: "Why do both the eyes and the buttocks sink very noticeably in those who indulge excessively in sexual intercourse, though the latter are near to and the former far from the sex organs? Is it because both these parts obviously co-operate in the act of coition by contracting at the time of the emission of semen? Consequently all the nourishment, which in these parts is easily dissolved, is forced out by pressure. Or is it because things which become overheated waste away most, and the sexual act operates through heat? And the parts which are moved in the act are most heated" (tr. Hett, p. 109).

22. Following the phrase "either entirely or in part" is an intrusive negative particle (ἢ πᾶς τί ἄλλο): see Hett's edn, p. 124.

23. That is, the medieval translator of the *Problemata*, Bartholomew of Messina.

24. This editor has not been identified in Cozensa's repertory of humanists, or in the catalogue of Renaissance edns of Aristotle in *Index Aureliensis: catalogus librorum sedecimo saeculo impressorum*, n.pl.: Aureliae Aquensis, 1966. Possible candidates are Alessandro Giustiniano, translator of John Philoponus's commentary on the *Prior Analytics* published in Venice in 1560, or perhaps Johannes Hospinianus, editor of a bilingual *Organon* pubished in Basel in 1573.

25. Guillaume Budé (1468–1540), French hellenist, humanist and jurist. Guastavini is probably referring to the great Greek-Latin dictionary *Lexikon Hellenoromaikon*, Basel: ex officina Henricpetrina, c.1565, compiled from the works of a number of scholars, but with Budé named first. See the entry *s.v.* εὐνουχίας, where indeed the word is defined as a synonym of εὐνούχος.

26. Matthew 19.12; the translation is that of the Revised Standard Version, slightly modified to agree with the Vulgate.

27. Though λαγνεία normally means "libido" or "sexual desire," Galen adds that Hippocrates used it to denote the sexual act itself, or (notably in *The Nature of the Child*) semen: *Linguarum seu dictionum exoletarum Hippocratis* or *Vocum obsoletarum Hippocratis explanatio*, ed. Kühn, vol. 19, p. 117. For Renaissance edns of this work, see Durling, "A Chronological Census," p. 294, no. 148.

28. Theodore is in fact translating correctly: *longe* renders the ὑπερ of ὑπερβάλλη "greatly abounds." On Guastavini's unusual reading of this passage, see my introduction.
29. Martial, *Epigrams* 13.34, my tr., modifying the Loeb's, by D. R. Shackleton Bailey.
30. Aristotle, *Movement of Animals* 6, 700b.
31. Lucretius, *De rerum natura* 4.1058–62; my tr., modified from that of Ronald Latham, *Lucretius: On the Nature of the Universe*, Harmondsworth: Penguin, 1951, p. 163.
32. Aristotle, *Generation of Animals* 1.20, 728a, slightly modifying A. L. Peck's Loeb tr.
33. *Problems* 30.1, 953b, slightly modifying H. Rackham's Loeb tr.
34. This last sentence is Theodore's attempt to resolve a lacuna in the text: cf. Hett's remarks in his Loeb edn, p. 128, n. *a.*
35. Hett's English tr. reads "in boys and adults" (p. 129).
36. Cf. Ian Maclean, *The Renaissance Notion of Woman*, Cambridge: Cambridge University Press, 1980.
37. On the force of this revised tr., see my introduction.
38. Aristotle, *Generation of Animals* 1.20, 728a.
39. The major alteration is to the first sentence. The Latin of Theodore reads: "Fit enim vt tam gestiant, quam cum agunt, vtque genituram nihilo minus ita emittere valebat." Compare to Hett's tr. (p. 131): "For men are accustomed to enjoy what they normally do, and to emit semen accordingly . . ."
40. Guastavini's point seems to be that Theodore's reading makes the pleasure follow on the habit, whereas Guastavini thinks that the habit is the consequence of the pleasure. Again, he seems to be focusing on the corruption of desire, rather than any mere behavioural conditioning.
41. For English tr. and commentary on this passage of the *Canon*, see Borris (ed.), *Same-Sex Desire*, pp. 127–30.

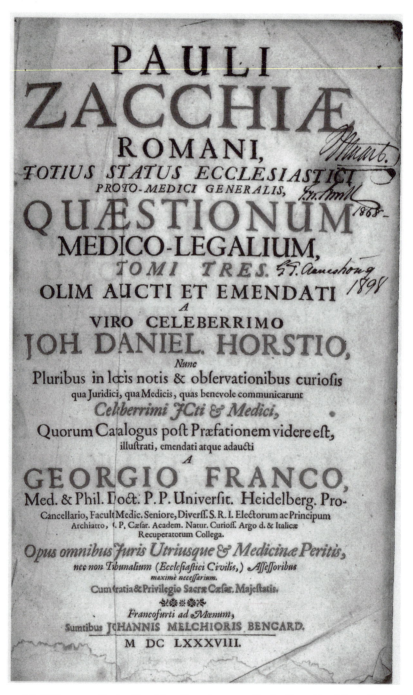

PAULI ZACCHIÆ

ROMANI,

TOTIUS STATUS ECCLESIASTICI
PROTO-MEDICI GENERALIS,

QUÆSTIONUM

MEDICO-LEGALIUM,

TOMI TRES.

OLIM AUCTI ET EMENDATI

A

VIRO CELEBERRIMO

JOH. DANIEL. HORSTIO,

Nunc

Pluribus in locis notis & obſervationibus curioſis

qua Juridici, qua Medicis, quas benevole communicarunt

Celeberrimi JCti & Medici,

Quorum Catalogus poſt Præfationem videre eſt,

illuſtrati, emendati atque adaucti

A

GEORGIO FRANCO,

Med. & Phil. Doct. P. P. Univerſit. Heidelberg. Pro-

Cancellario, FacultMedic. Seniore, Diverſſ. S. R. I. Electorum ac Principum
Archiatro, C. P, Cæſar. Academ. Natur. Curioſſ. Argo d. & Italicæ
Recuperatorum Collega.

Opus omnibus Juris Utriusque & Medicinæ Peritis,

nec non *Tribunalium (Eccleſiaſtici Civilis,) Aſſeſſoribus*

maximè neceſſarium.

Cum Gratia & Privilegio Sacræ Cæſar. Majeſtatis.

❄✱✿✱❄

Francofurti ad Mœnum,

Sumtibus JOHANNIS MELCHIORIS BENCARD.

M DC LXXXVIII.

Figure 4.1 Title-page, Paolo Zacchia, *Quaestionum medico-legalium,* Frankfurt: Sumptibus Johannis Melchioris Bencard, 1688. By permission of the Osler Library for the History of Science and Medicine, McGill University.

4 Policing the anus

Stuprum and sodomy according to Paolo Zacchia's forensic medicine

George Rousseau

Mid-nineteenth-century readers of the new sexology – the emerging science of sex just being invigorated in Europe – would have continued to stumble upon the name Paolo Zacchia (1584–1659) in primary texts, footnotes, and learned apparatuses.[1] Zacchia was usually glossed as the most eminent authority on forensic science of the Renaissance but without explanation why. It appeared to those readers curious about the new science of sex as if he had accomplished for the Renaissance what DNA testing has done in our generation. Yet rarely was Zacchia biographically or bibliographically discussed: his dates, life, and the titles and contents of his works. All they could find were brief comments to the effect that he was an authority on evidence, logic, rule, and exception in Renaissance law and medicine. For example, a reader of five representative forensic texts at mid-century – B. A. Morel's *Traité des dégénérescences physiques, intellectuelles et morales de l'espèce humaine, et des causes qui produisent ces variétés maladives*, Paris: J. B. Baillière, 1857, and four of Doctor Ambroise Tardieu's forensic works dealing with the status of sodomites, *Étude médico-légale sur les attentats aux moeurs*, Paris, 1862, *Étude médico-légale sur l'avortement*, Paris: J. B. Baillière, 1864, *Étude médico-légale sur la folie*, Paris: J. B. Baillière, 1872, *Question médico-légale de l'identité*, Paris: J. B. Baillière, 1874 – would have found Zacchia prominently named in all five. Readers must have wondered who this allegedly towering figure was.

Zacchia was one of the founding fathers of legal medicine.[2] His *Quaestiones medico-legales*, compiled in the 1620s, was first published in 1630, ran to several editions, and was an immensely influential text in forensic medicine until the eighteenth century (Figure 4.1).[3] The 1661 Lyon edition adds to his earlier text of 1630 a collection of *consilia*, or "consultations." He wrote these in his capacity as expert witness on behalf of one of the parties involved in the case at hand, or at the request of the legal authorities.[4] He also included a hundred *decisiones* – verdicts – of the Tribunal of the Sacra Rota, the ecclesiastical court in Rome whose prelates answered only to the Pope.[5] This edition of 1661 was usually the one consulted by the early commentators of the new sexology just mentioned, such as Tardieu.

Zacchia also enjoyed respect as a public figure within the medical-legal establishment of his epoch. He became the personal physician to Popes Innocent X and Alexander VII, legal adviser to the Rota Romana (a lower papal court not to be confused with the just mentioned Sacra Rota), and director of the health system of the Papal States.[6] He was a formidable polymath in the tradition of the most learned of Renaissance students and became known for these qualities after his death in 1659, particularly for having written widely on diverse subjects in addition to his specialty in forensic medicine and theology.[7] Within these realms where the law and medicine intersected he was savvy about hypochondriacal disorders in an era when their forensic implications were beginning to assert themselves (i.e. alleged hypochondriacs as malingerers, frauds, charlatans without genuine illness).[8] But his *Quaestiones Medico-Legales* was doubtlessly his greatest testimony to future generations, and would be translated into many languages early in the eighteenth century when Latin ceased to be the lingua franca. This was a seminal work within the sweep of forensic science, throughout the realms where medicine and the law intersect, for its brief commentaries on sodomitical sinners form only a miniscule portion of the work.[9]

The early sexologists curious about Zacchia in the mid-nineteenth century cannot have known a fraction of the information about him that has been retrieved by contemporary scholars. But they must have had an inkling that the substratum of the developing sexology in which their epoch was immersed owed him a debt. Why else refer so prolifically to him and in such reverential terms? Now, almost 400 years after his death and two centuries after the mid-nineteenth-century birth of sexology, he is generally less well-known in the English-speaking world than he was at any time except during the late eighteenth century, when he faded from the forensic limelight as the result of new leniency towards sodomites and because his works had not been translated into English or French.

Zacchia would have been surprised to discover his appearance in a book dedicated to the sciences of homosexuality in the early modern world. If he interested himself in gender, it was not gender in our modern sense but within the contexts of ecclesiastical and secular law; and his discussions of sodomy among males and females occur in narrow forensic contexts only, where the crucial matter is the accurate understanding of signs as forms of investigative evidence. At no time did he speculate about the cultural or psychological implications of sodomy, let alone the metaphysical dimensions of any "science of sex" beginning to emerge in the Renaissance. He harbored no sense that sodomy can be a state of mind rather than physical act. His interest in sodomy is entirely limited to the legal sphere: the area in which his eminence became legendary, not least for his wish to make forensic evidence in the courtroom as accurate a "science" as possible.

The purpose of my assessment is threefold. First, to introduce Zacchia to English-speaking readers who may not have come upon him, and to investigate how his legal mind shaped the presentation of the material. Here I seek to guide the reader to the relevant passages, pause over them – especially within the context of Zacchia's contemporaries – and reconstruct Zacchia's main points vis-à-vis sodomy as preserved in his *own* sequences of thought. Where necessary, I cite his contemporaries whom Zacchia himself often quotes. You could say that by using his text as the basis I reconstruct the universe of his thinking about a "science of homosexuality." Upon occasion it may seem that I have presented the flow of his ideas in an obsolete sequence; I do so to preserve his original logic, even where it differs from modern sense of cause and effect, hypothesis and conclusion. But I do not aim to compile and assess Zacchia's sources, except in passing – my aim remains to introduce him.

Second, I hope to explain precisely what his contribution to the developing science of sodomy was, albeit in the forensic domain, and in which of these forensic areas he had been innovative. Finally, and perhaps most crucially, to provide the reader with some sense of Zacchia's logic and reasoning in his writings themselves, especially in the *Quaestiones Medico-Legales*, so that the reader can form her own judgment about the quality of Zacchia's contribution. However, rather than provide biographical sketches or summarize his forensic works descriptively, I have selected a few of his most significant passages capturing this habit of mind – his logic and reason – to provide some indication of how he moved from point to point in his thinking about sodomy. I do this in the hope that by proceeding in this necessarily cautious philological manner I can convey the essence of his thinking as captured in its own cadences and contexts.

Such close interpretation of old texts based on literal translations (and the translations here strive to be as literal as possible) necessarily thrives on philological analysis, and I could not perform this tripartite task without entering into discussions of Zacchia's vocabulary and the often complex milieu of his key usages. This is not a fashionable approach in our time when cultural studies, however practiced, rules the collective mentality, but is the one that yields rewards for a figure who has practically dropped out of recent history – certainly out of recent sexual history.

Stuprum and the stuprator

Zacchia's conception of sodomitical evidence begins with an action: *stuprum*, or penetration. The word's grammatical profile is historically unclear: it functioned as both noun and verb in Latin. "Stuprum" originally meant dishonor, especially defilement having occurred through an unchaste act. In cases of violation through lewdness it could apply both to the active and passive participant, but it was not an exclusive synonym for penetration and even now it remains unclear precisely when it acquired this narrowed meaning or whether Zacchia was the first thinker to delimit it in this imaginative way. It may be that he reflects contemporary usage but further extensive research would be needed before endorsing this view. The main point is that Zacchia has delimited a word originally meaning dishonor – *stuprum* – and narrowed its connotation to defilement of a very specific type: *sodomitical anal penetration*.

Used in all his passages but one instead of "sodomia," the word "stuprum" guides Zacchia's thoughts about sodomy. Indeed he seems to construe it as a synonym of sodomy, viewing *sodomia* exclusively as anal penetration. Nothing about his conception of sodomy can be understood without starting from its facts. First among its many intricacies is the type of penetration it represents, and the affirmation that it can be known primarily against those to whom the action has been committed. By using a word that is often translated as "disgrace,"[10] Zacchia's language implies the antagonism of commission ("committed") because he assumes that rarely do the passive recipients of stuprum request it. From the start this issue of free will surfaces in his discussion of *stuprum* and must remain in full sight.

Stuprum, Zacchia maintains, is "not only committed against girls, and virgins, and spinsters" (*QML* 259).[11] It is also performed "against men by the most wicked of men who abuse Nature." In making such strong affirmation Zacchia joined with other eminent contemporary jurists, such as Prospero Farinacci, in the view that stuprum is *contra natura* – "against Nature" – as well as a distinct form of abuse.[12] It is specifically the act of stuprum – as inflicted by the *stuprator* – that renders sodomy *contra natura*. Hence sodomy (*sodomia*) in that legal view is not an abstract condition of existence or other state of being, nor a psychological state of mind, but explicitly an action whose complex components require disentangling.

Zacchia also declares that *stuprum* has generally been "punished with the greatest severity" (*QML* 259). As evidence he cites a number of authorities,[13] but not without calling attention to the perils involved to distinguish fact from fiction. Expert witnesses alone can decide the matter – Zacchia's reason for placing so much emphasis on them: "In the examination of this offence, in order that judges may be made more certain concerning the truth, they preside over [cases] through the doctors and surgeons observing those boys." Zacchia buttresses this view by reference to Sebastiano Guazzini, another contemporary jurist, and Prospero Farinacci, one of his main sources already mentioned.[14] The protocol is that doctors and surgeons report their findings for assessment; the judges, in turn, decide whether "there may be such signs confirming that the boys endured *stuprum*" (*QML* 259).[15] Specifically, they determine whether they were passive (Zacchia's word is "passus") in "submitting to another's lust."

The temporal element also plays a main part in Zacchia's conception as the clue to the frequency of the stuprator's crime. As Zacchia writes:

> There is a double distinction, because some show *stuprum* committed recently, truly others [show *stuprum* committed] a long time ago, and again there are those to whom *stuprum* has been perpetrated on only one occasion, or rarely, while there are certain ones who exhibit frequent *stuprum*. (*QML* 259)

Zacchia's temporal consideration appears lumbersome, yet his point clear: the anatomical evidence will depend on the frequency of stupration. Hence

> *stuprum* against a boy, which may have been performed recently, within a month, especially if it is frequent, is clearly apparent from tearings of the anus called *rhagadia*, which readily appear on account of the force of being entered, especially if the boy is of a more tender age, and the *stuprator* is richly endowed with a thick penis. (*QML* 260)

This temporal consideration is thus further complicated by the *stuprator*'s own anatomy. Zacchia's "tears" (*rhagadia*) are self-evident, even visible, he thinks, to the naked eye. But the penetrator's member, or penis – his *mentula* – also plays a major part. *Mentula*, originally an obscene slang term, is here a synonym for the *membrum*, or *membrum virile*. Zacchia's notion is not that the act of rape causes this organ to fill with fluid and blood and therefore enlarges it: hence the reason the judge can ascertain whether the rape has been committed within a month – such technical thinking exceeded Zacchia's view. He merely means that the member must be examined to determine the type of "tears" (*rhagadia*) that would most probably have been sustained. Zacchia repeats Guazzini's point when stating that "the consideration of size and of smallness of the penis of the alleged stuprator ought to be had in this case" (*QML* 260). The boy's anatomy must be examined, and the size of the *stuprator*'s penis must be shown to the court.[16] It is insufficient to state the size: the penis must actually be demonstrated before the court on grounds that a small penis could not have been as harmful as a large one.

The implications here are far-flung: all is understood literally, without a trace of our rich contemporary symbolism or doubt about the motives of those who pry. Both the predator's penis and the victim's anus must be examined with care. A small penis can clear an alleged *stuprator*'s name. The temporal element – whether the rape had recently been committed –would indicate the extent of the damage done and the intervening time for healing. But even so, the case would still stand or fall on the size of the alleged *stuprator*'s penis, and nothing except measurement and demonstration could establish the fact. The magistrate or judge must search for "the clearest evidences of a bruise where these parts join together" (*QML* 260). And where the boy is older, more grown up or larger in size if young, or in cases where the *stuprator* is not endowed with a thick penis, "occasionally this part [i.e. of the anus] will appear stripped of its skin, surely on account of that same cause of violence, and also at other times it is annoyed by inflammation" (*QML* 260). These symptoms are less serious than the brutal tearings (*rhagadia*) because the damage done is anatomically less drastic.

Further evidence is obtained by inspecting the anus. As Zacchia comments:

> But the inflammation appears more readily at the outset. Hereafter, when it has been made tender, a festering follows, and the color of his anus is changed into a livid bruise, with the blood having been entirely changed by clotting. He had this [bruise] where they [the folds] had joined together, on account of the violence and motion and heat. If the *stuprum* was very frequent, there appears also in this same fundament, a certain dilation and stretching of this part [i.e. the anus], which can also indurate after a long time and that can at the same time indicate frequent *stuprum*, also committed in time past.

Over and again frequency of assault provides the clue, and all the anatomic inspections lead toward that determination. For this reason, the male (and under other conditions the female) anus became a site as heavily policed among the accused as the penis. Here the evidence lay in *carunculae*, or "little bits of flesh" (*QML* 259). In modern medical texts "caruncles" indicate "any small fleshy eminence, whether normal or abnormal."[17] However, Zacchia's usage suggests our hemorrhoids; in his language "excrescent flesh more often signifies what in vulgar [speech] are called *cristas*."[18]

Quoting Juvenal's famous second satire Zacchia introduces a third term for these growths, or piles: *marisca*, a word that literally means "fig." In this satire against "moralists without morals," Juvenal had excoriated by rhetorical interrogation:

> do you rebuke foul practices, when you are yourself the most notorious delving-ground among Socratic reprobates (*cinaedi*)? A hairy body, and arms stiff with bristles, give promise of a manly soul: but sleek are your buttocks when the grinning doctor cuts into the swollen piles.[19]

Podice levi, or "sleek buttocks," is more accurately translated as a smooth or stretched anus; the suggestion is venereal disease through frequent illicit sodomitical contact. In Juvenal's Satire 2, it is the "grinning doctor" who discovers the secret behind the hypocrite's masculine swagger and bravado. Certainly, Zacchia's concern is less with the public–private chasm than with the anatomical evidence, but the fact that Juvenal's passage is the only directly quoted one in this discussion of *stuprum* suggests that Zacchia, as a doctor and a forensic authority, recognizes the physician's role in relation to the legal system. It is a matter of expert affinity – this is his new contribution.

Yet Zacchia himself omits any Juvenalian invective and instead directs his attention to the anatomical evidence: these "*mariscae* are taken for hemorrhoids by very many doctors, when they are swollen and opened or made sore, so that they resemble a certain kind of fig" (*QML* 259 for the remainder of this paragraph). By now Zacchia's view is firmly fixed on the fundament, and modern students of his text can only wonder about what he could have achieved with the help of a microscope. Pointedly he writes, "the condition of the anus will be able to indicate the much more frequent practice of such very abominable coitus, which is made smooth and flat from such a union, although it is wrinkled naturally." Indeed, he notes,

> these wrinkles which are in the ring of the anus are erased on account of incessant friction from a penis, the more that *stuprum* is repeated, the greater also the width of the anus stretches from day to day, largely because the most notorious catamites [*cinaedi*] are gathered together.

Here then was a rather detailed medical theory describing catamites and their partners for magistrates and judges; one entirely inflexible in its moral bases. At no point does the very correct and proper Zacchia entertain the possibility that authority, especially as invested in Church and State, is flawed. His task as a forensic theorist is to generate a rational and logical system accounting for the signs the judges will inspect. These acts are entirely heinous in his purview, as are, apparently, the organs and human beings perverted and corrupted. From our removal in time we marvel, perhaps, at his anatomical specificity, which is unsurprising when it is remembered that Zacchia's treatise was intended for judges sitting on frequent court cases. Yet consolation exists: for example, Zacchia describes new lubrications to assuage, "so that they may lessen the pain from this action, especially the first time, and so that they may endure more easily, medicines are used for relaxing and softening" (*QML* 260). Here Zacchia is momentarily attuned to the anatomical stresses of (what we would call) the homosexual couple on their first venture into sexual intercourse. His nod also acknowledges the existence of sodomitical subcultures engaging in these practices, even if they amount to *sex contra natura*. It also proclaims awareness of the pharmacological practices, however rogue, of his era – the sale of not merely popular lubricants but medicaments (his "medicamenta") – when conceding that not all "tears" derive from the hateful and illicit *stuprum*; that in a forensic case all other possible causes must be ruled out first: "it should be noted that more of the recounted signs can be from other causes, than can ascribe their origin to sexual violation." Therefore, "the greatest precaution must be used, to distinguish when they [the signs] have been caused by *stuprum* and when from other causes."

Next Zacchia ponders such other possibilities, as he aims to show that he is a fair-minded and balanced system-builder. "Truly," he writes, "tears can derive from the acrid and erosive *humore*, or from hard stools, from which inflammation and itching can be readily present." Precise interpretation proves nearly impossible here, as Zacchia's terms are not defined. He had glossed his other terms – *stuprum* and its cognates – but does not expatiate on his version of Galenism and the humors.[20] His treatment is nevertheless detailed, his logic infallible, his anatomy exquisitely honed. As he comments:

> If, nevertheless, the tears derive from the acrid and biting *humore*, this will readily be apparent through other such signs proving the abundance of the *humores* and through the occasional exudation of ichorous, golden yellow, citron-coloured, or green *humore* from those little ulcers and tears.

Therefore, defecations and stools now match what stupration, tears, and penis measurements earlier revealed.

> Even if they have been from the passing of too hard stool, this can easily be established from a consideration of the stool, except that where it is plain from these causes, there must not be bruises present, nor habitual redness in the anus, nor in fact can the boy endure as great a force from hard stool, as he is compelled to endure from the violence of *stuprum*. (*QML* 260)

Zacchia also assumes that the pox cannot be anally contracted. He believes that some anal tears among boys are caused by infections oozing ichor and causing ulcerations but that these have not been venereally contracted. In such cases the damage has been caused by erosive *humores* rather than sodomitical intercourse. He is vigilant to distinguish between the two types, while cautioning that erosive *humores* are rarely found among boys who are not catamites. Such erosive *humores* seen in ordinary boys who have not been sodomized prompt us to speculate about

Zacchia's Galenism: a topic of great complexity in the Renaissance. Determined not to omit any possible cause for the evidence of ulceration, Zacchia considers the possibility of innate biological, or temperamental, flaw, hereby repeatedly working as the consummate logician who leaves no stone unturned:

> However, the one other possible cause [for the signs visible upon examination in court], namely the flowing of erosive *humores*, scarcely has a place in boys, and this ailment is not usually very familiar to them, because the *humores* assigned [to them] are of a more benign nature.

These are not infections caused by "corrosive *humores*" and do not result from anal penetration but from hard stools and other sharp objects, or they may indicate some basic biological flaw innate since birth. In either scenario there has been no sexual infraction, the boy is no catamite, and there is no legal case to answer. Anal intercourse having been absent, the judge must not think such signs were owing to sodomy. Zacchia's continued insistence on logic and reason leads him to balanced views – no stone can be left unturned – even when his personal moral belief could have swayed him otherwise.

His conclusion ends logically at the point where it began: in the magisterial significance of stupration for the judge and for the medical doctors on whose evidence he will rely. "*Carunculae*, as well as the friction and flattening of wrinkles, are scarcely able to be from another cause, than from *stuprum*." He has proved, he thinks, that the action alone can cause the damage; and if violation has occurred, then punishment can be doled out. Even so, evidence that an offence had been committed was not in itself proof that a named suspect was guilty of the offence. Suspects often insisted on their innocence despite proof of stupration and cast doubt on the evidence presented against them. Anatomical size, as we have already observed, constituted further evidence but even it, of itself, did not prove that a named suspect was the guilty party. False accusations were common for all sorts of reasons, especially among children, with spite and revenge as chief motives. For all these reasons convictions could be difficult to make.[21]

Zacchia the forensic system-builder had no hard and fast solutions to these lingering obstacles to the gap between available evidence and proof of guilt. He had constructed a logical system that placed little weight on motive, intention, or extenuating circumstance other than the bio-anatomical ones listed. The suspected *stuprator* is guilty if these conditions obtain as evidenced in the signs that have been presented. It is an ostensibly foolproof semiology based on logic and incapable of fallibility. On this note Zacchia terminates his section in the *Quaestiones* about the forensic science applicable to sodomy:

> And so, with individual causes and signs having been considered concerning this [action], with great precautions having been applied, also with conjectures and presumptions not having been neglected, even those which can be held outside [their] skill, doctors can easily pronounce the truth concerning this matter. (*QML* 260)

Further implications

Zacchia's discussion of a forensic science of sodomy comprises little more than one thousand words embedded in the *Quaestiones*. Here, in this locus classicus celebrated in later centuries, is the brief text on which his later reputation as the avatar of sexually forensic science was based. It is important to emphasize, even at the expense of repetition, that he did not write the *Quaestiones* to pronounce exclusively on sodomy. To the contrary, he composed it as a general system of forensic science requiring a section on anal intercourse, particularly between males. Would he have included it two centuries earlier? This *what if* question is flawed and, moreover, tangential; if it must be answered the reply is in the negative. In c.1430 male same-sexual relations were not yet perceived in the Italian cities as the potentially divisive force, or threat, they later became,[22] and forensic science of Zacchia's variety then barely existed. Likewise for Zacchia's other medical pronouncements. If, as we have earlier observed, he wrote about medical hypochondria in forensic contexts, especially in cases where the malady was deployed by malingerers as an excuse for neglect, he wrote there too as an early modern forensic scientist, not as a philosopher of medicine or cultural commentator.

In one domain however – the hermaphroditic – his pronouncements shed further light on his science of sodomy. The chapter containing it complements his systematic semiology of homosexuality for forensic purposes. It too appeared in the *Quaestiones* as "Investigation VIII: On hermaphrodites," and the most relevant sections are 31 ("From Aristotle, the assigning of one dominant sex and one recessive sex to anyone born with both sexes") and 32 ("On Sodomy").[23] Like its companions at *Quaestiones* 259–60 the purpose of these two chapters (499–500) is forensic. Magistrates usually decided verdicts based on the gender or sex of a human creature; they, and the medical doctors on whose testimony they rely, needed the expert guidance Zacchia provides even though such cases were rare. Renaissance trials were permeated with cases of illicit impregnation; sometimes the accused defended himself, or herself, by claiming he/she was a hermaphrodite incapable of performing the act. It was left to the experts to decide. Epochs later the pioneer sexologists of the nineteenth century read Zacchia on hermaphroditism as closely as on the anatomies of the genital organs.

Zacchia begins by deferring to Aristotle: "With creatures assigned two sexes, Aristotle always determines them to have one that is dominant, and the other recessive." The dominant one is fixed, or established, from birth: the reason why hermaphrodites demonstrate the characteristics of one sex more than the other. Here Zacchia thinks of procreation: the dominant gender is the one that will be used to reproduce; it is the one capable of procreating, while the recessive gender is "impotent." This recessive one "is able to go under," while the other – the dominant – asserts itself for procreation. Zacchia does not expound on what happened when "recessive" females actually fell pregnant, but it seems logical to think that their gender would need to be legally reassigned after the event.

The implication, nevertheless, of this division for the law was considerable. Zacchia claims that female hermaphrodites have a "dominant" womb, which gives them the potential for copulating. He then enlists the histories of Hieronymus Montuus (1495–1560), a natural historian of reproduction, "to assess those women who declared positively that they have been made pregnant by hermaphrodites." Montuus had written accounts of women impregnated by hermaphrodites; Zacchia enlists his writings now to tease out the deception involved. That is, the women have perpetrated "a worthy deception" when claiming "they strengthened their womb to [be able to] bear from hermaphrodites." Womb-strengthening amounts to a type of pelvic exercise: performing motions of restraint and release so that the vaginal cavity becomes stronger. When a woman charged that a man had fathered her bastard, the villain often pleaded hermaphroditism. Zacchia's agenda here is the generation of a theory of signs permitting the matter to be decided in court. In such cases, the womb was to the hermaphrodite what the anus was to the catamite – all investigation must be focused there.

Hermaphrodites became the subject of forensic scrutiny when they deviated from their chosen gender, the gender nature has made dominant. As Zacchia notes:

> According to the authority of laws, when they order hermaphrodites to choose whatever sex is agreeable, as if they were to obtain of both sexes perfectly, in their will it may be placed to choose for themselves what sex they wish to use, by the imposition of punishments, if they don't remain thereafter as they have chosen, and they act abusively against the other sex. It is said they wish to choose the sex in which they are stronger, and therefore, abiding by it, they abstain from the other, and they renounce their free choice, because, it is certain, whichever sex dominates is the one in which they experience themselves stronger, and whose use Nature inclines and urges them with stronger provocation.

The thought is clear: allow hermaphrodites to choose their sex based on the inclination of their nature, but punish them with penalties if they waver from playing the accepted social role of that gender. Two centuries later, when sexology was formative in the mid-nineteenth century in Dr Tardieu's Parisian milieu, this earlier Renaissance homology of catamites and hermaphrodites proved of extraordinary interest to the new theorists.

In most cases the forensic solution worked. Where it did not, and where violation had occurred, it was because the offenders reverted to the "recessive sex." The substance of Zacchia's thought amounts to an infirmity model not so different from our modern addiction relapse. That is, addicts today often pledge to remain dry or substance free; when they lapse, or relapse, they harm themselves above all others and must start their recovery over again. In Zacchia's model they specifically commit the "sin of sodomy" because they have fraudulently used their "recessive" womb as if it were "dominant." On this point he is unequivocal, "For if they use their recessive sex they sin severely, Sodomy is the sin committed, or at least joining together what is not dissimilar, because they misuse Nature." The argument of *contra natura* returns, as it often does in Zacchia, and the specific violation these offenders have caused against Nature (the "misuse") occurs through dissymmetry "since it is not possible for them to procreate through the recessive sex."

Full circle we have returned to the Renaissance master principle of *contra natura*: all that goes against "Nature" in this domain of sex and gender, that defies what is given and inflexible. Here Zacchia specifies his "violation" through recognition that sodomy is an abstraction; if not a label then an abstract word ("sodomia") capable of many interpretations. He wishes to provide his experts – those doctors who will appear in court to testify and the magistrates who will base their decisions on what they have said – with concrete reasons why this "misuse" of the womb is criminal. So he explains: "no less great is this [sin committed] than another sin of sodomy." The *other sin* is explicitly "intercourse with a member of the same sex, or not in the natural vessel (*vase*)." *Non in vase naturali* refers to any coitus not in the vagina because "procreation is impossible to follow."

Hence Zacchia's logic allows him to theorize that "the sin of Sodomy is in fact not only the carnal union of man with man, but also of woman with woman." His entire sentence, although tortured, is worth citing:

> Sodomy is the sin committed, or at least the joining together of what is not dissimilar, because they [i.e. offending hermaphrodites] misuse Nature, since it is not possible for them to procreate through the recessive sex; in fact not less great is another sin of sodomy, which is intercourse with a member of the same sex, or not in the natural vessel, from which procreation is impossible to follow: and the sin of Sodomy is in fact not only the carnal union of man with man, but also of woman with woman.

Through rigorous logic the proposition has become QED: Zacchia has established his point about hermaphrodites and reasoned in such a way not only to enforce the established codes of Church and State, but also to outlaw all intercourse (*coitus*) outside the anatomical womb. Here it is a delicious irony of the Latin language that, according to Adams, *vase* is often a euphemism for *mentula*.[24] The *mentula*, or penis, is after all the "unnatural vessel" when it invades such foreign anatomy "from which procreation is impossible to follow." Can it be that the very learned Zacchia was impervious to the *double entendre*?

Conclusions

The nineteenth-century sexologists often wrote as if Zacchia was the only Renaissance scholar who had pronounced on these matters. For this reason primarily their reverence is pronounced. The names of his colleagues, some already mentioned, rarely appear in their writings. Yet Zacchia consulted Prospero Farinacci, Aegidius Bossius, Giulio Claro, Sebastiano Guazzino, Amato Lusitano, and others, and often relied on their ideas to construct his forensic science. His contemporaries, especially Lusitano, also deserve mention, however brief, in a discussion of the rise of the early forensic sciences of sodomy.

Farinacci and Guazzino have already been discussed above but so far I have said little about Amato Lusitano (1511–68), perhaps the first European writer to assess the possibly adverse effects of anal intercourse between males in his *Curationum medicinalium centuriae septem* (1551), reprinted frequently and annotated in the sixteenth century.[25] Born in Castelo Branco in Portugal and eventually the occupier of the Chair of Medicine in Ferrara, he was a Sephardic Jewish polymath of renown. His interests included botany and he collected specimens from as far afield as Asia. He also wrote commentaries on books 1 and 2 of Dioscorides (Antwerp, 1536) and worked for a time in the Netherlands. But it was Lusitano's medical commentaries on "excrescent flesh growing around the anus," which – as I have noted –the laymen of his era called *cristas*, that make him important within the context of Zacchia's forensic science. Lusitano singled out these "cristas" for discussion and observed that they occurred "not only in women but in young boys at Rome." He had seen them "at the origin of those cracks [of the anus], that is, similar to those [cracks or fissures] which occur on the lips on account of the frozen breeze of the North wind."[26] But his main contribution was advocacy of surgical excision: "after a little bit has been cut, the vestiges left behind are cured," and the remaining fissures "are extirpated by ointment from lead and especially by other drying [agents]." Almost a full century before Zacchia published in 1630, Lusitano is found using the same argument about sodomy as a sin *contra natura*, and pronouncing on sodomy as the most "vile" and "abominable" of diseases. You could read his commentary on sodomy and think you are reading Zacchia – eighty years earlier.

Like Lusitano, Aegidius Bossius (1487–1546) lived in the generation before Zacchia and published several treatises on criminal law. He was less interested in cracks and fissures than the others but intent upon establishing the immorality of sodomy. To do so he ransacked the *consilia* of authorities on jurisprudence prior to the sixteenth century to demonstrate that sodomy even transcended incest. Zacchia relied on his writings as reliable compilations of the *consilia* of the previous century. A generation later than Bossius, Guilio Claro (1525–75) took up some of the former's mantle. An Italian by birth he had gained favor with the court of Philip II of Spain, where he often worked, and in the great Spanish libraries of the day consulted *consilia* unavailable to Bossius. Nothing in his writing suggests that his model of sodomy deviated from the norm of these other thinkers. He merely read widely enough to solidify further their positions.

Other figures even more minor than these polymathic contemporaries of Zacchia could be mentioned, but they would not alter the main point: that Zacchia consolidated a body of knowledge developing for almost two centuries through *consilia* and other learned commentaries on the science of sodomy. By the time his *Quaestiones Medico-Legales* had been published and digested in the mid-seventeenth century, his name became synonymous with the forensic approach to sodomitical science. For four decades at least (1630–70) he would likely have been the leading continental authority on the forensic implications of sodomy. If further work needs to be gathered in this context it is the effect of Zacchia's texts and positions over the next three generations, from 1670 to 1760. Such research would clarify how the law changed in ways that relegated his views to obsolescence – dusty tomes unvisited in late eighteenth-century libraries. This chapter, which we cannot provide here, amounts to study of the aftermath of Zacchia and the decline of his authority.

Zacchia *au fin* is a pivotal figure in the developing sciences of sodomy in the early modern period because his example demonstrates how legal practice interacted with medical knowledge in sodomy cases. Hitherto sodomites had often been convicted by torture; medical evidence was rarely used among the suspects. Zacchia's writings encouraged the authorities, especially judges, to examine the medical evidence first before delivering guilty verdicts. He merits a secure place in the evolving history of same-sex relations in the early modern period, which so far he has not had, earned by combining various sciences, especially legal and medical, for his reforms.

Nevertheless, a final question must also be asked about Zacchia's work in the context of our times. The main legal minds who figure in this exploration – Zacchia and his colleagues – aimed to develop a forensic science of sodomy for courtrooms aiming to decide between the guilty and innocent. Any pronouncements they generated en passant about sodomy's *moral* status were insignificant in comparison to their primary purpose: a newly devised scientific system, grounded in medicine and the law, to detect offenders. Viewed collectively as a single group their view monolithically condemns sodomy as a "vile and wicked disease." Not one voice in this learned Renaissance company, in any of the countries from which they issued, deviated from this stance about *sodomy as sin*. It is a collective position capable of making some of our contemporaries in the twenty-first century paranoid: indeed, tolerant-minded current homosexuals could feel traumatized after reading these persecutory works; for not merely do they want to detect sodomites but they devise a "science" of detection aiming to be fool-proof. Why then should readers – even scholars –in the twenty-first century want to know about this tradition that is so antithetical to the more tolerant one largely found today?

The answer depends on the uses made of history. My goal has been to annotate an important, if understudied, moment in the early modern development of the science of sodomy. Most modern histories of homosexuality from the Greeks to the present time deal with the centuries from 1400 to 1700 in theological and legal terms and overlook its scientific contexts. Often and brilliantly, they explicate the social and aesthetic consequences of same-sex attraction and sodomitical practice but neglect the pronouncements of seemingly far-flung sciences: astrology to physiology, botany to medicine. They comment on gender and the construction of desire, even in affective senses, as if the participants were somehow free to follow their inclination. Yet most infractions then led to inquest and imprisonment. The significance of a Zacchia is that he intuitively combined legal practice and medical knowledge in ways that enhanced the accurate detection of sodomites while never consciously intending to condone homosexuality at all.

Notes

1. See e.g. Michel Foucault's treatment of Zacchia in his *History of Madness*. Whether correctly or not Foucault thought Zacchia had "summed up all Christian jurisprudence that related to the question of madness" (Michel Foucault, *History of Madness*, tr. Jonathan Murphy and Jean Khalfa, London: Routledge, 2006, p. 122), and Sylvia DeRenzi has confirmed the view for the injured body: see her "Witnesses of the Body: Medico-Legal Cases in Seventeenth-Century Rome," *Studies in the History and Philosophy of Science*, 33 (2002), 219–42. Foucault considered Ambroise Tardieu (1818–79) to be the pre-eminent forensic doctor of the nineteenth century; see the uses he made of Tardieu and the developing sexology of the mid-nineteenth century in *Herculine Barbin: Being the Recently Discovered Memoirs of a Nineteenth-Century French Hermaphrodite*, London: Harvester Press, 1980. Tardieu's forensic works were reprinted in French almost every year after they appeared and often used as textbooks for law students. Tardieu became interested in the forensic aspects of pederasty in the 1840s and published a treatise on the subject entitled *La pédérastie*. A modern edn has appeared; see Dominique Fernandez, *La prostitution antiphysique par François Carlier. Précédé de La pédérastie par Ambroise Tardieu; présenté par Dominique Fernandez*, Paris: Le Sycamore, 1981. I am grateful to N. L. Davidson of Oxford University who commented on versions of this chapter and significantly improved it.

2. The most important work in English and Italian about Zacchia, biographically and interpretatively, has been written by Silvia DeRenzi: see her articles "'A Fountain for the Thirsty' and a Bank for the Pope: Charity, Conflicts, and Medical Careers at the Hospital of Santo Spirito in Seventeenth Century Rome," in Jon Arrizabalaga *et al.* (eds), *Health Care and Poor Relief in Counter-Reformation Europe*, London: Routledge, 1999, pp. 102–31; "La Natura in Tribunale: Conoscenze e Pratiche Medico-Legali a Roma nel XVII Secolo" (Nature in the Courtroom: Medical-Legal Knowledge and Practices in 17th-Century Rome), *Quaderni Storici*, 36/3 (2001), 799–822; and "Witnesses of the Body: Medico-Legal Cases in Seventeenth-Century Rome," *Studies in History and Philosophy of Science*, 33 (2002), 219–42. For other useful information about Zacchia see Michel Porret, "La voie de Paolo Zacchias: medècine et crime," *Crime, Histoire et Sociétés*, 5 (2001), 129–33; Joseph Bajada, *Sexual Impotence: The Contribution of Paolo Zacchia (1584–1659)*, Rome: Pontificia Università Gregoriana, 1988; and Zdzislaw Traunfellner, "Paolo Zacchia: Vater der Gerichtlichen Medizin, 400 Jahre nach seiner Geburt," *International Journal of Legal Medicine*, 94/2 (April 1985), 159–63. For the fullest view of Zacchia in the eighteenth century see Nicolas François Joseph Eloy, *Dictionnaire historique de la médecine ancienne et moderne*, 4 vols, Mons: Chez H. Hoyois, 1778, *s.v.* "Zacchia." Zacchia figures in the background of Lucy Bland and Laura Doan (eds), *Sexology Uncensored: The Documents of Sexual Science*, Cambridge: Polity Press, 1998.

3. The edns of the *Quaestiones Medico-Legales* pose difficult questions about composition and organization. The 1st edn of 1630 is entitled *Quaestiones Medico-Legales, in quibus omnes eae materiae Medicae . . .* , Leipzig, 1630. The 1630 edn was followed by others published in Leipzig and Amsterdam in 1651, 1661, and 1676. The 1651 Amsterdam edn is the one I have used for all citations in this chapter. The edn of 1661 is the largest of Zacchia's compilations and most inclusive of the versions. All translations of Zacchia and his contemporaries were made by Meredith Donaldson Clark.

4. *Consilia* were collections of the diagnoses made by celebrated physicians and had existed in Italy from the thirteenth century. As such they constituted one of two main genres of "medical narrative about individual patients and their diseases," the other one being "anecdotes embedded in general medical or surgical treatises" (Nancy G. Siraisi, *The Clock and the Mirror: Girolamo Cardano and Renaissance Medicine*, Princeton: Princeton University Press, 1997, p. 201, see below). They were commonly used in Renaissance schools of medicine as a main component of medical education. *Consilia*

could be collected on account of the renown of either the doctor or the patient. The *consilia* of an authority as eminent as Zacchia would have commanded much attention in his writings. For the history and development of the consilia see the study just cited and also Nancy G. Siraisi: *Medieval and Renaissance Medicine: An Introduction to Knowledge and Practice*, Chicago: University of Chicago Press, 1990.

 5. For the Sacra Rota see Rienzi, 2002 (n. 2), pp. 221–2.

 6. For the flavor of the reports issued by the Rota Romana of the type Zacchia would have seen and commented upon, see Gero Dolezalek, "Reports of the 'Rota'" (14th–19th Centuries)," in John H. Baker (ed.), *Judicial Records, Law Reports and the Growth of Case Law*, Berlin: Duncker & Humblot, 1989, pp. 67–99.

 7. For useful comments about Zacchia and Farinacci in this context see Ian Maclean, *Interpretation and Meaning in the Renaissance*, Cambridge: Cambridge University Press, 1992, esp. pp. 245ff. Maclean demonstrates how Zacchia presided over the developing marriage between medicine and the law in many areas of human behavior where they had previously been considered apart. But by the late eighteenth century Zacchia had dropped out; see, for some examples, Sir Leon Radzinowicz, *A History of English Criminal Law and its Administration from 1750*, 3 vols, London: Stevens, 1948–86.

 8. Valerio Marchetti has addressed some of these matters in two important chapters: "La simulazione di santità nella riflessione medico-legale del sec. XVII," in G. Zarri (ed.), *Finzione e santità tra Medioevo ed età moderna*, Turin: Rosenberg & Sellier, 1991, pp. 202–27; and "Sul controllo medico-legale dell''ambiguità sessuale: L'archiatra romano Paolo Zacchia (1584–1659) e l'ermafroditismo," in A. Pastore and P. Sorcinelli (eds), *Sanità e società: Emilia Romagna, Toscana, Marche, Umbria, Lazio, Secoli XVI–XX*, Udine: Casamassima, 1987, pp. 67–104.

 9. The main section dealing with sodomy appears as part of Investigation V, "Signs of a Sexually Violated Boy," and is found on pp. 259–60 of the 1651 Amsterdam edn; it is the one cited throughout this discussion.

10. J. N. Adams, *The Latin Sexual Vocabulary*, London: Duckworth, 1982, pp. 200–1.

11. Zacchia's *vidua* may include the class of widows. The *Quaestiones Medico-Legales* are from now on abbreviated as *QML*.

12. See Prospero Farinacci (1554–1618), *De Delictis Carnis*, q. 148, num. 1, a chapter in vol. 2 of Farinacci's *Praxis et Theorica Criminalis*, Venice, 1608, which was reprinted in his collected works, *Opera* (9 vols). Farinacci's influence is so preponderant in Zacchia's thought that it is worthwhile to pause on him. Dooley notes that "he came from relatively obscure origins. The son of a notary, he was possibly even less advantaged when he came to study civil and canon law at the University of Rome . . . Immediately after graduation he received successive appointments to manage the small, semi-independent state of Bracciano for the Orsini family and to help Pierdonato Cesi manage the state of Civitavecchia for the papacy. In spite of a scandalous and violent style of life that landed him in jail more than once, Farinacci aspired to still higher things. In 1585 he completed the first installments of the masterwork on criminal practice . . . By the turn of the seventeenth century, having obtained a provincial governorship all for himself and ingratiated Pope Clement VIII by a deliberately flimsy legal defense in the notorious parricide trial of Beatrice Cenci, permitting the Aldobrandini pope to confiscate the fortune of the rival Cenci family, he could set his sights on the highest magistracy in papal government: the governorship of Rome." Brendan Dooley, *Morandi's Last Prophecy and the End of Renaissance Politics*, Princeton: Princeton University Press, 2002. Dooley draws his information about Farinacci from Niccolo Del Re, "Prospero Farinacci, giurisconsulto romano," *Archivio della Societa Romana di Storia Patria*, 3rd ser. 29 (1975), 135–220. Farinacci's turbulent life included accusations of violent penetration by Bernardino Rocchi; a trial in Rome was held and Farinacci was exculpated. The Roman trial naming him as a sodomite has many curious parallels with Zacchia's discussion here, not least the "creste" so important to Zacchia. When suspect Rocchi was interrogated why he recently left Rome, he

explained to the court that he had been injured by sodomy and fled to Suriano, near Viterbo, for medical assistance. The trial transcript survives in the Archivio di Stato, Roma, "Tribunale del Governatore," processi 1505–1599, vol. 290, fols. 113r–121v, the relevant extract having been published by Giovanni Dall'Orto in *Babilonia*, 135 (1995). Rocchi told the court that of the various men who sodomized him Farinacci had done him the most damage because his penis was larger. Rocchi's "creste" were subsequently surgically excised, but the court seems to have doubted Bernardino's story and may have been covering up for the offence of such a powerful figure as Farinacci.

13. Among them is Aegidius Bossius, *Tractatus varii, qui omnem fere criminalem materiam excellenti doctrina complectuntur*, Venice, 1574.

14. See Sebastiano Guazzini, *Tractatus ad defensam inquisitorum . . .* , Venice, 1639, vol. 4, ch. 7, num. 12, p. 185.

15. Guazzini is the source for this statement, which Zacchia has repeated. See, for comparison with Zacchia's text, Guazzini, *Tractatus ad defensam*, num. 13, p. 185.

16. Ibid.

17. *Black's Medical Dictionary*, 41st edn, ed. Harvey Marcovitch, London: A. & C. Black, 2005.

18. Adams, *Latin Sexual Vocabulary*, n. on p. 98: "Juvenal employed *crista* as an *ad hoc* metaphor [for the clitoris] at *Satires* 6.422." Amato Lusitano (1511–68) discusses *crista* present around the anus in sodomitical contexts in *Curationum Medicinalium Centuria Secunda*, Venice: Ex officina Erasmiana Vincentij Valgrisij, 1552, p. 222.

19. Juvenal, *Satires*, 2.11–13. Adams comments that as a synonym for *carunculae* and metaphor for *culus* (anus), the term *marisca*, or "the important metaphor of the fig," was used in a similar way. "The fig had a widely-felt symbolism in antiquity. In Greek, words for 'fig' are sometimes used metaphorically for the anus . . . The usual metaphorical sense of a sexual kind borne by Latin *ficus* and comparable words was "anal sore" (usually thought to have been induced by anal penetration). . . . A husband desiring to *pedicare* boys might say that *pedicatio* of his own wife would not be the same thing: he wants the Chian fig (*chia*), not the insipid *marisca*. . . . But it is worth pointing out that in late popular Latin *ficus* may have taken on the sense 'female pudenda'." *Latin Sexual Vocabulary*, p. 113.

20. The phrase *ab humore acri et erodente* is problematic and may not refer to one of the humors, especially if *humore* can be construed here just as another liquid or moisture rather than in its Galenic sense. The "stinging and eroding liquid" described may be some type of diarrhea or other discharge.

21. For further discussion of these complications see Mary Hewlett, "Women, Sodomy and Sexual Abuse in Late Renaissance Lucca," University of Toronto unpublished Ph.D. thesis, 2000, pp. 221–6.

22. The chronological point, now in the public domain, is documented in: Ottavia Niccoli, *Il seme della violenza: Putti, faniculli, e mammoli nell' Italia tra Cinque e Seicento*, Bari: Casa Labalme, 1995; Michael Rocke, *Forbidden Friendships: Homosexuality and Male Culture in Renaissance Florence*, New York: Oxford University Press, 1997; N. S. Davidson, "Sodomy in early Modern Venice," in Tom Betteridge (ed.), *Sodomy in Early Modern Europe*, Manchester: Manchester University Press, 2002, pp. 74–7. Rocke suggests that sodomy was not treated as a serious offence in Florence, a position whose statistical evidence has been contested. For the developing adolescent in the Renaissance and his sexuality see Ilaria Taddei, *"Puerizia, adolescenza e giovinezza*: Images and Conceptions of Youth in Florentine Society during the Renaissance," in Konrad Eisenbichler (ed.), *The Premodern Teenager: Youth in Society 1150–1650*, Toronto: University of Toronto Press, 2002, pp. 15–24.

23. All quotations in this discussion over several paragraphs are from *QML* 499–500.

24. Adams, *Latin Sexual Vocabulary*, pp. 41–2, 88.

25. See Harry Friedenwald, *Amatus Lusitanus*, Baltimore: Johns Hopkins University Press, 1937; Yedida K. Stillman and George K. Zuckers (eds), *New Horizons in Sephardic Studies*, New York: SUNY Press, 1993, p. 7; and Donald F. Lach, *Asia in the Making of Europe*, vol. 3, *The Scholarly Disciplines*, Chicago: University of Chicago Press, 1977, pp. 430–1.
26. See Lusitano, *Curationum Medicalium*, p. 222.

5 Syphilis and the silencing of sodomy in Juan Calvo's *Tratado del morbo gálico*

Cristian Berco

At Zaragoza's main hospital, Santa Gracia, in 1667, a doctor making his rounds in the syphilis ward stopped by the bed of Bernardo Martínez, an adolescent student at Vicente Ferrer University College, and remained long enough to interrogate him thoroughly, despite the unpleasant stench of nearby patients sweating profusely due to mercury poultices and the heavy nightgowns and blankets heaped on them.[1] For some unknown reason – possibly resulting from an examination *in situ*, received information, or Bernardo's behavior – the doctor asked Bernardo if he had gotten sick from sexual contact with a woman. The hospital constitutions and regulations from 1655 do not require this question. Bernardo must already have undergone a preliminary, even if verbal and probably hurried, exam.[2] Given the details of his sexual experiences that would surface later, Bernardo probably had anal syphilitic chancres.

Bernardo responded negatively. His answer opened the door for various possibilities, both apparently nefarious and innocent, such as transmission through a male sexual partner or, according to formerly prevalent medical theory, non-sexual modes of infection. Even the clothes of one suffering from the disease could supposedly have infected Bernardo.[3] But something on which the sources are silent happened in the course of the night. Possibly due to felt pressures of Catholic conscience, hospital officials,[4] or both, the young man not only confessed the next day to having had passive anal intercourse but also denounced his sexual partner – Juan Curán, an adult staff member of the college's kitchen – who had apparently sodomized Bernardo for over a year. Although Curán was tried for sodomy and condemned to six years of rowing in the king's Mediterranean galleys, no further records of Bernardo remain. It seems he was not tried as an accomplice and most likely received the hospital's usual treatment. Although "sodomy" formerly had various possible applications, the bulk of legal cases, both inquisitorial and secular, involved anal sex between males, so that in legal and everyday usage, the term tended to focus on male–male liaisons, particularly anal.[5] I use the term accordingly, throughout this chapter.

Bernardo and his sodomitical syphilis demonstrate a striking disconnection between early modern medical theory and practice. In fact, the tense dynamic between the doctor's question, "Did you get sick from a woman," Bernardo's eventual response the next day, and the ensuing efforts to restore legal and spiritual order all played to the theme of moral reform of those afflicted with venereal disease, a common goal of early modern medical treatment. In this case, the ultimate example of sexual sin – the unmentionable vice – was central, and its conjunction with syphilis produced the perfect setting for a morality play amidst the bedpans and agonizing screams of a baroque hospital. At no point did the circumstances appear to produce medical incredulity. And yet, according to the doctrines of sophisticated medical treatises, our anonymous doctor should have been shocked at the manifestation of an impossibility: sodomitical syphilis. Instead, his question to Bernardo may well have anticipated the possibility of sodomitical infection that it came to reveal. This disconnection between practical experience and published medical discourse requires further attention. The medical treatise on the French disease most widely read in the Spanish Golden Age – Juan Calvo's 1580 *Tratado del morbo gálico* – maintains absolute silence on the possibility of transmission through same-sex erotic contact. The extent of logical and argumentative legerdemain required to produce this silence only speaks to the substantiality of what it sought to obscure in the actualities of baroque morality and public appearance. Faced with a local social crisis manifested in the widespread prosecution of sodomy, Juan Calvo applied this strategy of silence in accounting for the etiology, contagion, and symptoms of the disease.

Etiologies

Early modern narratives of how syphilis appeared and became a raging epidemic in Europe interpreted its genesis and interaction with society according to particular suppositions and concepts concerning health, gender, and sex.[6] Most chroniclers agreed that a terrifying disease that caused excruciatingly painful buboes and joint pain spread like wildfire through Europe in the mid-1490s. Tommaso di Silvestro and Sigismondo dei Conti reported this epidemic was raging through parts of Italy in 1495–6.[7] By the summer of 1496 it had struck Germany, and the following year, prostitutes and sufferers of the disease were expelled from areas of Scotland and Paris's Hôpital Dieu.[8] By March 1498, the Spanish doctor Francisco López de Villalobos had published a treatise describing the appearance of syphilitic buboes in Madrid and the terrible and cruel pestilence that followed.[9] Fierce disputations erupted between traditionalists linking this disease to illnesses described in classical and Arabic sources, such as elephantiasis, and others who considered these buboes a new pestilence.

The foundational stories of syphilis delight the imagination with everything from severe divine punishment to mysterious heavenly movements, from damaging humoral imbalances to unrestrained sexual sinning. Although learned authors proposed and disputed myriad origins and combinations thereof, the theory of an American etiology, advocated by many eminent scholars including Gabrielle Falloppio, Jean François Fernel, and Ruy Díaz de la Isla, slowly became the most widely reported.

When Juan Calvo also claimed that syphilis originated in the New World in his *Tratado del morbo gálico* published in Valencia in 1580, his general notions thus followed the opinions of his peers. As one of the last great doctors of the Valencian school before its decline in the seventeenth century, Calvo had been well trained in this city and later in Zaragoza under Juan Murillo, but extended his scholarly knowledge by visiting various Italian universities and working for a few years in Montpellier before returning to Valencia itself in 1568.[10] So influential were his opinions that this work was republished ten times in Spanish and twice in French over the course of the next two centuries.

According to Calvo, the French disease originated in the Americas

> because in the Indies it is very common and well known, since [the natives] were very wanton, sensual, and voracious, as they not only ate the flesh of animals but that of men as well, so that during their feasts and banquets they used to kill their slaves, roast them and eat them as we can see from the histories of the Indies.[11]

This crucial passage must be read in the light of both medical views on the geographic origin of syphilis and the moral discourse accompanying and seeking to legitimate the American conquest. The combination of these two currents of thought to posit a novel medical–moral assessment of the origins of the disease makes Calvo unique. Combining and thus reshaping both the medical and historical traditions, he added moral censure of American culture to the former, and modified the latter by substituting cannibalism for sodomy as the depraved behavior that engendered syphilis.

The first medical author to assign an American origin to syphilis was Ruy Díaz de la Isla,[12] a Spaniard who not only seems to have treated this disease in different parts of Aragon and Castile but also spent ten years as a surgeon specifically in charge of it at the All Saints Royal Hospital in Lisbon, Portugal.[13] In his *Tratado contra el mal serpentino* first published in 1539, Díaz classified syphilis as a new disease, never before seen in Europe, that first appeared when Columbus arrived in Barcelona in 1493 and met with the Catholic Monarchs. Claiming that he had even treated some of the sailors from the voyage, Díaz insisted that its birthplace was "in the island which is now called Hispaniola."[14] Moving on to discuss the evolution of the disease and the ways of treating it, Díaz leaves aside any possible moral issues relating to its American origin. Except for stating that "divine justice served to send us unknown diseases never before seen nor described in medical books," Díaz wrote about the European manifestation of syphilis as a scientific fact almost completely divorced from morality.[15]

After Díaz de la Isla, various authors further propagated the notion of an American origin for the disease, such as Gabrielle Fallopio in his 1563 treatise *De morbo gallico*, and Jean François Fernel in *De lues venerae curatione* published posthumously in 1579.[16] In the *Historia medicinal de las cosas que se traen de nuestras Indias Occidentales*, an important treatment of American pharmacology published in 1565, the Spaniard Nicolás Monardes assumed syphilis arose in the New World when commenting on various plants, including *guayaco* and *zarzaparrilla*, used to treat the disease in the Americas. Within a hundred years, forty-two editions of his work were published in six languages.[17]

Citing foreigners such as John of Vigo, Antonio Musa Brasavola, and the latter's student Falloppio regarding the American origin of the disease, Calvo was obviously well versed in the various theories. Eagerly tackling the debates of the time, he praised both Brasavola and Falloppio for arguing, quite against canon, that this illness was a "whole substance disease" – affecting the body at an interior, essential level – rather than one only acting through "manifest qualities," such as the outward forms of syphilitic lesions. Yet he attacked Nicola Leoniceno, the famous Galenic teacher, for declaring that the French disease originated in antiquity, and also Nicola Massa for stating that it exhibits the characteristics of coldness and dryness (p. 566). He even disagreed with Girolamo Fracastoro's emphasis on the disease's pituitary nature.

Calvo's support of the still developing notion of a whole-substance disease places him at the crossroads of new medical thought as doctors tried to make sense of diseases like syphilis by modifying and extending traditional Galenic knowledge. Indeed, these new ideas helped introduce a notion of disease as an invading entity wholly separate from the patient.[18] Calvo's approval of Falloppio and Brasavola indicates a theoretically innovative bent. He might have met the former during his visits to Italian universities in the early 1560s before Falloppio's death in 1562.

Calvo's opposition to some traditional aspects of Galenic medicine and to claims that the French disease had already been described by ancient authorities probably contributed to his acceptance of the American etiological theory. Greco-Roman authors could thus not have encountered the disease. Most academically trained early modern doctors were widely read and imbued with humanistic notions, just as Fracastoro incorporates learned literary references in *Syphilis sive*.[19] However, instead of relying on generalized tropes about God's punishments for sins, Calvo more innovatively appropriates contemporary historical sources about then-current issues like the conquest of the Americas, so as to introduce moral commentary into his scientific discussion of the disease's origin. Although that presumed historical knowledge was used to justify the oppression of American natives, its topicality in relation to contemporary European expansion made it quite "modern," and in that sense so was Calvo's thinking. As we have seen, his treatise claimed that the general licentiousness of the American natives, and particularly their cannibalistic tastes, led to the widespread existence of syphilis in the New World. For Calvo, the prevalence of this disease was directly proportional to the amount of sinful activity, for the natives did not merely misbehave but were "*very* wanton, sensual, and voracious" (p. 569).

Even by the standards of Renaissance medicine, as we can see by comparison with Díaz, Calvo's argument was primarily moral and polemical, designed to teach a lesson, rather than treat a scientific reality objectively. Although he could have argued his connection of syphilis with cannibalism on a supposedly physical basis, he rejects that theory. Some physicians, such as Leonardo Fioravanti, had already attributed the appearance of syphilis in Naples in 1496 to consumption of dead soldiers by the invading French army.[20] This theory of contagion assumed that rotting flesh produced a miasmic putrefaction, and so eating it could corrupt humors and thus cause various diseases.[21] But against the great surgeon Andrés Alcazar's assertion of this cannibalistic theory of syphilis in his *Chirurgiae libri sex* published in 1575,[22] Calvo declares "there have been other civil wars in which soldiers have consumed bad food, even horse and human flesh, without knowing it, and we do not find any reliable author asserting that this resulted in this illness" (p. 568).

To Calvo, then, the relation of syphilis to cannibalism was not defined by mere physical cause and effect, something that occurred through the act itself of consuming human flesh. Instead, it was a function of (im)moral behavior, of a conscious and repeated disavowal of everything that God and civilized people held right. For Calvo it was important that the French soldiers "consumed bad food, even horse and human flesh, *without them knowing it,*" for their transgression was not deliberate (p. 568). But he assumed the natives deliberately killed their own slaves to satiate their voracious appetite for human flesh. This behavior signaled an irrepressible moral failing on the part of the natives, in his view, that brought syphilis as divine punishment.

Although Calvo's knowledge of native cannibalistic rites was gleaned from his careful reading of histories of the Indies, as he pointed out, those sources do not discuss syphilis in the context of cannibalism, nor do they even associate the latter with Hispaniola, where Columbus' sailors had to contract syphilis according to the New World etiology. But Calvo refocused that theory on cannibalism, while simultaneously silencing the sodomy his sources generally designated as the greatest sin of the Hispaniolan natives.

At the time Calvo was writing his *Tratado del morbo gálico* the two rival camps of the Dominican friar Bartolomé de las Casas and Ginés de Sepúlveda were debating the moral status and consequent rights of the American natives, and Calvo's etiology of syphilis reflects Sepúlveda's kind of censures. Las Casas and his followers – which had included a young Prince Philip – argued that natives should be treated with the respect afforded to free subjects and that Spanish abuses against them should be curbed. Aided by historians and even Dominican enemies of Las Casas, Sepúlveda argued that the natives' enslavement (and thus mistreatment) followed naturally and justly from their barbarous inferiority and subhumanity, demonstrated by their unnatural vices.[23] But Las Casas represented them as the noblest and most innocent of beings with no malice whatsoever, who "did not commit against the Christian a single mortal sin that is punishable by man."[24] Las Casas's monumental *Historia de las Indias*, not published until 1875, argued that the natives of the Caribbean were wrongly accused of engaging in cannibalism and sodomy.[25] Another authority on the Indies, Alvar Nuñez Cabeza de Vaca, found evidence of cannibalism not among the natives of Florida, but only among starving Spaniards.[26] Though Cabeza de Vaca noted the natives' practice of male same-sex marriages in passing, his view of their societies was positive enough that Las Casas relied on him heavily for his accounts.[27]

Calvo's censorious view of the New World thus accords more with the camp that legitimated the conquest, and he most likely relied on Sepúlveda's own source and official history of the Columbian encounter, Gonzalo Fernández de Oviedo y Valdés's *Historia general y natural de las Indias*, and on Francisco López de Gómara's immensely popular *Historia general de las Indias*. First published in 1526 in Toledo, the former was translated into English by 1555 and French the following year. Having appeared in Zaragoza in 1552, the latter was widely republished, as at Venice, London, and Paris. Yet, though both claimed syphilis originated in the New World,[28] neither associated the disease with a specific moral failing of the natives. For Oviedo, this disease was natural to the Indies from whence it spread to the rest of the known world. At a time when Spanish intellectuals complained that the riches of the Americas were effectively ending in the hands of Italian and Northern financiers, Oviedo felt the spread of syphilis meant justice was served so that other Europeans shared both the spoils and the hardships of the Spaniards. Laughing at those who call it the French or Neapolitan disease, he argued that "they would correctly guess the name if they called it the Indian disease."[29] After enumerating the many first-hand witnesses he interviewed from Columbus's second voyage and reiterating the common claim that Spanish soldiers defending Naples from the French spread the disease to the rest of Europe, Oviedo declared, "from this island of Haiti or Hispaniola this hardship passed to Europe … and here it is very common among the Indians, and they know how to cure themselves and have excellent herbs, trees, and plants appropriate to this and other illnesses, like *guayacan* and *palo santo.*"[30]

Oviedo's connection between disease and wrongdoing in these pages is relatively tentative. He seems much more interested in presenting this illness as a divine test of human patience that must seek to emulate Job in reckoning with both pleasure and pain.[31] Various chroniclers had associated Job with the French disease when it appeared in different parts of Italy, but much of that message involved divine punishment and it never was quite clear whether God was punishing individual or collective sins or even testing the innocent.[32] Oviedo's reading of this illness remained mildly equivocal as to who was to blame and why. After mentioning the great curative properties of American plants for the treatment of this disease he continued, "such is divine clemency, that wherever it sends *us* hardships for *our* faults, right there beside them it wills the remedies with their mercy."[33] Oviedo may have meant Spaniards when referring to *our* faults, included the natives, or been ambivalent, as in the rest of his discussion of this disease.

Gómara's *Historia de las Indias* invited even less moral interpretation of the disease, for he mentioned it only in passing and rehashed well-known stories as matters of fact. "All the [Indians] of … Hispaniola are syphilitics," he mused, "and since the Spaniards slept with the Indian women, they immediately got covered in these buboes, an extremely contagious illness that tortures with great pains."[34] Then he merely retold the famous Neapolitan story, ending with the small comfort that "just as the illness came from the Indies, so did the cure, which is another reason to believe that it originated there."[35]

However, although neither Oviedo nor Gómara specifically singled out sinful native practices as harbingers of syphilis, both stressed the natives' moral failings, thus justifying the Spanish conquest and ostensibly civilizing mission. Calvo merely had to take such foundational rhetoric of conquest one step further and apply it to his own concern with syphilis itself.

Consider Gómara once more. The section just prior to his comment on syphilis alleges the iniquity and barbarity of the natives of Hispaniola. They worshiped the Devil, he claims, who not only appeared before them in various guises, but engaged in sexual relations with the women, engendering children "with two crowns, as a signal that their god fathered them."[36] The natives walked around naked and the men married as many women as they wanted. Moreover, "they readily couple with the women, and even like crows, snakes, and worse; all this aside from the fact that they are great sodomites, lazy, lyers, ingrates, fickle, and vile."[37] In Spanish law, sodomy was one of the worst of crimes, second only to treason in the eyes of God. Ascribing the nefarious sin to native communities – the ultimate sign of their iniquity – became a standard trope in Spanish historiography of the conquest of the Americas.[38]

Oviedo fully detailed alleged sodomitical practices in Hispaniola. After outlining marriage customs and the polygamy of native chiefs, he lamented that these were constituted "not only for the use and coupling that married men naturally undertake with their wives, but for other bestial and nefarious sins, as the chief Goacanagari had certain women with whom he coupled like the snakes do."[39] Citing Albertus Magnus and Isidore of Seville, Oviedo discourses on the sexual habits of vipers and serpents, and declares unnatural sin to have permeated native society. Here Oviedo launched a tirade alleging widespread sodomy among native males:

> So what I have said about the people in this island and its lands is public knowledge, and even in the mainland it is known that many of these Indians were sodomites. And consider to what degree they relish their guilt, in that, just as some people like to wear some necklaces made of gold and precious stones, in some parts of these Indies they would wear a gold necklace depicting a man on top of another, performing the diabolical and nefarious act of Sodom. I saw one of these necklaces from the Devil that weighed twenty *pesos* in gold, hollow and well crafted, that was found at the port of Santa Marta on the mainland in the year 1514.[40]

However, despite the nefarious moral failings of the Hispaniola natives for Gómara and Oviedo, neither ever referred to them – the ones who supposedly first infected Spaniards with syphilis – as flesh eaters. How then did Calvo find cannibalism a root cause of syphilis in the Americas while ignoring sodomy? It seems he interchanged these two factors, partly because they were so interconnected in the European moral worldview.

Just like sodomy, cannibalism was a central theme in early modern writings on the Americas. Indeed, one of the first questions Columbus asked the natives of the Caribbean upon his arrival was where he could find the cannibals. Granted, he was referring to the people of the Can – that is, Asians – but he also associated this in his writings with flesh eating. As other scholars have noted, his focus on that issue allowed him to characterize the natives as particularly uncivilized and thus rightly subject to a variety of normalizing coercive tools, including slavery.[41]

Because of Columbus's early obsession with the Caribs and their apparent cannibalism, the consumption of human flesh constituted a necessary frame of reference for the New World, a persistent rumor to be either explained away, as by Las Casas, or confirmed. Referring to the natives of San Juan – today's Puerto Rico – Oviedo stated that "some people say that the [natives] of this island did not eat human flesh, but I doubt this, for the Caribs, who knew and helped them, do eat it."[42] Aside from the issue of cannibalism, he found the natives of San Juan and those of Hipaniola quite similar, since most of their religious practices, political organization, and marriage customs appeared to be the same. As with most early modern descriptions of the Aztecs, Oviedo's likewise featured human sacrifice and cannibalism: "they eat human flesh; they make human sacrifices, killing many Indians, and opening their chest and taking out their hearts they throw them to the sun."[43] However, according to Oviedo, and other authors like Gómara and later Bernal Díaz del Castillo, the Aztecs, and especially their priests, despised sodomy. Just as in the case of Hispaniola, then, sodomy and cannibalism did not necessarily coexist in any given particular culture according to Spanish accounts.

However, chroniclers and their readers nevertheless tended to associate cannibalism and sodomy, for they both appeared as signs of (un)civilization and its repercussions, and in that sense were synonymous. Both could appear to justify actual atrocities against the natives, for legal scholars argued that either or both of these practices authorized a just war and subsequent enslavement.[44] We see how interconnected these behaviors were in some learned minds of the time when Oviedo addressed the issue of slavery, even as he disagreed with it. The explorer Juan de la Cosa's enslavement of hundreds of natives along the Venezuelan coast was conceivably legal, Oviedo observed, but nevertheless affronted the morality of conquest:

> this manner of discovery and capture might best be called devastation. I do not know if the license for this voyage was given to these ship owners because these peoples had been declared enemy slaves or not, or because they are idolaters, warlike, and sodomites, as well as because they eat human flesh, but I know that Juan de la Cosa later paid for this assault and theft on that land, as will be said later.[45]

Oviedo abhorred the mistreatment of native peoples and thus negotiated, in effect, between Spanish behavior and the need to extirpate the natives' perceivedly barbarous practices. His discussion of cannibalism and sodomy indicates how inextricably linked they often seemed to early modern mentalities.

Cannibalism and sodomy indeed constituted two members of an unholy trinity that focused Spain's presumed civilizing, correcting mission in the New World.

When Gómara summarized his findings about most native cultures encountered by the Spaniards (except for the Aztecs, dealt with later) he used the heading "Praise to the Spaniards" and proclaimed:

> Good is the Glory of our monarchs and men of Spain, who have made the Indians take and keep one God, one faith and one baptism, and have removed the idolatry, the human sacrifices, the consumption of human flesh, the sodomy, and the other great and evil sins that our good God well abhors and punishes.[46]

Apologists for the conquest and exploitation of native peoples tended to conflate human sacrifice, cannibalism, and sodomy as barbarous transgressions of moral and divine order jointly endemic to the New World, and justly demanding forceful intervention.

When Calvo pointed to cannibalism as the epitome of perversity that birthed syphilis in the Americas, he was thus borrowing from a generalized trope found in the histories, rather than specifying an actual trait ascribed to the natives of Hispaniola. Moreover, since they were alleged to be sodomites, and cannibalism and sodomy had been so interconnected in representations of American natives, Calvo's choice of cannibalism and silence on sodomy make little logical sense, and almost seem purposeful. This silence is not an isolated occurrence, a mere slip on the part of our author, for it is consistent throughout the treatise, including discussion of contagion as well as etiology.

Contagion

If, in the introductory case of Bernardo Martínez, the doctor at Zaragoza's Royal Hospital had taken Juan Calvo's views literally, he might not have asked Bernardo whether he had contracted the French disease from sexual contact with a woman, and Bernardo's admission that he had done so from a man would have appeared a striking medical anomaly and discovery. For Calvo, following Falloppio, the French disease was transmitted through

> contact that one has with women exhibiting buboes, in such a way that when a healthy man engages in sexual intercourse with a woman who has these, or a healthy woman with an infected man, that venereal act between the two is the immediate cause for this illness to pass from one to the other. (p. 569)

Syphilis thus spread through necessary vectors of male and female in copulation.

However, that theory did not apply equally to both sexes. Assuming a male readership, Calvo begins with hypothetical victimization of males by women ("the contact one has with syphilitic women"). Medical theory indicated females would more readily fall prey to syphilis than men. According to Calvo, following Galen, women enjoy coitus far more than men, for they "not only enjoy pleasure when they climax but also when the uterus attracts and binds the man to itself" (pp.

569–70). As women found intercourse more pleasurable, their humors heated more than their male partners' and thus females were more apt to contract the disease. To Calvo and most medical practitioners, the possibility of acquiring a sexually transmitted disease was proportional to the enjoyment of the act. In an aside on the various names of syphilis – specifically the propensity to call it *mal de siment* –Calvo argued that "just as from a grain or seed many others are born and multiply, a woman who has buboes, or illness of the seed, will infect many men who have intercourse with her: the same will a man do to women" (p. 568).[47] He again first thinks of transmission from female to male, rather than the reverse.

In tending to gender the disease in this way, Calvo was merely repeating oft-mentioned theories. The connection of presumed female sexual voracity to the spread of venereal disease had become almost an early modern medical topos.[48] In Calvo's own beloved Valencia female prostitutes were routinely singled out for the spread of syphilis.[49]

This gendered view of syphilis squares quite nicely with silence on sodomy, and Calvo's attribution of syphilitic contagion to male–female sex depended on the posited commonality of promiscuous women. How else would so many men acquire the disease, if not through women they shared? Most of the syphilitics a doctor like Calvo would have seen were male, especially young and single,[50] and his theory of contagion demanded whores and "loose women" to continue the chain of transmission. If women were chaste, the thinking went, the disease would disappear. Once prostitution had been outlawed, this was an argument used in the seventeenth century to maintain its illegality.[51] But the unchaste woman was also a necessary figure to occlude, deliberately or otherwise, the far more nefarious and socially uncomfortable possibilities of sexual transmission between men.

Even when Calvo examined what he thought was the first transmission of syphilis to Europe, he strove to create and maintain a female–male causal chain. When Columbus returned in 1493 "with many male and female Indians, some healthy and some sick, for the king to see them," Calvo argued, "some of the soldiers, seeing the Indian women, had intercourse with many of them without knowing whether they were healthy or sick, and thus many of them were left with the same illness, and they in turn, as they had relations with other women, gave it to them as well" (p. 568). Here we find the Renaissance stereotypes of the libidinous soldier and the sexually available native woman.[52] With these people, according to Calvo, syphilis in Europe began.

Of course many questions remain. The vague "other women" are probably not American but European, to continue and extend the chain of transmission. What about the sick native men? They most obviously appear for factual precision: Columbus brought back both native men and women, and both would presumably have been infected. Nevertheless the admitted presence of infected native men makes possibilities of sodomy rather more audible than altogether silent. Calvo's account here erroneously substitutes Naples for Barcelona as Columbus' European port of arrival. If that was not simply an inadvertent slip of the pen, and Calvo really assumed his hypothetically sick natives had arrived at Naples and thus directly occasioned the Neapolitan outbreak of syphilis, the coherence of his account depended on these native men. Practically the whole army stationed at Naples and much of the city became infected, and Columbus had not brought back enough native women to justify such a rapid spread. Calvo did not, and perhaps could not, envision the possibility of sex between the native men and European women. Instead, he supposes that the former functioned as agents of transmission to Europeans because "the Indian men ... slept with some soldiers, gave them the same buboes, and the latter did the same to others" (p. 568). Hence he allowed for a mode of contagion from male to male, just as same-sex bedsharing was formerly common, and living quarters on early modern ships were extremely cramped.

Native men sleeping with virile soldiers, and the latter in turn doing so with their comrades, helped spread the disease. The implications are less than sacrosanct, especially if we remember that most descriptions of syphilis at the time, including Calvo's, focused on ulcered chancres that appeared in the sexual organs. Here the silence on sodomy is about to shatter, and the ill-founded edifice of purely opposite-sex sexual transmission collapse. Only by allowing for some means of male to male transmission could Calvo credibly account for the rapid, almost ferocious, spread of this disease.

However, all the uncomfortable sodomitical questions implicated in the medical construction of this disease could be evaded by hypothesizing non-sexual contagion. Like most physicians, Calvo assumed that syphilis could be spread more easily than influenza. Thus, continuing to recount the genesis of the pandemic in Naples, he asserted that "many of the male and female Indians died in Naples, and since other people then wore their garments and the soldiers were also infected, because this illness is contagious, it has successively moved from one to others who have been infected" (p. 568). Not only could this terrible affliction be contracted by simply sleeping with those who were ill, but also from sharing their bedsheets, or their clothing, even through their breath, and drinking from the same cup, though only "if it is not first washed well" (pp. 564–5).

The rapid spread of the disease could thus be conveniently reconciled with presumed social decorum and the preservation of such appearances. Infected married women, ecclesiastics, and nobles had a respectable alibi. Even a much later Spanish medical writer declares, "this illness is proved to be contagious because, as we see every day, infants, virtuous maidens, and monks and nuns of very holy life suffer it."[53] Allowance for nonsexual transmission could also save social appearances by helping to hide the actual extent of supposedly "nefarious" and hence exceptional sexual contact between males.

Calvo's theories of the etiology and contagion of syphilis, and those of his scientific peers, fascinate because of the remarkable malapropisms, so to speak, required to support such impossible notions, and because they consequently reveal social fictions of sex and gender that had to be preserved at whatever costs to reason and common sense. Allowance for casual, nonsexual transmission was socially essential. Of course I do not suggest here that the whole theory of contagion developed by Calvo and others only responded to some perceived need to maintain a silence regarding sodomy. Male homoeroticism only constituted one factor that required adroit and subtle handling, like the sexual desires and potential behaviors of young unmarried women or cloistered nuns. Calvo's model of transmission nevertheless necessitated some allowance for male-to-male contagion, often in ways that were suggestive of what he silenced, consciously or otherwise.

Symptomatology

For Calvo, perhaps more so than other writers, the heteronormative model of syphilis led him to yet more logical legerdemain when he discussed the disease's symptoms. Because countless doctors had already documented the progression of the disease, a variety of signs could reveal a patient's contraction of the illness. Low energy, pain that extended over a few days to the knees and joints, some fever, and the apparition of small pustules all over the body could mark the advent of the buboes. All these symptoms, including with some patients the onset of gonorrhea (in its early modern sense of a possible contributing factor to the French disease),[54] preceded the apparition of both buboes and chancres, the classic syphilitic symptoms that Calvo discussed at length. Regarding the buboes themselves, inflammations of the lymph nodes usually appearing in the groin, he prescribed a variety of treatments including the ubiquitous mercury ointment (pp. 590–1). Either mercury ointments or powder were utilized to treat the syphilitic ulcers which appeared in the sexual organs.

Calvo's discussion of these ulcers again awkwardly ignores sodomitical possibilities. Doctors rightly realized that these ulcers could appear anywhere on the body because contact – whether sexual or not – with one of them meant transmission of the disease at the point of touch. While recognizing this, Calvo focused on the areas of the body which, according to Galen, "produce many excrements and so are more ready and apt to be corrupted and receive an ulcer than others" (p. 596). On this point, he somewhat deviates from other doctors who, while likewise ignoring sodomy, had directly connected the genitals, coitus, and these ulcers.[55] Calvo was well aware of that medical view, and indeed he had already discussed sex as one of the main means of transmitting the illness. Nevertheless, to him the ulcer manifested itself in both sexual and non-sexual organs that involve apertures subject to evacuation of fluids, principally "the mouth, the nose, the penis, and the vagina" (p. 596).

Thus it seems unreasonable for Calvo to ignore the possibility of anal ulcers. Whether assessed in view of the anus's sexual potential or of Calvo's own emphasis on openings emitting bodily fluids, his omission of the anus in his syphilitic symptomatology is puzzling. While not an aspect of syphilis that most doctors were willing to discuss openly, as we will see later, anal infection does not seem to have been altogether inconceivable. Almost a century later, when sodomy was so taboo that inquisitors had ceased to burn men publicly for fear of advertising sodomitical pleasure,[56] Pedro Lopez Pinna described a type of syphilitic wart in his *Tratado del morbo galico* that appeared in the "man's penis, the opening of the vagina in a woman, and around the bottom."[57] Closer to Calvo's time, Andrés de León, former doctor to the Spanish king's army, argued that many patients suffered a type of psoriasis – itchy skin lesions – in the legs, arms, testicles, "and other [people] in hidden places, difficult to know and cure."[58] Since various chapters had already surveyed the body's skin in general, including the two main sexual organs, these hidden places seeming to affect only some patients could well include the anus.

Nevertheless, early modern medical discussion of syphilis is overwhelmingly heteronormative, and very rarely acknowledges even the possibility of same-sex sexual transmission. The foregoing examples might provide such hints, but the norm, as in Calvo's case, is utter silence. This reticence could be related to a long tradition in some medical circles of either minimizing or ignoring anal ailments. The same Villalobos who wrote the first Spanish treatise on syphilis also authored a much larger compendium of various illnesses and their cures. After providing a short description of hemorrhoids and their treatment, Villalobos entitled his next section, "Explanation for not discussing the other illnesses that afflict this body part," and instructed those who wanted to learn about them to read Avicenna, for "this is a speech that might lead to reproach when the tongue treats such dirty places."[59] Already at the waning of the fifteenth century, the intellectual climate in Spain was such that matters of the anus were unspeakable.

This situation appears to have deeply contrasted with both popular notions and everyday medical practice. At least some men inclined to the unmentionable vice seem not to have been so foolish as to believe that such same-sex contact could not be infectious, even if popular notions condemning women as carriers of disease were often used as justifications for male homoeroticism.[60] Thus in 1623 Pierre Delgado, a Frenchman involved in the silk weaving business – a major part of the Valencian economy, though already at the time in decline after the expulsion of the Moriscos – attempted to seduce a youngster with whom he shared a bed in a Valencian inn. He probably wished to penetrate the youth, for the latter complained that "he was not a woman to be treated in such a fashion."[61] However, before going to bed, Pierre asked his desired partner "if he was healthy."[62] Given the prevalence of various types of venereal diseases, including syphilis, Pierre need not have waited for doctors like Calvo to pronounce on the possibility of same-sex transmission to make his mind up on the matter.

Doctors themselves could encounter anal lesions from syphilis and these would probably not have been unknown or unheard of to someone like Calvo. As part of normal proceedings in inquisitorial cases involving sodomy, often doctors were asked to perform detailed exams on the passive partners. Although few of these descriptions have survived, they include anal ulcers. Thus in 1650, Vicente Morales, a 14-year-old boy sexually involved for at least a year with a variety of older men, was found to have "the sphincter muscle … very dilated from tears and ulcers."[63] Pus and matter from them continuously flowed into the lad's gown. Although the doctors' objective was to determine whether sexual intercourse had occurred – and they dutifully concluded that it had – the description of anal ulcers points to venereal disease acquired through same-sex intercourse. Moreover, these doctors experienced in forensic examination of sodomites were not surprised: their assessment appeared routine.

Even surgeons not dedicated to inquisitorial activities would have encountered anal venereal infections. In the early modern Mediterranean region, including Valencia, sodomy between adult men and feminized adolescents or even effeminate adults was commonplace and part of a masculine culture of penetrative sex.[64] In 1578 around the time Calvo was writing his masterpiece, Valencia was shocked by the trial of one of the city's Franciscan friars from the monastery of Saint Sebastian – Pedro Pizarro, or as his friends knew him, "La Pizarra," his *nom de guerre* when he sauntered the city cross-dressed in search of virile young men. Swirling rumors reached even the ears of the order's provincial at court in Madrid, Friar Romero. Concluding that Pizarro was not in fact being treated for hemorrhoids as he had been claiming for the last year or so, Romero declared "this illness was no other than one caused by having had intercourse against nature with some man, because it was rumored that [Pizarro] was being treated with the John of Vigo powders which are very strong and not suited for hemorrhoids."[65] The Inquisition's prosecutor categorically stated that,

> because of [Pizarro's] frequent habit of engaging in the nefarious sin as the passive partner (*pecado nefando siende paciente*), *it stands to reason* (*a lo que es de creer*) that he has suffered many ulcers in the behind and to cure them it was necessary to apply the John of Vigo powders which are very strong and appropriate for the treatment of such ulcers [my emphasis].[66]

Apparently, Pizarro had obtained this medicament from Juan Nuñez, a Valencian surgeon, or at least one of his servants who applied it to the friar.[67]

The John of Vigo powder was a mercury-based product used to treat especially obstinate syphilitic ulcers. In his chapter "corrosive ulcers," which seem to have been especially malignant and problematic, Calvo's possible remedies include this powder (p. 597). Its usage in Renaissance treatment of syphilis was common, although its preparation could vary, and many attempted to safeguard its exact recipe and thereby enrich themselves. Miguel Juan Pascual, the Spanish translator of Vigo's work, and Professor of Medicine at the University of Valencia in the 1550s, opined that this powder reigned supreme among all medicines designed for this purpose, and that it was "the secret of the corrosive secrets." The doctor for Pope Julius II had gained considerable wealth and fame in Rome, Pascual says, from administering this miraculous powder.[68] Those seeking its use around the time of Calvo should have been ready to pay considerably: 10 percent of someone's rent for a single application of this powder gives a sense of its price.[69] At least in the case of Pedro Pizarro, our cross-dressing friar, this price was warranted.

We cannot be certain Juan Calvo was aware of the unmentionable use that could be given to this powder, but he likely did. Friar Pizarro had obtained this powder from a surgeon or at least had it applied by the latter's servant, so this use could not have been very obscure. Moreover, even if Calvo had not already known of this application, he could have heard of it when Pizarro was sentenced in his *auto-da-fé*, for at that time sodomy sentences were still read with merits – that is, with a full disclosure of the articles of accusation, which would have included this one. Even if Calvo had been absent from the *auto*, news of such an interesting tidbit should nonetheless have reached him, especially when we consider that Valencia was at that time no more than an overgrown village in size.[70] Most medical doctors extensively informed their writing from their practice, so that Calvo would presumably have been keen to collect information on current treatments.[71]

It seems unlikely that Calvo was unaware that syphilis could possibly be transferred through same-sex sexual contact. The local use of John of Vigo's powder in such an unmentionable way and the everyday experience of a practicing surgeon should have alerted him to the existence of sodomitical transmission. It stood to reason, as Pizarro's prosecutor said. Calvo's silence in the matter thus seems all the more obstinate and strange to modern ears. Yet when we contextualize the Valencia of Calvo's time, his rhetorical choice of silence, no matter how deafening it actually might have been, rings true.

Silencing sodomy in a society under siege

Calvo's silencing of sodomy in his writing was by no means unique. If anything, he was following traditional interpretations that emphasized women as carriers of disease and opposite-sex transmission. In this sense we can think of Calvo's silence as normative and conventional. What sets Calvo apart from predecessors and contemporaries is his obstinate silencing of sodomy in the face of almost overwhelming local evidence of same-sex erotic activity and its link to syphilis. Calvo's silence then might not merely be inadvertent – the result of faulty assumptions, ambiguities about the symptoms of syphilis, or just theoretical blindness – but rather deliberate and willful.

The case against Friar Pizarro already discussed was not exceptional in bringing sodomy to the forefront of Valencian public life when Calvo was writing his masterpiece. If anything the prosecution of sodomy can be seen as a normative reaction to a generalized crisis of confidence in Valencia at the time. The 1568 Morisco revolt of the Alpujarras in Granada had not only shaken all of Spain, but Valencia in particular. Outside Granada, Valencia had the largest concentration of Moriscos anywhere in Spain. After the revolt, Moriscos in Valencia faced increasing repression of traditional Arabic cultural practices as church and state leaders came to see them as a foreign cancer to be extirpated, a process that would end unhappily with their expulsion in 1609.[72] Economically the kingdom was faring no better as structural stresses – the inability to participate in trade with the America, inflation, dwindling Mediterranean trade – ensured that Valencia was on the verge of an economic collapse that would be realized by the turn of the century.[73] And the kingdom of Valencia itself was politically divided, on account of widespread banditry, endless conflict between inquisitors and secular authorities, and increasing attempts by the crown to control an uncooperative city of Valencia.[74]

It was in this context of socio-economic instability, potential rebellion from a religious minority, and royal intromission into Valencian affairs that inquisitors launched a wide-ranging prosecution of sodomy in a feat of unique cooperation with state authorities. The Inquisition had gained the ability to prosecute this offense in the Crown of Aragon when a papal brief granted them a jurisdiction in 1524. However, it was only in the 1570s, and particularly after the trial against the Master of the Order of Montesa, Rodrigo Garcerán de Borja, that Valencian inquisitors began energetically to prosecute the unmentionable vice. In the long run, as William Monter argues, the prosecution of this crime appears to have been a means to foster goodwill among the general populace, particularly as trials involved mostly outsiders to the community.[75] In the short term, however, and at least until Calvo published his treatise in 1580, the Inquisition seemed intent on punishing, often quite severely, not only the usual cadre of low-lifes and foreigners but also well respected members of the community and clergymen. Thus throwing the gauntlet, the inquisitors probably shocked many Valencians.

The trial of the Master of the Order of Montesa, one of the most distinguished Valencian noblemen, not only provided sensational gossip but warned that sodomitical vice would not be tolerated even, or perhaps especially, when it involved the local elite. Apparently, Garcerán de Borja had for some time kept the company of a charming ruffian, Martín de Castro, who claimed not only to have sodomized him but also other noblemen such as the Count of Ribagorza. When Martín was apprehended in Madrid, the Master's household knew no rest, for they did "nothing but cry, fearing that Martín de Castro may have rocked the boat."[76] When the Valencian Inquisition obtained more witnesses and the young man's testimony, Garcerán de Borja was apprehended for the "nefarious crime" and his sentence (short-term exile from Valencia), with full details of his actions, became public. Dishonored, destitute, and almost ruined, the former Master of Montesa (as the crown effectively took control of it) showed that absolutely nobody was safe from the inquisitorial tentacles.

Although the best remembered and most sensational Valencian trial of the century, the case against the Master of Montesa reflected a wider pattern of inquisitorial persecution. Between 1570 and 1580 Valencian inquisitors condemned three Trinitarian friars to execution.[77] The members of this order, while not necessarily on par with the Dominicans or the Franciscans in terms of influence, still had enough money to sponsor at least two popular Marian sanctuaries in the kingdom of Valencia.[78] Friars held a special place in local society, one of respect as shepherds of the flock. Yet it was precisely their exalted station that drove inquisitors to target them. In the case of Alonso Pizarro, the cross-dressing Franciscan afflicted with a "nefarious carnal appetite" in the words of his prosecutor, he faced a difficult trial because

> The crime and sin against nature being so nefarious and detestable that Our Lord sends and has sent severe punishments and hardships on the lands where it is committed, and the aforesaid owing a greater obligation than others as a regular clergyman of remaining immune of this nefarious sin of sodomy as a great example of chastity and Christianly behavior, not only has the

> defendant not done these things but has nonetheless committed the following nefarious crimes against nature.[79]

During the 1570s the Inquisition targeted clergymen suspected of nefarious sexual activities precisely because their behavior should have been a beacon of exemplary chastity to others.

The prosecutions of the Master of Montesa, local friars, and other clergymen, such as a Valencian sacristan, probably shook Calvo's small-town society. Clergymen accounted for four of seven executions for sodomy in that decade. The *autos-da-fé* were lengthy public events adorned with pomp and purpose, in which the culprits started a procession in the early morning and all sentences were read, replete with details designed to impart a lesson to the populace. For Valencians in the 1570s, their once quiet city must have seemed suddenly to be teeming with depravity and on the verge of utter breakdown. When those whom people were supposed to admire and look up to filed past, guilty of apparently the worst of crimes, the world must have seemed fragile indeed.

Sodomy in Valencia was more visible than ever, then, when Calvo was writing his treatise on syphilis. Despite this apparent local currency of sex between males, and its potential to transmit syphilis officially acknowledged in the legal case against Pizarro, Calvo still chose to ignore sodomy within his treatise. While this silence was conventional among medical writers at the time, and the status of sodomy as severe crime could not have encouraged its inclusion in a treatise, at least Calvo's silence cannot be reduced to mere ignorance. Just as the prosecutor in Friar Pizarro's case had argued that it stood to reason that the accused had anal syphilis, so too does it stand to reason that Calvo's silencing of sodomy in his treatise was willful and intentional.

Juan Calvo's treatise on syphilis indicates the intimate connection between local socio-political context and former scientific discourse impinging on sexual relations. As with any piece of medical writing on such topics, Calvo's didactic treatise veers from pursuing a pure and unobtainable objectivity through usage of rhetorical constructions and assertions that promote a certain image of society, disease, and sex. In his discussion of the origin, contagion, and symptoms of syphilis, Juan Calvo focused on opposite-sex transmission to the point where his silence about sodomy defies logic and even the daily realities of medical practice at the time. Given the success and multiple editions of Calvo's treatise, his deliberate silencing of sodomy only served to enshrine as medical truth intentional misrepresentations of the facts of the disease. Although only a small part of a wider medical heteronormativity, Calvo's silence reminds us that its construction was not necessarily accidental and unintentional, an unfortunate consequence of ignorance. In this case, maintenance of the normative silence clearly required effort and intent. Calvo thus indicates that, after the late fifteenth-century advent of syphilis in Europe, the characteristic early modern exclusion of sodomy from published medical discourse about the disease was not simply inadvert or casual, but reflects, at least in some cases, deliberate obfuscation.

Notes

1. This case is summarized in Archivo Histórico Nacional, Madrid (hereafter AHN), Inquisición, libro 998, 77v–81r. The full case has not survived.
2. The thoroughness of the initial examination at the hospital's entrance depended on the availability of doctors. All potential patients needed to be cleared for admission and then sent to the appropriate wards. However, the chaplain manning the entrance could perform this task. *Ordinaciones del Hospital Real y General de Nuestra Señora de Gracia de la ciudad de Zaragoza*, Zaragoza: Miguel de Luna, 1656, pp. 64–5. Biblioteca Nacional, Madrid (hereafter BN), 2-50622.
3. As most early modern doctors believed. Cf. Jon Arrizabalaga *et al.*, *The Great Pox: The French Disease in Renaissance Europe*, New Haven: Yale University Press, 1997, pp. 35, 122. For studies specifically on Spain see the bibliography in Cristian Berco, "Between Piety and Sin: Zaragoza's Confraternity of San Roque, Syphilis, and Sodomy," *Confraternitas*, 13/2 (2002), 3–16. See Kevin Siena (ed.), *Sins of the Flesh: Responding to Sexual Disease in Early Modern Europe*, Toronto: Centre for Reformation and Renaissance Studies, 2005, for further references in the wider European context.
4. Hospital chaplains were supposed to continuously seek sacramental confession from those patients who had failed to do so at reception. *Ordinaciones*, p. 66.
5. Sex with animals, same- or opposite-sex anal intercourse, and under very specific circumstances sex between females could fall under the rubric of "sodomy." The Aragonese Inquisitions, comprised of the tribunals of Barcelona, Valencia and Zaragoza, commenced to try sodomy cases in earnest around the 1560s, and most of all prosecuted anal intercourse between males as sodomy. Anal sex, especially when it involved ejaculation inside the rectum, constituted the gravest of crimes punishable by death. "Imperfect" sodomy, on the other hand, involved anal intercourse without ejaculation and, though not legally as serious, could also be punished with severe sentences, even death if proved to be a repeated occurrence. Inquisitors also utilized the term *molicies* to prosecute any and all sexual activity between males that they considered ultimately conducive to sodomy, such as mutual masturbation, kissing, fondling, and oral intercourse.
6. Cf. Marie E. McAllister, "Stories of the Origin of Syphilis in Eighteenth-Century England: Science, Myth, and Prejudice," *Eighteenth-Century Life*, 24 (2000), 22–44.
7. Arrizabalaga *et al.*, *Great Pox*, pp. 20–7.
8. Paul A. Russell, "Syphilis, God's Scourge or Nature's Vengeance? The German Printed Response to a Public Problem in the Early Sixteenth Century," *Archive for Reformation History*, 80 (1989), 286–307. On Scotland see Johannes Fabricius, *Syphilis in Shakespeare's England*, London: Kingsley, 1994, p. 58. For early measures against patients see Peter Lewis Allen, *The Wages of Sin: Sex and Disease, Past and Present*, Chicago: Chicago University Press, 2000, p. 42.
9. Francisco López de Villalobos, *El sumario de la medicina con un tratado sobre las pestíferas bubas*, Salamanca: Universidad de Salamanca, 1973, p. 153.
10. José Luis Fresquet Febrer, "Los inicios de la asimilación de la material médica americana por la terapéutica europea," in José María López Piñero (ed.), *Viejo y Nuevo Continente: La medicina en el encuentro de dos mundos*, Madrid: Saned, 1992, pp. 281–307.
11. Juan Calvo, *Primera y segunda parte de la cirugía universal: Segundo tratado del morbo gálico*, Valencia: Herederos de Chrisóstomo Garriz, 1647, p. 569. BN, R-5581. Cited parenthetically within my text hereafter.
12. Although Girolamo Fracastoro in his famous poem *Syphilis sive morbus gallicus* spoke of his unfortunate shepherd suffering the gods' wrath of this disease while in the Americas, he is quite ambivalent about a single point of origin, for he notes that the disease appeared at once in many European cities. Whether syphilis originated in the Americas is still controversial. See A. M. Setton, "The Great Pox that was ... Syphilis," *Journal of Applied Microbiology*, 91 (2001), 592–6; Bruce M. Rothschild,

Fernando Luna Calderon, Alfredo Coppa, and Christine Rothschild, "First European Exposure to Syphilis: The Dominican Republic at the Time of Columbian Contact," *Clinical Infectious Diseases*, 31 (2000), 936–41.

13. Amélia A. B. de Rincon-Ferrz, MD, "Early Work on Syphilis: Diaz de la Ysla's Treatise on the Serpentine Disease of Hispaniola Island," *International Journal of Dermatology*, 38 (1999), 222–7.

14. Ruy Díaz de la Isla, *Tratado contra el mal serpentino*, Seville: Dominico de Robertis, 1539, 3r. BN- R-28825. Cf. Ian Michael, "Celestina and the Great Pox," *Bulletin of Hispanic Studies*, 78 (2001), 103–38.

15. Díaz de la Isla, *Tratado*, 3r.

16. See Charles Scott Sherrington, *The Endeavour of Jean Fernel: With a List of his Editions and Writings*, Cambridge: Cambridge University Press, 1946, and *Man on his Nature*, 2nd edn, Cambridge: Cambridge University Press, 1963; José Keny-Turpin (ed.), *Jean Fernel: Médecine et philosophie*, Paris: Corpus, 2002. Fallopio was at the forefront of the battle against syphilis, and in his *De Morbo Gallico*, Padua: Gryphium, 1563, he actually argued against the use of mercury as treatment.

17. Monardes probably had much contact with Italian scientists and doctors as he was the son of a Genoese merchant established in Seville. See Francisco Guerra, *Nicolás Bautista Monardes: Su vida y su obra*, Mexico City: Compañia Fundidora de Fierro y Acero de Monterrey, 1961.

18. See Arrizabalaga *et al.*, *Great Pox*, pp. 262–4.

19. Cf. Vivian Nutton, "The Reception of Fracastoro's Theory of Contagion: The Seed that Fell among the Thorns," *Osiris*, 6 (1990), 196–234; Stephen Jay Gould, "Syphilis and the Shepherd of Atlantis," *Natural History*, 109/8 (2000), 38–82; Richard Frank, "Fracastoro: Poetry vs. Prose," *International Journal of the Classical Tradition*, 9/4 (2003), 524–34.

20. Walter Eamon, "Cannibalism and Contagion: Framing Syphilis in Counter Reformation Italy," *Early Science and Medicine*, 3/1 (1998), 1–31.

21. See Vivian Nutton, "The Seeds of Disease: An Explanation of Contagion and Infection from the Greeks to the Renaissance," *Medical History*, 27/1 (1983), 1–34.

22. See Luis Sánchez Granjel, "La obra de Andrés Alcazar," *Clin Lab (Zaragoza)*, 67 (1959), 154–60.

23. See Lewis Hanke, *All Mankind is One*, De Kalb, IL: Northern Illinois University Press, 1974. For Prince Philip's admiration for Las Casas see Henry Kamen, *Philip of Spain*, New Haven: Yale University Press, 1996, pp. 32–4.

24. Bartolomé de las Casas, *Brevísima relación de la destrucción de las Indias occidentales*, ed. José María Reyes Cano, Barcelona: Planeta, 1994, p. 26.

25. Bartolomé de las Casas, *Historia de las Indias*, Madrid: Alianza Editorial, 1994, p. 1855. Las Casas also argued in this work that syphilis originated in the Americas.

26. Alvar Nuñez Cabeza de Vaca, *Naufragios y Comentarios*, Madrid: Espasa-Calpe, 1999, p. 46.

27. Rolena Adorno, "The Discursive Encounter of Spain and America: The Authority of Eyewitness Testimony in the Writing of History," *The William and Mary Quarterly* (April 1992), 210–28.

28. Las Casas also supported this notion in his manuscript *Historia de las Indias* (unpublished until the nineteenth century).

29. Oviedo, *Historia general y natural de las Indias*, Madrid: Editorial Atlas, 1959, vol. 1, p. 53.

30. Ibid., p. 54.

31. Ibid., p. 53. In *The Pre-Columbian Mind*, London: Seminar Press, p. 57, Francisco Guerra claims that Oviedo thought syphilis originated in the New World as punishment for the natives' allegedly widespread sodomitic practices. But Oviedo's "veiled remark" that Guerra produces as evidence merely refers in traditional terms to the various

tribulations God would send upon any people, not just natives, who practiced sodomy, and does not imply that syphilis was "caused" by New World sodomy.

32. Arrizabalaga, *Great Pox*, pp. 52–4.
33. Oviedo, *Historia general*, vol. 1, p. 53 (my emphasis).
34. López de Gómara, *Historia general de las Indias*, Madrid: Editorial Iberia, 1982, p. 54.
35. Ibid.
36. Ibid., p. 50.
37. Ibid., p. 52.
38. The Valencian legal commentator Tomás Cerdán de Tallada argued precisely this point just before Calvo published his work, with fiery allusions to the fate of sodomites, and defines sodomy as one of the most heinous offences to God. *Visita de la carcel y de los presos*, Valencia: Pedro de Huete, 1574, pp. 196–8. BN, R-745. On usage of sodomy to legitimize conquest, see Pete Sigal (ed.), *Infamous Desire: Male Homosexuality in Colonial Latin America*, Chicago: University of Chicago Press, 2002, p. 3.
39. Oviedo, *Historia general*, vol. 1, p. 118.
40. Ibid., pp. 118–19.
41. Philip Boucher, *Cannibal Encounters: Europeans and Island Caribs, 1492–1763*, Baltimore: Johns Hopkins University Press, 1992.
42. Oviedo, *Historia general*, vol. 2, p. 107.
43. Ibid., vol. 4, p. 243.
44. Sepúlveda utilized the notion of "just war" against sodomites and cannibals in his debate against Las Casas. See John Langan, "The Elements of St. Augustine's Just War Theory," *Journal of Religious Ethics*, 12/1 (1984), 19–38.
45. Oviedo, *Historia general*, vol. 3, p. 131.
46. Gómara, *Historia general*, pp. 384–5.
47. To some authors, women were particularly dangerous because vaginal ulcers could be difficult to detect. Sixteenth-century medical views of syphilis displayed an increasing misogyny.
48. Winfried Schleiner, "Infection and Cure through Women: Renaissance Constructions of Syphilis," *Journal of Medieval and Renaissance Studies*, 24 (1994), 499–517.
49. Already as early as 1502 a Flemish traveler to Valencia described the public brothels and the municipally appointed doctors designed to examine the women for venereal disease. By 1589 municipal laws required prostitutes to obtain a certificate of health from the General Hospital even to work in a brothel. See Maria Amparo Vidal Gavidia, *La casa de arrepentidas de Valencia: Orígen y trayectoria de una institución para mujeres*, Valencia: Generalitat Valenciana, 2001, pp. 39–41.
50. For example, at the syphilis hospital in Toledo men constituted 78 percent of patients treated in the years for which records have survived. ADPT, Libro H-55.
51. Pedro Vergés, *Discurso sobre si conviene o no se restituya en Zaragoza la casa pública*, Zaragoza: Pedro Vergés, 1637. BN, R-3597.
52. Early modern soldiers had a terrible reputation, especially for sexual violence. See Richard Trexler, *Sex and Conquest: Gendered Violence, Political Order and the European Conquest of the Americas*, Cambridge: Polity Press, 1995; Alan Shepard, *Marlowe's Soldiers: Rhetorics of Masculinity in the Age of the Armada*, Aldershot: Ashgate, 2002. Most Spanish authors believed American women were promiscuous. Cf. Ramon Gutierriez, *When Jesus Came the Corn Mothers went away: Marriage, Sexuality, and Power in New Mexico, 1500–1846*, Cambridge: Cambridge University Press, 1991.
53. Pedro Lopez Pinna, *Tratado de morbo galico*, Seville: Juan Gomez de Blas, 1664, 5r. BN, R-5793.
54. Early modern doctors did not necessarily distinguish between syphilis and gonorrhea so that symptoms for either one could be conflated under accepted definitions of the French disease.

55. Already in 1498, the first Spanish treatise on the buboes had focused on sexual contact as the cause of this disease. See Francisco López de Villalobos, *El sumario de la medicina con un tratado sobre las pestíferas bubas*, Salamanaca: Universidad de Salamanca, 1973.

56. Cristian Berco, "Social Control and its Limits: Sodomy, Local Sexual Economies, and Inquisitors during Spain's Golden Age," *Sixteenth Century Journal*, 36 (2005), 331–57.

57. Lopez Pinna, *Tratado*, 71v.

58. Andrés de León, *Práctico de morbo gálico*, Valladolid: Luis Sánchez, 1605, 19v. BN, R-7385(2).

59. López de Villalobos, *Sumario*, p. 96.

60. See e.g. the 1647 inquisitorial sodomy case against Pedro Masic who attempted to seduce a younger man by arguing that sexual intercourse with women was so harmful that it was best for men to satisfy each other. AHN, Inquisición, libro 993, 384v–388r.

61. Ibid., 509v–510r.

62. Ibid.

63. AHN, Inquisición, libro 941, 375v–379r. Likewise AHN, Inquisición, libro 731, 376r–377r.

64. Berco, "Social Control." On Renaissance Florence see Michael Rocke, *Forbidden Friendships: Homosexuality and Male Culture in Renaissance Florence*, New York: Oxford University Press, 1996.

65. AHN, Inquisición, legajo 844, no. 3.

66. Ibid.

67. Pizarro might have obtained the powder from a servant, for health care in Valencia at the time extended well beyond the normal official and academic channels. See María Luz López Terrada, "Las practicas médicas extraacadémicas en la ciudad de Valencia durante los siglos XVI y XVII," *Dynamis*, 22 (2002), 85–120.

68. Cited in Miguel López Pérez, "Los polvos solutivos de Juan de Vigo," *Panacea*, 3 (Dec. 2001). *Panacea* is a recently discontinued online journal from the Universidad Complutense in Madrid. This article is still accessible through http://web.archive.org/web/20030107102435/http://www.ucm.es/info/folchia/LAS+BOTICAS+O VETENSES+A+FINES+DEL+SIGLO+XVI.htm

69. A *dragma* or 1/8 of an ounce of this powder cost one *real* in 1591 in Oviedo in northern Spain, whereas the cost of an ounce of the basic mercury ointment normally used for syphilitic lesions cost one *real* and a half, if the patient were poor, and two *reales* if rich. At the same time the monthly rent for a normal house in Toledo ran to almost 10 *reales*. For prices in Oviedo see Víctor Manuel Rodríguez Villar, "Las boticas ovetenses a fines del siglo XVI: la tarifa de medicinas de Melchor de Olibares," *Panacea*, 5 (Aug. 2002).   http://web.archive.org/web/20030107102435/http://www.ucm.es/info/folchia/LAS+BOTICAS+OVETENSES+A+FINES+DEL+SIGLO+XVI.htm   In 1582 the syphilis hospital of Toledo charged rents for a variety of houses in the city averaging 4000 mrs per year. As 1 real= 34 maravedis, the average monthly rent came to 9.8 reales. The account books for the Hospital de Santiago in Toledo can be found in AHN, Ordenes Militares, carpeta 328, número 33.

70. The population of Valencia and the other Aragonese capitals like Zaragoza and Barcelona could not rival that of the great Castilian cities like Seville and Madrid. For the basic demographic imbalance between Castile and Aragon, see Gregorio Colás Latorre, *La Corona de Aragón en la Edad Moderna*, Madrid: Arco Libros, 1998, pp. 11–18.

71. José Luis Fresquet Febrer, "La práctica médica en los textos quirúrgicos españoles en el siglo XVI," *Dynamis*, 22 (2002), 251–77.

72. For the Alpujarras revolt see Luis de Mármol Carvajal, *Rebelión y castigo de los moriscos*, Málaga: Arguval, 1991. Emilia Salvador Esteban, *Felipe II y los moriscos valencianos: Las repercusiones de la revuelta granadina (1568–1570)*, Valladolid: Universidad de Valladolid,

1987, discusses its effects on Valencia. Cf. Ronald Surtz, "Morisco Women, Written Texts, and the Valencian Inquisition," *Sixteenth Century Journal*, 32 (2001), 421–33.

73. Álvaro Castillo, "La coyuntura de la economía valenciana en el siglo XVI y XVII," *Anales de historia económica y social*, 2 (1969), 239–88; Eugenio Císcar Pallarés, *La Valldigna, siglos XVI y XVII: Cambio y continuidad en el campo valenciano*, Valencia: Diputación de Valencia, 1997.

74. Cf. Gregorio Colás Latorre, *La Corona de Aragón en la Edad Moderna*, Madrid: Arco Libros, 1998, pp. 45–9; Emilia Salvador Esteban, *Cortes valencianas de Felipe II*, Valencia: Universidad de Valencia, 1973; Sebastián García Martínez, *Bandolers, corsaris i moriscos*, Valencia: E. Climent, 1980.

75. William Monter, *Frontiers of Heresy: The Spanish Inquisition from the Basque Lands to Sicily*, Cambridge: Cambridge University Press, 1990, pp. 276–99.

76. AHN, Inquisición, libro 936, fol. 90v.

77. For a list of cases of sodomy tried by the Valencian Inquisition in these years, ibid., fols. 50v–210v.

78. Jesús Bravo Lozano, "Santuarios marianos en el reino de Valencia," *Revista de Historia Moderna: Anales de la Universidad de Alicante*, 21 (2003), 7–54.

79. AHN, Inquisición, legajo 844, num. 3.

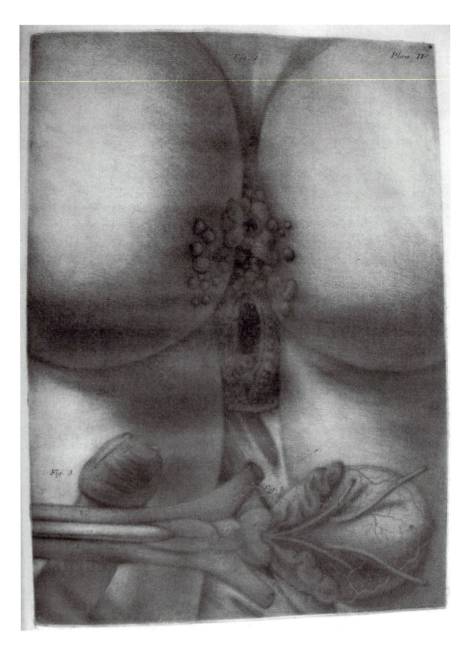

Figure 6.1 Poxed female posterior, Plate IV from Jacques Gautier d'Agoty, *Exposition anatomique des maux vénériens* (Paris: J. B. Brunet & Demonville, 1773). Courtesy of the New York Academy of Medicine.

6　The strange medical silence on same-sex transmission of the pox, c.1660–c.1760

Kevin Siena

Before there was AIDS, there was GRID, so-called "Gay-Related Immune Deficiency," "gay cancer," or "gay pneumonia."[1] The nomenclature of the early response to HIV/AIDS reminds us of how strongly forged were the links between male same-sex love and sexually transmitted infection in recent times. But how closely wed were same-sex love and sexual disease in previous centuries? Focusing on English medical treatises on "the venereal disease" (usually, though debatably, translated as syphilis[2]) between roughly 1660 and 1760 we find we must explore silence, for they say remarkably little about same-sex transmission, whether male or female. For a collection of reasons, including notions of decorum in doctors' professional self-fashioning, scientific constructions of the disease, and aspects of the doctor–patient relationship, the vast majority of early Enlightenment doctors do not appear to have envisioned the possibilities of same-sex contraction, despite the appearance of hundreds of Enlightenment treatises on the disease in London alone.

This silence is particularly strange because medical discourse on the disease performed clear policing roles. Various cultural anxieties and political agendas penetrated medical discussions of the disease. The pox was evocative and frightful, providing an effective discursive tool to demonize perceived social ills, and doctors gave voice to these agendas.[3] So Puritans hoping to close down alehouses found an ally in surgeon William Clowes, who warned readers that they risked infection there from poxed vagabonds.[4] Those trying to supplant the tradition of employing wet nurses with maternal breastfeeding found support from doctors who publicized stories of bourgeois babes infected by filthy plebeian nurses.[5] Medical discourse on the pox performed its most obvious cultural work supporting anti-prostitution efforts,[6] but more surprising was its role in the now well-documented anti-masturbation campaign.[7] Excessive masturbation, doctors warned, could cause gonorrhea.[8] Yet, even though the eighteenth century witnessed an increasingly intense campaign to rid England of the nefarious sin of sodomy – with numerous public executions for the crime[9] – sex between men was not policed in this medically discursive way. Medical treatises on venereal disease rarely give any hint, still less any warnings, that men could contract it from each other. And medical discussions of such female same-sex possibilities seem altogether nonexistent.

A rare and important exception was surgeon John Marten, whose 1708 discussion of male-to-male transmission was recently included in Kenneth Borris's anthology on early modern same-sex desire.[10] As an aside within a discussion of the dangers of prostitutes Marten reminded himself:

> I had almost forgot to acquaint the Reader that there is yet another way of getting the *Venereal* Infection (which indeed I should have taken notice of in its first place), and that is by one Man's conversing with, or having the carnal use of another Man's Body, *viz.*, B——ry, an abominable, beastly, sodomitical, and shameful Action: an action as it's not fit to be named, so, one would think, would not be practiced in a Christian Country, more especially since the Laws of God and Man are so directly in force against it. But, I say, by that means we have known the distemper to be contracted, and I am afraid is what is too commonly practiced in this dissolute Age.

Marten proceeded to tell readers that, in addition to "B——ry," the disease could also be passed through oral sex, highlighting an example involving two men:

> And which is still worse, this Distemper is also gotten after another manner of Conversation, *viz.* By a Man putting his erected Penis into another Person's (Man or Woman's) Mouth, using Friction, &c., because at the mentioning, or but thinking of it, the utmost detestation and loathing. But by that means also has it been gotten, and a man so infected (one that I know not nor where to find) had I in Cure not long since, who assured me (though with seeming concern for the committing so foul a Crime) that he contracted it no other way; and that the Person from whom he got it (being a Man) had at the same time (as he has since been assured) several Pocky Ulcerations, &c., in his Mouth . . . O Monstrous! Thought I, that Men, otherwise sensible Men, should so vilely debase themselves, and become so degenerate; should provoke God so highly, condemn the Laws of Man so openly, wrong their own Bodies so fearfully; and which is worse (without sincere Repentance) ruin their own Souls eternally.

At which point Marten begins quoting biblical chapter and verse.[11]

Later he recounts a physical examination in which he inspected the rectal cavity of a "lovely Stripling" whom he declared poxed by way of anal sex. Marten took the young man into his care and proscribed medicines covertly to the patient's "Sodomitical Keeper" who self-medicated while in hiding. Marten remarked, "I was somewhat uneasy with these people, as knowing that they might, and indeed ought, to fall under the Cognizance of the Civil Magistrate."[12] Yet, although Marten's discussion contains the sense of shock, the apology for even discussing the topic and the evocation of legal punishment conventional in early modern discussions of sodomites, within medical literature it was, as Borris observes, quite unique.[13]

A survey of twenty-five other medical treatises on the pox published in London in the century that roughly surrounds Marten's text reveals just how unique; fully twenty-one make absolutely no mention of male same-sex transmission, and none mention woman-to-woman transmission.[14] In terms of chronology, the texts spread fairly evenly over the period, written by surgeons, physicians, apothecaries and empirics, including books by foreign practitioners published in English translation. Standard topics include the origin of the disease, modes of contagion, symptomology, treatment, case histories, descriptions of mercury and other therapeutic agents, and warnings about the dangers of quacks.

However, two of the four apparent references to same-sex transmission are remarkably ambiguous. In his 1678 treatise surgeon Charles Peter's account of transmission allowed, "There are several other ways by which this *Disease* may be gotten: as by *Sodomy*, &c."[15] Yet this is all he says on the topic, for he immediately proceeds to discuss infection through kissing, wet nursing, or using the same cup, sheets, or privy as an infected person. His single reference to sodomy *et cetera* seems almost purposefully undefined. Moreover, "sodomy" in the period could stand as a metonymy for a variety of sexual practices deemed excessive and, in the absence of supportive context, cannot certainly be equated with same-sex intercourse.[16] For example, sodomy was sometimes linked to bestiality in the period, and one sixteenth-century theory presented the pox initially resulting from "sodomitical" bestiality with a diseased animal.[17] Everad Maynwaring was even more ambiguous than Peter, writing that "untainted persons using immoderate, unusual, and bestial Venery, may produce the first symptoms leading to this *Lues*."[18] "Bestial" could itself function as a metaphor for behaviors deemed improper for rational humanity.[19] Peter and Maynwaring may have meant to acknowledge same-sex intercourse, but we cannot say for sure. Even if they did, their brevity and discretion underscore just how unusual John Marten's lengthy passages were.

Decorum seems to have been one factor in the virtual silence on same-sex transmission in medical treatises on the pox. Marten's treatise was unique was because he was unique. He may well have been a legitimate surgeon, but he was widely accused of writing lurid prose thinly veiled as medical science. The titillating details of his case studies lead one scholar to describe his work as a kind of "paramedical erotica."[20] Consumers responded, and Marten quickly brought out new editions of his treatise, expanding the sixth edition with an appendix, *Gonoslogium Novum, or a New System of all the secret Infirmaties and Diseases,* which was essentially a sex manual comparable to such other notorious Enlightenment titles as *Onania, Aristotle's Masterpiece* or Nicholas Venette's *The Mysteries of Conjugal Love Reveal'd,* the last of which Marten seems to have plagiarized.[21]

While London readers devoured Marten's daring prose, it produced significant outcry. Considering Marten a worthless libertine for publishing such "scandalous" "smut" and "obscenity," rival surgeon John Spinke accused him of "mak[ing] Anatomical Disquisitions [merely] a pretext to . . . Bawdy Lectures,"

> intended only to stimulate the Youth to Lewdness; Debauch their Morals, and prompt them to vicious Courses of Life, thereby to encrease the number of

Clap't patients: So that I conceive your Appendix well merits to be presented by the Grand Jury at Hick's hall as being published with an Intention to Debauch Youth, and so far as in you lies, encourage Vice and immorality.[22]

Marten was indeed indicted in 1709 on charges (later dismissed) of intending to corrupt the public.[23] Spinke targeted Marten's passages on same-sex fellatio and anal sodomy as the prime examples of just how far beyond acceptable civility Marten had gone. "What is it that could move him," Spinke asked,

to make so ample a Collection of Bawdry . . . in such fulsome, rank and plain terms [?] . . . . Witness his account of Huffling [i.e. oral sex] and Buggery, which are represented by him in so lively Expressions, and most abominable Circumstances, that I am sure he has exceeded in this Point, all that has been publish'd, even [by] the most Profligate Wretches in the Universe.[24]

Venereal disease offered the medical community opportunity for sober, socially acceptable discussions of what in other contexts would have been considered beyond the pale. Topics like the pox helped establish medical discourse as a focal point for discussions of sexuality in the Enlightenment and helped promote the medicalization of sex that Foucault and others have explored.[25] However, there were limits, and most doctors refused to follow Marten's lead. Doctors like Thomas Garlick promised to be circumspect: "I have taken all Imaginable Care to avoid, as much as the nature of the thing would admit of, all obscene Language throughout the whole work, that I might not give offence to the most modest reader."[26]

Doctors who traded in the pox thus walked a precarious line. Its scandalously offensive nature and the odium of their clientele threatened to impugn their personal and professional honor.[27] Key to a successful medical practice was casting oneself as a gentleman with whom members of polite society would associate. Yet to demonstrate their expertise, doctors writing on the pox had to go further and further into detail about modes of sex and describe vaginal ulcers, genital discharge and other offensive topics ever more vividly. Daniel Turner advised young surgeons to keep their poxed clientele at arm's length: "I must dissuade you by all means from being their Companions," he warned, fearing that young doctors might find themselves drawn into their patients' debauched lifestyle. Besides possibly catching the disease themselves, he cautioned them,

you will hereby make your selves mean, be despised of all those of Reputation; and when 'tis the Mishap of any such, *who are always the best Patients* . . . they will doubtless apply to those, who if not more remarkable for the Cure, are less so, for a Conversation with loose People.[28]

More than their relations with patients, doctors had to govern their pens if they wished to keep a good reputation. For example, Winfried Schleiner has observed that prophylaxis was a sensitive topic, because to many in early modern England it encouraged vice.[29] Doctors like Daniel Sennert, Joseph Cam, John Spinke and

Daniel Turner all refused to disclose information on so-called "preventatives" lest they facilitate debauchery, helping libertines to sin without consequence. "I do not beleave," Sennert exclaimed, "that those things can be taught with a good conscience, by which so many men are encouraged to lust, whom perhaps the fear of this Disease might have frightened from it; and therefore we will say nothing of these medicines."[30] When faced with certain topics impinging on sex, image-conscious doctors censored themselves.

Likewise in the third of the four aforesaid exceptions in the twenty-five surveyed texts, where a doctor may appear to acknowledge possibilities of same-sex transmission, surgeon Joannes Sintelaer raised the issue only to explain why he *refused* to discuss it. After detailing forms of contagion commonly highlighted – copulation, nursing, infection of a fetus *in utero*, and "lascivious kisses"[31] – Sintelaer atypically mentions sodomy, but only to censor himself: "I forbear on Purpose to speak here of the Venereal Infection gotten by the Brutish Sin of Sodomy, Friction, or Suction, being Actions so beastly and unnatural as not to be related among Christians."[32] While clearly an attempt at self-fashioning in the name of bourgeois respectability, this comment likely rebukes John Marten, for Sintelaer was John Spinke's partner in bringing criminal charges against Marten that very year.[33]

They were in good company because still other practitioners attacked Marten for his risqué passages. Daniel Turner, ever concerned with keeping up appearances, rebuked Marten's frankness by censoring the *Gonoslogium*. "There are several other more uncommon Ways of giving as well as receiving the *Venereal Venom*," Turner said,

> but the Thought of such vile Monsters, and their execrable Practices, is too shocking (unless to the Dregs of humane Nature) to bear even a repetition of Circumstances, and fit only for a detestable *Gonologium*[sic], or Collection of Smut and Obscenity . . .[34]

Turner does not name "sodomy," "buggery" or "huffling" by name, but that indeed seems the point. His need to distance himself from their discussion is so great that it drove them from the page, leaving scholars just their negative relief as a kind of fossilized imprint.

However, while doctors worried about discussing the topic, the risks they ran hardly compared to those of their patients. It may therefore be useful to shift perspectives. When trying to explain doctors' silence, we should also consider their *patients'* silence. Connections between the pox and same-sex love would have been much obscured for medical commentators by the reticence and deceptions of patients who contracted the disease in this way. The exchange of information between doctor and patient, or patient-narrative, was central in early modern medicine.[35] For diagnoses, what the patient related orally – the patient's "history" – was as important as his or her physical symptoms. The age of the silent patient who sat passively through the poking and prodding of a physical exam still lay ahead in the early eighteenth century.[36] Before then, medical knowledge was heavily dependent on verbal exchanges. When did the patient fall ill? What were the initial symptoms? What was he or she doing before falling ill? What was the malady in the patient's view?

The patient's sexual history had particular importance for identifying the pox in early modernity, because the disease was notoriously hard to identify. Not only was "the venereal disease" in any case a conflation of syphilis, gonorrhea and a host of other genito-urinary disorders,[37] but its wide range of symptoms caused doctors routinely to confuse it with other illnesses. John Archer devoted his entire treatise on how to differentiate the pox from scurvy. Discussing the pox's wide and confusing symptomology, physician Gideon Harvey exclaimed "There is scarce any malady, but one time or another is noted to attend the Pox,"[38] while a contemporary called the disease "Pandora's Box, out of which all other diseases and Mischiefs issue," for its victim "has not one Single disease alone, but a legion of Maladies."[39] Even the great Jean Astruc admitted difficulty identifying the disease from its physical symptoms alone.[40]

The body confused, so doctors relied heavily on what patients told them. When listing the criteria to determine whether a woman's vaginal discharge signaled the pox or merely "the whites" (a name given to simple, non-venereal, infections), surgeon John Douglas advised practitioners to consider: (1) the quantity of the discharge; (2) its persistence over time; (3) whether her husband became infected; and (4) "the account the patient gives of herself, or her husband."[41] To Douglas, the patient's report of her sexual history was just as crucial as her corporeal signs. For Astruc too, such details were crucial "to form a Judgment concerning the certainty or Uncertainty of the Venereal Disease."[42] In short, patients' reports of their sexual pasts were vital medical facts.

Case studies contained in medical treatises clearly demonstrate the importance of the patient narrative. According to the stories that two patients told him, Thomas Garlick reached diametrically opposed diagnoses. As a man of about 40 years of age reported that he had recently slept with a prostitute, so the surgeon proclaimed him poxed. But "a gentleman of good Character" with quite similar symptoms "protested he knew no Woman but his own wife, and she was a Person of undoubted Character." Garlick thereby concluded "this Gentleman's Case was not Venereal."[43] Steven Shapin has well demonstrated that "proof" in the era of the scientific revolution had as much to do with civility as with observable data, so that early modern truth claims relied heavily on the reputation for honesty of the man making the assertion.[44] Thus, medical knowledge produced from a negotiated, largely oral, exchange between doctors and patients fell right in line with other branches of contemporary scientific culture.

Since we know that patients facing the possible diagnosis "venereal" displayed enormous creativity explaining their symptoms and sexual histories, the former importance attached to patients' stories goes far to explain the gaps and confusion in early modern theories of transmission. Hospital evidence shows that for over two centuries patients tried to avoid entering the stigmatized venereal wards by lying about their diagnosis. Patients often sought to avoid letting others know that they even had the disease by self-medicating, seeking discreet care or claiming to suffer from something else.[45] They also frequently sought to convince their doctors (along with their husbands, wives, neighbors and employers) that they had contracted the disease innocently. Medical treatises discuss such patients constantly. Most people still believed that the disease could be contracted nonsexually, affording patients a ready alibi: they must have caught the disease from someone's sheets or drinking cup. "Various are the Contrivances and Pretensions made use of by some to conceal the Shame of having contracted the Venereal Disease," Sintelaer observed, for "they tell their Doctors strange stories of having drunk out of the same glass with a person afflicted with this foul distemper; or to have lain and sweated in the same Bed with him."[46] I. F. Nicholson likewise reported that "many bashful People have made those innocent Ways of contracting the disease, their Excuses, only to hide their shame by not discovering the more criminal manner after which they had receiv'd the Infection."[47]

Note the term "criminal." A man who had contracted the pox through same-sex sodomy in late seventeenth- or early eighteenth-century London had especial cause to conceal his sexual history. Marten's infected sodomites, we will remember, exhibited great unease "knowing that they might . . . fall under the Cognizance of the Civil Magistrate."[48] Sodomitical anxieties about public exposure are documented not only by the periodic waves of prosecution,[49] but also by blackmail trials, which show sodomites were targets for extortion.[50] Moreover, early Enlightenment patients could not yet assume the privacies of medical confidentiality.[51] Hence they could not be sure that disclosures to doctors would not become public. Any man wishing to obscure sexual contacts with men could blame his infection on a drunken trip to a prostitute, a story likely to deflect further questions. Facing the possibility of a hangman's noose, many men surely did just that.

Hence most early Enlightenment doctors probably never heard a patient report infection from an act of same-sex love. Insofar as doctors writing on the disease included patients' testimonies among their dependable facts encountered in their private practices, same-sex transmission would have appeared nonexistent, or at most extremely rare. This dynamic helps explain why so many medical writers ignored same-sex encounters in their theories of transmission. Daniel Turner readily believed the man who reported he had caught the disease by sharing a bed platonically with an infected man-servant, presenting the case as an example of the danger of sharing sheets. He similarly failed to suspect same-sex transmission in the case of an infected cabin boy brought to him by a ship's captain.[52] Even though treatises on the pox typically discussed both oral and rectal lesions, symptoms which male patients presented quite commonly, doctors show little sign of suspecting same-sex oral or anal sex in such cases.[53]

Figure 6.1, a lithograph from the influential medical illustrator Jacques Fabien Gautier d'Agoty's *Exposition Anatomique des Maux Vénériens* (1773), indicates just how pronounced such symptoms could be. D'Agoty does acknowledge the possibility of same-sex transmission, albeit briefly. Describing transmission he noted:

> Experience also shows that one can catch the Pox from pederasty: it then comes with cankers, mucous warts on the anus & other signs, either on

these parts or in the vicinity. This type of Pox is very difficult to cure, even incurable.[54]

A survey of French treatises from the period after 1750 would be needed to show just how common or rare such passages were in French medicine of the late Enlightenment. While d'Agoty here connected rectal symptoms to same-sex infection, he omitted anal sodomy when he discussed these symptoms more fully. This is curious because doctors otherwise commonly pointed to ulcerated regions as likely points of contact; just as genital lesions signaled sexual infection, so did ulcerated nipples or mouths signal points of contact in cases of infant–nurse transmission. Yet, when presented with symptoms like those in Figure 6.1, most doctors did not present anal sodomy as an explanation. Instead, they detailed how the disease's poison crept through the far reaches of the body, first entering the genitals but eventually attacking the victim's entire system, anus included. D'Agoty followed suit. When his discussion turned to the symptoms portrayed in his striking image, he explained rectal lesions not by way of anal sodomy, but stressed they "are always infallible marks that the virus has infected the mass of blood" and thus spread to the wider vicinity (*"voisinage"*) of the genitalia, which included the rectum.[55]

In discussing same-sex sexual transmission of the pox, then, doctors would have risked their professional reputations, and patients gross social opprobrium and criminal prosecution. At least to some extent medical silence on same-sex love and the pox expresses the old reluctance to speak its name. However, this silence remains somewhat curious, for the subgenre of pox treatises was by definition so impolite that concerns of decorum alone might nonetheless have been overcome in more texts. Further influencing the absence of same-sex transmission from most treatises was the current scientific understanding of the disease itself. For early Enlightenment doctors, the disease was firmly heteroerotic in nature. Both its production and its transmission were attributed to the conjunction of two distinct anatomies, one male and one female.

Generally assuming a male patient, early modern treatises on the pox predominantly featured a narrative structure presenting men as the disease's victims and women as the source of infection.[56] More importantly, theories about the disease's etiology increasingly stressed the combination of both male and female principles in the production of the disease, thus presenting the pox as a result of a union between men and women and helping to exclude considerations of same-sex production of the disease. Jacques Béthencourt's 1527 treatise was likely the first to suggest that the pox was generated either by the mixture of the male and female reproductive seeds in the womb, or of the male seed and the menses.[57] The menses had long been linked to disease, and numerous Renaissance theorists, Paracelsus foremost among them, similarly attributed the pox to uterine sores that became pathogenically corrupted during male–female intercourse.[58] But it was Béthencourt's notion of mixing seed that most influenced later theories on the pox. However, by 1596 a subtle change had taken place, for Italian physician Aurilius Minadoi argued that the disease arose from a mixture of *multiple* men's seed, rather than the corruption of the seed of one man and one woman.[59] It was not until after the Interregnum that the theory made its way into print in England. In 1660 Daniel Sennert explained "[Minadoi] thinks this evil proceeded first, when women were made very unclean, when they had received a mixture of seeds."[60]

Though it had its roots in the early sixteenth century, the theory became most influential in the early Enlightenment. Popular for various reasons, it presented scientific "proof" of the dangers of prostitution or female promiscuity, and thus assisted those seeking to corral female sexuality.[61] But it acquired further vogue from adaptation to emerging iatrochemical and iatromechanical branches of science, which grew steadily in popularity in the later seventeenth century.[62] For Helmontian iatrochemists, the properties of the tiny particles they termed acids, alkalis and salts were crucial to understanding health and disease. Rather than presenting the pox in terms of Galenic humoral imbalance, a medical paradigm that was fast waning, surgeons like Nicholas de Blegny and others revised the theory of heterogeneous seed in light of emerging chemistry. "The pox," Blegny proposed,

> is a contagious distemper occasioned by contact, and by means of a venemous salt, proceeding from the mixture and corruption of the seeds of divers persons received and contained in the wombs of publick women; by which all liquid substances wherein it mixes do thicken and corrupt the nerves, skin and in general the flesh to which it adheres becomes prickt, gnawed and dry, lastly the bones and cartileges that it penetrates do rise up and corrupt.[6]

The putrefied material produced from this mixture constituted a volatile "poison," which scientific thinkers increasingly described as made up of razor-sharp particles that fiercely damaged the body as they moved through it.[64] Discussed by nine of the doctors from our list –as well as many others –this theory garnered significant support well into the late eighteenth century.[65]

Although Winfried Schleiner may have rightly suggested that the fear of conjoining male seed may have reflected, in part, former "homophobic shudder,"[66] doctors clearly held that the female womb played a vital role in the process of putrefaction by which the disease was born anew. "These seeds being mixed together," Blegny asserted, "may pass from their fermentation to corruption due to the heat and moisture of the part that contains them."[67] Here early Enlightenment thinkers were merely recasting positions staked by much earlier physicians. Andrew Boorde's 1547 *Brievyary of Helthe* had long ago linked the pox to the womb's supposed pathogenic agency:

> Vulva is the Latyn word. In greke it is named a womans secret member the which is the gate or dore of the matrix or belly, and there may brede many diseases as ulcers, skabbes, apostumes, fissures, fystles, festures, the Pockes and burnynge of an harlot.[68]

Moreover, doctors presented women's traditionally cold physiology as overheated by frequent intercourse. Promiscuous male–female intercourse appeared to cause a preternatural multitude of circumstances: not just a mixture of different men's semen, but its presence within an unnaturally hot womb that allowed a pathological chemical transformation to take place. This two-sex theory of the pox's production galvanized what we might call an essentially heteroerotic understanding of the disease. Two separate and distinct sexes thus jointly contributed in *different* ways to the production of the disease, demonstrating that late Stuart venereology was influenced by – and contributed to – the sexual dimorphism now seen to characterize European culture after about 1590.[69]

The influence of the emerging two-sex anatomical model appears also in the heterogeneous seed theory's omission of the female seed in the disease's production. As the one-sex anatomical paradigm faded, so that male and female genitalia no longer appeared homologous, so too did the notion that women contributed seed through orgasm.[70] In Béthencourt's original theory the female seed had played a role. But by the seventeenth century the pox was said to result from the conjunction of *men's* seed in the womb – not different men's seed *and* the woman's seed. In the two-sex model of humanity female anatomy became increasingly passive; it housed and nurtured the now all-important male seed. Just as the female body became a less active contributor in pregnancy, so too did doctors now portray it as a passive participant in disease production, so that the crucial feminine principle in the pox came to be the womb as incubator.[71] Such ideas did not just concern the production of the disease *ex nihilo*, for doctors also attributed important roles to the two distinct sexes in theories of transmission. Detailed discussions expounded how men's and women's different genital structures enabled them to give and receive the disease's poison.[72] The increasingly influential theories representing the disease as a malady produced by and transmitted between two *distinct* sexes helped further to obscure not only the topicality but the possibility of same-sex transmission.

And yet a great exception to this rule appeared in 1736, Jean Astruc's *De Morbis Venereis*, translated from the Latin the following year as *A Treatise of the Venereal Disease in Six Books*. Born in 1684, Astruc attended and later taught at the medical school of Montpellier, before acceding to the medical faculty at the University of Paris and becoming the king's physician.[73] Astruc's treatise on venereal disease appeared in many editions, and achieved almost legendary status in the eighteenth century.[74] He researched every treatise on the disease that he could find to write an account of the pox that, at times, reads more like a history of the disease than a medical exploration of it. Books 5 to 9 of his expanded nine-book 1754 English edition included summaries of no less than 542 medical writers on the disease, dating back almost three centuries. Decades later London doctors routinely endorsed it as the most comprehensive source available.[75]

When explaining transmission, Astruc mentions only five modes of contact: male–female intercourse, nursing, kissing, sharing sheets, and manual contact when midwives or surgeons touched the genitals of an infected patient.[76] However, much later, when discussing buboes (inflamed glandular swellings, often associated with plague), he asks, "whether Venereal Buboes are formed in *Catamites* and *Pathics* by the unnatural Use of Venery? and if they are produced by these means, in what parts is it usual for them to appear?" He proceeds:

> As to the first Question I never observed myself, nor do I imagine that any other Person has ever observed Buboes upon *Catamites* which could certainly be determined to arise from the Infection just contracted by the unnatural Use of Venery. For I do not imagine that there are any *Catamites*, who are so fond of playing the pathic, that they never attempt it the Part of the Agent; but it is enough to have once played the virile part, to make it Matter of Doubt whence the Bubo arises, if it should happen to follow upon this Action.

He then cast even further doubt on the presence of buboes in "catamites," based on his understanding of the lymphatic system and the unlikelihood of lymph pooling in the glands of the lower abdomen and rectum. Astruc oddly raises the issue of same-sex anal sodomy only to question whether men having receptive anal sex could contract the disease by that means.

However, having raised the subject he seemed unable to resist wagging a judgmental finger.

> But let not these Wretches congratulate themselves upon this Account, since besides many very grievous Disorders that are peculiar to that filthy Vice, of which see below *Chap. X.* they are exposed to Buboes of as bad, if not a worse kind than the inguinal ones; for it frequently happens in them that the Lymph that returns from the Extremity of the Rectum, and the parts near the *Anus*, being inspissated by the poisonous Particles exhaling from the *Semen*, enlarges, distends, and swells the lymphatic Glands which are very small, but situated in great Numbers in the Fat about the *Podex* [i.e. buttocks]; whence arises a Kind of annular Bubo, with which the *Podex* is surrounded, attended with Heat, Redness, Hardness, and excessive Pain, especially at the Time of Excretion of the Faeces. This is to be cured by the same Remedies, and treated after the same Manner with the inguinal Venereal Buboes.[77]

By presenting infected semen as volatile and acidic material that structurally damages the rectum, Astruc's text pathologized same-sex sodomy more clearly than perhaps any other venereal disease treatise.

Yet in a subsequent chapter on ulcers Astruc detailed a long list of symptoms among men, women, and in many instances "catamites," without these moral warnings. Instead, we find rather mundane descriptions of symptoms and treatments. Comparing ulcerations of the penis, and then the vagina, Astruc states,

> Something of this kind is observed in *Catamites* and *Pathics*, if they contract foul Ulcers in the *Anus*, by the unnatural Use of venery: From these Ulcers they

are tormented with a violent Inflammation at the extremity of the *Rectum,* and a Tightness or *Phimosis* of the *Podex.*[78]

As he proceeds, in numerous examples, the catamite appears its own category, discussed alongside of, but distinct from, the male and the female. Astruc explains how the pox inflames the foreskin of the penis preventing its retraction, and then describes a parallel symptom affecting the labia in women. "'Tis the same Case with Catamites and Pathics," he adds,

> in whom the neighbouring Parts of the Anus are afflicted with Chankers, and *Phimosis*: hence the excretion of the Faeces becomes difficult and the Malignity of the Disease daily increasing, if it be neglected, *Chrystalline Bladders* frequently push forth at the Margin of the *Anus* exactly like those [on the penis and labia] we have just described.[79]

For many pages Astruc details the symptoms of men, women, catamites, and in some cases wet nurses, in that order. For example, emphasizing the importance of the structural make-up of ulcerated areas, he states: "the Tumour of the Prepuce or Glans in Men; of the different parts of the Vulva or Vagina in Women; of the Margins of the Anus in Catamites; lastly of the Nipples in Nurses, is obvious to the senses." Later, addressing treatment, he draws the same parallels:

> All that we have hitherto advised to be practiced upon Male Patients, will be of equal Service in the female ones, whether the Nipples or the *Pudenda Muliebria* are swelled or inflamed with the Venereal Poison. The same also, only changing a few Circumstances, will hold good with regard to Catamites.[80]

Likewise, "The advice above given concerning the Inflammation of the Genitals in Men, will be equally useful to Women, if their Pudenda, or Nipples, or to Catamites, if the neighbouring Parts of the Anus, are swelled with a Venereal Inflammation." And "Whatever has been said of the *Venereal Phymata* upon the Pudenda in Men, is to be equally understood as belonging to the *Phymata* which happen to Women from impure Venery, or which affect the parts near the *Anus* in *Catamites*." Also, "if a cancerous *Phyma* in the Glans in Men, in the *Labia Vulvae* in Women, *or* in the *Anus* in Pathics is buried deep . . . it is to be eradicated in the same manner." Finally, "the *Sphacelus* is easily extirpated, if it only affects the *Prepuce* in Men, the *Nymphae* in Women, or the *Christa Ani* in Pathics."[81]

Throughout this substantial chapter, Astruc assigns the anally receptive male sodomite a category all his own, on equal footing with the sexually penetrative male and the vaginally receptive female. Moral condemnation has now faded away, allowing the physician to present same-sex love with what seems like modern scientific detachment. There is no reference to the "bestial" or "criminal" nature of anal sex, merely a straightforward cataloguing of symptoms and treatment. Seemingly freed from perceived necessities of overt condemnation, at least for the moment, Astruc offers a rare early modern taxonomy of sexual differences developed for medical analysis. Here the catamite is neither a legal category, as in sodomy law, nor a term of derision, as in instances of slander. It is a medical category, its distinctions grafted onto the body. Astruc's men, women, and catamites each have their sexual inclinations and practices written onto a specific body part: men are represented by their penetrative penis, women by their receptive vulva, and catamites by their receptive anus. Throughout his many claims concerning the sexual health of male sodomites, Astruc largely ignores the possibility that a man contracting the pox through penetrative anal sex could develop symptoms on his penis. Those "playing the part of the Agent," to use Astruc's terms, seem instead subsumed within the penetrative male category, as if he assumes that the effects of the pox are the same for them whether contracted through vaginal or anal intercourse. By contrast, the catamite's sexual health (and therefore his sexual nature itself) revolved entirely around his anus, as the receptive partner in anal sex. Astruc's influence assured that these categories would be taken up by at least some of the writers who studied his work. Physician John Armstrong summarized the abovementioned passages in his 1737 précis of Astruc's text, while in 1772 surgeon Nikolai Falck cited Astruc repeatedly and similarly appropriated these categories. Speaking of venereal excrescences, Falck proclaimed "They are sometimes scattered over the glans and prepuce in men; praepuce, clitoris, and carunculae myrtiformes in women; and about the anus in pathics."[82]

Such medical categorization may appear to offer support to Randolph Trumbach's differently argued claim for the effeminate male sodomite as a third gender, arising in the eighteenth century alongside the heterosexual man and woman.[83] However, this is debatable, for such a distinction has been claimed to date from the ancient Roman *cinadeus*,[84] and related penetrative/receptive categories appear in various medical and scientific texts dating from the ancients through their medieval inheritors to the Renaissance.[85] The remarkably erudite Astruc may well have known some of these precedents and this may have influenced his venereal taxonomy. What is clear is that by the eighteenth century this tripartite categorical distinction of men, women and catamites becomes capable of being used explicitly as a basis for published, extensive and respectable medical discussion.

Astruc's exclusive focus on rectal symptomatology of catamites also meant that when he turned his attention to such symptoms in a later chapter, his discussion of same-sex love continued.[86] However, the brief – and rather rare – tone of scientific objectivity that he momentarily struck two chapters earlier seems to have been too difficult to sustain. As if realizing four hundred pages into his text that his discussion of sodomy between men may offend, he seeks to stave off the kind of criticism that John Marten faced decades earlier.

It is very irksome, so frequently to repeat such horrid Nastiness, but the End for which this Work was wrote, would by no means suffer me to stifle a fact, which to the great scandal of Mankind, Experience teaches us to be a too certain Cause of *Venereal Disease*. Nay, Honesty itself seemed to require that I should frequently include this Cause, that such as are fired with so mad a Lust, being admonished, may at last grow wise; and if they are neither to be

> recalled by a Sense of what is natural, nor to be deterred by the Vengeance
> of Heaven, at least being made certain of the Evils that arise from this filthy
> Vice, they may at length be reclaimed from it.[87]

Astruc is nothing if not honest. By pathologizing sex between men he hopes that
the profound emotion of unnatural lust might be countered by a more profound
fear of venereal infection. If eternal damnation cannot convince men to resist
their urges, perhaps the terror of cancerous rectal tumors will do the trick.

Although Astruc's discussion is rich and revealing, we still face the question
of why such a discussion appears so rarely. Perhaps only a physician so driven to
comprehensiveness that he researched 542 authors and penned a nine-volume,
700-page epic was thorough enough. If so, same-sex transmission apparently
remained an issue dispensably minor to most people writing on the disease. Even
to Astruc, it hardly seems to have been an issue of primary importance, buried
as it is almost four hundred pages into his treatise – unless this was a deliberate
strategy to obscure the discussion from casual and nonprofessional readers.

In the vast landscape of early Enlightenment venereology, we are thus left with
a few fleeting acknowledgements and just two substantial discussions of same-sex
transmission – neither of which are typical of medical discourse. One author was
one of the most erudite and detailed medical writers of the age, and the other
one of the most scandalous! Moreover, even when set against the volume of their
own writing on the pox, Astruc's and Marten's relatively few pages of same-sex
commentary seem slim. What they tell us about contemporary attitudes towards
same-sex transmission is vital. However, it is far overshadowed by an enormous
medical silence on the issue.

Professional self-fashioning and codes of politeness led some doctors to refuse
to discuss the topic in the hopes of attracting genteel patients. And whereas some
Renaissance concepts of the disease's etiology and transmission had tended to
focus on women as sources and agents, the Enlightenment's new anatomy and
changing sexual economy contributed to theories that it arose from conjunction
of two distinct sexes, further obscuring the role of male same-sex love. Meanwhile,
according to conventions of medical practice, patients' reluctance to divulge their
sexual histories left doctors with very little evidence of links between the pox
and same-sex love for either gender. There were just too many other ways that
one could explain away infection, too many other ways to account for symptoms
that might have aroused suspicion, and too much riding on the diagnosis for the
patients involved. There was likely a real crisis of STD infection among men
having sex together in early modern London. But most doctors missed it.

Notes

1. Mirko D. Grmek, *History of AIDS: Emergence and Origin of a Modern Pandemic*, tr. Russell
   C. Maulitz and Jacalyn Duffin, Princeton: Princeton University Press, 1990, pp. 10,
   32–3; Randy Shilts, *And the Band Played on: Politics, People and the AIDS Epidemic*, New
   York: St Martin's Press, 1987, pp. 120–71.

2. "The venereal disease" encompassed many conditions we now separate, including syphilis and gonorrhea. I agree with those who advise employing early modern terms, in this case "the venereal disease" or "the pox," rather than the modern anachronism "syphilis." See Jon Arrizabalaga *et al.*, *The Great Pox: The French Disease in Renaissance Europe*, New Haven: Yale University Press, 1996, pp. 16–19.

3. Kevin Siena, "Pollution, Promiscuity, and the Pox: English Venereology and the Early Modern Discourse on Social and Sexual Danger," *Journal of the History of Sexuality*, 8 (1998), 553–74; and Roze Hentschell, "Luxury and Lechery: Hunting the French Pox in Early Modern England," in Kevin Siena (ed.), *Sins of the Flesh: Responding to Sexual Disease in Early Modern Europe*, Toronto: Centre for Reformation and Renaissance Studies, 2005, pp. 159–86.

4. William Clowes, *A Short and Profitable Treatise Touching on the Cure of the Disease Now Called Morbus Gallicus*, London, 1579, ch. 1, fol. 2.

5. Charles Peter, *A Description of the Venereal Disease*, London, 1678; Walter Harris, *A Treatise of the Acute Diseases of Infants*, London, 1742, pp. 16–17; John Profily, *An Easy and Exact Method of Curing the Venereal Disease*, London, 1748, unnumbered preface.

6. See esp. the call to transport prostitutes to the New World in the name of disease prevention in L.S., Προφυλακτικον: *Or Some Considerations of a Notable Expedient to Root Out the French Pox from the English Nation*, London, 1673, pp. 82–6.

7. Thomas Laqueur, *Solitary Sex: A Cultural History of Masturbation*, New York: Zone Books, 2003, pp. 168–245.

8. Joseph Cam, *Thoughts on the Consequences of the Venereal Disease in Three Parts*, London, 1729; J. H. Smyth, *A New Treatise on the Venereal Disease, Gleets, Seminal Weaknesses*, London, 1771.

9. For discussion and further references see Tim Hitchcock, *English Sexualities, 1700–1800*, New York, St Martin's Press, 1997, pp. 60–70.

10. Kenneth Borris (ed.), *Same-Sex Desire in the English Renaissance: A Sourcebook of Texts, 1470–1650*, London: Routledge, 2004, pp. 154–6.

11. John Marten, *A Treatise of all the Degrees and Symptoms of the Venereal Disease*, 6th edn, London, 1708, pp. 68–9; repr. in Borris (ed.), *Same-Sex Desire*, pp. 154–5.

12. Marten, *Treatise*, pp. 150–1; repr. in Borris (ed.), *Same-Sex Desire*, pp. 155–6.

13. Borris (ed.), *Same-Sex Desire*, p. 154.

14. Lengthy subtitles have been omitted. Daniel Sennert, Nicholas Culpeper, and Abdiah Cole, *Two Treatises: The First of the Venereal Pocks*, London, 1660; John Wynell, *Lues Venerea, or, A Perfect Cure of the French Pox*, London, 1660; Richard Bunworth, *A New Discovery of the French Disease and Running of the Reins*, London, 1662; P.B., *Pilulae Antipudendagriae: or Venus's Revenge*, London, 1669; Gideon Harvey, *Great Venus Unmasked: Or a More Exact Discovery of the Venereal Evil or French Disease*, London, 1672; Everad Maynwaring, *The History and Mystery of the Venereal Lues*, London, 1673, L.S., Προφυλακτικον, 1673; Nicholas de Blegny, *New and Curious Observations Concerning the Art of Curing the Venereal Disease*, tr. Walter Harris, London, 1676; Charles Peter, *A Description of the Venereal Disease*, London, 1678; John Archer, *Secrets Disclosed of Consumptions, Shewing How to Distinguish between the Scurvy and Venereal Disease*, London, 1684; W. Wall, *A New System of the French Disease*, London, 1696?; Johannes Sintelaer, *The Scourge of Venus and Mercury: Represented in a Treatise of the Venereal Disease*, London, 1709; Anon., *The Tomb of Venus*, London, 1710; I. F. Nicholson. *The Modern Siphylis*, London, 1718; William Cockburn, *The Symptoms, Nature, Cause and Cure of a Gonorrhoea*, London, 1719; Thomas Garlick, *A Mechanical Account of the Cause and Cure of a Virulent Gonorrhoea in Both Sexes*, London, 1719; Bouez de Sigogne, *A New Method of Curing the Venereal Disease*, London, 1724; Daniel Turner, *Syphilis: A Practical Dissertation on the Venereal Disease*, London, 1724; Daniel Turner, *A Discourse Concerning Gleets*, London, 1729; J.S., *A Mechanical Dissertation upon the Lues Venerea*, London, 1731; Vincent Brest, *An Analytical Inquiry into the Specifick Property of Mercury, Relating to the Cure of Venereal Diseases*, London, 1732; John Douglas, *A Dissertation on the Venereal Disease*, London, 1738; Joseph Cam, *A Rational Account of the*

Venereal Disease, London, 1740; John Watson, *An Account of the Effects of Mr Hauksbee's Alternative Medicine, as Applied in the Cure of the Venereal Disease*, London, 1742; Jean Astruc, *A Treatise of Venereal Diseases, in Nine Books*, London, 1754.

15. Peter, *Venereal Disease*, p. 5.
16. Cf. Alan Bray, *Homosexuality in Renaissance England*, London: Gay Men's Press 1982, p. 25.
17. Cf. Turner, *Syphilis*, pp. 1–2; P. G. Maxwell-Stuart, "'Wild, filthie, execrabill, detestabill, and unnatural sin': Bestiality in Early Modern Scotland," in Tom Betteridge (ed.), *Sodomy in Early Modern Europe*, Manchester: Manchester University Press, 2002, pp. 82–93.
18. Maynwaring, *Venereal Lues*, p. 12.
19. Cf. e.g. Sintelaer, *Scourge of Venus*, p. 24.
20. Peter Wagner, "The Discourse on Sex – or Sex as Discourse: Eighteenth-Century Medical and Paramedical Erotica," in Roy Porter and G. S. Rousseau (eds), *Sexual Underworlds of the Enlightenment*, Manchester: Manchester University Press, 1987, pp. 47–9.
21. Roy Porter, "'Laying Aside Any Private Advantage': John Marten and Venereal Disease," in Linda E. Merians (ed.), *The Secret Malady: Venereal Disease in Eighteenth-Century Britain and France*, Lexington, KY: University of Kentucky Press, 1996, pp. 52–3.
22. John Spinke, *Quackery Unmask'd: or Reflections on the Sixth Edition of Mr. Martin's Treatise of the Venereal Disease and its Appendix*, London, 1709, pp. 8, 82. On the Spinke–Marten feud see Philip Pinkus, *Grub Street Stripped Bare*, London: Constable, 1968, pp. 51–66; and Anon., *An Apology for a Latin Verse in Commendation of Mr. Marten's Gonosologioum Novum*, London, 1709.
23. Wagner, "Discourse on Sex," p. 47.
24. Spinke, *Quackery Unmask'd*, appendix, p. 28.
25. Michel Foucault, *History of Sexuality*, vol. 1, New York: Vintage, 1990; Ludmilla Jordanova, *Sexual Visions: Images of Gender in Science and Medicine between the Eighteenth and Twentieth Centuries*, Madison, WI: University of Wisconsin Press, 1993.
26. Garlick, *Virulent Gonorrhoea*, p. vii.
27. Margaret Pelling, *Medical Conflicts in Early Modern London: Patronage, Physicians, and Irregular Practitioners 1550–1640*, Oxford: Oxford University Press, 2004, pp. 239, 269.
28. Turner, *Syphilis*, unnumbered preface. Emphasis added.
29. Winfried Schleiner, "Moral Attitudes towards Syphilis and its Prevention in the Renaissance," *Bulletin of the History of Medicine*, 68 (1994), 389–410.
30. Sennert *et al.*, *Two Treatises*, p. 27; Cam, *Venereal Disease*, p. 5; Spinke, *Quackery Unmask'd*, pp. 28–32, 64; Turner, *Syphilis*, p. 84. Preventatives had some defenders. See Astruc, *Venereal Diseases*, pp. 279–83.
31. Sintelaer, *Scourge of Venus*, pp. 11–24. Compare Sennert *et al.*, *Two Treatises*, pp. 5, 17; Bunsworth, *French Disease*, pp. 3–5; P. B., *Venus's Revenge*, pp. 5–6; Harvey, *Great Venus*, pp. 58–64; Maynwaring, *Venereal Lues*, pp. 72–82; L.S., Προφυλακτικον, p. 5; Blegny, *Curious Observations*, pp. 18–22; Archer, *Secrets Disclosed*, pp. 31–4; Anon., *Tomb of Venus*, p. 10; Nicholson, *Modern Syphilis*, p. 90; Turner, *Syphilis*, p. 8; Douglas, *Venereal Disease*, p. 2; Astruc, *Venereal Diseases*, pp. 122, 129.
32. Sintelaer, *Scourge of Venus*, p. 24.
33. Wagner, "Discourse on Sex," p. 48; Anon., *Marten's Gonosologioum Novum*.
34. Turner, *Syphilis*, p. 15.
35. For discussion and further references see e.g. Andrew Wear, *Knowledge and Practice in English Medicine, 1550–1680*, Cambridge: Cambridge University Press, 2001, pp. 105–16.
36. Roy Porter, "The Rise of the Physical Exam," in Porter and W. F. Bynum (eds), *Medicine and the Five Senses*, Cambridge: Cambridge University Press, 1993, pp. 179–97; Mary Fissell, "The Disappearance of the Patient's Narrative and the Invention of Hospital

Medicine," in Roger French and Andrew Wear (eds), *British Medicine in an Age of Reform*, London: Routledge, 1991, pp. 92–109.

37. Claude Quétel, *History of Syphilis*, Baltimore: Johns Hopkins University Press, 1992, pp. 82–3.
38. Harvey, *Great Venus*, p. 33.
39. L.S., Προφυλακτικον, pp. 13–14.
40. Astruc, *Venereal Diseases*, vol. 1, pp. 50–1, vol. 2, p. 35; Peter, *Venereal Disease*, p. 9; Sintelaer, *Scourge of Venus*, p. 23; Archer, *Secrets Disclosed*, p. 31; Anon., *Tomb of Venus*, pp. 61–2, 82; Cam, *Venereal Disease*, p. 10.
41. Douglas, *Venereal Disease*, p. 3.
42. Astruc, *Venereal Diseases*, vol. 2, p. 50.
43. Garlick, *Virulent Gonorrhoea*, pp. 57, 59–60.
44. Steven Shapin, *A Social History of Truth: Civility and Science in Seventeenth-Century England*, Chicago: University of Chicago Press, 1994, pp. 65–125.
45. Kevin Siena, *Venereal Disease, Hospitals and the Urban Poor: London's "Foul" Wards, 1600–1800*, Rochester, NY: University of Rochester Press, 2004, pp. 30–61, 79–82, 90, 106–7, 117–18, 239–40.
46. Sintelaer, *Scourge of Venus*, pp. 19–20. See also p. 13.
47. Nicholson, *Modern Syphilis*, p. 12.
48. Marten, *Treatise*, pp. 150–1; repr. in Borris (ed.), *Same-Sex Desire*, pp. 155–6.
49. Hitchcock, *Sexualities*, pp. 70–2.
50. Ibid., p. 68.
51. For discussion and further references see Siena, *Venereal Disease*, pp. 49–52.
52. Turner, *Syphilis*, pp. 16, 301.
53. On rectal symptoms and treatment see Sennert *et al.*, *Two Treatises*, p. 4; Wynell, *Lues Venerea*, p. 50; Harvey, *Great Venus*, p. 75; Maynwaring, *Venereal Lues*, p. 57; Archer, *Secrets Disclosed*, pp. 34–46; Wall, *French Disease*, unnumbered preface; Cockburn, *Gonorrhea*, pp. 236–9, 249, 252; Garlick, *Virulent Gonorrhoea*, pp. 17–18; Sigogne, *Venereal Disease*, pp. 42, 53, 90; Turner, *Syphilis*, pp. 72, 240; Douglas, *Venereal Disease*, pp. 9, 15, 62–3, 67; Cam, *Venereal Disease*, pp. 7–8, 21, 27, 48; Watson, *Venereal Disease*, pp. 16–17; Astruc, *Venereal Diseases*, vol. 1, pp. 193, 203, 260 and ch. 10, book 3. On oral symptoms see Sennert *et al.*, *Two Treatises*, p. 3; Wynell, *Lues Venerea*, p. 50; Bunsworth, *French Disease*, p. 5; Maynwaring, *Venereal Lues*, pp. 58, 82; Peter, *Venereal Disease*, pp. 8, 11; Anon., *Tomb of Venus*, pp. 62–3; Douglas, *Venereal Disease*, pp. 21, 57; Watson, *Venereal Disease*, pp. 46, 51; Astruc, *Venereal Diseases*, vol. 1, p. 122, vol. 2, p. 14.
54. Jacques Gautier d'Agoty, *Exposition Anatomique des Maux Vénériens*, Paris, 1773, p. 3. Thanks to Jennifer Drouin for translation help.
55. Ibid., pp. 2–3, 7.
56. Bruce T. Boehrer, "Early Modern Syphilis," *Journal of the History of Sexuality*, 1 (1990), 199.
57. Quétel, *Syphilis*, pp. 53–5; J. D. Oriel, *Scars of Venus: A History of Venereology*, London: Springer-Verlag, 1994, p. 16.
58. Winfried Schleiner, "Infection and Cure through Women: Renaissance Constructions of Syphilis," *Journal of Medieval and Renaissance Studies*, 24 (1994), 503–4; Laura J. McGough, "Quarantining Beauty: The French Disease in Early Modern Venice," in Siena (ed.), *Sins of the Flesh*, p. 211.
59. Aurelius Minadoi, *Tractatus de Virulentia Venerea*, Venice, 1596, ch. 30; Sennert *et al.*, *Two Treatises*, p. 15; Astruc, *Venereal Diseases*, vol. 1, p. 11.
60. Sennert *et al.*, *Two Treatises*, p. 14.
61. Schleiner, "Infection and Cure," pp. 505–6; Siena, "Promiscuity and the Pox," 562–9; Marie E. McAllister, "Stories of the Origin of Syphilis in Eighteenth-Century England: Science, Myth, and Prejudice," *Eighteenth-Century Life*, 24 (2000), 34–40.
62. Lester King, *The Philosophy of Medicine: The Early Eighteenth Century*, Cambridge, MA: Harvard University Press, 1982.

63. Blegny, *Curious Observations*, p. 3.

64. Cf. Harvey, *Great Venus*, pp. 43–4, 132–3.

65. Sennert *et al.*, *Two Treatises*, p. 15; P.B., *Venus's Revenge*, p. 5; Blegny, *Curious Observations*, pp. 3–5; Nicholson, *Modern Syphilis*, pp. 3–4; Sigogne, *New Method*, p. 59; Turner, *Syphilis*, pp. 3–4; Brest, *Analytical Inquiry*, p. 6; Garlick, *Virulent Gonorrhoea*, p. 36; Astruc, *Venereal Diseases*, vol. 1, pp. 92–3; See also J. S., *A Short Compendium of Chirurgery*, London, 1678, p. 114; Steven Blanckaert, *A New Method of Curing the French-Pox*, London, 1690, p. 27; William Salmon, *Praxis Medica: The Practice of Physick*, London, 1707, pp. 655–7; Richard Boulton, *Phisico-Chirurgical Treatise of the Gout, the Kings Evil, and the Lues Venerea*, London, 1714, p. 252; John Atkins, *The Navy Surgeon*, London, 1734, pp. 207–8; Pierre Desault, *A Treatise on the Venereal Distempers*, London, 1738, pp. 4–14; Walter Harris, *A Treatise of the Acute Diseases of Infants*, London, 1742, pp. 198–200; Jaques Daran, *A Complete Treatise of the Virulent Gonorrhoea both in Men and Women*, London, 1767, p. 70.

66. Schleiner, "Infection and Cure," p. 506.

67. Blegny, *Curious Observations*, pp. 12–14.

68. Andrew Boorde, *Brievyary of Helthe*, London, 1547, ch. 237.

69. Thomas Laqueur, *Making Sex: Body and Gender from the Greeks to Freud*, Cambridge MA: Harvard University Press, 1992; Londa Schiebinger, *The Mind Has No Sex? Women in the Origins of Modern Science*, Cambridge, MA: Harvard University Press, 1989, pp. 160–213.

70. Laqueur, *Making Sex*, pp. 99–103.

71. Debating whether gonorrheal discharge in women represented pus or instead, as many believed, corrupted seed, Garlick argued for the former: "For Women have no Seed." *Virulent Gonorrhoea*, p. 20. See also Nicholson, *Modern Syphilis*, p. 21, and Cockburn, *Gonorrhea*, pp. 9–10.

72. Cf. Garlick's description of giving and receiving gonorrhea, *Virulent Gonorrhoea*, pp. 28–36.

73. J. Doe, "Jean Astruc (1694–1766): A Biography and Bibliography," *Journal of the History of Medicine*, 15 (1960), 184–97.

74. The 1754 edn consulted here expanded on the 1st English edn, published in London in 1737, and available in facsimile: Jean Astruc, *A Treatise of the Venereal Disease*, tr. William Barrowby, 2 vols, New York: Garland, 1985. For the passages discussed below in the 1737 edn, see vol. 1, pp. 419–48. A later edn appeared in 1770, tr. (with considerable commentary) by Samuel Chapman, *A Treatise on the Venereal Disease; Being Chiefly Designed as a Translation and Abridgment of the Practical Part of Dr. Astruc's work*, London, 1770. See esp. pp. 197, 466–71.

75. Cf. William Fordyce, *A Review of the Venereal Disease, and its Remedies*, London, 1767, p. 17; John Leake, *A Dissertation on the Properties and Efficacy of the Lisbon Diet-Drink*, London, 1790, p. 145; Jesse Foot, *A Complete Treatise of the Origin, Theory and Cure of the Lues Venerea*, vol. 2, London, 1792, p. 21.

76. Astruc, *Venereal Diseases*, vol. 1, pp. 121–3.

77. Ibid., pp. 339–40.

78. Ibid., pp. 365–6.

79. Ibid., pp. 368–9.

80. Ibid., p. 374.

81. Ibid., pp. 375, 378, 382, 386. For many more examples see also pp. 377–91.

82. John Armstrong included a 109-page "abstract" of Astruc's treatise as an appendix to his book, *A Synopsis of the History and cure of Venereal Diseases*, London, 1737, pp. 410–519. For his summary of the relevant passages see pp. 454–5; N. D. Falck, *A Treatise on the Venereal Disease*, London, 1774, p. 209, also pp. 211–15.

83. Randolph Trumbach, *Sex and the Gender Revolution*, vol. 1, *Heterosexuality and the Third Gender in Enlightenment London*, Chicago: University of Chicago Press, 1998, pp. 3–22, 430. Michel Foucault and Jeffery Weeks both date this development later to the

nineteenth century. See Foucault, *Sexuality*, vol. 1, and Weeks, *Sex, Politics and Society: Regulation of Sexuality since 1800*, London: Longman, 1989.

84. David Halperin surveys this discussion in *How to Do the History of Homosexuality*, Chicago: University of Chicago Press, 2002. See index, *s.v.* "kinaidos."

85. See e.g. texts by Pseudo-Aristotle, Firmicus Maternus, Caelius Aurelianus, Avicenna, Pietro d'Abano, Lodovico Ricchieri, and Theodor Zwinger in Borris (ed.), *Same-Sex Desire*.

86. Astruc, *Venereal Diseases*, vol. 1, pp. 398–404. Astruc also briefly mentions catamites in *A Treatise on the Fistula of the Anus*, London, 1738, pp. 12, 18–19.

87. Astruc, *Venereal Diseases*, vol. 1, p. 399.

Part II

Divinatory, speculative and other sciences

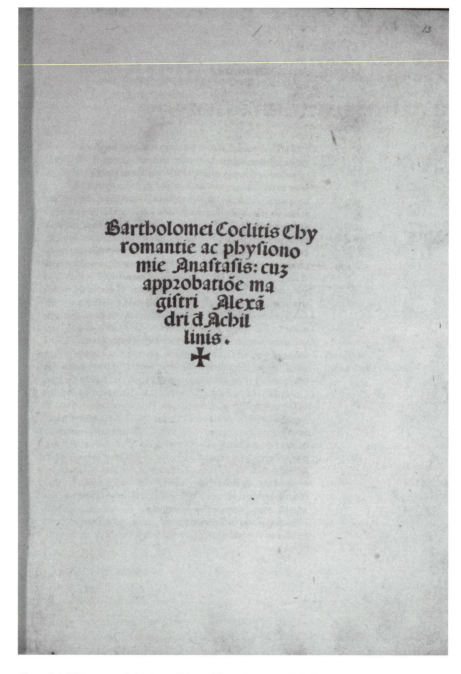

Bartholomei Coclitis Chy
romantie ac physiono
mie Anastasis: cuz
approbatiõe ma
gistri Alexã
dri d Achil
linis.
✠

Figure 7.1 Title-page of the first edition of Bartolommeo della Rocca, or Cocles, *Chyromantie ac physionomie anastasis* (Bologna: Per Joannem Antonium Platonidem Benedictorum, 1504). National Library of Medicine. By permission.

7 Sodomizing science

Cocles, Patricio Tricasso, and the constitutional morphologies of Renaissance male same-sex lovers

Kenneth Borris

The nineteenth-century homosexual became a personage, . . . a type of life, a life form, and a morphology, with an indiscreet anatomy and possibly a mysterious physiology . . .

(Michel Foucault[1])

Much sexual historiography assumes that premodern same-sexual acts were adventitious to the actors, as if somehow performed at random and unrelated to their actual or imputed temperamental interiorities.[2] But premodern physiognomics entailed much reflection upon differences of biological sex, gender, and sexual affinities, and the means by which they may be perceived, classified, and interpreted.[3] Its ancient authorities had established assessment of a person's conformation to conventional masculine and feminine norms as a principal technique of the discipline.[4] At least since its revival as a medieval science, sexual behaviors had been readily conceivable as functions of corresponding intrinsic inclinations that were encoded upon the body. The physical signs of varied sexual types could thus be studied, identified, inventoried, and publicized. Francesco Casoni's sixteenth-century forensic handbook recommended general usage of physiognomics in criminal investigations.[5] Moreover, an individual's sexual potential was not necessarily conceived as if it were, as some have claimed,[6] a chaos of equally possible and congenial options or "one undivided sexuality." Early modern physiognomics allowed for bestiality, incest, adultery, marital fidelity, promiscuity, "cinaedi" or male passives,[7] their insertive counterparts or "pedicators,"[8] lovers of boys, prostitution, and many other sexual possibilities. But it assumed that, depending on a subject's nature as evinced in bodily signs, he or she could be characterized by indiscriminate lust, *or* by some specific sexual desires, *or* by one in particular. For the physiognomer and prototypical sexologist Cocles or Bartolommeo della Rocca c.1500, we will find, a certain chiromantic sign indicates maximum constitutional inclination to pederasty.

Just as physiognomers conceived particular sexual affinities in a quasi-essentialist way long before the nineteenth century, they assumed their discipline's sexual applications and typologies were transhistorical. Like Cocles, they commonly cited extant accounts of ancient personalities as if those persons were as relevant to codifying current sexual types and practices as anyone alive in their own time, and on the same basis. Cocles repeatedly uses comments of the eleventh-century Arab Avicenna to explain why some males are cinaedi. Moreover, some of their main physiognomical traits alleged in the later Middle Ages and Renaissance derive from the discipline's ancient authorities. Essentialist understandings of particular sexual alignments were much more characteristic of those times than most recent historiographies of sexuality would lead us to expect.

For study of the intersections of early modern science with same-sexual history, Cocles is the single most important exponent of physiognomics.[9] Born illegitimately in 1467, he overcame unfortunate origins to become a barber-surgeon in Bologna, and despite having been largely an autodidact, attain posthumous European fame as probably the leading "modern" authority in the burgeoning field of physiognomics throughout most of the sixteenth century. He continued to be cited, engaged, and published in epitomes or compilations marketed under his name throughout the seventeenth. The early modern intellectual celebrity Girolamo Cardano (1501–76) pronounced Cocles "the admiration of his own age," worthy of inclusion in Cardano's survey of the horoscopes of renowned personalities.[10] Among the plethora of early modern physiognomical treatises, it is Cocles's compendious *Chyromantie ac physionomie anastasis*, first published in 1504 at Bologna and widely disseminated in various formats thereafter,[11] that engages sexual topics most extensively (Figure 7.1). He does so always within the frameworks of physiognomics, complexional physiology,[12] natural philosophy, astrology,[13] and independent observational experience.

While adducing many ancient, Arabic, medieval, and contemporary authorities in those fields, Cocles sought to present his own case studies of individuals to test, refine, and supplant former hypotheses, even in his sex research. Whereas premodern physiognomics typically repeated traditional aphoristic generalizations without presenting the writer's personal experience and observations, Cocles's more exploratory treatise offers a superior breadth of theoretical reference, concrete social reportage and insights, and a relatively open-minded fascination with all human phenomena. It bore the introductory endorsement of the Averroist professor of logic, natural philosophy, and medicine Alessandro Achillini (1463–1512), whom Cardano called "the foremost philosopher of his time."[14] Physiognomics and its subdisciplines, Achillini declares, are "valid forms of knowledge (*scientiae speculativae*) based, like medicine or astronomy, on principles of natural philosophy."[15] But soon after publishing the *Anastasis* Cocles was murdered, either by a disgruntled student or by order of one of the Bentivoglio, Bologna's ruling family, to avenge the physiognomer's prophecy of his ruin.[16]

The early modern European history of sex research could have turned out somewhat differently if the Dominican monk and rival physiognomer Patricio Tricasso (1491–c.1530), scandalized by Cocles's frank disquisitions on same-sexual types and practices, had not given him a verbal *auto-da-fé* in 1525. The Tricasso–Cocles controversy clarifies how early modern culture tended to discourage application of its diverse sciences to same-sexual research: Cocles's *Anastasis*, though widely consulted in various versions, did not inspire new proto-sexological advances in print. Even though many premodern physiognomical treatises assign particular morphologies and corresponding constitutions to one or more male same-sexual types (most often the cinaedus), the *Anastasis* appears to do so most thoroughly. Whereas some sexual historians maintain that same-sexual relations could only be experienced and conceived in terms of "sexual acts" until some particular date each proposes between 1650 and the late 1800s, many had long before conceived those acts as manifestations of corresponding constitutions, temperaments, interiorities, morphologies, and sexual identities.[17]

I use "physiognomics," "physiognomical," and "physiognomer" to denote the full range of early modern endeavors to interpret bodily features as signs of personal characteristics, health, fortune, conditions of life and death, and future prospects. "Physiognomy" denotes the subdiscipline assessing outward bodily parts, aspects, and mannerisms; "chiromancy" (now called palmistry) observation of the hands.[18] I use the formerly complex word "sodomy" and its cognates much as it is defined in a standard early modern encyclopedia first published c.1503, the *Margarita philosophica*, and still is in the much later forensic manual of Paolo Zacchia (1584–1659): the sexual coupling of "male with male or female with female."[19] The term applies to either or both types here according to context. Though "sodomy" had various taxonomic, metaphoric, and polemical applications in the period, its most common meaning, both socially and in legal practice, was sex between males: primarily anal, but comprehending their other "sodomitical" options.[20]

Elements of early modern same-sexual physiognomics

According to the discipline's complexional and astrological assumptions, a bodily sign evinces conditions of the subject's life or constitution that conduce the behavior or future prospect signified.[21] Such a behavioral inclination can be permanent or vary with age, depending on the case, so that it may pertain only to youth or maturity, say, or possibly increase with age. A sign associated with a certain sexual behavior indicates an intrinsic inclination producing that legible outward inscription. At any given point inner and innate factors substantially influence a physiognomical subject's particular sexual desires and behaviors. Cocles's text furnishes various examples. A lower lip particularly red and loose, he reports, indicates that a boy "is or *will become* a cinaedus, especially if his face and eyes are laughing." And Cocles has observationally verified this principle, as in "a certain nobleman."[22]

Since physiognomics claimed to disclose not only current personal character and behaviors but also future prospects, it had to define its observed physical signs as substantially definitive revelations of a subject's physical and mental constitution and the forces shaping his or her destiny. From physiognomical viewpoints, then, various same-sexual behaviors implied corresponding constitutionally defined types of person, especially after the conceptual invention of sodomy.[23] Though early modern physiognomers sought to downplay their discipline's deterministic hence heterodox implications, it nonetheless tended to restrict free will and hence reduce moral responsibility for alleged sins, sexual and otherwise.[24] Physiognomics posed such challenges to orthodoxy more dramatically than could either astrology or complexional theory alone, because it claimed not only to reveal and document an individual's characteristic tendencies toward certain sins, but do so as they are inscribed upon his or her body.

While physiognomy had assimilated complexional physiology by categorizing bodily features as expressions of dominant qualities and humoral combinations, learned chiromancers much elaborated those principles so that their discipline appeared to have greater analytic and predictive capacities. Both physiognomy and chiromancy thus attended, for example, to the skin's tone, color, and condition; relative fleshiness and muscularity; amount, color, and type of hair. Blonde hair, pale skin, soft fleshiness, and lack of body hair all appeared to signify a cold and wet, hence relatively effeminate complexion contrary to normative masculinity's heat and dryness. Hence physiognomy claimed to define and identify viragos and male effeminates of various types. Chiromancy further mapped the hand into zones that supposedly manifested all of a subject's conditions and prospects. Its several competing schemes and schools mainly observed lines and relative elevations, termed "mounts." Certain universal lines were assigned primary importance. As three of them corresponded to the supposedly principal organs, the heart, brain, and liver, so chiromancy claimed to assist medical diagnosis and prophylaxis.[25] Some leading chiromancers were also medical practitioners, such as Cocles himself, Cardano, Johannes Rothmann (fl. 1592–5), and Marin Cureau de La Chambre (1594–1669), physician in ordinary to Louis XIV of France.

Cocles adopted what was probably the most widely used scheme of learned chiromancy in early modernity. As his range of variant terms for certain lines indicates in Figure 7.2, those who followed this general system used different synonymous names for the hand's features.[26] Names for the line corresponding to the heart included the Line of Life, or the Cardiac, Cordial, or Vital Line (in Cocles, *Linea vite seu cordis vel cardica*); for the brain and head, the Middle Natural or Cephalic Line (*Linea cerebri seu media nālis*); for the liver, the Line of the Liver or Stomach, or Hepatic Line (*Linea epatis seu basis triāguli*). Together these formed the Triangle, held to reveal much about a subject's insides, like some other features such as the Mensal or Table Line, or Line of Fortune (*Linea mēsalis seu moralis*). The latter broadly indicated the body's general health, condition, and future prospects, besides revealing those of the bladder, intestines, and sexual organs.

Supplemented by complexional assessments of skin, hair, and other bodily features, chiromancy promised profound insights into a subject's amorous and sexual nature, inclinations, and behaviors. In the common scheme that Cocles used, four features, some universal and others not, have most importance for such analysis. The Mount of Venus, the mound of the thumb adjacent to the palm, registers a subject's relation to that planet and to things venereal (Figure 7.3, *Venus*). The universal Vital Line may have a so-called "Sister" running parallel to its sibling alongside or through the Mount of Venus, and further evincing sexual inclinations (Figure 7.3, *Soror in mōte pollicis*). Some conformations of the Girdle of Venus, a relatively rare line extending from between the index and second finger to between the fourth and fifth, denote strong affinities for corresponding

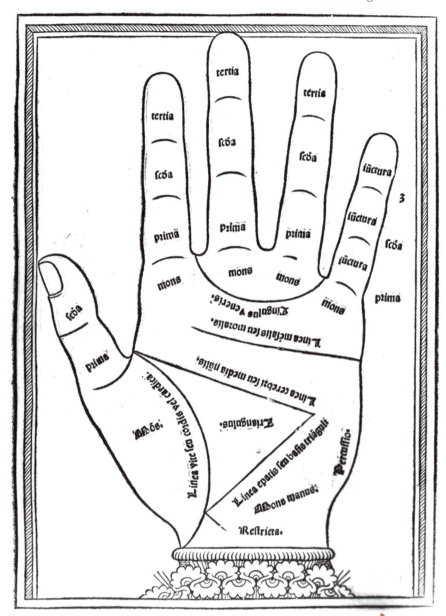

Figure 7.2 First chiromantic paradigm, from Bartolommeo della Rocca, or Cocles, *Chyromantie ac physionomie anastasis* (Bologna, 1515), fol. 71a. By permission of the British Library.

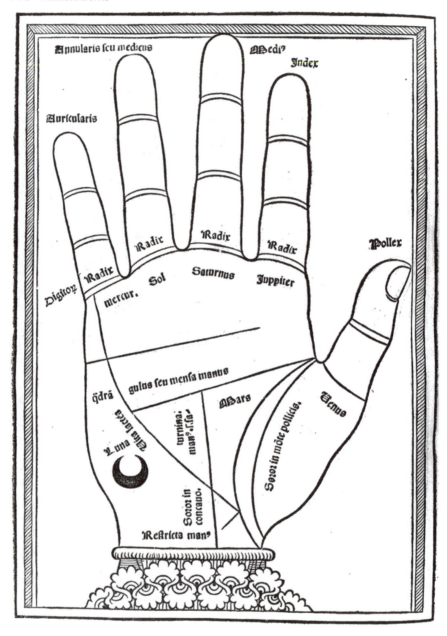

Figure 7.3 Second chiromantic paradigm, from Bartolommeo della Rocca, or Cocles, *Chyromantie ac physionomie anastasis* (Bologna, 1515), fol. 71b. By permission of the British Library.

sexual deviances or excesses (Figure 7.2, *Cingulus Veneris*). Likewise the Milky Way, a diagonal line going from the wrist at the Mount of Venus towards the little finger (Figure 7.3, *Via lactea*). A relatively red, elevated, fleshy Mount of Venus, for example, indicates a constitution venereally hot and sanguine, thus prone to "inordinate lusts" that could well be sodomy if that were corroborated by other physiognomical indicators. Various specific marks in these areas and others evinced the subject's affinities for, among numerous possibilities, adultery, incest, rape, marital fidelity, chastity, prostitution, general debauchery, or, as we will see, male same-sex amours and sexual roles. Much was likewise inferred from the Table Line's appearance, which appeared to summarize the subject's complexion and prospects.

Some recent research has uncanny similarities to early modern sexual physiognomics. Marc Breedlove *et al.* report in *Nature* that "animal models have indicated that androgenic steroids acting before birth might influence the sexual orientation of humans."[27] Lesbians, they find, tend to have a hyper-androgenized finger pattern in which the index finger is proportionally shorter than the fourth, and so do homosexual males who have an exceptionally high number of older brothers. Fetal hyper-androgenization, they conclude, appears to promote development of female and male homosexuality. Their research objectives differ from those of early modern physiognomics, for Breedlove *et al.* seek to clarify prenatal and natal causes, while their interest in subjects' hands wholly serves that end. Conversely, early modern physiognomics assumed that complexional and astrological theories had already accounted for innate or constitutional causality, so that same-sexual inclinations and behaviors were thus conduced by particular temperaments and legibly evinced in outer physical signs. However, since Breedlove *et al.* maintain that "finger-length patterns vary with gender, sexual orientation, and birth order,"[28] their linkage of constitutional factors and particular physical traits with same-sexual relations parallels that of former physiognomics. From both these contemporary and early modern scientific viewpoints, same-sexual acts express the distinctive natures of the actors. Hence those acts appear signifiers of corresponding intrinsic constitutions indicated also by other identifiable bodily signs. In effect, those who have same-sexual relations are thus constitutionally differentiated from other sexual sectors of humankind, to be studied and documented in their various aspects and subtypes. The categories, terminologies, and concepts used for that inquiry now and in early modernity differ.

Cocles's physiognomics of male same-sex lovers

While Cocles, unlike any other early modern physiognomer I know, at least frankly acknowledges sex between females,[29] he is one of sixteenth-century Europe's most extraordinary and extensive commentators on male same-sexual relations. Although accounts of fellatio are extremely rare in early modern print, even in the major proto-pornographic texts,[30] Cocles notes and deliberately breaks the prior silence of physiognomics on this subject in his brief chapter "On Fellators" (book 6, ch. 86). While allowing in conclusion that some are female, his comment assumes most are male, and advises they typically swallow the sperm. "This detestable vice is found in many," Cocles advises, "above all in a certain city of Italy, which I will not name." Fellators have certain distinctive signs. "When they see someone pleasing to them, they move their lips as if in action, like children (*pueri*) being breastfed." Their eyes become happy, their faces flush expectantly. Invoking fellatio's classical pedigree, Cocles quotes Martial's *Epigrammata*, 14.74: "Welcoming crow, why are you considered a fellator? In your head no penis has entered." Since the physiognomer applies the term "cinaedus" to fellators, he assumes it denotes males sexually penetrated in general, not just anally.

Aside from many incidental comments on cinaedi, male effeminacy, and pedicators,[31] Cocles dedicates two chapters to the former and one to the latter. Pedicators, he assumes in a telling simile, are as magnets to the cinaedi's iron: they really go together.[32] The *Anastasis* has two main segments – books 1 to 3 on physiognomy proper, books 4 to 6 on chiromancy – and each segment includes a chapter on cinaedi.

Book 1's general survey of physiognomics ends with a chapter headed, "Chapter 41 is philosophical statements in metaphors concerning . . . cinaedi." Cocles initially cites two main pronouncements about them from "Aristotle's" *Physiognomics* (now considered pseudonymous): they normally lean to the right in walking; second, their voices are high, soft, or cracking, like women's (808a, 813b). Cocles's subsequent commentary probably takes a further pseudo-Aristotelian dictum for granted: the brave man's carriage is erect (807a). From physiognomical standpoints that posture would have been normatively masculine, since females were supposedly timid. Cocles proceeds to reason that since heat rises and a male is relatively hot (*hoc de natura est calidus*), the cinaedus' bent or leaning posture reflects his leaning *from* masculine nature toward femininity. This trait is a complexional index of deviation in gender conformation and sexual affinity. For Cocles the cinaedus' relatively "soft" (*mollis*) and "moist constitution" (*complexio humida*) further conduce this leaning, presumably by impairing uprightness. The cinaedus' constitution is feminine relative to masculine norms, hence complexionally less hot and dry, Cocles assumes, and that physiological difference accounts for this sexual type's outward signs and definitive behaviors.

Now according to Aristotle's *Parts of Animals* 3.9, Cocles observes, the right side is naturally hotter, stronger, superior, and elevated; yet the cinaedus leans to and depresses his right, as if his left predominates. That further evinces effeminate complexional moisture and softness, for Aristotelians associated femininity with imperfection relative to natural norms, and the right was deemed masculine relative to the left.[33]

Then this prototypical sex researcher adds his own first-hand observations. "I see that such people have soft flesh, fine throats, effeminate and often slender legs, large soft ankles, pale faces, and quarrelsome dispositions, and many other signs." Another indicator is their relative comeliness, which appears "effeminate" because physiognomics assumed that female physiques evince charm and attractiveness rather than strength.[34] Pallor and softness were phlegmatic complexional traits, hence also relatively feminine (cool and moist).

Despite some ignorant authorities, Cocles declares, receptive roles in sex between males are not only favored by some boys (*pueri*):

> I have observed this passion in many "boys" 40, 50, 60, 65, and 70 years old. And currently a certain ruler who is imprisoned was so because of these matters. And there is a man of 60 from Lucca who leans to the left in walking, has a roseate lovely throat like a woman's, quarrelsome aspect, splendid coiffure, and soft voice. He is the utmost cinaedus and not a boy.[35]

For his time, Cocles's efforts to make and report his own observations were scientifically advanced. Not only disputing some current assumptions here, he notices and records an instance contrary to the presumed Aristotle's doctrine that cinaedi lean to the right. The physiognomer then presents extracts from Avicenna's medically prestigious *Liber canonis* that, in Cocles's view, recognize the existence of adult cinaedi and deal with them as males whose atypical sexual desires appear somehow mentally characteristic or physically constitutional.[36]

Finally Cocles addresses the supposed Aristotle's association of cinaedi with high or soft or cracking voices. Male voices normally undergo a process of change after childhood, Cocles explains, whereby they deepen with maturity and regularize at the lower level.[37] His implicit point is that cinaedi's contrary voices reflect the profound difference of their natures from normative masculinity. They either do not commence the voice-change process typical of masculinity (those with high or soft voices) or end mid-way, unresolved (cracking voices). Instead, their voices retain some prepubertal moist and smooth qualities. As we will see, Cocles assumes with Aristotle that all males prior to late adolescence are complexionally effeminate relative to adult males (e.g. book 6, ch. 76). The comparatively unchanging voices of cinaedi bespeak their distinctive developmental and sexual relation to an abiding physiological effeminacy.

Cocles's heading for this chapter stresses that it discusses cinaedi according to philosophical metaphors (*philosophi in methaphoricis*), and most of its details figure forth a type of male constitutional effeminacy that is sexually definitive. That condition not only produces bodily signs identifying the cinaedus, but accounts for his desires for receptive (hence perceivedly somewhat "feminine") sex, and for their continuation in maturity. The Coclean cinaedus is a complexional pseudo-hermaphrodite. The relatively fixed type Cocles explains here (he also posits a transitory one later) is constitutionally hot enough to be genitally male, but too moist, cool, or both for his appearance, behaviors, and amorous affinities to become normatively masculine.

For this physiognomer, the cinaedus and pedicator are complementary aspects of what his contemporaries Niccolò Leonico Tolomeo (1456–1531) and Lodovico Ricchieri (1469–1525) call "masculine love."[38] Cocles's book 6 surveys persons distinguished by certain behaviors, and the means to discern them according to their bodily signs, mainly chiromantic. In doing so he conjointly presents a further chapter on cinaedi and one on pedicators – chapters 76 and 77 – and the one on pedication follows its companion's rear. Their physical conjunction cannot be fortuitous, for book 6 has 328 chapters on various sexual and other topics. To Cocles, then, cinaedi and pedicators appeared correlative aspects of a general phenomenon of sex between males to be distinguished from other sexual behaviors. The chapter on fellators is presumably not contiguous because a minority, Cocles assumes, are female. For him, as for Leonico Tolomeo, Ricchieri, Jean Tixier (c.1475–1524), and Theodor Zwinger (1533–88), male same-sex lovers constituted a distinct erotic genus, in effect, with two main species: passive and active.[39] Many sodomites presumably had much more elaborate ideas about masculine love than these writers constrained by print and relative lack of experience. But in Cocles's view insertive and receptive male same-sexual affiliations arise from innate or currently prevalent temperaments legibly expressed by the subjects' bodies. Every trait he mentions in these chapters outwardly expresses and signifies a corresponding inner condition. Since he assumes readers have some knowledge of complexional physiology, the human body according to natural philosophy and medicine, and his preceding five books of physiognomical explications, his exposition is somewhat telegraphic.

Chapter 76 on cinaedi has two sections: the first discussing complexion and physical characteristics, the second presenting a case study. In general accord with Aristotelian natural philosophy, Cocles observes that all males younger than 20 have an effeminate physiological complexion to some extent, evinced by their habits, appetites, voices, and softness of flesh.[40] Until age 18 to 20, they continue to share somewhat in the humidity and relative coolness of female constitutions, but as they mature through adolescence, masculine heat increases (and would thus somewhat dry them). Masculine physiology involves a transitional effeminacy of complexion. But somehow, Cocles implies, that becomes sexually definitive in cinaedi, whether in adolescence alone or also thereafter. Cocles first reviews their five main chiromantic signs: "a swollen, coloured, and striped Mount of Venus"; a Mount of Venus cross-hatched by lines, like a chessboard; a Sister of the Line of Life "very prominent and red in the Mount of Venus"; "a continuous Milky Way with good proportion"; "a fleshy and red hand." Most of these signs evince excesses of moisture, sanguine humors, and venereal heat in the subjects' amorous constitutions. Then he adds physiognomical signs. Do the complexion, bodily composition, and lineaments appear effeminate? Are the lips and eyes notably "cheerful" (too gay, as it were)? Cocles had already discussed such perceivedly feminine complexional indicators elsewhere. Is the skin "white and bright with visible veins": so clear and translucent that some veins subtly appear, producing an interplay of white and red? He had earlier assigned such skin to the influence of the planet Venus, promoter of amorous sensuality (book 3, ch. 5). Women with this trait, he says, tend to be prostitutes. The variety of signs adduced implies that a particular physiognomical subject evinces a sample to be assessed *in toto* to determine his sexual affinities.

Then Cocles considers an exemplary problem of identification. Suetonius, Plutarch, Petrarch, and others say Julius Caesar was both a great adulterer and cinaedus, indeed "a man to all women and a woman to all men."[41] Yet some deny that Caesar could have been a cinaedus, since such males are effeminate and feminity is timid, whereas Caesar was brave. But there are two basic types of cinaedi, Cocles argues. One evinces a feminine aspect in fleshiness and color, yet with "width of chest and well-formed neck," and such a male, "lubricious" by nature, audaciously receives "lascivious actions in his back parts." He tends to cease doing so as his complexion masculinizes toward his twentieth year. But the second type, with a somewhat different coloring, evinces a "constriction of the chest and weakness of complexion, which causes faintheartedness and true effeminacy." Relative to supposed masculine norms, such a constricted chest and weak complexion (presumably too cold) would have indicated a permanent effeminacy arising from the intrinsic condition of the heart: in Aristotelian natural philosophy the body's principle of vital heat and hence the formative agent of embryonic differentiation in biological sex.[42] The heart was deemed the wellspring of courage, an ostensibly masculine trait,[43] while timidity was feminine, and cardiovascular physiology rationalized these gendered assumptions. Caesar's type of cinaedus was instead the transitional one.

Cocles further argues that masculine boldness and magnanimity arise in the eighteenth to twentieth year as males mature, their complexion changes, and constitutional heat predominates over moisture. Those who say Caesar's bravery shows he could never have been a cinaedus have disregarded the dynamics of human development, for the physiological complexion indicated by Caesar's courage postdates male adolescence and hence his youthful sexual behaviors. According to Suetonius,[44] Cocles adds, Caesar had the skin type associated with Venus that, in males, indicates a cinaedus: "a white . . . mixed from white and red" on account of its translucency, "veins . . . apparent but faint." Hence "he was full in all lasciviousness (*plenus omni lascivia*)," just as his sexual roles included receptive ones with men. According to Cocles's flexible scheme male receptivity to phallic penetration need not simply correspond to apparent gender inversion, but has additional configurations.

If a cinaedus, the physiognomer observes, were well proportioned in body, with "radiant eyes," the Venerean white skin, and "brown or black clothing" that is "shining and elegant" (dark colors accentuating this prized skin tone), he "would draw the hearts of pedicators to himself as a magnet draws iron (*attrahit ad se pediconum corda: ut magnes attrahit ferrum*)." Such considerations of appearance, Cocles adds, determine the attractiveness of male and female prostitutes, mistresses, and concubines.

Proceeding to report his own examinations of a young cinaedus similar to Caesar's type, Cocles finds much to admire, and nothing he says indicates the boy is a prostitute. In cinaedi Cocles seems to valorize an interplay of feminine and masculine traits, as opposed to feminization. The youth's body has good proportions, a proper, somewhat raised chest, distinct pectorals, firm flesh (a sanguine, masculine trait), and muscular definition. Yet he also has characteristics deemed feminine, such as blond hair, a small mouth, and small feet, and further displays the sanguine sensuality of full rosy lips and notably red tongue and palate. Both "celestial" and lustily "caprine," his shapely eyes with "handsome" lashes "laugh like boys' eyes when seeing things they desire."[45] And his skin has the

Venerean translucent whiteness that Cocles, a studied connoisseur of skin tones, treasures. This youth bashfully reddens when looked at, has modestly downcast eyes, some freckles, stammers slightly, and when he speaks, does so "sweetly," while his eyes and lips smile with his whole face. His knees press together a little, an age-old signifier of the cinaedus.[46] His hands epitomize the chiromantic signs that Cocles and others associated with the cinaedus and sodomitical behaviors: Mount of Venus "very much raised" and abundantly lined; continuous and intensely colored Sister of the Line of Life; continuous Milky Way; as well as the appropriate Girdle of Venus. Rather than being revolted by these hands, as physiognomers such as Cardano and Rothmann would have proclaimed,[47] Cocles sees much beauty. They are Venerean translucent white yet "muscular," "some lines flowed all around as stars," and some others are "most beautiful." As physiognomics had come to include genital examinations,[48] so Cocles finds the boy's penis "veiny, firm, and pointed at its top," "a hand's breadth in length, two inches in width," with "uneven testicles, . . . the right somewhat larger." His buttocks are "muscular and smooth, crevice finely formed (*intersticium formosū*)."

Thanks to this youth's special lozenges that he prepares himself, from gum-tragacanth softened with rose water, cane sugar, and fine musk, his breath has "pleasing, . . . excellent odor," Cocles reports, like "a rosy apple." When about to have intercourse "in his back parts," the boy sucks one of these, so as "thus to kiss the person joined to him." His erotic behaviors yield hints on amorous etiquette instructive for all tastes. Relative to early modern discursive norms for comment on sex between males, Cocles reports this with stunning equanimity. "Briefly by way of metaphor," his chapter concludes, the exemplary subject was "milk and blood compounded and in age sixteen years."

Though Cocles says nothing explicitly judgmental about cinaedi,[49] his following chapter on pedicators, the insertive partners, assumes they are more transgressive and morally responsible. He assumes cinaedi are often young, and though European standards in prosecuting sex between males varied, some allowances for youth tended to be made.[50] Venice treated youthful partners less severely than their lovers, and Florence most leniently.[51] Michael Rocke's study of fifteenth-century Florentine legal evidence showed that the anally receptive role in masculine love was usually linked there with males younger than 18 to 20.[52] Now Cocles enables us to see how that cultural phenomenon corresponded to certain natural philosophical assumptions. It was thus probably quite widespread in late medieval and early modern Europe. Those normative upper ages correspond precisely to Cocles's demarcation of complexionally and physically matured masculinity. According to the Aristotelian categorization of boys according to biological sex and gender affinity, they are all intermediate between female and male, for their bodies are comparable to women's and yet they have nascent or maturing male genitals and masculine potential.[53] Their status varies as they pass from the relatively feminine condition of childhood through the growth of their capacities for masculinity culminating, Cocles assumes, around ages 18 to 20. In that sense, all younger males to some extent appeared transitionally hermaphroditic in their complexion, physique, and general nature, while their youth was presumed to render them inherently lascivious. They amounted to a variously intermediate category of sex and gender, and for pedicators the desirability of male youths would have partly reflected that particular cultural status and its associated attributes. Pedicators themselves would have defined their own amorous affinities in terms of that somewhat paradoxically same-sexual attraction. But the manifestations and cultural expressions of such paradoxes are not only early modern, for Foucault and many others have stressed the relation of modern homosexuality to gender transitivities, inversions, and hermaphrodisms of the soul.[54]

For both Cocles and Tricasso, some male youths seemed more constitutionally apt to fulfill the same-sexual potential of this notionally intermediate category than others, and some of the former remained so even in maturity. Compared to males of correlative ages, Cocles assumes, the bodies of cinaedi evince distinctive modes of effeminacy that are sexually definitive: either the transitional Caesarian type that matures to become more conventionally masculine, or the enduringly effeminate one. Together forming a unique sexual species of male humankind, with further subspecies, these two basic types each have particular complexional implications, apparent, for instance, in the sanguine aspects of the case study, or the other type's constricted chest and heart.

Figure 7.4 Chiromantic sign of a pedicator susceptible to genital disease. Andreas Corvus, *Excellentissimi et singularis viri in chiromantia exercitatissimi Magistri Andree corui mirandulensis* (Lyon: Jean de Vingle, 1510), sig. I5b. By permission of the British Library.

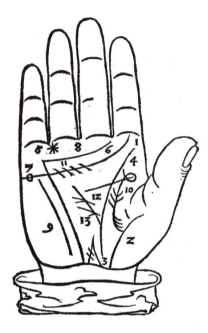

Figure 7.5 Chiromantic sign no. 7: a pedicator susceptible to genital disease.   Patricio Tricasso, *Enarratio pulcherrima principiorum chyromantiae* (Nurnberg: Apud I. Montanum & U. Neuberum, 1560), sig. Q2b. By permission of Houghton Library, Harvard University.

Cocles may well have assumed that, since receptive same-sexual relations are thus natural to cinaedi, they are somewhat exempt from harshly adverse judgment. His natural philosophical and medical readings in Aristotle, Avicenna, and Pietro d'Abano (1257–1315/6) could have led to such conclusions. Cocles's relatively uncritical portrayal of cinaedi does not simply result from allowances for youth. His captivating Eros of buggery has such marked temperamental propensities for sex "against nature" that, if he were later to cease being a cinaedus, he would most likely become a pedicator. He has the deviant Girdle of Venus, and, much as in Cocles's subsequent case study of a pedicator, the swollen Mount of Venus and strong Sister of the Line of Life. Also, since one of Cocles's two categories of cinaedi is constitutionally permanent and he recognizes many are adult, youth would not reduce their responsibility in all cases. But because the pedicator appeared more conventionally male, Cocles and others seem to have held him to a higher judgmental standard. Though his typically greater maturity relative to his sexual partners would have been a factor, masculinity was itself supposed to ensure stronger reason and self-control.[55] Yet the very complexional profiles that guaranteed pedicators' masculinity – particularly sanguine, according to Cocles's next case study – inclined them also to sodomitical transgressions, so that their condemnation was not logically consistent.

Chapter 77 addresses pedicators insofar as they are the insertive partners in primarily anal sex with boys (*pueri*).[56] Though the age range of boyhood was elastic,[57] 20 would be the likely upper limit here, since that is Cocles's ultimate border between complexional male youth and maturity, after which a male who had receptive sex would indubitably be an adult cinaedus. In treating sex between males, the *Anastasis* summarily delineates some main paradigms without seeking to be comprehensively systematic. Cocles assumes fellatio between males is common in chapter 86, for example, and allows for adult and even old cinaedi in book 1. What sorts of males had sex with them? Cocles does not say. On pedicators, he starts by summarizing the legal, medical, and social implications. "This vice is much condemned by the laws," he begins, "although Avicenna in the third book [of his *Liber canonis*] says that intercourse with boys (*pueris*) is less harmful" than with women, because the former drains less spermatic vital fluid.[58] Yet in the *Metaphysica*, Cocles adds, Avicenna says that since marriage conduces the maintenance of civil societies, the state should seek to prevent "fornication and sodomy."[59] However, the Arab would be shocked to find how much the sexual and other misdeeds of nominally Christian monks and nuns, including seduction of both boys and girls, have disturbed marital and civil order.

Cocles then reviews the chiromantic signs of male complexions conducive to sex with male youths. In males a Table Line divided near the end and reaching about to the index finger indicates aversion to women and love of boys (*inimicus mulierum: et amabit pueros*). If such a man were to have sex with a female virgin, her virginity in front would remain uncompromised. A man with a pit or trench in that line across from the fourth finger attracts and sexually misuses (*abutetur*) clerics or educated boys (compare Figures 7.4 and 7.5). Or if the Table Line has "thick and disordered fissures," that indicates "nefarious lust with boys" (presumably anal), "especially if its color is intense." A sign like an "E" beneath the ring finger signifies both coitus with boys and "nefarious lust" with women. A full, rounded Mount of Venus "moderately smooth and well colored signifies intercourse with boys" and "lust with women in the place of boys," so that women would assume the latter's sex roles.

"There are many deceivers who exclaim against pedicators with . . . curses," Cocles adds, but "act worst with boys in secret." And when or if such a man has sex with a woman, he "misuses" her, sometimes causing rectal damage: "a breaking of circles (*circulorum*)." Then a surgeon must be consulted and discovers the man's sexual tastes. Referring to his own surgical practice, Cocles declares he has encountered "many such," and medically treated women in this condition.[60] The physiognomer partly seeks to disseminate means to pierce the pretenses of abusive sexual hypocrisy.

A very strong Sister of the Line of Life in the Mount of Venus, he continues, "denotes the greatest inclination to sex with boys (*maximum inclinationem ad puerorū cōcubitus*)," especially if red (hence sanguine). Similarly a Line of Life with many parallel lines nearby. If small, forked lines extend from the thumb's base through its mount, the subject will have sex with that many boys, and thick clefts in the Table Line further signify pedication. The letter "D" on the Mount of Venus shows the subject is "filled with repulsive lust (*turpi luxuria*)": contextually pederastic.

The extent and type of pederastic inclination varies according to the indicator, as do those of disinclination toward sex with females. But Cocles's account of these signs assumes that pedicators tend to avoid vaginal sex. In antiquity, *pedico* meant "'bugger,' with object usually male, but sometimes female."[61] Some Coclean signs indicate only love of boys, one as a maximum commitment; others that anal sex with women may also occur; still others that a subject has such sex with boys or women, as if his partner's gender is insignificant so long as the penetration is not vaginal. Nevertheless, for the physiognomer pedication primarily involves sex between males, just as he arranges book 6, which has 328 chapters, to conjoin the two on cinaedi and pedicators.

Cocles then adduces his case study: a "sodomite" (*sodomitam*) whom the chiromancer considers "the worst, for he himself pretended to abhor such a vice." In the four chapters considered here – one on fellatio, two on cinaedi, and this one – the rhetoric of *sodomia*, fraught with theological and legal condemnation, only appears in this chapter, and does so twice.[62] Cocles could nonetheless take for granted that the cinaedus too would appear sodomitical from many viewpoints. The physiognomer's selection of his sample pedicator is deliberately somewhat contrary to type rather than representative. The subject has married and does not seem averse to vaginal intercourse with his wife. But he is nonetheless committed to pederasty.[63] Cocles may focus on this case because it has added interest, being atypical, or warns how deceptive marital appearances can be, or displays a particularly full or classic repertoire of bodily signs. "With his confidential friends he completely uncovered his nature," the physiognomer observes, "for he declared he had never deflowered virgins or committed adulteries with wives, so that his own [pederastic] pursuit (*studium*) has never been hindered." While appearing "most virtuous," then, this "distinguished" scholar and pedagogue has seduced numerous (*multis*) boys who sought his instruction. Their attachments to him have not been amorous, for they sought material or educational gains.[64] The scholar insisted that he did not obstruct procreation, Cocles reports, for he had taken a wife for that purpose and fathered "many sons," and he further maintained that neither his knowledge nor his abilities opposed his desire for boys. He "touched many and often," and assigned "the cause" of that "lascivious thing" to "natural disposition (*ingenium*), honor, and letters in the extreme."

This pedicator was resourcefully prepared to argue that pederasty honorably accorded with his own or human nature, and the ardent pursuit of humanist learning. If such desires were pursued without precluding reproduction, and frustrating the divine purpose of sexual capacities alleged by celibate theologians, how could sex between males be "against nature"? While apparently condemning such sex in *De amore*, the homophile Marsilio Ficino (1433–99) clarifies how its advocacy would have proceeded.[65] The male was deemed intellectually superior to the female, and could thus appear more apt for love. Much Greco-Roman literature and philosophy extolled the beauty and erotic desirability of male youths, so that, in the heady Platonizing atmosphere of the later Quattrocento, such desire could readily have seemed intrinsic to the humanistic rebirth of classical culture and learning. Cocles's intellectual sodomite would have grasped that current medical theory tended to naturalize such intergenerational sex between males, for it was not only thus a function of his own complexion, but the boys were either an intermediate sex, in effect, or in some cases even intrinsically cinaedi, and sexually eager by nature. Moreover, masculine health required periodic discharges of sperm, which otherwise turned poisonous.[66]

Reviewing the scholar's bodily attributes, Cocles finds his look "cheerful and pleasing," his face "large and fleshy," nose and lips "somewhat large." The complexion is a sanguine type, associated with sensuality: "hot and moist" (*calidam et humidam*). Insofar as the subject is hotter than the masculine norm, he is hypermasculine, and his many sons would have appeared to confirm that.[67] Generally attractive, his body is "hairy" (indicating strong, libidinous masculinity), its parts well formed, their fleshiness "everywhere muscled." His gait is measured and meditative, his "eyes cast down and charming, like boys looking at very desirable things." Cocles admires this man's "fleshy" hands. There are "lovely lines joined together as a glittering and flowering star." And marks associated with complexions conducive to pedication. The Mount of Venus has a long and strong Sister of the Line of Life, even "with triple proportion and intense color." There is "a lovely groove in the Mensal Line under the Auricular Mount": the little trench, pit, or *fossicula* that chiromancers associated with this sexual type (Figures 7.4–5).

Cocles's case study and general account of pedicators show that not only the receptive male sodomite but his insertive counterpart readily appeared a deviant sexual species with a repertoire of observable outer traits expressing the inner condition that conduced pedication. It too was a sign, in effect, of that distinctive interiority. Though recent sexual historiographies have often assumed that the insertive male sodomite did not appear particularly abnormal, inwardly perverse, or outwardly distinctive, to Cocles this constitutional morphology made sense around 1500, and he publicized it.[68]

In closing the chapter, Cocles declares "I do not praise such a man, for Christian theologians, the pagans likewise[69] and all laws . . . condemn him, for we ought to do everything to conserve human generation, and whosoever lives outside the divine standard should be cast away." Cocles affirms he has not said anything here to contradict other learned authorities, nor "those whose natures are elevated rather than debased." "If I have transgressed order in my chapters," he concludes, that was "for the increase of knowledge (*doctrine ampliatio*)." "In my six books [of the *Anastasis*] I have undertaken to record all things that could be said in this art for the full and useful satisfaction of all readers."

Though seeking to forestall criticism of his frankness, Cocles does not share many early modern writers' horror of sodomy, nor the intimidation implied by others' studied silence. He refuses to betray his science by excluding anything to which it applies. And his selection of these case studies challenges readers. The boy seems appealing and same-sexually desirous. The sample pedicator is a learned man of great talents yet a complexional "sodomite." Although the latter outwardly conforms to the sexual mores of his culture, no doubt to protect himself, he can contest them incisively whenever he wishes, and has a like-minded coterie. Cocles reports rather than suppresses his subject's sexually subversive thought. The physiognomer condemns adults who seduce male or female youths, and describes the pederastic scholar's behaviors and views with sarcastic verbal irony. Yet Cocles's position is complex and exploratory. His chapter on pedication begins by claiming that Avicenna says sex with boys is healthier, yet notes the civil value of marital controls upon sex, not just "sodomy" but "fornication" in general. So may pedication be no worse than adultery or premarital sex? Moreover, Cocles also records his exemplary pedicator's riposte: despite avid pursuits of male youths, this man has done his procreative marital duty. The physiognomer finally urges a religious objection, but the sodomitical humanist, implicitly appealing to Greco-Roman norms, has set that aside, and the chapter begins by condemning Christian sexual hypocrisy. Cocles writes in such a way as to invite freer thought about sex in general.

"That filthy beast": the Tricasso–Cocles controversy

The *Anastasis* is the only early modern physiognomical text to have been republished with a seriatim commentary. This was first printed in Latin then also Italian, both in 1525, and had several further editions.[70] However, the commentator, the Dominican monk Patricio Tricasso, omits books 1 to 3, deals solely with books 4 to 6 on chiromancy, and renumbers them 1 to 3 as republished with his commentary. As he no doubt hoped, this intervention strongly affected Cocles's reception. Tricasso's annotated text would have curtailed the market for further editions of the complete *Anastasis* by appearing in a relatively cheap format that seemed more accessible. The edition of Cocles's whole volume that had been published in 1523 was indeed to be its last. Typically appending a comment to each Coclean chapter, Tricasso is his author's avowed antagonist from the start and bowdlerizes him, so that this so-called commentary does not even reliably present the text discussed. His savaging of Cocles's passages on same-sexual relations reveals much about the possibilities of early modern responses to such topics within the discourses of natural and divinatory inquiry. In this section my references follow Tricasso's renumbering of Cocles's books on chiromancy (the latter's books 4, 5, and 6 now become 1, 2, and 3).

Although Tricasso had various objections to the *Anastasis*, and likely hoped to boost his chiromantic reputation and income by appearing to crush the most substantial "modern" authority, he had a profoundly personal animus against Cocles that most emerges whenever the latter discusses female or male same-sexual relations. Those are the passages Tricasso bowdlerizes: incest, female prostitution, homicide, and adultery are relatively uncontroversial. This procedure begins in book 1, question 11, "The Signs of Nefarious Lust on a Woman's Hands."[71] Tricasso's comment begins thus: "All the pleasure and recreation of this filthy and dirty beast [i.e. Cocles] persisted solely in filth and dirt and shamefulness, and especially with boys. If this beast had known worse actions of such a kind he would have adduced them also." The insinuations "especially" include pederasty. On the sexual actions that Cocles reports in this question, Tricasso sarcastically announces he will include some in his commentary's more generally accessible

Italian version, yet others he will "cover in shadow," not just "to remove [them] from women" (much more likely to read a vernacular language than Latin), but also "in consideration of the dignity of that beast." Thus he will render mock-tribute to Cocles's reputation by striking scandalous passages from his text. The Italian version indeed abbreviates Cocles's discussion here, while erasing its reference to sex between females. Even the commentator's Italian definition of "nefarious lust" as "any kind of sex except what accords with the usual order and course of nature" (that is, penis ejaculating in vagina) mentions just incest and, euphemistically, masturbation ("when they make the best that they can").[72]

Likewise, in question 6 of book 1, Tricasso's Italian silently compresses a Coclean passage on "cinaedi" so that they become "those that suffer [i.e. allow themselves to be sexually penetrated] in a lost fashion." But in that context Cocles had been relatively detached and scientifically informative:

> These are men who are said to suffer "alluminati." Indeed those are the men who cannot copulate without submitting to another's lust [i.e. being penetrated]. And Avicenna recounts the true cause in the particular chapter [on this subject] in [his *Canon's*] book 3. As it is related in [my] First Book of Physiognomy [i.e. ch. 41].[73]

When Tricasso comes to Cocles's companionate chapters on the cinaedus and pedicator, he follows the same procedure (book 3, chs. 76–7). His Latin and Italian texts present Cocles's general discussion of cinaedi but erase the whole case study of the youth, as well as the preceding sentence on attractive cinaedi as magnets to the pedicators' iron. Tricasso's brief Latin comment ends sarcastically: "*having experience* (perhaps), he shows off his holy trinkets in this chapter and following ones" (my emphasis).[74] The Italian comment makes similar same-sexual insinuations. In both the Latin and Italian versions, Tricasso finally refers readers to his comment on Cocles's eleventh question in book 1,[75] which calls Cocles a filthy beast, and avows sexual censorship of his text.

Tricasso truncates Cocles's chapter on pedicators so that it just summarizes nine chiromantic signs of such a complexion in the Latin, and little more in Italian. Tricasso's Italian comment summarizes his Latin broadside:

> I think that Cocles is more pig than man. And furthermore he does not delight in anything but dirtiness and maledictions, and . . . ribaldries. And in the beginning this pig pretends that he abominates this vice, yet nevertheless in the beginning as well as throughout the chapter he tolerates, praises, and glorifies it.

Tricasso alleges that Cocles's initial censure of pedication is a hoax exposed by his inclusion of neutral or positive material. The commentator provides a few brief pointers on the signs distinguishing pedicators, then in the Latin text closes with the proverb *intelligenti pauca*: this is enough for the prudent, who will seek to know no more about such persons and sexual pursuits.

Tricasso's abuse of Cocles when the latter addresses same-sexual relations does not result from any basic intellectual disagreements about physiognomics. Both assume that individuals are distinctively characterized by specific sexual inclinations and behaviors, and that these are functions of complexional and astrological factors physically evinced in various signs that can and should be publicly codified. They both consider sex between males accordingly. Commenting on Cocles's discussion of cinaedi, his nemesis agrees that all males prior to 20 are somewhat betwixt masculinity and feminity (book 3, ch. 76). As Cocles himself implies by surveying the signs of cinaedi, Tricasso adds that "not all" young males "are of equal complexion," for some are thus constitutionally "more inclined than others" to such sex. Broadly agreeing with Cocles on the particular signs that identify cinaedi and pedicators, Tricasso only cautions that chiromantic assessment should be based on a number of concurrent signs and stresses that some have more than one possible meaning. Cocles would not have disagreed on either point. Tricasso too catalogues the signs of pedicators and cinaedi (the latter quite vaguely) in his own Latin texts on chiromancy.[76] But unlike Cocles, Tricasso's treatment is aphoristically tight-lipped. His Italian handbooks on chiromancy become far more vague and general on such matters ("nefarious lust," "abominable lust"), presumably to address the broader vernacular readership with greater restraint.[77]

Intelligenti magna

Much of the Tricasso–Cocles controversy revolves around considerations of decorum as they affect the study of sex and sexual affinities within the natural and divinatory domains, particularly in print. This conceptual and methodological schism within early modern physiognomics exposes former cultural barriers obstructing same-sexual inquiries in the sciences generally.

For Cocles, the scope of his inquiries legitimately embraces all human behaviors, however anathematized, and the investigator is to enhance understanding of those phenomena. His numerous citations of the physician, philosopher, astrologer, and physiognomer Pietro d'Abano, whose likewise wide-ranging intellectual curiosity earned him a posthumous immolation for heresy that Cocles contests in the *Anastasis*, show that Pietro profoundly inspired Cocles's attitudes and methods. Though the latter presses his published sexual inquiries very far indeed for his time, precedents existed in ancient and late medieval physiognomics, the supposed Aristotelian corpus (most of all book 4 of the *Problemata*),[78] Avicenna, and Pietro, besides the antique astrologers Ptolemy and Firmicus Maternus, among others. Unlike most other early modern writers, Cocles pursued such leads energetically and in print.

Yet although his diverse sexual inquiries included identifying and studying a range of sodomites, even he felt restricted by publication. At various points his comments indicate that his full knowledge of same-sexual relations exceeds what he has committed to print, so that his proposed schemes and taxonomies are deliberately provisional. He closes the second chapter of his sequential pair on cinaedi and pedicators with efforts to forestall religious and moral criticism, and urge that reportage of this same-sexual research is proper to the enhancement of knowledge. That may be the first such claim by an early modern author in print.[79]

Though Tricasso insinuates that Cocles himself enjoyed sex with males, the latter's same-sexual discussions seem credibly distanced, and his gestures of disapproval spontaneous rather than posed. Cocles's account of the 16-year-old cinaedus would not likely have been so relaxed if he had wished to hide sodomitical practices of his own. His freer exploration of same-sexual issues seems motivated by his manifest interest in gossip, broad intellectual curiosity, fascination with human diversity, commitment to studying it at first hand, and belief in the legitimate sexual scope of natural and divinatory inquiry. These are Coclean traits evident throughout the *Anastasis*, not specific to his treatment of sodomy. Yet physiognomics partly sought to enhance its adherents' social power by disclosing others' personal secrets. While Cocles's comments on cinaedi are relatively mild, he deplores pedicators' hypocritical pretenses and covert seductions of male youths, so that his inventory of pedicators' signs presumably aims to provide means of exposure. But physiognomers could not control the uses to which their discipline was put. A sodomite could seek to use the *Anastasis* to identify boys likely to enjoy masculine love, for example, while a cinaedus with a taste for large penises could likewise seek such men.

For the monk Tricasso, on the other hand, the disciplines of natural and divinatory knowledge must maintain far more discretion, and same-sexual relations are simply abominable. He is relatively unperturbed by Cocles's comments on incest, female prostitution, adultery, and masturbation. But in contexts addressing same-sexual relations, Tricasso's phobic reactions and excisions demonstrate homophobia's premodern foundations in what we may call "sodomophobia."[80] For Tricasso, Cocles wantonly betrayed an obligatory code of self-censorship and made himself a deserving scapegoat, for his discussions of sodomitical phenomena seemed too exploratory, hence ambiguous, evocative, and potentially subversive. From Tricasso's viewpoint, the material he expunges from the *Anastasis* so violates the sexual decorums of learned inquiry that its circulation must be curtailed while its scandalous author is held to account. Sodomitical types can be acknowledged in Tricasso's commentary and Latin chiromantic manuals, but only in a censoriously closed rather than open-ended manner, not in ways that might possibly occasion sympathy, questioning of conventional condemnations, apparent humanization, or erotic interest. For Tricasso, Cocles's relatively open way of treating same-sexual topics sodomizes natural and divinatory knowledge, implies covert sodomitical practice, and demands public vilification.

The cultural taboo of sodomy likewise tended to stifle same-sexual researches and reportage across the entire range of late medieval and early modern sciences.[81] Such projects could certainly be conceived and pursued. Collating the resources of medical, natural philosophical, astrological, and physiognomical disciplines with his own first-hand observations, Cocles sought to codify and publicize the basic morphologies and constitutions of various sodomitical types c.1500. But if an investigator were to show what might seem too much knowledgeable interest in such sexual phenomena in print, he could come to appear sodomitically tainted himself. Tricasso's attack on Cocles in 1525 epitomizes that danger: *"intelligenti pauca."* The growing official repression of sexual freedoms across Europe following the advent of syphilis in the 1490s, the Reformation, and the Counter-Reformation would only have increased constraints upon applications of the sciences to same-sexual phenomena.

Both Tricasso's and Cocles's distinct approaches to dealing with sexual physiognomics in print had early modern followers and counterparts. Particularly in vernacular treatises, various writers on physiognomy and chiromancy surpassed even Tricasso in suppressing their disciplines' same-sexual lore and applications. Their citations include ancient and Neo-Latin treatises involving such discussion, yet ignore it.[82]

Other exponents of physiognomics were much more open to acknowledging the full range of sexual inclinations and behaviors, and yet, among them, no one offered reportage as open, frank, and deliberately observant as Cocles's, and his proto-sexological development of the discipline remained unequalled. What physiognomers were willing to say in print would have differed from their oral and investigative practices. Michelangelo Biondo (1497–1565), Cardano, Jean Taisnier (1508/9–62?), Antonio Piccioli (fl. 1587), and Giambattista della Porta (1535?–1615) all display some relative sexual frankness.[83] This aspect of their intellectual and discursive conduct would likely have been influenced by their reading of Cocles, whom they all cite, engage, or in some cases plagiarize. Providing a long chapter on chiromantic signs of the diverse types of lust, Taisnier takes much on cinaedi and sodomites from Cocles.[84] Porta parallels Cocles in devoting chapters to discussion of cinaedi, yet provides different information.[85] However, unlike Cocles, who breezily discusses fellatio and "receiving in the back parts," as we have seen, both Taisnier and Porta avoid mentioning specific sexual acts. Tricasso's abuse of Cocles would have tended to deter others from developing his free-ranging kind of sexual physiognomics further.

Moreover, after Cocles's *Anastasis* was published in 1504, censorship of print progressively increased and the Inquisition was founded. Not only theologically heretical, antipapal, lascivious, or obscene writings came to be at issue, but the divinatory sciences in general, for they appeared to compromise divine providence, free will, and human moral responsibility by claiming to predict the future and by treating personal characteristics and inclinations as functions of bodily constitution. Beginning in the 1550s various printed Indexes of Prohibited Books particularly condemned Cocles and some other notable exponents of learned divination (including Tricasso, ironically), while including predictive physiognomics in the general condemnations of all divinatory books.[86] Sixtus VI further condemned the divinatory sciences in the papal bull *Coeli et Terrae* in 1586. Both Cardano and Porta, for example, had major difficulties with censors and the Inquisition, and c.1571 Cardano was forbidden to publish further. The Indexes and the papal anathema forced writers on physiognomics to become more defensively concerned with apologetics and pursuit of respectability. Like medical texts, these books were partly marketing tools for the authors' professional services, and that purpose promoted discretion in addressing controversial sexual topics, particularly sodomy.[87]

Nevertheless, Cocles had much sixteenth-century impact intertextually and otherwise, and was still cited in the seventeenth.[88] From his viewpoint, inquiry into all sexual phenomena is wholly legitimate, admissible for learned discussion in print, and yields knowledge worthy of accumulation, collation, and transmission. He gave male same-sexual affiliations an influential public articulation according to his considerable medical, natural, divinatory, and experiential resources, at some remove from the repressive standpoints of theology and law. In 1571 Thomas Hill published an English physiognomical text drawing on the continental Coclean vernacular epitomes and including a good many comments on cinaedi from the *Anastasis* itself, while anglicizing "cinaedus" as "cyned." Cocles to some extent animated the sixteenth-century currency and conceptualization of this same-sexual term in English vernacular as well as European Latin discourse.[89] The recent demolition of a wall in a Spanish house dating from this period revealed a cache of eleven books hidden from Inquisitorial depredations c.1560. Among them was found, in a fascinating conjunction, books 4 to 6 of Cocles's *Anastasis* in Tricasso's Latin version with commentary, and a manuscript copy of Antonio Vignali's frankly sodomitical *La cazzaria*.[90] The *Anastasis* was one of the main contemporary sources that discussed the varieties of sexual affiliation and experience from a scientific standpoint. The man who hid these books, it is thought, was a Spaniard who had lived in Italy, sympathetic to masculine love.[91]

Notes

1. Foucault, *The History of Sexuality*, vol. 1, *An Introduction*, tr. Robert Hurley, New York: Vintage, 1980, p. 43.
2. On this controversial "acts paradigm," see Ch. 1, this volume.
3. For an overview and bibliography of ancient and early modern physiognomics in relation to sexual history, see Kenneth Borris (ed.), *Same-Sex Desire in the English Renaissance: A Sourcebook of Texts, 1470–1650*, New York: Routledge, 2004, ch 5. Also Joseph Ziegler, "Sexuality and the Sexual Organs in Latin Physiognomy 1200–1500," *Studies in Medieval and Renaissance History*, 3rd ser. 2 (2005), 83–108; Michael Camille, "The Pose of the Queer: Dante's Gaze, Brunetto Latini's Body," in Glenn Burger and Steven F. Kruger (eds), *Queering the Middle Ages*, Minneapolis: University of Minnesota Press, 2001, pp. 57–86.
4. As in e.g. the pseudo-Aristotelian *Physiognomics* that had much late medieval and early modern influence. See Maud W. Gleason, *Making Men: Sophists and Self-Presentation in Ancient Rome* Princeton: Princeton University Press, 1995, chs 2–5.
5. Francesco Casoni, *De indiciis et tormentis tractatus duo*, Cologne: Johann Wickede, 1594, tractate 1, chs 6–9; tractate 10, chs 7–9. 1st edn 1557 or before. Casoni does not discuss same-sexual applications specifically. Cf. Richard Saunders, *Physiognomie and Chiromancie, Metoposcopie*, London, 1653, Wing S754, p. 16.
6. E.g. Alan Bray, *Homosexuality in Renaissance England*, 2nd edn, New York: Columbia University Press, 1995, ch. 1 (e.g. p. 25). Likewise the first edition (1982).
7. In Renaissance usage a "cinaedus" was a male who enjoyed being sexually penetrated. Some cinaedi might also enjoy being sexually insertive, possibly with females too. The penetration was typically presumed to be anal, though it could possibly be oral, as in Cocles's own usage. See further Ch. 1, n. 75.

8. Though allowing that some pedicators may also have anal sex with females, and even procreate, Cocles strongly associates the term with insertive roles in sex with cinaedi or seduced boys. Reflecting cultural change, such as the conceptual invention of sodomy and its minoritizing, "othering" effects, his usage of the term is narrower than the ancients'. Compare J. N. Adams, *The Latin Sexual Vocabulary*, London: Duckworth, 1982; Craig A. Williams, *Roman Homosexuality*, Oxford: Oxford University Press, 1999, general index, *s.v.* "pedicare."

9. Based on my survey of over 100 Neo-Latin, Italian, French, and English physiognomical texts printed between 1475 and 1700.

10. Cardano, *Libelli duo*, Nuremburg: Apud Jo. Petreium, 1543, no. XVIII.

11. The complete *Anastasis* had Latin edns in 1503/4, 1515, 1517, and 1523. Patricio Tricasso republished books 4 to 6, on chiromancy, in bowdlerized Latin and Italian versions that had various printings beginning in 1525. A flood of unauthorized physiognomical books under Cocles's name appeared in German, Latin, Italian, French, and English between c.1511 and 1700. Though their relationships to the *Anastasis* are still unclear, Lynn Thorndike proposes that most are epitomes, in effect, summarizing book 1 up to ch. 25. See his *A History of Magic and Experimental Science*, 8 vols, New York: Columbia University Press, 1927–58, vol. 5, pp. 63–5; and NUC pre-1956. Martin Porter claims these texts actually reproduce Michael Scot's physiognomy. But he offers no evidence, and dates their vernacular inception far too late. Thomas Hill's 1571 English version of the epitome/s contains unique Coclean observations from the *Anastasis* up to the end of book 1 and even into book 2 (see n. 89 below). Porter, *Windows of the Soul: Physiognomy in European Culture 1470–1780*, Oxford: Clarendon Press, 2005, p. 123. J. M. de Bujanda *et al.* (eds) also seek to clarify Cocles's complex publication history in *Index des livres interdits*, 10 vols, Sherbrooke: Centre d'études de la Renaissance, 1984–96, vol. 5, pp. 316-18, vol. 8, pp. 291–2. Their Italian edns of the *Anastasis* are actually Tricasso's version (see above), and their German edns are probably epitomes (vol. 5, p. 318).

12. On complexional physiology, see Ch. 1, this volume. I use "complexion" and its cognates in this temperamental sense throughout this chapter.

13. On astrology's relation to physiognomics, see Ch. 1, this volume; on astrology, Chs 8–9.

14. Cardano, *Libelli duo*, no. XVIII.

15. Brian P. Copenhaver, "Astrology and Magic," in Charles B. Schmitt *et al.*, eds, *The Cambridge History of Renaissance Philosophy*, Cambridge: Cambridge University Press, 1988, p. 271.

16. Cf. Thorndike, *History*, vol. 5, pp. 50–65. Also Elisa Ruiz García and E. Sánchez Solar, introductions, in Patricio Tricasso, *Comentarios clarisimos sobre la quiromancia de Cocles hechos por Tricasso de Mantua*, 2 vols, Mérida: Regional de Extremadura, 2000, vol. 2, pp. 9–102. Use Solar with caution. He claims e.g. Andreas Corvus was Cocles's principal source for book 6 (book 3 in Tricasso's edn), without (as Solar admits) having examined Corvo's text (vol. 2, pp. 86, 89). It is totally different.

17. Cf. Ch. 1, this volume.

18. Cf. Charles S. F. Burnett, "The Earliest Chiromancy in the West," *Journal of the Warburg and Courtauld Institutes*, 50 (1987), 189–95. On premodern sources, see Thorndike, *History*; and (less reliably) Gino Sabattini, *Bibliografia di opere antiche e moderne di chiromanzia e sulla chiromanzia*, Reggio Emilia: Nironi & Prandi, 1946.

19. Gregor Reisch, *Margarita philosophica*, Basel: J. Schottus, 1508, sig. 2O4^b. Indexed under "*Sodomia*." On Zacchia, see Ch. 4, this volume.

20. On "sodomy," see Ch, 1, nn. 19, 22.

21. As in the learned physiognomics typical of the later fifteenth and sixteenth centuries. This tradition began to break down in the seventeenth century; variant theories developed, such as Marin Cureau de La Chambre's, while the older ones persisted.

22. Cocles, *Chyromantiae ac physionomie anastasis*, Bologna: Per Joannem Antonium Platonidem Benedictorum, 1504, book 2, q. 20; emphasis mine. Since the questions and chapters are short, I dispense with page references. Most translations are Meredith Donaldson Clark's, otherwise collaborative or mine.

23. See further Ch. 1, this volume.

24. See Borris (ed.), *Same-Sex Desire*, pp. 179–84.

25. E.g. Jean Taxil, *L'astrologie et la physiognomie en leur splendeur*, Tournon: R. Reynaud, 1614, pp. 112ff.

26. Cf. Saunders, *Physiognomie*, pp. 5–6.

27. Breedlove *et al.*, "Finger-Length Ratios and Sexual Orientation," *Nature*, 404 (2000), 455–6.

28. Ibid., p. 455.

29. Borris (ed.), *Same-Sex Desire*, pp. 182, 185–6.

30. Cf. Ian Frederick Moulton, "Introduction," in Antonio Vignali, *La cazzaria: The Book of the Prick*, ed. and tr. Moulton, New York: Routledge, 2003, pp. 48–9. Michael Rocke concludes that fellatio was "fairly widely employed in [male] homoerotic relations in Florence." Cf. *Forbidden Friendships: Homosexuality and Male Culture in Renaissance Florence*, Oxford: Oxford University Press, 1996, index, *s.v.* "sexual practices between males – fellatio" (quoting p. 93).

31. These remain to be fully studied, for the *Anastasis* is long, complex, and demanding.

32. Contrast Rocke, who claims that pedicators and cinaedi had little in common, less indeed than pedicators and men who penetrated women. *Forbidden Friendships*, p. 14. Yet he observes the mutual pleasures and attachments of males who had sex together, pp. 94, 129, 167, 172, 190. See Borris (ed.), *Same-Sex Desire*, p. 374, n.32.

33. Cf. Ian Maclean, *The Renaissance Notion of Woman*, Cambridge: Cambridge University Press, 1980, pp. 2–3, 30–2, 44–5.

34. E.g. Pseudo-Aristotle, *Physiognomics*, 809b, 810a.

35. On Florentine legal records of adult cinaedi, see Rocke, *Forbidden Friendships*, pp. 101–5, 129, 207, 233–4.

36. For Avicenna's text, cf. Borris (ed.), *Same-Sex Desire*, pp. 128–9. Cocles equates Avicenna's discussion here with cinaedi, males who enjoy having receptive sex with males, and does so repeatedly in the *Anastasis*. For Jacques Despars, c.1450, the application of Avicenna's passage may have been less straightforward (Ch. 2, this volume).

37. Compare Aristotle, *Generation of Animals*, 776b, 787b–788b.

38. Cf. Borris (ed.), *Same-Sex Desire*, pp. 6–8, 205–8.

39. Ibid., pp. 204–23, on Tixier and Zwinger. Rocke, e.g., contrarily assumes that early modern male "actives" and "passives" appeared to have little in common. *Forbidden Friendships*, p. 14. But they were not so represented in these and other texts. See above, n. 32.

40. Aristotle assumes "a boy . . . resembles a woman in physique" and begins to become differentiated at puberty as masculine heat increases and enables concoction of sperm. *Generation of Animals*, 728a, tr. A. L. Peck.

41. Suetonius, *Divus Iulius*, 49–52. Cocles may mean that Plutarch and Petrarch confirm Caesar's particular skin color. Plutarch's *Life of Caesar* does not comment on his sex life, but says his skin was white and soft (17.2). Petrarch's long life of Caesar appears to ignore the claims he was a cinaedus in youth, but acknowledges his notably white skin (*candidus*). Francesco Petrarca, *De viris illustribus vitae*, ed. Luigi Razzolini, 2 vols, Bologna: Romagnoli, 1879, pp. 656–60.

42. Aristotle, *Generation of Animals*, 734b–735a, 740a, 766a–b.

43. E.g. Plato, *Timaeus*, 70A–D.

44. Suetonius, *Divus Iulius*, 45: *colore candido*, a shining, clear white, contrary to the perceivedly unattractive "alban" dull white. For Cocles, the former corresponds to his Venerean translucent white.

45. The narrow (or possibly sunken) caprine eye indicated a most lustful nature. Cf. Lodovico Ricchieri (Caelius Rhodiginus), *Lectionum antiquarum libri triginta*, Frankfurt: Apud heredes A. Wecheli, C. Marnium, I. Aubrium, 1599, ch. 10 (pp. 680–1). 1st edn 1516.

46. Cf. pseudo-Aristotle, *Physiognomics*, 808a, 810a. W. S. Hett's Loeb edn translates the Greek equivalent of "cinaedus" as "morbid" or "lustful."

47. Compare Cardano, *De utilitate*, in *Opera omnia*, vol. 2, Leiden: Sumptibus Ioannis Antonii Huguetan & Marci Antonii Ravaud, 1663, p. 178b; Johann Rothmann, *Chiromantiae, theorica, practica concordantia genethliaca*, Erfurt: Joannes Pistorius, 1595, fol. 17b.

48. Cf. Ziegler, "Sexuality and the Sexual Organs," pp. 87–94.

49. The perceived effeminacy of cinaedi may be implicitly pejorative, since physiognomics privileged masculinity. Although ch. 76 on cinaedi closely follows ch. 74 on female prostitutes, so too does the one on pedicators.

50. Cf. Borris (ed.), *Same-Sex Desire*, pp. 75–86.

51. Guido Ruggiero, *The Boundaries of Eros: Sex Crime and Sexuality in Renaissance Venice*, Oxford: Oxford University Press, 1985, pp. 110, 118, 121–5; Rocke, *Forbidden Friendships*, pp. 51–2, 68, 82, 101–2, 232–3.

52. Ibid., pp. 88, 95, 101, 113–19.

53. Aristotle, *Generation of Animals*, 728a. Compare Guglielmo Gratarolo: women's "nature is similar to that of boys." *De praedictione morum naturarumque hominum facili*, in *Opuscula*, Basel: Nicolaus Episcopius, 1554, p. 92.

54. Foucault, *Sexuality*, vol. 1, p. 43, whence that last phrase. Compare David Halperin, *How to Do the History of Homosexuality*, Chicago: University of Chicago Press, 2002, p. 169 n. 45.

55. See Maclean, *Renaissance Notion of Woman*, *passim*; e.g. pp. 49–52.

56. Although *puer* can mean either "boys" or "children" when plural, Cocles focuses ch. 77 on adult male sex with boys. *Pueri* patently means boys in the chapter on cinaedi in book 1 (ch. 41), and the chapter on pedicators in book 6 follows one on cinaedi (by definition male). Its case study is a scholar who seduces his students, who would have been male. On Florentine usage of *puer* in sodomy cases, cf. Rocke, *Forbidden Friendships*, pp. 115–16.

57. See Borris (ed.), *Same-Sex Desire*, pp. 20–1.

58. Compare Ch. 2, this volume, on earlier representations of this passage in Avicenna. For Cocles it contextually applies to boys, whether wholly or in part.

59. Avicenna, *Metaphysica sive prima philosophia*, Venice, 1495; repr. Frankfurt: Minerva, 1966, book 10, ch. 4.

60. On early modern anal sex with women and resultant injuries, see Ruggiero, *Boundaries of Eros*, pp. 117–21. Further references in Chs. 1 and 4, this volume, re Zacchia.

61. Adams, *Latin Sexual Vocabulary*, p. 123.

62. Premodern Florentines usually reserved "sodomite" for the anally insertive, mature partner. Cf. Rocke, *Forbidden Friendships*, pp. 14, 24, 110. However, it does not follow that "men who sodomized boys and men who penetrated women had more of a common character and identity than did two males who coupled sexually" (p. 14). E.g. unlike men who did not sodomize, men who did so together were sodomites in a particular sense – an important distinction in early modern Europe. Cf. nn. 32, 39, above.

63. On premodern Florentine sodomites' marriages of convenience, see Rocke, *Forbidden Friendships*, pp. 41, 119, 127–32. "The magistrates charged with policing sodomy were much more likely to convict single men than husbands" (p. 131).

64. This is not a universal pattern, for Cocles recognizes e.g. constitutional cinaedi, who would have had various motivations. On mutual desire and the role of gifts in Florentine intergenerational same-sexual relations at this time, see Rocke, *Forbidden Friendships*, pp. 94, 129, 165–72, 190.

65. See Borris (ed.), *Same-Sex Desire*, pp. 260–71.
66. E.g. Johannes de Ketham (attr.), *Fasciculus medicinae*, tr. Luke Demaitre, Birmingham, AL: Gryphon–Classics of Medicine, 1988, p. 50. First printed 1491.
67. From an Aristotelian and Avicennan perspective, the male seed is the active principle in procreation, so that the conception of a female betokens some failure of the seed to beget its like. Siring many boys thus betokened dominant masculinity. I thank Faith Wallis for consultation on this.
68. For attribution of such perceived conventionality to the insertive sodomite, see e.g. Halperin, *History of Homosexuality*, pp. 113–16; compare p. 169 n. 44. Likewise Rocke, *Forbidden Friendships*, p. 14. Cocles's contrary account builds on prior traditions; see Joseph Ziegler, "Sexuality and the Sexual Organs," pp. 83–108.
69. E.g. Plato's *Laws*, Maximus of Tyre, and the Augustan *Lex Julia*, formerly alleged to have proscribed all sex between males. Here Cocles ignores pagan homoerotic advocacy. Compare Johannes Thuilius's citations, in Borris (ed.), *Same-Sex Desire*, pp. 48–9.
70. E.g. Latin: Venice, 1525; Mantua, 1525. Italian: Venice, 1525; 1531, 1535.
71. Compare *Anastasis*, book 4, q. 10, tr. in Borris (ed.), *Same-Sex Desire*, pp. 185–6. Tricasso, *Super chyromantiam Coclytis dillucidationes praeclarissimae*, Venice: Helisabetta de Rusconi, 1525. Since most chapters are short, I dispense with page references. I thank Meredith Donaldson Clark for assistance with translations.
72. Tricasso, *Expositione del Tricasso Mantuani sopra il Cocle*, Venice: Helisabetta de Rusconi, 1525. Since most chapters are short, I dispense with page references. I thank Nicola Martino for assistance with Italian translations.
73. "Alluminati" is a Latinized variant of Avicenna's Arabic term for this, alternatively Latinized as "alguagi" or "alubuati." Cf. Ch. 2, this volume.
74. "Et ex experientia (fortassis) iam habita. in hoc cap. & sequēti multu[m] phylateria amplat." Hans Ramminger informs me that "phylateria amplat" implies showing off on account of the reception traditions surrounding pharisaical display in Matthew 23:5.
75. *Anastasis*, book 4, q. 10.
76. E.g. Tricasso, *Enarratio pulcherrima principiorum chyromantiae*, Nurnberg: Johann vom Berg & Ulrich Neuber, 1560, e.g. sigs. P1a, Q1a, Q3a–4a, R4a, S2a, 2A3a, etc. De Bujanda *et al.* seek to unravel the publication histories, relationships, and variant titles of his chiromantic books in *Index des livres interdits*, vol. 8, pp. 304–6 (omitting Tricasso's Cocles commentary).
77. Tricasso, *Epitoma chyromantico*, Venice: Agostino de Bindoni, 1538; *Chyromantia del Tricasso*, Venice, 1534.
78. Cf. Ch. 3, this volume.
79. On medieval precursors, see Joan Cadden, "'Nothing Natural Is Shameful': Vestiges of a Debate about Sex and Science in a Group of Late-Medieval Manuscripts," *Speculum*, 76 (2001), 66–89.
80. See Borris (ed.), *Same-Sex Desire*, pp. 18–20, 23–35, 73–86, 204.
81. Cf. Cadden, "Vestiges of a Debate."
82. E.g. Saunders's *Physiognomie* almost omits same-sexual relations altogether, yet nonetheless cites authors such as Cocles, Jean Taisnier (see below), and Firmicus Maternus, who provide much information on that (e.g. sig. A1b, pp. 48–9). Saunders largely translates Jean Belot. Some physiognomers maintained that deliberate silence even in Neo-Latin, such as the priest Johannes ab Indagine.
83. Biondo, *De cognitione hominis per aspectum*, Rome: Apud Antonium Bladum Asulanum, 1544. For Cardano, see Chs 9–10, this volume, and his posthumously published *La metoposcopie*, tr. Sieur Claude Martin de Laurendière, Paris: T. Jolly, 1658, also published in Latin, 1658. See Figure 1.2. Piccioli, *De manus inspectione libri tres*, Bergamo: J. B. Ciotti, 1587. Much of his p. 29 e.g. draws on Cocles's *Anastasis*, book 4, q. 10.

84. Taisnier, *Opus mathematicum octo libros complectens*, Cologne: Apud Theodorum Baumium, 1583. 1st publ. 1562. See Figures 1.3–5.

85. Porta, *De humana physiognomonia*, Vico Equense: Apud Josephum Cacchium, 1586, book 4, ch. 11. Porta expanded this discussion in later edns. For comment and translation, see Borris (ed.), *Same-Sex Desire*, pp. 191–5. Much incidental comment on cinaedi appears in book 2. See also Porta, *Coelestis physiognomonia*, ed. Alfonso Paolella, Naples: Edizioni Scientifiche Italiane, 1996, vol. 4, chs 20–1.

86. Cf. de Bujanda *et al.* (eds), *Index des livres interdits*, vol. 3, p. 226; vol. 5, pp. 316–18; vol. 8, pp. 126–7, 140, 271, 291–2, 304–6.

87. Compare e.g. the almost universal silence on same-sexual transmission of the pox in medical print prior to 1700 (Chs 5–6, this volume).

88. E.g. Honorat Nicquet, *Physiognomia humana libris IV*, Lyons: Petri Prost, Philippi Borde, & Laurentii Arnaud, 1648, pp. 170, 210.

89. Hill, *The Contemplation of Mankind*, London, 1571, STC 13842. For comment and excerpts, see Borris (ed.), *Same-Sex Desire*, pp. 184–91. Hill cites some clearly Coclean observations on cinaedi from the *Anastasis* (e.g. book 1, ch. 41: Hill, fols. 11b–c; book 2, q. 20: Hill, fol. 121a–b). Hill's earlier *Brief and Most Pleasaunt Epitomye of the Whole Art of Phisiognomie* seems also at least somewhat derived from Cocles but does not contain those comments, nor the word "cinaedus" in any form, London, 1556, STC 5468. On "cinaedus" as an English loan-word, cf. Gordon Williams, *A Dictionary of Sexual Language and Imagery in Shakespearean and Stuart Literature*, 3 vols, London: Athlone, 1997, *s.v.* "cynede."

90. Cf. Vignali, *La cazzaria: The Book of the Prick*.

91. See García and Solar, introductions, in Tricasso, *Comentarios*, 2.9–17, 23–5. On "masculine love," see Borris (ed.), *Same-Sex Desire*, pp. 6–9.

8 Representations of same-sex love in early modern astrology

P. G. Maxwell-Stuart

The person who supposes that everything issues from the planets because it *must* do so is removing merit and therefore blame as well . . . In that case, moral rectitude suffers injustice on account of this error because the sinner refers his or her responsibility back to the planets.

(Heinrich Institoris[1])

Sodomy is the most serious of all sexual sins because it violates nature and denies procreation.

(Lodovico Gabrielli da Ogobbio[2])

For over 1,700 years astrology was an integral part of a shared culture. People regulated their health, planned voyages and marriages, tried to foresee disasters, and even chose the date of coronations according to its directions. High and low, learned and unlearned, sought and tended to accept its predictions even if an increasing number of the learned during the sixteenth and seventeenth centuries began to question the validity of its complex propositions. Interpretation of planetary and astral influences upon humankind and the earth itself depended on a division of the sky above and below the horizon into a zone of twelve zodiacal signs through which the heavenly bodies moved. The very term "influence" referred to the rays transmitting the planets' and stars' effects to those passive recipients which lived or grew or simply existed beneath the moon. Everything – human beings, animals, plants, minerals – was affected by and subject to these influences, and in consequence an extensive knowledge of astrology could well seem essential for a proper understanding not only of physical change within created beings and objects, but also of human temperament, disposition, and character. So Keith Thomas describes astrology as "probably the most ambitious attempt ever made to reduce the baffling diversity of human affairs to some sort of intelligible order."[3]

Astrology, however, increasingly confronted unresolvable difficulties. Its universe, and the techniques it employed to explain influences within that universe, were essentially those of Greek and Roman antiquity, and the bible of astrologers continued to be Claudius Ptolemy's *Tetrabiblos* written in the second century CE.

LIBER QVARTVS,

DE VARIETATIBVS NON NATV-
ralis partus, & earundem curis.

G 2 Quando-

Figure 8.1 Astrologers assessing an infant's future at birth, from Jakob Ruff, *De conceptu, et generatione hominis* (Frankfurt: Apud P. Fabricium, Impensis S. Feyrabendii, 1587), p. 26. By permission of the Thomas Fisher Rare Books Library, University of Toronto.

The impact of advances in mathematics, the struggle to refine interpretative techniques to address an apparently bewildering plethora of variables, and the advent of a new picture of the universe post-Copernicus, threatened to overwhelm astrologers with intractable tasks, although they continued to strive to cope with their problems well into what might be called the modern era.

One such difficulty was the vexed relationship between astral influence and human free will. Were human lives and characters astrally determined, or could they be changed in spite of the heavenly bodies? When Shakespeare made Cassius say to Brutus, "The fault, dear Brutus, is not in our stars, / But in ourselves that we are underlings," and Duncan to Malcolm that "There's no art / To find the mind's construction in the face," he was, whether deliberately or not, having them take sides in this kind of debate which had already been argued for several centuries.[4] "The stars incline but do not compel" was an apologetic cliché to which defenders of astrology regularly resorted. Nevertheless, there were disparities between the way astrologers expressed themselves and the broader social reception of certain possible traits they thought could be innate and accordingly predicted.

From astrological viewpoints, particular predilections for each one of the range of sexual behaviors, or, in the case of some individuals, combinations thereof, were astrally inscribed at birth or conception (compare Figure 8.1). Hence astrology implicitly challenged notions of sexual "sins against nature" such as sodomy, for which individuals were theologically and legally responsible on account of human free will. Like Helmut Puff, I shall use "sodomy" pragmatically in its formerly common general sense referring to sex between males, primarily anal, but including other male same-sexual possibilities.[5]

In the Middle Ages and Renaissance, censure of astrology focused on its predictive ambitions and deterministic implications, especially in usages that appeared to compromise providence and free will. Following Keith Thomas's analysis, we may distinguish four chief types of predictive or judicial astrology: general predictions; nativities or horoscopes; elections; and horary questions. They all sought to interpret the influence of the celestial bodies by tracking the movements and positions of the seven planets in relation to each other and to those of other stars whether single or gathered in patterned groups. The first type dealt with a range of matters concerning society in general, from eclipses, weather, and harvests to epidemics, political conditions and warfare. The second, which can be called genethliacal or natal astrology, assessed the personal implications of the state of the skies at birth (although there was a continuing argument that this should be the moment of conception instead). Natal predictions could be refined through "annual revolutions," whereby an astrologer assessed a client's situation in the year to come. Genethliacal data further enabled a client to seek advice on elections, to choose the most auspicious time for a certain action or event. In addressing horary questions, an astrologer resolved a client's query according to its own horoscope, in effect, at the time asked. This was the type most likely to be used by physicians. Simon Forman, for example, frequently cast figures for patients, read their diseases from the current position of the stars, and so "mapped" them (in Lauren Kassell's phrase) onto his clients' ailing bodies. Applications of astrology to predictions of natural phenomena such as tides, weather, and eclipses were least controversial. Indeed, the Inquisition permitted astrological inquiry for medical, agricultural and navigational purposes.[6]

Objections to astrology could, nonetheless, be methodological. The English mathematician Henry Briggs went up to Cambridge as a student in 1577, and there applied himself to the various branches of mathematics so that he would be well-equipped to study astrology, but abandoned it when he found "there was no certainty" in the rules of judicial astrology. Probably because of anxieties about astrology's religious implications, Luther similarly claimed that its outcomes could not be deduced from its fundamentals. "Astrology," he said, "is not a science because it has no principles and proofs. On the contrary, astrologers judge everything by the outcome and by individual cases and say, 'This happened once or twice, and therefore it will always happen so'." This sounds like a condemnation of judicial astrology, although elsewhere Luther swats horary astrology – "whoever governs his life and work according to certain days, celestial signs, and the advice of fortune-tellers [breaks the first commandment]." Occasionally he targets attempts to predict the future of religions according to the astrological conditions of their origins: "the Christian religion is not the result of a blind accident, or of a fate determined by the stars." Yet Luther's coreligionist Philipp Melanchthon, as in his *Initia doctrinae physicae* (1549), was an enthusiast for astrology.[7]

The most substantial critique of divinatory types of astrology was Giovanni Pico della Mirandola's *Disputationes adversus astrologiam divinatricem* (1496). The third book argued, for example, that the sky had a general, not a particular effect, and that the self-evident differences in the characters of people born at the same moment in the same latitude demonstrate that the physical, not the psychic, influence of the heavenly bodies is effective. Several others took his argument further. Giovanni Pontano noted that

> the sun's heat is not distributed in equal measure everywhere, topography is not the same everywhere, and the sun, along with the planets, is sometimes nearer, sometimes further away from the inhabited parts of the earth. Therefore its effects cannot be the same, or equal, everywhere.

He also noted, however, that from the sky flowed down everything relevant to arousal to action and to procreation and, via the modification and condition of the blood, "the application and inclinations of people's minds, as well as people's characters." Pontano also countered the objection that astrologers often made errors. Doctors, sailors, and farmers not infrequently made mistakes in their observations: "hence, therefore, the empty predictions of astrologers, because not all causes agree at one and the same time with respect to those things which seem to be portended by the stars."[8]

Pontano also raised the important question of free will, and this brings us to genethliacal astrology in particular, and hence the astral determination or otherwise of sexual preferences. Here at least, though not elsewhere as we shall see, Pontano was quite clear that people behave the way they do because they wish to, not because they are under some kind of compulsion. If human beings allow themselves to be ruled by their senses, he argued, they are bound to be weak and easily subdued by whatever particular malignancies inhere in their individual natures, a proposition he illustrates with the example of the Emperor Nero.

> Nero Augustus was renowned for his singular cruelty. But who will refuse to acknowledge the sensible notion that during Nero's procreation the temperature of the semen and the humours from which the foetus was formed was to a high degree malign, and that the stars made a very real contribution to that situation, with the result that Nero was inclined and excited to savagery by his very own nature? Therefore the causes of this situation were (a) Nature herself which gave rise to Nero, because she had been badly leavened; and (b) the evil condition of the stars and their unnatural configuration, which either followed the humour – that malign [humour] indeed! – which had been affected contrary to the proper order of things, or affected him by its own malignity and distortion.

Nevertheless, concludes Pontano, the responsibility for Nero's evil actions rests with his bloody will, not with the stars and the sky, or his intrinsically bad nature. Nero did them because he wanted to. The senses are themselves physical and thus subject to astral influences. "The effects of the stars are turned upon bodies below them and only upon those things which are made from the elements, and those elements are like some open field on which the stars exercise their forces." But people's minds, not being physical objects, are immune to this kind of influence; and since the will is the mind's most powerful property, human beings can exercise independent control over the astral forces influencing their bodies and bodily impulses.[9]

Now, how do these points relate to same-sexual relationships? Is the impulse to these relationships predestined and thus unavoidable, or can it and should it be subdued by an exercise of the will? Astrological commentators seem to be largely of one mind. Sodomy, effeminacy, lewd and "filthy" sexual behavior *contra naturam*, all variously result from a person's being born under some correlative combination of planetary or astral influences. Girolamo Cardano is clear on this point. The stars, he says, exercise great power in sexual matters because these are concerned almost entirely with the senses, and the sexual proclivities of whole national groups are governed by the stars. Hence, Poles are not sodomites, whereas Turks and Moors are considered to be so "because the way the stars are arranged indicates this."[10]

Some such notion may lie behind a curious medieval misinterpretation of a phrase in the ninth-century Arab Abū Ma'shar's *De magnis coniunctionibus*. In part 6, chapter 5, section 8 he says that if Mercury is transiting over Mars, it is a sign of various disasters including "the dismissal of the slaves in the houses of worship." The Latin translators of the twelfth century, with no apparent linguistic justification, rendered this as "the slaves commit sodomy in the houses of prayer." Mars is one of the key planets involved, and most commentators emphasize the genethliacal role played by Mars and Venus in determining sexual proclivities. If these are found simultaneously in a masculine sign, Cardano says, women will actively seek out sexual partners and assume the masculine role, whereas *natural* sexual intercourse happens if the Sun is in a masculine sign and the Moon in a feminine. When both Moon and Sun are in feminine signs, however, men are deprived of their masculinity and take the passive role in sexual intercourse. If Venus is in a feminine sign, men will be effeminate and "keen for acts of sexual intercourse unknown in Nature"; and if Mars is in a feminine sign, men will behave like sodomites "to the point where the general anger and religious feeling of the people [render them] notorious."[11]

Sometimes the texts are a little difficult to interpret. When, for example, Luca Gaurico says that a combination of Venus and Mars in the twelfth house made the eminent humanist Francesco Filelfo burn "with every kind of lust for virgins (*virginibus*), and especially *pueris*," does this mean "for boys" or "for children"? Since *pueris* is conjoined with *virginibus* which can mean "girls," "especially boys" seems most likely. Which were the years commonly designated as *pueritia*? Or does *puer* have an extended, metaphoric sense like "male youths" here? Pontano makes a similar point. "Those in whose nativities Mercury and Venus are situated at the same time and in like manner, and within the same influences of the sign (especially if it is unfavorable), will be abusers of the male sex and of *puerorum*, because Mercury has significance in regard to boys/children." According to Johann Schöner, Mercury governs the period of *pueritia* which covers the ages from 14 to 22. These "children" associated with sexual abuse of males may well have played the passive role, and evidence from late fifteenth- and early sixteenth-century Florence suggests that most passive partners were males between the ages of 13 and 18, more or less between the canonical age of puberty (14) and that of transition to young manhood (about 18 to 20).[12]

This question of passivity in sexual roles is one which occurs over and over again in the astrological commentaries. Pontano, as usual, provides essential details. When Venus and Mars are found only in masculine signs in a woman's horoscope, they predict that she will be sexually unrestrained and promiscuous, "with the result that perhaps she will abandon customary feminine [sexual] practice and begin to do what is more appropriate to a man." She will be assertive and aggressive, will not conceal her lust, and will abuse her own sex. If both Mars and Venus are both found in feminine signs, however, a woman will not be subject to any extraordinary effects, "but the man will rather tend towards those things which are out of line with Nature, and to a passivity appropriate to women (*ad muliebra patienda*), and he will be sensitive (*mollis*) and effeminate in his behaviour." If Venus is in a feminine sign, she turns a man into a *cinaedus* which, Pontano explains, means a *pathicus*. The word "cinaedus" has been the subject of some debate, but it seems reasonable to say that even though it appears in several classical Latin contexts which suggest his sexual activity is not necessarily limited to playing the passive role in a same-sex relationship, the intention of medieval and early modern commentators was to designate just such a sexually passive male, and at the same time to indicate moral disapproval of what he was alleged to do. If there is an equal number of masculine and feminine signs in the horoscope, and Venus is the ruling planet, the child (*natus*, implying a male) will be a hermaphrodite, which in this context is more likely to mean, as Leone Ebreo put it, that he would love men and find it not at all shameful to be both active and passive in sexual intercourse.[13]

Although "effeminate" formerly had a range of specific applications different from current usage, including libidinousness and supposedly excessive sexual pursuit of women, it was often applied to males who assumed a sexually passive role.[14] Even a cursory reading of the astrological texts suggests such sexual behavior was commonly thought to be associated with other feminine traits, and in some cases the description of sodomitical "likes" and "preferences" is clearly intended to imply that. Thus Antoine Mizauld offers a vivid portrait of bitchy queens:

> Those who are born under the rising of the Pleiades bring back the following behaviour. They follow Bacchus and Venus. They will always be conscious of the way they look and their elegant expression. Extravagance and allurements please them, and a golden pin secures their curly hair. In addition, their remarkable, gentle good looks shine with their rosy mouths. His [*sic*] attire is like that of a girl and his chest is fragrant with Assyrian myrrh. Wines, amusing jokes, and impudent language please him. They always love caustic witticisms and words dipped in poison, and anxiety awakens new fires. But lust reigns victorious in his heart. He is no less ambitious and struggles for honours; but they quickly regret the kind [of person they are] very much indeed. Consequently, they want to make themselves look like a woman, to polish their hairy arms and legs with hollow pumice stones. It is never enough for them to love; they want to be seen to love.[15]

So much so stereotypical, for Mizauld is here almost certainly following Manilius's *Astronomica*, 5.140–56, which describes the preoccupation of "people," but clearly men rather than women, born under the rising Pleiades, who take pains over their personal appearance and affect feminine dress and gait. Schöner makes an interesting connection between religion and a type of *cinaedus* who is also *effoeminatus*. "[Venus] in the house of Mercury[16] makes him keep company with monks and nuns," and "those born under the unlucky aspects of Venus and Jupiter will love to dress their hair, enjoy showing themselves off to people of good character, and take delight in things connected with the Church." Mark Jordan has noted a similar "correlation between ritualism and 'effeminacy' in Roman Catholicism and Anglicanism," expressed particularly in those he calls "liturgy queens" – men (not necessarily priests) who find an emotional satisfaction in the trappings of worship.

The terminology applied by Florentines to boys and youths who allowed themselves to be sodomized also reflected this alignment of sexually passive males with women – prostitute, bitch, woman, wife. Nevertheless, as Rocke points out, there is no evidence that these boys were either feminine or androgynous in appearance, or that they dressed in women's clothes, or behaved as though they were in any other way female. Now, the Latin term most frequently used by astrological commentators in this context, *effeminatus*, may certainly imply what we call "effeminacy," but it may also do no more than suggest that the man involved is playing the expected role of a woman in sexual intercourse – that is, passivity. This, for example, is how eleventh-century Peter Damian interpreted the word "sodomite." In his view, "sodomite" does not imply any particular style of dress or behavior, but is associated with "effeminacy," by which he means that a sodomite behaves sexually in ways the culture expects a woman to behave. The *effeminatus* of the texts thus wavers between "sexually passive" and "camp" to an extent which is difficult, often impossible, to disentangle.[17]

Effeminacy was feared and condemned because it was believed to make men (and also women after a somewhat different fashion) cross accepted social boundaries. A man was to be sexually insertive, produce children and look, dress and sound a certain way. Women were to be sexually receptive to men, bear children, and have their distinctive appearances, dress and speech. Sodomites appeared to blur and confuse these distinctions, so that they tended to seem to be out of bounds.[18]

These conventional expectations of sex and gender also influenced astrological commentators. According to Mizauld, those born under the rising of the Kids, two stars in the constellation Auriga, will run away from fighting and noble acts. "Courage never drives them [to inflict] a wound, but foul lust [does]." "The filthiness and shamefulness of sexual intercourse is not of one kind," writes Pontano, noting that different people have different sexual inclinations. "There are those who hate girls and pursue elderly women (*vetulae*), [and] some who take no notice of free-born females and fall desperately in love with maid-servants and slave-girls." His sentiments are echoed by Schöner. If a male's horoscope has Saturn and Mars unfavorably situated, "he will be a sodomite, [and one] choosing to do the act with old and repulsive people rather than with good-looking ones." Though unspecified, the gender of these partners is most likely male, since Helmut Puff has shown that "sodomy" in German contexts "most commonly" referred to sex between males. Sodomites also appeared to lack sexual self-control. Robert Burton's *Anatomy of Melancholy* (1621) not only represents sodomy as a sin, but also condemns it as an expression of inordinate lust, restlessness and insatiability, characteristics which ran directly counter to that rational self-control the Renaissance prized so highly in men. Time and time again the astrological writers, too, characterize excess as a mark of the sodomite. If a man's horoscope has Venus and Mars in masculine signs in the east, says Schöner on one sodomitical type, he "will have a lot of sex, and to a somewhat excessive degree." Ptolemy says that if females have Mars and Venus, or only one of them, in a masculine sign, they "will be addicted to that which is contrary to their nature, and will be very lustful and intemperate." It is this inordinacy of passion which Luther, commenting on Romans 1:26–8, explained was the punishment inflicted on people by God for their lapse into idolatry.[19]

Sodomy was made to seem much worse by being associated quite often with other reprehensible and forbidden acts. Thus Pontano: "Some [people] … do not hesitate to violate the law of consanguinity, that is, their daughters and nieces." Or Schöner: the child born when both Saturn and Mars are unfavorably situated "will be wretched, committing adultery, … and will want to fornicate with animals." Although it might appear that in these contexts Pontano and Schöner are conflating sodomy with other forbidden sexual behaviors, such an inference would be mistaken, for astrological discourse actually distinguished a wide variety of specific sexual predilections, according to different horoscopes. One man could be a *cinaedus*, another a sodomite, another incestuous, another adulterous, another prone to sodomy *and* incest, and so forth.[20] The sometimes strong language of disapproval used by early modern astrological commentators mirrored their own societies. Thus Schöner writes, as above, that if a man's horoscope has Venus and Mars in masculine signs in the east, he will not be content with "natural" sex, but will strive for a debauched type, to the extent that he rejects women and abuses men. It is even worse if the planets are in feminine signs, in the west, and if they are aspected by Saturn, because then "sexual intercourse will be unnatural and dirty." Those born under the rising of the Kids, says Mizauld, will be lascivious, unwarlike, indolent, effeminate, sluggish, and obscene; and it is their effeminacy which leads them to be like this and worse. Pontano offers more general condemnations of sexual behaviors which do not conform to society's expectations. "When men and women perform sexual acts on their own kind and gender, and when women start doing what men do, and men what women do, it is more violent and more indecent than appropriate."[21]

Most noteworthy, however, is Pontano's comment on pseudo-Ptolemy, *Centiloquium*, aphorism 80. The long paragraph is replete with such phrases as "filthy and debased" (on some people in their love-making), "filthy intercourse" and "filthy lust," along with "loathsome," "tainted" and "corrupt" to vary the pattern. But Pontano also makes quite specific the apparent inevitability of these conditions – he does not call them "inclinations" – to which the sodomite or *cinaedus* is born. If Saturn and Mars are in opposition in a man's horoscope,

> it determines that he will be a *cinaedus* and that he will have a bad reputation because of this vice . . . Venus in a feminine sign, and placed together with Saturn in the seventh house of the horoscope, determines that men will be *cinaedi*, if Mars, the Sun, Jupiter, and the Moon are all in detriment in the horoscope.

The verb "determines" is *decernit*. It is used of determining something as a matter of fact, declaring a judicial decision, making up one's mind, issuing a decree. So there is no room for doubt or inclination. People, the language seems to be saying, are predestined to be what they are and the stars do not so much incline as determine people's characters and fates. It was a theory with a long past history, of course. Ptolemy had been quite clear on the subject. If people could predict the weather from observing the motions, qualities, and aspects of the stars and planets,

> why not also predict respecting man? For, according to the state of the Ambient [i.e., firmament] at the time of their formation, the general quality and temperament of each may be known at the time of birth, both as to body and mind, and from the same cause also future events may be foretold . . . Predictions of this kind may be made with certainty.[22]

The Church, as one might expect, opposed astral determinism on the grounds that it ran counter to the gift of free will endowed upon humanity by God. Thus, in his bull of 1586, *Coeli et terrae*, Pope Sixtus V condemned "those who dare to cast and interpret people's birth-horoscopes with a view to foretelling future events – be these contingent, successive, or fortuitous – or actions dependent on human will, even if the astrologer maintains or testifies he is not saying anything for certain." But opposition also came from elsewhere. Paracelsus had no time for it, nor even for "inclination" which he regarded as nonsense. "People say that humankind receives an 'inclination' from Mars, Saturn, the Moon, and so on … It would be more reasonable to say that Mars imitates humankind, for humanity is greater than Mars or the other planets." Others were prone to take the middle view, as had Robert Grosseteste much earlier. The constellations did indeed affect free will and behavior, but an astrologer should hesitate before pronouncing on these matters, because he cannot rely on the accuracy of his observations, and in any case free will is governed, not by the stars, but by God.

These arguments and counter-arguments received particular force during the early sixteenth century in fresh debates on free will and determinism by reformers and Catholic apologists, as in Calvin's summary of what was to be his most characteristic doctrine:

> Whoever will want to be considered a God-fearing man will not dare simply to deny predestination, by which God has ordained some to salvation and assigned the rest to eternal damnation . . . When we attribute prescience to God, we mean that everything is and remains for ever in His sight, with the result that He recognises no future or past at all. Everything is present to Him . . . We call "predestination" the eternal decree of God, by which He has decided what He wants to make of each person.[23]

Predestination was not a new doctrine, of course. It had been a thread running through theological discourse since St Augustine; but astrological debate about whether the stars determined but not inclined had also had a long history, which in a way ran parallel with its theological companion. The third-century Neoplatonist Plotinus, for example, had accepted that the stars radiate influences and can indicate a present or future happening. But he flatly denied that stars were the causes of any sublunary event, and his views ran deep with both St Augustine and Marsilio Ficino. In the fifteenth century, scholarly interest had been stimulated not only by

Giovanni Pico della Mirandola's *Disputationes adversus astrologiam divinatricem* (which rejected materialist astrological determinism while acknowledging and laying bare the various difficulties and inconsistencies in current astrological interpretations), but also by Marsilio Ficino's *Liber de vita* (1489), whose third book is devoted to explaining how one should make one's life harmonize with the beneficent influxes from the heavens. Ficino recognizes their power while seeking to retain free will in managing them. Using free will to combat these influences, in fact, was the obvious way to resist astral determinism, and it represented the simplest and most effective compromise between outright acceptance of astral direction and outright hostility to it. "The last rule, (which has always been held by astrologers)," said Francis Bacon, who was a reformer not a rejecter of astrology, "is that there is no fatal necessity in the stars, but that they rather incline than compel" – a defence which, like so much else in early modern astrology, goes back to Ptolemy.[24]

Attacks on and defences of astrology continued long after Pico. These intensified as the great conjunction of 1524 approached, when Mars, Jupiter and Saturn were due to unite at the tenth degree of Pisces. At this time Erasmus and Luther were disputing the nature of free will – Erasmus's *De libero arbitrio* (1524), Luther's reply, *De servo arbitrio* (1525) and Erasmus's rejoinder, *Hyperaspistes* (1526). Zwingli joined in on the side of predestination in *De vera et falsa religione commentarius* (1525), followed by Calvin's definitive statement in the first edition of his *Institutio* (1536). Preoccupation with astral determinism and with predestination thus seem to have sprung more or less together into the public domain of scholarly disputation from one of the deepest layers of the Renaissance psyche.

Exercising free will, however, was not the only way to resist the stars. Tommaso Campanella was quite clear that God did not allow any evil to happen to humankind without providing a remedy for it, and showed that just as He had bestowed moral teaching to counteract diseases of the mind, medicine to deal with those of the body and politics and the law to cure the ills of the state, so "against damages brought by the stars, [He has provided] the branch of knowledge dealing with the stars." Astrology itself therefore contains the remedies for avoiding astrally predicted disasters by alerting the individual to them so that he or she may exercise free will and so take avoiding action. Della Porta claimed that *cinaedi* could lose their effeminacy by living in hot, windy places, altering their diet and taking up exercise.[25]

Although Della Porta's regimen suggests a physical basis for sexually receptive male behaviors, it was difficult for people to disentangle physical bases from astral causes because astrologers (such as Della Porta himself) assumed that differences in horoscopes were at least a main factor in differences in human character, anatomy, and physiology, as with the generation of hermaphrodites. Aristotle had suggested that in some cases the desire of males to be penetrated anally sprang from a natural deformity, and in others, from early habituation to abuse (implying sexual abuse); while Parmenides proposed that effeminates or *cinaedi* originated because of something which took place during their parents' sexual intercourse and were therefore, as we should say, "genetically determined." Pseudo-Aristotle's *Problemata* claimed the impulse in men to submit to anal intercourse resulted from an excess of semen which, finding itself blocked on the way to the seminal ducts and the penis, diverted itself to the anus and stimulated the desire for friction in that place; and from here it is not difficult to see a line of descent to the Renaissance's unease over masturbation and flagellation. But only a little of this finds any explicit reflection in astrology. Schöner observed that certain astral conditions – the elevation of unlucky stars above lucky ones – mean that the child will be physically weak and have a wretched constitution; and he lists ways in which planets govern a person's physical and psychological states, with Saturn (as one might expect) exerting a particularly baleful influence. Outside the domain of astrology, sodomy could somewhat similarly be likened to an infectious disease. "It is said to be a contagious disease," wrote Albertus Magnus, "and infects one person from another"; while the Franciscan Francesc Eiximenis tells us that "when men with men or women with women act against the ways of nature, the temperament of these sinners becomes corrupt. Thus corrupted, the air around them becomes contaminated, resulting in terrible plague-like conditions." [26]

Disease, corrupting and potentially revolutionary inclination, innate physiological condition, astrally determined trait, sin against nature – sodomy in its former sense of sex between males might appear all or any of these things but, regardless of whether it was a matter of choice or determination, seemed to constitute a threat to society by perverting men into women, or at least inducing womanly behavior, and avoiding procreation.[27] In consequence, it evoked repressive legislation, although the variance in both numbers prosecuted and executed, and the type of law passed and enforced could be quite considerable. In fifteenth-century Bruges, for example, large numbers suffered – an expression of politically motivated rather than theologically inspired suppression – while Venice and Florence notoriously went out of their way to investigate accusations and pursue them to prosecution, although Venice also tried persuasion by requiring prostitutes to stand bare-breasted on the Ponte delle Tette to entice young men away from their penchant for sodomy.[28]

Again, the astrologers mirror contemporary views. They do so partly, at least, in the adverse language which characterizes their comments on same-sex relationships and practices, and occasionally by implication, as when Gaurico relates the violent death of the notorious Pier Luigi Farnese, Pope Paul III's natural son, in 1503. After lunch one day, indulging his "cupidinous pleasures" (*cupidineisque voluptatibus*) with "up to three lovely youths" (*adulescentulis formosis*), he was brutally attacked in his bedroom by his enemies, stabbed to death, and hung from a window to be a public spectacle. His testicles were cut off and so was his enormous penis (*mentula sesquipedalis*). While dealing with Francesco Filelfo, however, Cardano goes further than implication and points to the peculiar combinations in Filelfo's horoscope which clearly indicate that he was "a person on fire with every kind of lust," involving sex with "boys" (*ob puerorum concubitus*) and rape of women.[29]

Early modern astrological commentaries, then, attribute inborn, specific same-sexual affiliations to genethliacal horoscopes, but are limited in a number of ways. Despite their wide currency in Europe, so that they had a strong formative impact on former beliefs and attitudes, they constantly hark back to Ptolemy and, to a lesser extent, Firmicus Maternus as their primary authorities, and hence to astrological interpretations designed for the antique rather than the early modern world. In consequence, they also inherit the assumption that particular characteristics based upon a socio-culturally defined polarity between what constitutes masculinity and femininity can be read in the planets and other elements of the horoscope. Hence, for example, Ptolemy's identification, in *Tetrabiblos* 1.6, of the Moon and Venus as "feminine" planets, and the Sun and Mars as "masculine," along with their attendant attributes of moistness on the one hand and dryness on the other. If such assumed differentiations are taken as the norm, it follows, of course, that apparent anomalies will be read and interpreted as deviations from that norm, with the result that negativity in relation to these perceived differences is built into the system of interpretation. On the other hand, sodomitical sin did not exist in antiquity, and so the ancient sources also challenged early modern condemnation of same-sexual relations in various ways.

The early modern commentaries' evident hostility towards sodomy and contempt for male sexual passivity, however, also reflect certain social and theological attitudes which, while not confined to the early modern period, were notable within it. Lauren Kassell's suggestion that the astrologer-physician Simon Forman "charted the stars and then mapped the disease on the patient's body" rings true of Cardano's observations upon Francesco Filelfo's horoscope, inasmuch as he weds planetary and astral positions to the man's known sexual activities. The texts agree in seeing the stars as determining rather than inclining people towards sodomy and same-sexual relations, and their acceptance of astral determinism ran somewhat parallel with renewed theological controversy over predestination. Here both disciplines seem to be tapping into a widespread and deep-seated concern over the relationship between now and the hereafter, a concern made sharper by the confessional conflicts within contemporary Christendom.

Secular legislation, however, concentrated on punishing people for *what* they did, without addressing *why* they did it, although the degree of severity with which same-sex activities were punished often varied according to social, political and demographic considerations. In Venice, for example, the passive partner was usually given a less heavy punishment than the active, partly because boys and women (relatively rare in prosecutions of the legal offence of sodomy) were thought likely to suffer physical damage from anal intercourse.[30] Thus, while astrological assumptions impinged on theology and to a certain extent on medical theory, especially that relating to humoral temperament, they played no part in legal proceedings which, unlike astrology, looked to determine the fact or absence of specific deeds rather than to explain the motives behind them, possible innate factors, and causal etiologies.

Observations relating to female same-sex relations treat them as though their astral causes simply reverse those conditioning men. So when Mars and Venus are both found in feminine signs, said Pontano – and there are many more such examples in the texts – a woman will follow the nature and law of her sex; a man, however, will incline to things which are out of line with nature and towards a passivity more appropriate for a woman. The key planets are almost always Venus and Mars, with contributions from Saturn and Mercury. "Venus is the mother of loves and lasciviousness', wrote Nicolas de Bourdin, "and the association of this planet with others determines the kind of love": "shameless with Mars', "filthy and dirty with Saturn." This is quite at odds with the assumptions of modern astrology that Uranus (not available to antique or early modern astrologers, of course) plays a leading role in determining a person's sexual proclivity. When the Dutch astrologer Wim van Dam recently applied Hindu methods to the interpretation of genethliacal charts, he found that Uranus, by itself and not in conjunction with Venus, was more significant in the case of homosexual women, and the Moon in the case of homosexual men. Those, it turned out, were distinguished from heterosexual men by their *lack* of femininity – a complete reversal of the antique and early modern view.[31]

Representations of same-sex love in early modern astrology, then, both reflect and run counter to lines of inquiry and investigation in contemporary theology, law and the medical sciences. Hamstrung, to a certain extent, by its dependence on antique models and commentators, early modern astrology fell back on stereotypes, injecting a kind of pseudo-life into them by the occasional reference to its own period, but interpreting the genethliacal horoscope in very much the same way its *fons et origo*, Claudius Ptolemy, had done before. By thus importing assumptions of the Graeco-Roman sex/gender system into Europe from the later Middle Ages onward, however, astrological thought, which continued to enjoy a great deal of prestige well into the seventeenth century, varied from and hence unsettled the standard legal and theological accounts of same-sexual love.

Acknowledgements

I am very grateful to Professor Kenneth Borris for supplying me with copies of many of the relevant astrological writers, and for Darrel Rutkin's helpful comments on the first draft of this essay. All translations are my own unless acknowledged otherwise.

Notes

1. *Maleus Maleficarum*, Frankfurt, 1588, part 1, quest. 5.
2. *Methodo di confessione*, Venice, 1572, p. 217.
3. Keith Thomas, *Religion and the Decline of Magic*, London: Weidenfeld and Nicolson, 1971, p. 287. See also Ann Geneva, *Astrology and the Seventeenth-Century Mind*, Manchester and New York: Manchester University Press, 1995, pp. 8–9. Sara Schechner Genuth, *Comets, Popular Culture, and the Birth of Modern Cosmology*, Princeton: Princeton University Press, 1997, pp. 5–12.
4. Shakespeare, *Julius Caesar*, 1.2.141–2; *Macbeth*, 1.4.11–12. *Complete Works*, ed. Stanley Wells *et al.*, 2nd edn, Oxford: Clarendon Press, 2005.
5. Helmut Puff, *Sodomy in Reformation Germany and Switzerland, 1400–1600*, Chicago and London: University of Chicago Press, 2003, pp. 12–13. On same-sex love in early modern astrology, see Kenneth Borris (ed.), *Same-Sex Desire in the English Renaissance: A Sourcebook of Texts, 1470–1650*, New York and London: Routledge, 2004, ch. 4.

6. Thomas, *Religion and Decline*, pp. 338–40. On Forman, see Lauren Kassell, *Medicine and Magic in Elizabethan London*, Oxford: Oxford University Press, 2005, pp. 141–3. Debate about the value and propriety of astrology did not necessarily involve complete condemnation. Martín Del Rio concluded that "the astrologer who does not depart from general principles and those guiding premises which are immediately relevant can, in accordance with the canons of his art, predict with accuracy general events many years, perhaps, before they happen unless either his calculations or his instruments deceive him . . . Astrology which goes further . . . and predicts that *something is bound to happen is definitely illicit and superstitious*" (my italics). *Disquisitiones Magicae*, Leiden, 1608, book 4, ch. 3, quest. 1. In classical Latin, *horoscopus* (a Greek borrowing) refers to the ascendant, that is, the constellation, star, or planet which is said to be most powerful in determining a person's character. *Nativitas* was the common term used for a chart of the sky at the moment of one's birth (or conception), and so it appears in early modern astrological texts.

7   John Geree, *Astrologo-Mastix*, London, 1646, pp. 14–15. Luther, *Table Talk*, 54.173 (references are to the various volumes of his collected works, St Louis: Concordia, 1958–). Cf. *Lectures on Genesis*, 1.45. *Personal Prayer Book*, 43.17. *Lectures on Romans, Scholia* 25.145. Contrast Roger Bacon: "by this mean of astrology not only are we assured anent our profession [of Faith], but are protected against the system of Antichrist, to which astrology gives consideration at the same time as it considers the system of Christ." *Opus Maius*, ed. J. H. Bridges, 3 vols, Oxford: Clarendon Press, 1897– 1900, vol. 1, p. 254. For Melanchthon, see P. G. Maxwell-Stuart, *The Occult in Early Modern Europe: A Documentary History*, Basingstoke: Macmillan, 1999, pp. 93-4; Sachiko Kusukawa, *The Transformation of Natural Philosophy: The Case of Philip Melanchthon*, Cambridge: Cambridge University Press, 1995.

8. Pontano, *Dialogus*, in Antoine Mizauld, *Planetologia*, Lyon, 1551, pp. 88–90. Pontano, *De rebus coelestibus*, in *Opera Omnia*, Basel, 1551, preface to book 1. Cf. Paracelsus, *De vera influentia rerum*, in *Sämtliche Werke*, ed. Karl Sudhoff, 14 vols, Munich and Berlin: Oldenbourg, 1919–33, vol. 14, p. 227. Luther, too, maintained the stars' general as opposed to particular influence in *Table Talk*, 54.458, as did Tomasso Campanella in *De siderali fato vitando*, in *Opusculi Astrologici*, ed. G. Ernst, Milan: Biblioteca Universale Rizzoli, 2003, ch. 2, art. 1, s. 1. These problems are still with us. Cf. Maarit Laurento, "Astrology and Science: A New Millennium," in Nicholas Campion, Patrick Curry, and Michael York (eds), *Astrology and the Academy*, Bristol: Cinnabar, 2004, p. 71. On astrology's natural philosophical foundations, see H. Darrel Rutkin, "Astrology, Natural Philosophy and the History of Science, c. 1250–1700: Studies Toward an Interpretation of Giovanni Pico della Mirandola's *Disputationes adversus astrologiam divinatricem*," PhD thesis, Indiana University, 2002.

9. Pontano, *Dialogus*, in Mizauld, *Planetologia*, pp. 91, 93–4, 95–6.

10. Cardano, *In Claudii Ptolemaei de astrorum iudiciis commentaria*, Basel, 1578, book 4, ch. 8, arts. 4 and 5. See also Ptolemy, *Tetrabiblos*, 2.3 and 3.19, and *Claudii Ptolemaei . . . centum sententiae* (i.e. *Centiloquium*), Rome, 1540, p. 71. The Jews, too, were accused as a nation of sodomy. See A. Maggi, *Satan's Rhetoric*, Chicago and London: University of Chicago Press, 2001, p. 93.

11. The masculine signs are Aries, Leo, Sagittarius, Gemini, Libra, and Aquarius; the feminine signs are Taurus, Virgo, Capricorn, Cancer, Scorpio, and Pisces. Leone Ebreo (Judah Abravanel), *Dialoghi d'amore*, Vinegia, 1558, p. 178. There may have been some reason other than racial denigration for the notion that Muslim countries were more tolerant than their Christian counterparts of same-sex acts between men. In Algiers e.g. such acts could even be performed in public, and in both Jewish and Muslim Spain same-sex pleasures were considered to be more refined than heterosexual ones. See Daniel Eisenberg, "Juan Ruiz's Heterosexual 'Good Love'," in Josiah Blackmore and Gregory S. Hutcheson (eds), *Queer Iberia: Sexualities, Cultures, and Crossings from the Middle Ages to the Renaissance*, Durham, NC, and London: Duke University Press, 1999, pp. 255,

256. Cf. Gregory S. Hutcheson, "The Sodomitic Moor: Queerness in the Narrative of Reconquista," in Glenn Burger and Steven F. Kruger (eds), *Queering the Middle Ages*, Minneapolis: University of Minneapolis Press, 2001, pp. 99–122. Abú Maŝhar, *On Historical Astrology*, ed. Keiji Yamamoto and Charles Burnett, 2 vols, Leiden: Brill, 2000, vol. 1, pp. 366–7, 448–9. Firmicus Maternus distinguishes a type of *cinaedus* who serves in temple choirs, *Mathesis*, 3 vols, Paris: Les Belles Lettres, 1992–4, 7.25.4.

12. Luca Gaurico, *Tractatus Astrologicus*, Venice, 1552, fol. 62a. Cardano discusses Filelfo likewise in *De exemplis centum geniturarum*, in vol. 5 of *Opera Omnia*, Leiden, 1663, pp. 459–60. See Ch. 9, this volume. Pontano, *De rebus coelestibus*, fol. 292r. Schöner, *De iudiciis nativitatum*, Nuremberg, 1545, fol. 96r. Georgius Fendulus noted that Venus governs every kind of sexual activity both natural and *contra naturam* in both sexes, including mutual love between men and the love of a male child (*nati*). *Liber astrologiae Abumazaris*, 7.9, in Dieter Blume, *Regenten des Himmels: Astrologische Bilder in Mittelalter und Renaissance*, Berlin: Akademie, 2000, p. 222. The word *natus* has a range of meanings similar to those of *puer*. The singular is masculine, the plural not necessarily gender-specific. On ages in Florence, see Michael Rocke, *Forbidden Friendships*, Oxford: Oxford University Press, 1996, pp. 96, 100–1. Cardano makes the disconcerting observation that *pueri* who have been raped die at an advanced age, provided their constellation is not in a feminine sign, in *Claudii Ptolemaei . . . commentaria*, book 4, ch. 8, art. 5.

13. Pontano, *De rebus coelestibus*, fols. 290v–291r. He says *cinaedi* will be produced by the presence of Venus and Mars in feminine signs, either in quartile or in opposition, too, fol. 292v. According to Firmicus Maternus, Saturn in any kind of aspect to Venus turns men effeminate and makes them *cinaedi*, *Mathesis* 3.6.4. Cf. Schoner, *De iudiciis nativitatum*, fols. 93r, 18r, and Leone Ebreo, *Dialoghi d'amore*, p. 159. On definitions, see John Boswell, *Christianity, Social Tolerance, and Homosexuality*, Chicago: Chicago University Press, 1980, pp. 41–59. But see also David M. Halperin, *How to Do the History of Homosexuality*, Chicago and London: Chicago University Press, 2002, pp. 121–3.

14. Cf. Ch. 1, this volume.

15. Antoine Mizauld, *Asterismi*, Paris, 1553, sig. D7v–8r, "Those born under the rising of the Pleiades." Cf. Giovanni Battista della Porta, *De humana physiognomonia*, Vico Equense, 1586, book 4, ch. 11. Drawing upon ancient writers and his own experience, he describes "the face of a cinaedus', who turns out to be what we should call extremely "effeminate."

16. That is, a zodiacal sign ruled by Mercury, namely Gemini or Virgo.

17. Schöner, *De iudiciis nativitatum*, fols. 93r, 34r. Mark D. Jordan, *The Silence of Sodom*, Chicago and London: University of Chicago Press, 2000, pp. 186–93. Mark Jordan, *The Invention of Sodomy in Christian Theology*, Chicago and London: University of Chicago Press, 1997, p. 57. He also makes the important observation that "effeminacy of one kind or another is regularly alleged as a consequence of same-sex copulation or of any other form of *luxuria*," p. 169. Rocke, *Forbidden Friendships*, p. 109. Peter Damian, *Liber Gomorrhianus*, ch. 1, in *Patrologia Latina*, 145.161, where the sodomy he describes consists of acts, not desires, an important distinction.

18. Cf. Bruce O'Brien, "Male Friendship and the Suspicion of Sodomy in Twelfth-Century France," in Matthew Kuefler (ed.), *The Boswell Thesis: Essays on Christianity, Social Tolerance, and Homosexuality*, Chicago and London: University of Chicago Press, 2006, pp. 179–82. Barbara Weissberger, "'A tierra, puto!': Alfonso de Palencia's Discourse of Effeminacy," in Blackmore and Hutcheson, *Queer Iberia*, pp. 295–6. Linde M. Brocato, "'Tened por espejo su fin': Mapping Gender and Sex in Fifteenth- and Sixteenth-Century Spain," ibid., pp. 328–38. Mario DiGangi, "How Queer was the Renaissance?," in Katherine O'Donnell and Michael O'Rourke (eds), *Love, Sex, Intimacy, and Friendship between Men, 1550–1800*, Basingstoke: Palgrave, 2003, pp. 138–9, 141.

19. Mizauld, *Asterismi*, "Hoedorum exortu nati." Pontano, *Commentationum in centum Ptolemaei Claudii sententias*, in *Opera omnia*, vol. 3, p. 2823. Schöner, *De iudiciis nativitatum*, fols. 33v, 55r. Puff, *Sodomy*, pp. 12–13. On Burton, see Mark Breitenberg, *Anxious Masculinity in Early Modern England*, Cambridge: Cambridge University Press, 2003, pp. 58–65. Ptolemy, *Tetrabiblos*, book 3, ch. 19. Cardano discusses an effeminate man's horoscope, *Centum geniturarum*, no. 35; see Ch. 9, this volume. Luther, *Lectures on Romans*, in *Works*, 25.12–13.

20. Pontano, *Commentationum*, in *Opera omnia*, vol. 3, p. 2823. Schöner, *De iudiciis nativitatum*, fol. 33v. Cf. Pontano, *De rebus coelestibus*, fols. 290v–291r, on the unnatural behavior of women, born under Mars and Venus, with prostitutes.

21. Schöner, *De iudiciis nativitatum*, fol. 55r. Mizauld, *Asterismi*, poem cited. Pontano, *Commentationum*, in *Opera omnia*, vol. 3, pp. 2822–3. Pseudo-Ptolemy uses the word "filthy" (*rhyparos*) to describe the man born when Venus is conjoined with Saturn in the seventh house, meaning he will be sexually filthy.

22. Pontano, *Commentationum*, in *Opera omnia*, vol. 3, p. 2823. Ptolemy, *Tetrabiblos*, book 1, ch. 2 (tr. James Wilson).

23. For Sixtus V's bull, see Maxwell-Stuart, *The Occult*, pp. 111–12. Paracelsus, *Opus paramirum*, in *Werke*, vol. 9, p. 114. See further W.-D. Müller-Jahncke, *Astrologisch-Magische Theorie und Praxis in der Heilkunde der frühen Neuzeit*, Sudhoffs Archiv, Beihefte 25, Stuttgart: Franz Steiner, 1985, pp. 67–74, 78–89. Robert Grosseteste, *Hexaemeron*, London: Oxford University Press, 1982, chs. 9 and 10. Calvin, *Institutes of the Christian Religion* (1536 edn), London: Collins, 1986, 3.21.5.

24. On the astrological debate, see R. Catani, "The Polemics in Astrology, 1489–1524," *Culture and Cosmos*, 3 (1999), 16–30. John Dillon, "Plotinus on Whether the Stars are Causes," in Rika Gyselen (ed.), *La science des cieux, sages, mages, astrologues*, Bures-sur-Yvette: Groupe pour l'Étude da la Civilisation du Moyen-Orient, 1999, pp. 87–92. Bacon, *De dignitate et augmentis scientiarum*, in *Works*, ed. James Spedding *et al.*, 7 vols, London: Longman, 1857–9, vol. 1, book 2, ch. 4. For Heinrich Institoris, exercise of free will was a moral consideration. See my first epigraph. Cardano wedded physiology with theology to defend the stars, suggesting that "since black bile is excessive and is moved especially in configurations of the Moon, the Devil uses that foul humour and [things which are] sooty-black to terrify the animal spirits and the mind by their means, especially in lunar cycles . . . so that he may give a bad name to the heavenly bodies and God their originator." *In Claudii Ptolemaei . . . commentaria*, book 4, ch. 8, art. 2.

25. Campanella, *De siderali fato vitando*, ch. 1, art. 1, ss. 1 and 2. Della Porta, *De humana physiognomonia*, book 6, ch. 10.

26. Aristotle, *Nicomachaean Ethics*, 7.5.3. His use of the passive participle *hybrizomenos* here indicates that the people concerned have had an outrage or a personal injury inflicted on the *ek paidon*, since childhood. The context suggests that this refers to sexual penetration. Pseudo-Aristotle, *Problemata*, 4.6 (879a36–880a5). Concerning female same-sex relationships, Heinrich Kornmann condemns both the relationships and their attendant masturbation, in *Sybyla Tryg Andriana, seu De virginitate, virginum statu et iure tractatus*, Frankfurt, 1610, ch. 10. Parmenides, fr. 19, in A.H. Coxon, *The Fragments of Parmenides*, Assen and Maastricht: Van Gorcum, 1986. Paracelsus devoted a pamphlet to discussing the role of sodomy in producing homunculi or monsters. *Liber de homunculis*, in *Werke*, vol. 14, pp. 325–36. Cf. also his *De natis animalibus ex sodomia* (ibid., pp. 381–8), which describes sodomitical interbreeding between animals, a copulation which gives birth to extraordinary creatures. Schöner, *De iudiciis nativitatum*, fols. 20r, 26r–v. Notice the link between physical (representing moral) disability, when the angels strike the inhabitants of Sodom with blindness, in Martin Del Rio, *Disquisitiones Magicae*, book 2, quest. 8. Albertus Magnus, *In evangelium Lucae*, Hageman, 1540, 18.29. For Eiximenis, see Michael Solomon, "Fictions of Infection: Diseasing the Sexual Other in Francesc

Eiximenis's *Lo llibre de les dones*," in Blackmore and Hutcheson, *Queer Iberia*, pp. 277, 286.

27. Compare my second epigraph, from Lodovico Gabrielli da Ogobbio.

28. Cf. Trevor Dean, *Crime in Mediaeval Europe, 1200–1500*, Harlow: Longman, 2001, pp. 59–61; Dean and K. J. P. Lowe, "Writing the History of Crime," in Dean and Lowe (eds), *Crime, Society, and the Law in Renaissance Italy*, Cambridge: Cambridge University Press, 1994, pp. 11–12; Rocke, *Forbidden Friendships*, pp. 215–16; Rudolph M. Bell, *How to Do it: Guides to Good Living for Renaissance Italians*, Chicago and London: University of Chicago Press, 1999, p. 181.

29. Gaurico, *Tractatus Astrologicus*, fol. 109. On Cardano's Filelfo, *Centum geniturarum*, see Ch. 9, this volume.

30. Guido Ruggiero, *The Boundaries of Eros: Sex Crime and Sexuality in Renaissance Venice*, Oxford: Oxford University Press, 1985, pp. 110, 118, 124. On the legal status and treatment of lesbianism in various European countries, see Valerie Traub, *The Renaissance of Lesbianism in Early Modern England*, Cambridge: Cambridge University Press, 2002, pp. 42–3.

31. Cf. Kassell, *Medicine and Magic*, p. 141, and Robert Mills, *Suspended Animation: Pain, Pleasure, and Punishment in Medieval Culture*, Chicago: University of Chicago Press, 2005, pp. 91–2. Pontano, *De rebus coelestibus*, fol. 291r. De Bourdin, *Le centilogue de Ptolémée*, Paris, 1651, p. 243. Van Dam, *Astrology and Homosexuality*, tr. York Beach, Maine: Weiser, 1985, pp. 39, 41, 53.

9 Astrological conditioning of same-sexual relations in Girolamo Cardano's theoretical treatises and celebrity genitures

H. Darrel Rutkin

Girolamo Cardano (1501–76) inaugurated the early modern vogue for celebrity geniture collections, a form of astrological literature in which famous people from popes and kings to artistic and literary figures were subjected to unauthorized astrological analysis.[1] His first edition had ten horoscopes (1538), the second 67 (1543), the third 100 (1547).[2] The topic of sexual proclivities was of great interest then as now (and in antiquity),[3] and some of the genitures involve same-sexual relations, just as astrology extensively treated questions of sex in general.[4] Indeed, Cardano's dedicatory letter for the 1547 edition announced that his collection would treat, among others, pedicators, cinaedi, prostitutes, and adulterers: a statement which would today undoubtedly appear in the publisher's dustjacket blurb to attract prospective buyers.[5] Cardano provides two relevant horoscopes with interpretations: Francesco Filelfo's and an anonymous effeminate's.

To appreciate Cardano's standpoint and theory, we should first consider the broader natural philosophical and medical framework for understanding premodern sex and gender differences.[6] Premodern men and women were positioned on a sex/gender spectrum that ranged from hyper-masculine men to ultra-feminine women, where the normative patterns (and their deviant antitypes) were interpreted in terms of the oppositions male–hot–active and female–cold–passive. Indeed, masculine and feminine were conceived as contrary qualities subject to quantitative analysis within an Aristotelian conceptual framework. Cardano will help us articulate and historicize this framework.

Astrology was formerly used as a language to analyze and interpret individual sex differences of all types and to translate them into the qualitative discourse of constitutions and temperaments within the overall sex/gender framework. This system claimed to yield understanding of an individual's particular nature through analysis of his or her characteristic astrological makeup both at birth and over time. For the former it used nativities (birth horoscopes, also called genitures); for the latter, revolutions and directions (discussed below). Constitution and temperament then influence actions, but the choices an individual makes further determine how much the soul itself is affected by the actions undertaken. Along with astrology, natural philosophy, medicine, and physiognomy were used to negotiate this highly charged domain.[7]

For astrological assessment of a subject's sexual proclivities,[8] one first studies his or her particular configuration of masculine and feminine planets in relation to masculine and feminine zodiacal signs.[9] In Ptolemy's *Tetrabiblos*, the fundamental text in this tradition, the moon and Venus are the two feminine planets because they are the moistest (1.6). The sun, Mars, Jupiter, and Saturn are masculine, because they are hotter, dryer, or both, with Mercury going in either direction depending on which other planet or planets influence it most. One primary interpretive factor is whether Mars and Venus, the masculine and feminine planets par excellence, are in masculine or feminine zodiacal signs. All the signs of the zodiac are either masculine or feminine in turn, beginning with Aries as masculine; Taurus, feminine; Gemini, masculine; and so on (1.12). The two major elements of astrological analysis, the planets and the zodiacal signs, are both explicitly gendered, so that gender becomes a cosmic system, integrating the heavens and earth.

The relationship of Mars to Venus in the horoscope is also highly significant for sexual analysis, as Ptolemy tells us in *Tetrabiblos*:

> Allied with Venus, in honorable positions, Mars makes his subject [among other things][10] lovers (*amatores*), pleasure-loving (*voluptuarios*), masculine, given to sexual vices (*in venerea vitia pronos*), and passionate for both young men and young women (*iuvenum amatores, masculorum et feminarum*).
>
> In contrary positions, he [i.e., Mars] makes them leering, lascivious, profligate, adulterers, seducers of those both in their own families and in those of others, insatiate of pleasure, corrupters of women and maidens (*mulierum ac virginum constupratores*),[11] sometimes profligate, disposed to base practices (*perversos*) and shameless. (3.13; pp. 353–5; *textus* LXXIII, pp. 277–8)[12]

The particular significance of these astrological factors for the native, the person whose horoscope has been cast, depends crucially on his or her biological gender. For example, whether Mars, the masculine planet par excellence, is in a masculine or a feminine zodiacal sign in a man's chart strongly affects his overall sexual inclinations, as we will see. Likewise, Venus' location for a woman. Indeed, the interpretations of men's and women's nativities are strikingly symmetrical and complementary. The semiology of these basic factors is quite straightforward, with complications only arising as the interpretive factors compound.

These basic sex/gender determinants are then further nuanced by several other considerations. What actual signs do Mars and Venus occur in (beyond whether those are simply masculine or feminine signs)? What are their astrologically significant angular relationships with the other planets in their respective signs (the so-called astrological "aspects")?[13] Also, what are their relationships with the four cardinal points of a horoscope (the ascendant, midheaven, descendant, and lower midheaven, which affect the intensity of planetary influences)? These are all basic features of the geniture, the natal horoscope, and concern the person's root nature or constitution. The astrologer should also consider: (1) astrological developments affecting the native after birth as revealed by directions and revolutions (discussed below); and (2) significant non-astrological factors, such as overall cultural patterns and personal experiences.[14] In practice, however, most astrologers do not provide a full analysis, Cardano complains, because it requires too much work.[15]

Cardano addresses procedures for astrological assessment of sexual vices in chapter 8 ("On the Native's Vices") of his *De iudiciis geniturarum*, first published in *Libelli quinque* with the third edition of his geniture collection, in 1547.[16] All the examples he provides are sexual, and some relate to same-sex contacts. In the introductory section, Cardano relates astrologically conditioned sexual natures to choices and circumstances (personal, cultural, and historical), and the moral consequences thereof:

> You should know that many things come to me by chance (*casu*) rather than by nature (*natura*). For a girl or a boy in the hands of a violent master or a soldier, prostitute themselves without any vice of their soul, but such knowledge will not be had from a geniture; rather, from directions and revolutions with that infinite consideration of so many things which hardly anyone would dare to explain.

Cardano expands on these points in chapter 26 ("On the Perfection of the Art"):

> You should know that of things which are predicted, some are consistent, such as the temperament, customs, form of the body, powers and intelligence, which, although they can be changed, nevertheless always exist (except when they depart from their original nature by some violent accident), retaining a connection to their root (*radix*). And all of these are known from the geniture alone. But others are acquired over time, such as erudition, fame, wealth, honors, offices, scars, disfigurations of the body, and sexual habits (*usus venereorum*). Such things are understood from three [astrological procedures]: from the geniture, and this is the least [i.e. one can know the least from this]; from directions, since corresponding things come to pass without impediment, and in their appropriate time; [and] from revolutions, since many things signify the same thing with one [factor] following another.

The geniture establishes the native's root qualitative nature, the constitution, with its correlative temperament. Revolutions and directions, on the other hand, inform and predict changes over the native's life, including acquisition of habits, sexual and otherwise. Revolutions are also known as transits. When a person is born, the planets are wherever they are in his or her nativity. But they keep moving, so when they conjoin or otherwise aspect a planet or significant point in the natal horoscope, that transitory planetary influence is then brought into a person's life. Directions, on the other hand, are more like seeds planted in the nativity that unfolds over time. In addition to the planets, the ascendant and midheaven points can also be directed, moving a specific angular distance per year. For example, the sun moves one degree per year. When such a directed planet or point meets or otherwise aspects another natal planet or point, a significant event will supposedly occur at that time.[17]

Let us now return to chapter 8, where Cardano insists that, in assessing how an individual's astral circumstances relate to his or her prospects for sexual vice, much depends on the cultural context:

> only those are called shameless (*impudici*)[18] who prostitute themselves of their own volition (*sponte*) – as girls frequently, boys extremely rarely – in which it is also fitting to examine the laws and region, for it [i.e. male prostitution, presumably] was allowed in ancient times. And according to the law of Mohammed, many shameless men [i.e. same-sexually] are found, but rarely among Jews and Christians. Fear of the law accustomed their grandparents and parents and children that they should abstain from these [activities]. Also, over a long period of time forcible acts [*violenta* – i.e. non-natural shaping] transform into [one's] nature. Thus in Germany this [i.e. male same-sexual vice] is altogether monstrous, less so in Italy, although all are Christian; and adulteries are ignored by the Italians, and even more so among the French, whence a very small conjecture[19] from the stars will signify an adulteress in France, a greater [conjectural leap] will be necessary in Italy, and even greater in Germany and Spain.

Further refining his analysis, Cardano encourages the astrologer also to assess the person's socio-economic circumstances: "poor people become shameless without shame, by fear sometimes, and often by necessity."

Three levels may be distinguished here, all of which must be taken into account for a full analysis, including the evaluation of perceived moral rectitude: (1) a "natural" level, the biologically gendered person, body, mind, and soul; (2) a "cultural" level, which immediately upon birth begins to impart a precise historico-cultural configuration composed of language(s), customs, and laws, including the range of gender norms and expectations (any person born into any society is culturally imprinted in a way that continues to develop during the course of his or her life through various sorts of education); (3) a level of personal circumstances, beginning with the family a subject is born into, his or her parents, siblings, and relatives. Level 3 also includes a subject's actual experience as shaped by socio-economic, political, and religious status, and by the range of actual individuals who interact with him or her. Following Ptolemy, Cardano considers these different levels of analysis the proper framework for fully interpreting an individual's astrological configuration, which he determines according to three specific assessments: nativity, directions, and revolutions.

After Cardano's introductory comment, he turns to discuss the two main categories of sexual vices in males from his perspective: passive and active.[20] Here he provides astrological details, beginning with the passive vices:

in the case of sexual passivity (*in patiendo*) consider three planets: Venus; the moon when it is in the form of Venus; and Mercury when it has been feminized (*cum fuerit effeminatus*). Moreover, I call Mercury effeminate when it is in a feminine sign, in a (celestial) house of Venus [i.e. in Taurus or Libra], when it is southern, and when it is at the bottom of its epicycle.

For different reasons, Taurus, Libra, Capricorn and Pisces signify these things. Because Taurus is a feminine sign, and both feminine planets [i.e. the moon and Venus] rejoice (have their *gaudium*) in it.[21] Because Libra is a [celestial] house of Venus, the exaltation of Saturn, and signifies the *pudenda* [i.e. female sexual organs]. Capricorn because it is a feminine sign, and [because] both unfortunate planets [i.e. Mars and Saturn] have their *gaudium* in it.

I say, Venus was in Capricorn on the ascendant in the genitures of two men. While they were both boys, they desired to experience sexual acts no differently than women (*non aliter quam foeminae venerea pati desiderabant*), nor have I seen a more powerful indicator in this [respect]. Moreover, Pisces signifies [this] because it is Venus's exaltation, a feminine sign, and very cold and moist. But where Venus in Capricorn does not signify this, as among Germans and Scythians, it will signify adulterers. Moreover, in Italy it signifies both, [each] in its [appropriate] time.

In this last example, the astrological inclinations are the same, but cultural constraints limit the range of practicable options for expressing them, thus precluding any simple astral determinism.

Cardano then turns to sexually "active" vices of males:

> Look at Mars, Saturn and Venus, for when they are mixed together, they make adulterers, pedicators, and committers of incest. Mercury assists with this, and it does so by itself when it is in the form of Saturn and Mars. Mars makes more proclivities for adultery and incest. Moreover, Saturn makes proclivities for sleeping with boys (*ad puerorum concubitus*). Mercury accords with the nature of the planet to which it is assimilated. Nevertheless, these are changed by their location, just as Saturn with Venus, when it is in a feminine sign, and at the top of its epicycle, makes adulterers and committers of incest. Moreover, Mars when in Aquarius or Libra, [or] with Venus, at the bottom of its epicycle makes one desire sleeping with boys. Only Venus in Scorpio, if it rules the ascendant, can make cinaedi.[22]
>
> But if Mars, Saturn, Venus and Mercury are mixed in Taurus, Libra, Scorpio, Capricorn, Aquarius or Pisces, that makes men now adulterers, [now] womanly passives (*patientes muliebria*), and much more so from childhood, adulterers, committers of incest, masturbators, male prostitutes, and those who have been polluted with every infamy of lust (*omni libidinis infamia deturpatos*).[23] Moreover, in these [matters] a conjunction does more, after [that] an opposition, then a square; a trine and sextile less so.

After discussing aspects, Cardano turns to certain mitigating and malignant factors of both planets and signs: "The sun and Jupiter protect these things and diminish the negatives, sometimes even removing them, to the extent that the sun and Jupiter become even stronger. The houses which help are the first, seventh, sixth and eighth." But the influence of Saturn and Mars magnifies ills.

Perhaps inadvertently as a result of working with ancient astrological theories and sources, or more likely because he found the classification congenial himself, Cardano here articulates an astral typology of male sexual vices that follows the ancient Greco-Roman sex/gender system, where active and passive (or insertive and receptive) are the fundamental categories. He groups same-sexually active males with adulterers and committers of incest (whose sexual partners could well be female), apart from male passives. That does not mean he considers all these "actives" the same; only that they are correlative in his view insofar as they are sexually insertive, but disparate otherwise.[24]

Cardano came to treat related issues in his 1554 commentary on Ptolemy's *Tetrabiblos*, especially in discussing book 3, section 14, "On the Diseases of the Soul."[25] This chapter is divided into two parts. The first half treats illnesses of the active part of the soul, namely the intellect; the second half treats illnesses of the receptive–passive (*pathetikon*) or passionate part, including sexual vices.[26] In *textus* LXXIX, Cardano provides Ptolemy's analysis of the soul's defects (*vitia*) and sicknesses (*morbi*), which relates directly to what we have seen from chapter 8 of Cardano's own *De iudiciis geniturarum*, but now with a more developed psychological dimension. Ptolemy states:

> The corresponding perversion of the [soul's] passive portion, as in the former instance viewed in its extreme cases, is most apparent in excesses and deficiencies in matters of sex, male and female (*circa masculini aut foeminini sexus excessum ac defectum*), as compared with what is natural (*iuxta utriusque naturam*), and in inquiry is apprehended in the same fashion as before, though the sun is taken, together with the moon, instead of Mercury, and the relation to them of Mars, together with Venus, is observed. (p. 369)

Among his comments, Cardano discusses why the astrologer should analyze Venus and Mars to assess a subject's passive soul, instead of Saturn and Mars:

> insofar as we observe Venus instead of Saturn, [we also observe] the affect of the soul which drives it forward, that is, the sensitive [part], which is subject to the intellective; we understand about love (*amor*) and the desire for sleeping together (*concubitus desiderium*). (p. 285)

We will see that the subjection of the soul's sensitive part to the intellective is key for Cardano's interpretation of the moral implications of astrally induced proclivities for sexual vices, at least in his commentary.

Cardano then presents an informative doubt (*dubitatio*) concerning the relative power of the stars, laws, and cultural patterns, as we saw in chapter 8 of *De iudiciis*:

why is it that defects of the higher mind, such as epilepsy, insanity, *daemonium* [i.e. demonic possession?][27] are found everywhere, and are generally subject to the course of the stars? And among all nations they are subject to the laws of the stars. Not so sleeping with a wicked person; for among the Germans and those who worship Christ you will hardly even find one who takes pleasure in sleeping with boys, even if the stars openly decree that. But among Egyptians and worshippers of Mohammed, even if the stars do not openly and constantly decree this, nonetheless they are easily held captive by these vices.

Therefore, I say that the cause is this, that the *anima sensibilis* [i.e. the lower soul] is subject to the rational, and because of this, such vices are subject to laws; but stupidity and *daemonium* and epilepsy, since they are defects of the rational soul, are subject to the stars themselves, and cannot be averted by any force, since the supreme force of the person himself has been weakened and afflicted. For which reason indeed you will predict absolutely concerning the prior defects [i.e. those discussed earlier concerning the *anima rationalis*], just as also about bodily [deformities] because they are not subject to the rational soul. (pp. 285–6)

The upshot of Cardano's argument here, a development of his position in chapter 8 of *De iudiciis*, is that sexual vices are much more tractable both by society and the individual's will – as a vice of the *anima inferior* – than either defects of the higher soul or those of the body, precisely because they are presumed to be subject to control by the higher soul, namely intellect and will. Sicknesses or defects of the higher soul itself, by contrast, have no higher force in the soul to correct them. Perhaps surprisingly, Cardano does not characterize sexual vices as sicknesses of the body, but of the appetitive/passionate soul, thus rendering them theoretically corrigible by the rational soul. He continues:

Moreover, about these things described here, and whatever pertains to sex (*ad Venerem*), they do not turn out altogether similarly, but some differ, since such things are subject to [the influence of] laws and customs. Among the Germans, for example, someone who sleeps with boys defiles himself with his own hands [i.e. masturbates], or will consummate such things with another man, or sleep with handmaidens or people of lower station. And, so that I may finish the matter briefly, it is necessary [for the astrologer] to know the custom of the people in such matters. (p. 286)

Cardano's example is vaguely worded but clarified by the context. If an astrologer encounters a horoscope indicating that the native inclines to pederasty ("someone who sleeps with boys"), those signs must nonetheless be reconsidered according to cultural context, for the laws and customs of the Germans are such that those tendencies would likely be expressed in some other way or ways involving perceivedly unnatural sex or at least violation of class distinctions.

After these introductory remarks, Cardano presents Ptolemy's account of the sun and moon in masculine signs in *textus* LXXX: "if the luminaries are unattended in masculine [signs], males excel in masculine nature and women pass over to an overly manly disposition and nature" (p. 369).[28] Cardano comments:

> The luminaries alone make emotions (*affectus*) either too masculine or feminine when they both come to be in signs of the same kind, namely both masculine or both feminine. But this distinction is not serious. However, if the sun comes to be in a masculine [sign] and the moon in a feminine, this will be precisely in accordance with nature (*secundum naturam*). But if they come to be in the contrary mode (*contrario modo*), namely the sun in a feminine and the moon in a masculine sign, then they [i.e. the subjects] will be similar to natural men, but not perfectly so. Sometimes more masculine than is fitting and sometimes more effeminate (*effoeminati*), and this [is the case] if Mars is in a masculine sign but Venus in a feminine. (p. 286)

The language of nature and the natural in this text is straightforward: masculine planets in masculine signs are natural for men, and feminine planets in feminine signs for women. Nature here seems to refer to the unspecified norm or mean, which can sometimes be exceeded (too masculine) and sometimes be deficient (not masculine enough or too effeminate) in the astrological gender calculus.

Textus LXXXI of Cardano's commentary presents Ptolemy's discussion of the sexual implications of Mars and Venus in masculine signs. Ptolemy begins with the effects of excessive masculinity, first for men, then for women:

> if likewise Mars or Venus as well, either one or both of them, is made masculine (*masculini fuerunt*), the males become addicted to natural sexual intercourse, and are adulterous, insatiate, and ready on every occasion for base and lawless acts of sexual passion, while the females are lustful for unnatural congresses (*coitus praeter naturam*), cast inviting glances of the eye, and are what we call tribades; for they deal with females and perform the functions of males (*virilia munia*).[29] If Venus alone is constituted in a masculine manner, they do these things secretly and not openly. But if Mars is likewise so constituted, [they do them] without reserve, so that sometimes they even designate the women with whom they are on such terms as their lawful "wives." (pp. 369, 371)

Here Ptolemy further clarifies the usage of "natural" and "unnatural" within this gender calculus. For men with an excess of masculinity, they lose their self-restraint (moderation) but otherwise act "naturally." Women with an excess of masculinity, on the other hand, act "unnaturally" (literally, beyond nature) because they perform the function of males, namely, penetrating. The public/private axis is also evoked here, with Venus encouraging discretion and Mars abusing it. This astrological gender calculus strikes me as very similar to the assessment of "dignities" in a standard astrological interpretation, where the balances of different qualities of different strengths are assessed and analyzed.[30]

Cardano's comment begins with illegitimate sexual practices. In his view, naturalness and legitimacy seem closely related, but not identical:

By illegitimate sex he [i.e. Ptolemy] understands *stuprum*, adultery, incest, and sleeping with boys, and with girls in a different manner (*alieno modo*). Nevertheless, these will not be *extra naturam*, that is, sleeping together as passives (*concubitum patientes*). But women sin more in quality than in quantity when they mingle in the masculine manner (*masculino modo*), which vices sometimes rule among monastic or holy virgins;[31] just as also sleeping with men (*masculorum concubitus*) among monks . . . But it [i.e. the sinfulness] is lacking among those . . . only, who [have done so] not of their own free will (*sponte*), but who have been deceived (*decepti deceptaeve*), or compelled (*compulsi compulsaeve*) by their parents (*a parentibus*),[32] or entered (*introducitur?*)[33] by force. It disturbs me to say such things, but truth compels me. (p. 286)

Cardano's language here indicates a close conceptual relationship between natural and legitimate, unnatural and illegitimate, but he sharply distinguishes at their borders between illegitimate (whether illegal or unusual) and unnatural practices or acts. "Illegitimate" is beyond proper decorum, but "unnatural" appears to reverse the gender polarities. Cardano uses a vocabulary of quality and quantity here to make the distinction, which I will discuss further below. As in *De iudiciis*, he also takes pains to absolve those – whether male or female – who have committed apparent sexual transgressions, because they have been deceived or forced into compromising situations. Volition remains fundamental for Cardano in the moral evaluation of sexual acts, which are thus not to be considered apart from the corresponding sexual interiorities.

In Cardano's last relevant *textus* from Ptolemy, LXXXII, the latter again discusses the sun and moon, Venus and Mars, but this time their occurrence in feminine signs, so that here he deals with perceivedly excess femininity in both sexes: [34]

when the luminaries in the aforesaid configuration are found in feminine signs, women do not know the [proper] manner in those [practices?] which fit with their nature, and the males incline beyond their nature (*praeter naturam*) to the softness (*mollitiem*) of women and effeminacy.[35] If Venus is also made feminine, women become depraved, adulterous and lustful, with the result that they may be dealt with in the natural manner on any occasion and by any one soever, and so that they refuse absolutely no sexual act, though it be base or unlawful. But if Mars also is effeminate, their shamelessness is outright and frank and they perform the aforesaid acts of either kind, assuming the guise of common bawds who submit to general abuse and to every baseness until they are stamped with the reproach and insult that attend such usages. (p. 371)

Cardano comments:

In two words the thing is established. These four signifiers – sun, moon, Mars, Venus – in signs corresponding to the sex of the native make a passion (*libido*) immoderate in quantity (*immoderatam in quantitate libidinem efficiunt*); nevertheless they do not make it unruly or contrary to the sex of the native. But in signs contrary to the sex of the native, they do not so much augment an immoderacy of passion in quantity, but they incite [the native] to sexual congresses contrary to their proper sex. This comes to be in such a way that tribades do not desire to act (*agere*) with girls so often, nor boys desire to have passive sex (*pati venerea*) like women, or to act as men (*agere*), so often. (p. 287)[36]

Cardano's comments upon *textus* LXXXI and LXXXII from Ptolemy reveal the deeper structures of the former's thought. In the first, Cardano states that "women sin more in quality than in quantity," whereas in the latter he discusses passion "immoderate in quantity," but not "contrary to the sex of the native." Cardano's language is precise here, and is informed by Aristotelian natural philosophy, namely the ten categories, two of which are quality and quantity, which are themselves two of the four categories subject to change (kinesis, *motus*).[37] Both inhere in actually existing substances, here a male or a female human being. Likewise, "active" and "passive" are two further categories, but they are not subject to change. The astrological analysis takes place in this philosophico-medical context.

Cardano's view seems to be that "masculinity" and "femininity" are conceived in his gender calculus as a pair of complex and contrary qualities composed of a characteristic set of prior simpler qualities – like a medicinal simple in relation to a compound medicine – including hot, dry, and active for masculine, and cold, wet, and passive for feminine, with all their attendant strengths and weaknesses. The normative nature for a man is a moderate masculinity and for a woman a moderate femininity, but imbalances of excess and defect arise. These are changes (imbalances) of quantity, which are to be sharply contrasted with changes or transformations in quality, as when a woman is sexually active or a man passive. Then a man becomes apparently feminine and a woman masculine at least with respect to their sexual desires and behaviors. The model for this transformation seems to be that articulated in Aristotle's *De generatione et corruptione*, book 1, where elements (earth, air, fire, water) transmute from one into another by means of one of their two constitutive qualities (hot and cold, dry and moist) transforming into its contrary. But with gender, the constitutive substratum is more complex.[38] With this conceptual background, we may now turn to the horoscopes.

The geniture of the *effeminatus*

In Cardano's collections of celebrity genitures, each astrological chart in the series normally identifies the subject by name in the central square. However, the second and third editions (1543, 1547) include a horoscope, number 35, that pointedly conceals the subject's identity, designating him only as a type, an "Effeminatus" (Figure 9.1). Cardano's subsequent comment says that he is still alive in 1543. His birthdate can be inferred from the planetary data. The subject seems to have been

born on (or very close to) 19 September 1511, making him 32 or so in 1543.[39]
Cardano provides this explanation of the chart:

> Mars, which is the lord of manhood (*dominus est virilitatis*) is (a) in a feminine
> sign and (b) on the angle of the setting side and located with the moon. Venus,
> the lord of the ascendant, falls in Scorpio. Now this [configuration] has an
> interpretation which is not subject to doubt, except that Jupiter being in
> square with it could help, but Jupiter is weak and in Saturn's house.

Mars at 4.5 Virgo (a feminine sign) and the moon at 8.4 Virgo are conjunct
in the seventh house, which is ruled by Venus, although Cardano does not say
this. Mars is also on the setting side angle (the descendant), thus increasing its
feminizing influence. The moon here also feminizes the native. The rising sign
(ascendant) is Pisces, the sign in which Venus is exalted, one of a planet's essential
dignities. Venus thus rules the ascendant. Cardano refers here to the multiple
feminizing of Mars, and to Venus in Scorpio on the ascendant, just as he says in
chapter 8 of *De iudiciis*, as we have seen, "Only Venus in Scorpio, if it rules the
ascendent, can make cinaedi."

In that chapter of *De iudiciis* we also saw that Cardano mentions Jupiter as
a potentially mitigating, positive factor. In this geniture, Jupiter at 18 Aquarius

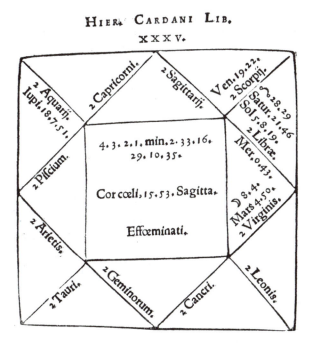

Figure 9.1 The geniture of an effeminate, from Girolamo Cardano, *Libelli duo* (Nurnberg: Apud Jo. Petreium, 1543), No. XXXV. By permission of the Osler Library for the History of Science and Medicine, McGill University. Biblioteca Osleriana 2228.

is indeed in a squared 90 degree angular relationship with Venus at 19 degrees Scorpio. Precision is not required for this aspect to have force. However, Jupiter is in Aquarius here, one of the two zodiacal signs (celestial houses) that Saturn traditionally "rules" (Capricorn is the other). So the former planet, astrologically considered the great benefic, is thus in a sign of Saturn, the great malefic, which weakens Jupiter's normally salutary influence.

Cardano adds:

> It is obvious that he will undoubtedly die a bad death. He has not died yet; nevertheless he has been in extreme danger. His morals are bad by necessity (*necessario*), but still they are free because Saturn is distant (*abest*).[40] He will die from a revolution, not a direction only, because his geniture is lacking in bad aspects.

Except for the weak square of Jupiter to Venus, there are indeed no bad aspects for any planet or point to be directed toward, but a revolution (a transit) could itself generate a bad aspect.

Also, Cardano says,

> He made a load of money from people unknown to him and was prepared for honors . . . , but they were all minor, because Jupiter and Venus [i.e. the planets indicating honors and wealth] were both unhappily located, and in his life infinite inconveniences came to pass and he was talked about abysmally. For the moon in the seventh house was also located with Mars, and because of these things this [misfortune] ran through everything [in his life], and he will never find an end to so many misfortunes. Nevertheless he was erudite and lived off the goods of the church. For the unfortunate moon, and Venus cadent in the ninth [house, and in Scorpio] inflames every vice of lust (*omni libidinis vitio flagrabit*).

Cardano is very forceful in his language, using phrases like "without doubt" and "necessarily" (*dubitabilem rationem non habet; absque dubio; necessario*). Although his comment's definition of the subject's sexual behaviors is vague, that context plays off and is partly defined by the horoscope's title, "Effeminatus." The final comment on "every vice of lust," then, seems designed to suggest scandalous enormity without getting into sexual specifics, while the title indicates the behaviors at issue here. So putatively outrageous that the native cannot even be named, they pertain to perceivedly feminine sexual roles – as we saw with the vices *in patiendo* – and that is the big scandal. The data make clear he has the geniture of a cinaedus: Venus in Scorpio, "not subject to doubt."

The geniture of Filelfo

The third horoscope in Cardano's collection, that of the notorious poet and courtier Francesco Filelfo (1398-1481), is the only other one involving explicitly alleged sexual vices.[41] The chart's identifying box provides the normal information: date and time of birth (24 July 1398, 6.50 p.m.), degree of midheaven, and the name (Figure 9.2). After noting Filelfo's remarkable longevity and learning in both Greek and Latin, and the features of his horoscope relevant to those traits, Cardano turns to his sexual character:

> since Venus was in Cancer, in the twelfth [house], with Mars in sextile to Mercury, and with Mercury also in square to Saturn, and herself [i.e. Venus] with *Canis Ardens* and with stars of the nature of Saturn and Mars, clearly this man was enflamed with every lust (*omni libidine flagrare*); whence on account of sleeping with youths and raping women (*ob puerorum concubitus et mulierum raptum*), he acquired a bad reputation, was publicly harassed by his enemies, and endured many inconveniences. For what disgrace (*quid flagitii*) could be added if Venus were joined with either maleficent [planet]?[42] Also, a bad and seditious temperament is indicated.

The main problem for Filelfo's sexual nature is that his Mars is, first of all, conjunct Venus in a feminine sign (Cancer) and in a feminine house (the twelfth), which is

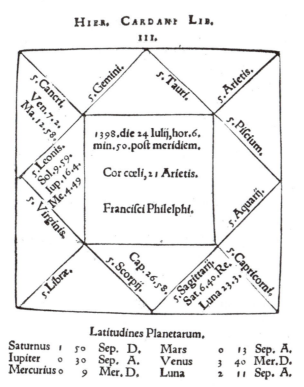

Figure 9.2 The geniture of Francesco Filelfo, from Girolamo Cardano, *Libelli duo* (Nurnberg: Apud Jo. Petreium, 1543), No. III. By permission of the Osler Library for the History of Science and Medicine, McGill University. Biblioteca Osleriana 2228.

Figure 9.3 Portrait of Francesco Filelfo, frontispiece of his *Francisci Philelfi satyrarum hecatostichon prima decas* (Milan: Christoph Valdarfer, 1476). By permission of the Thomas Fisher Rare Books Library, University of Toronto.

also ruled by nature by Pisces, a feminine sign in which Venus is exalted. Saturn too is important. The native thus embodies a range of "active" sexual vices, where Mars, Saturn, Venus, and Mercury are in play.

The rest of Cardano's astrological commentary on Filelfo further expatiates on his humanistic renown, studiousness, "many wives (raping the first)," and the astral configurations of learned men (compare Figure 9.3).

Cardano mentions revolutions and directions in the effeminate's chart, but not in Filelfo's, which mainly contains aspects. There is also a crucial difference in language in the two horoscopes: the former's is emphatically effeminate, as the title announces. The latter's does not use that vocabulary anywhere, so that Filelfo does not appear, from Cardano's viewpoint, a cinaedus, but rather a sexual deviant due to an excess of masculinity, as Cardano discussed in his commentary to Ptolemy, *Tetrabiblos*, 3.14. In Luca Gaurico's similar geniture for Filelfo, which reaches the same sexual conclusions, the subject allegedly had three testicles.[43] Though repeated in both horoscopes considered here, Cardano's phrase *omni libidine flagrare* is not to be taken literally, as if these two people are sexually the same. It once again serves to register perceived sexual scandal with a decorous vagueness that the associated information serves to clarify somewhat.

* * *

Cardano's approach in his horoscope collection markedly differs from what he advises in chapter 8 of *De iudiciis geniturarum*. There he says that, in considering sexual practices, an astrologer must reassess the indications of a subject's geniture according to directions, revolutions, and his or her cultural and other circumstances. But for his representative cinaedus and for Filelfo, he absolutely assigns their sexual affinities in later life to their natal astrological makeup. In practice, then, he assumes that, at least in the cases of some subjects, genitures can be sexually definitive. This discrepancy between his theory and practice corresponds to the larger one between his and other astrologers' protestations that the stars incline but do not compel, and their frequently determinist wording and interpretations.[44] Further research should investigate other early modern commentaries on passages of Ptolemy's *Tetrabiblos* addressing same-sexual relations, and inquire more deeply into how directions and revolutions were used in practice as a means of detecting and predicting astrally instilled inclinations and behaviors, especially sexual ones, that arise in later life from developments in a subject's astrological configurations after birth.

Acknowledgments

I dedicate this chapter to the memory of my extraordinary teacher at Stanford, John J. (Jack) Winkler, and to David Halperin and Maud Gleason for much stimulating conversation and encouragement. My thanks to Katharine Park for her detailed comments and suggestions on an early draft, and to Kenneth Borris for his assiduous editorial labors; this chapter is much the better for them.

Notes

1. See Anthony Grafton, "Geniture Collections: Origins and Use of a Genre," in MarinaFrasca-Spada and Nick Jardine (eds), *Books and the Sciences in History*, Cambridge: Cambridge University Press, 2000, pp. 49–68. On Cardano himself, see Anthony Grafton, *Cardano's Cosmos: The Worlds and Work of a Renaissance Astrologer*, Cambridge, MA: Harvard University Press, 1999; Nancy Siraisi, *The Clock and the Mirror: Girolamo Cardano and Renaissance Medicine*, Princeton: Princeton University Press, 1997. On astrological techniques, see J. C. Eade, *The Forgotten Sky: A Guide to Astrology in English Literature*, Oxford: Clarendon Press, 1984; Gerolamo Vitali, *Lexicon Mathematicum Astronomicum Geometricum* (anastatic repr. of the 1668 Paris edn), ed. G. Bezza, La Spezia: Agora Edizioni, 2003. I cite them as Eade and Vitali. All translations are mine unless otherwise indicated.
2. For Cardano's 1543 collection, *Libelli duo*, and for his 1547 collection, *Libelli quinque*, I use Petreius's Nuremberg edns.
3. See John J. Winkler, *The Constraints of Desire: The Anthropology of Sex and Gender in Ancient Greece*, New York: Routledge, 1990; Maud Gleason, *Making Men: Sophists and Self-Presentation in Ancient Rome*, Princeton: Princeton University Press, 1995; David M. Halperin, *How to Do the History of Homosexuality*, Chicago: University of Chicago Press, 2002; his *One Hundred Years of Homosexuality: And Other Essays on Greek Love*, New York: Routledge, 1990; Craig A. Williams, *Roman Homosexuality: Ideologies of Masculinity in Classical Antiquity*, Oxford: Oxford University Press, 1999.

4. Astrological evidence is a vast and relatively untapped source for cultural attitudes toward and scientific explanations of human sexuality, same-sex and otherwise. For an overview and bibliography, see Kenneth Borris, "Astrology," in Borris (ed.), *Same-Sex Desire in the English Renaissance: A Sourcebook of Texts, 1470–1650*, New York and London: Routledge, 2004, ch. 4.

5. Cardano, *Libelli quinque*, sig. A3b.

6. See Joan Cadden, *Meanings of Sex Difference in the Middle Ages: Medicine, Science and Culture*, Cambridge: Cambridge University Press, 1993; Ian Maclean, *The Renaissance Notion of Woman: A Study in the Fortunes of Scholasticism and Medical Science in European Intellectual Life*, Cambridge: Cambridge University Press, 1980.

7. See Jole Agrimi's groundbreaking *Ingeniosa scientia nature: Studi sulla fisiognomica medievale*, Florence: Galluzzo, 2002.

8. I use "proclivities" and "inclinations" in a loose premodern sense; these do not indicate the modern psychologized and subjectivized sexual categories of heterosexual, homosexual or bisexual.

9. See Borris, "Astrology," in his *Same-Sex Desire*. In the sources, usage of the terms "sign" and "house" is often ambiguous. When I use the term "sign," I always refer to zodiacal signs (which are sometimes also called (celestial) "houses"). When I use the term "house," I always mean the mundane houses, first through twelfth, beginning with the ascendant; the term *locus* is often used. These houses are subject to several different rules of house division. See John D. North, *Horoscopes and History*, London: Warburg Institute, 1986. In my translations, where the Latin is *domus* but refers to a zodiacal sign, I will use "(celestial) house" for clarity.

10. I have elided everything but the sexually relevant features.

11. On *stuprum* in antiquity, see Williams, *Roman Homosexuality*, pp. 96–124.

12. For Ptolemy, I use the Loeb text, tr. F. E. Robbins, but in a way compared to and sometimes modified in light of the Camerarius–Gogova Latin translation of Ptolemy that Cardano himself used in his *Tetrabiblos* commentary (cited and discussed below). Cardano designates each excerpt of Ptolemy on which he comments a numbered *textus*, and I cite them accordingly.

13. The main "aspects" are: 0°, conjunction; 60°, sextile; 90°, square or quartile; 120°, trine; 180°, opposition.

14. See Ptolemy, *Tetrabiblos*, 1.2–3. Although Ptolemy considers celestial influences the most important, he is clear that there are other causal factors as well: material, familial, cultural, etc. Cardano develops Ptolemy's ideas in the texts examined below.

15. Cardano, *De iudiciis geniturarum*, in his *Opera omnia*, ed. Charles Spon, 10 vols, Lyon: Sumptibus Ioannis Antonii Huguetan & Marci Antonii Ravaud, 1663, vol. 5, p. 453. I cite this text by chapter numbers alone, hereafter.

16. For an Italian translation with useful apparatus, see Cardano, *Come si interprano gli oroscopi*, tr. T. Delia and O. P. Faracovi, Pisa: Istituti Editoriali e Poligrafici Internazionali, 2005.

17. In *De iudiciis geniturarum*, chs 4 and 5, Cardano tells us how to calculate directions and what they signify, but not what they are. Chapter 6 treats revolutions. To learn more about both, see Vitali and Eade.

18. On *impudici*, see Williams, *Roman Sexuality*, pp. 172 ff.

19. That is, a very small conjectural step or inference is required for the interpretation.

20. In antiquity, "active" and "passive" were fundamental categories for assessing normative and aberrant patterns of masculinity. This is also the case for Cardano and many other Renaissance writers.

21. A planetary dignity increases its influence, a debility decreases it. On dignities and debilities, including rulership, *gaudium* and exaltations, see Eade, pp. 60–5. Cardano uses "gaudium" loosely here. Strictly speaking, Venus's proper *gaudium* is Taurus, one of the signs it "rules" (along with Libra), whereas the moon has its "exaltation" in Taurus. Because both are so positive, Cardano says they both rejoice in Taurus. This

is also the case for Mars and Saturn just below. Saturn's proper *gaudium* is Capricorn, in which Mars is also exalted.

22. Firmicus Maternus provides many astrological configurations that "make" (*efficere*) cinaedi. See *Mathesis*, ed. P. Monat, 3 vols, Paris: Belles Lettres, 1992–7, 7.25.4–16.

23. This phrase also appears in Cardano's two genitures to be discussed, for the anonymous effeminate and for Filelfo.

24. For contexts where Cardano clearly differentiates same-sexual pursuits from other modes of sex in various ways, not least concerning the consequences for personal reputation, see Ch. 10, this volume.

25. Cardano, *In Cl. Ptolemaei Pelusiensis. IIII de astrorum iudiciis, aut … quadripartitae constructionis, libros commentaria*, Basel: Heinrichus Petri, 1554. For the text of Ptolemy's *Tetrabiblos* presented there, Cardano used the Camerarius–Gogova Latin translation in Antonio Gogova's 1548 Louvain edn. It reproduces the first two books as translated by Joachim Camerarius for his 1535 *editio princeps* of the Greek text. Gogova translated books 3 and 4 afresh. There were several earlier medieval Latin versions from Arabic translations. Cf. Robbins's Loeb introduction. A full study of the *Tetrabiblos* translations, edns and commentaries is needed.

26. This chapter is worthy of fuller treatment than I can give it here.

27. Ptolemy discusses demonic possession in *Tetrabiblos*, 3.14, and associates it with "water on the brain," as Robbins notes in the Loeb edn. But this aspect of Ptolemy's text may have meant something different to Cardano.

28. My translation here is much closer to Gogova's Latin translation of Ptolemy than to Robbins's English one.

29. See Katharine Park, "The Rediscovery of the Clitoris: French Medicine and the Tribade, 1570–1620," in David Hillman and Carla Mazzio (eds), *The Body in Parts: Fantasies of Corporeality in Early Modern Europe*, New York: Routledge, 1997, pp. 170–93.

30. On astrological "dignities," see Eade, pp. 59–88.

31. See Judith Brown, *Immodest Acts: The Life of a Lesbian Nun in Renaissance Italy*, New York: Oxford University Press, 1986.

32. In the sense of being prostituted? Or using "parent" as a metaphor for religious superior?

33. The *Oxford Latin Dictionary*'s second meaning for *introduco* is "to insert."

34. Especially here, Robbins offers much more a paraphrase than a translation in the Loeb.

35. On *mollitia*, see Williams, *Roman Homosexuality*, index.

36. The emphatic negatives are clear and repeated in the text, but the meaning is not clear.

37. The main texts articulating this view are Aristotle's *Categories* and *Physics*.

38. See Cadden, *Sex Differences*, pp. 214–16 and in n. 164, for a parallel with Pietro d'Abano. I hope to develop this analysis further in subsequent research.

39. The planets relevant for dating are Saturn at 21 Libra, Jupiter at 18 Aquarius, the sun at 5 Libra and the moon at 8 Virgo. I use the ephemerides at www.astrodienst.com. Some additional information appears in the box: 4.3.2.1 min. 2.33.16. The next line has 29.10.35. I do not know what these sets of numbers refer to.

40. Namely, distant from the ascendant and its lord, which rules *mores*.

41. See Diana M. Robin, *Filelfo in Milan: Writings, 1451–1477*, Princeton: Princeton University Press, 1991; Paolo Viti, "Filelfo, Francesco," in *Dizionario biografico degli Italiani*, vol. 47, pp. 613–26.

42. Namely, Saturn and Mars.

43. Luca Gaurico, *Tractatus astrologicus*, Venice: Apud Curtium Troianum Navo, 1552, fol. 62a.

44. See Borris, "Astrology," in his *Same-Sex Desire*, pp. 162–3.

Figure 10.1 "Boy Playing a Lute," Caravaggio. The Hermitage, St. Petersburg. Scala/Art Resource, NY.

10 *"Bolognan boys are beautiful, tasteful and mostly fine musicians"*

Cardano on male same-sex love and music

Guido Giglioni

A writer of insatiable curiosity and far-reaching scope, Girolamo Cardano (1501–76) became involved in almost every domain of Renaissance learning. He left his characteristic mark in such diverse disciplines as mathematics, astrology, medicine, physiognomy, and oneiromancy. Also an author of a lost treatise on lovesickness, he sometimes comments on male same-sex love in his scientific and philosophical oeuvre, insisting on its moral deficiencies, but says almost nothing about its female counterpart.[1] Especially when dealing with music he refers, not so infrequently and not so obliquely, to the unmentionable loves of male musicians and singers, describing a social environment in which he perceived overt ethical unreliability and sexual depravity. After examining Cardano's rather bleak representation of love, I will survey most of the relevant *loci* on sexual love between males in his vast production of scientific, ethical, autobiographical, and musical texts (the main exceptions being his commentary on Ptolemy's *Tetrabiblos* and posthumously published treatise on metoposcopy). In each case, I will focus on his ways of addressing the theme of male same-sex love and forms of manly sociability in the various disciplinary domains that he considered. Cardano offers a number of differing diagnostic descriptions, sometimes attributing such sexual desires to the result of a defined physiognomic profile, an astral inclination, a moral deficiency of character, or excessive indulgence in esthetic pleasure. In Cardano's treatment of music, finally, male same-sex desires become interlaced with that art, its pleasures, and those of young singers.

When Cardano discusses sexual love between males, he almost exclusively addresses varieties involving a youth or boy with a relatively mature male, or the behaviors of a so-called effeminate male of whatever age. In all these cases, his condemnation is firm. He would have known of other kinds of male same-sexual relations, such as ones without hierarchically patterned sexual intercourse, or receptive/insertive role distinctions, or sexual subordination according to youth, at least from his reading, if not from his social milieu.[2] But in his own writings, Cardano distinguishes between two main categories of male engaging in sex with males: the relatively mature pedicator (*paedico*), characterized by an insertive or otherwise assertive and hence sexually "active" and "manly" gender identity; and the receptive and relatively "passive" *cinaedus*, who may be a youthful catamite, or an adult.

The perceived distinction is important, especially because considerations of age can increase or decrease the alleged gravity of the sexual transgression. Cardano exclaims that if we can excuse Britannicus' and Nero's same-sexual experiences because of their young age (the former just a *puer* and the latter an *adulescens* – an age "inclined to all sorts of inordinate desires," Cardano assumes), who can defend Caesar, an old man, "lying in bed with Octavius, his sister's nephew"?[3] And yet rumors of pederasty swirled around Cardano himself. Although he clearly valued the company of male youths, he rejects the resultant innuendos and was never charged with sodomitical offences. The truth of the matter cannot now be known. For Cardano boyhood (*pueritia*) shifted into adolescence (*adulescentia*) around age 14, although a *puer* or "boy" could well be older, for he applies that term to a 15 year old in *Paralipomena* as we shall see.[4]

Cardano on love and male same-sex love

Cardano does not have a reassuringly edifying view of love. Although his more theoretical and speculative treatises evince Neoplatonic patterns of argumentation, this does not seem so with love. For Cardano, it is a bitter and unnatural experience that is not preparatory to any revelation of truth: "a torment full of pleasure and a madness of a unique kind."[5] Marred by passions of hope and fear and by claims of possession, amorous experience is remorselessly precarious, suspended between bliss and misery.[6] Compliance with love's allurements marks a weak character, and it is for this reason that "love usually takes possession of tender hearts, like women, adolescents, and people of gentle habits."[7] Cardano often warns against the dangers of unrestrained love (*nihil amare immodice*) because it brings about either "great losses" or "great damages."[8] Starting from the twelfth century, love in an aspect called *amor hereos* had become part of Western nosography, a perceived disease or morbid syndrome. "I have suffered from *amor heroicus* to the point of thinking to kill myself," recounts Cardano in his autobiography.[9] Sometimes he does not hesitate to describe himself as a man incurably addicted to sex (*veneri deditus*);[10] at other times, as a patient successfully recovering from sexual intoxication. From a purely anatomical point of view, man, birds aside, is the most salacious land animal. In males, phallic erection may be provoked by all sort of physical and emotional causes, from being flogged to imagining "someone else's pain."[11] Refraining from sex, Cardano acknowledges more than once, adds strength to one's body and lengthens one's life. It is for this reason that "eunuchs and women are more long-lived than men." Moreover, sexual intercourse risks infection (such as, for example, *lues indica*), to the point that impotence may even be thought a blessing. "How many people wish they were impotent!" cries Cardano.[12]

No matter if your beloved is a young woman or a boy: the drawbacks are the same. If the boy you desire is chaste but you cannot possess him, you will suffer from insane jealousy; if he is a prostitute, hence dissolute, the sexual gratification will be worthless, "no matter if the boy is a musician, delightful, and pretty."[13] As

Figure 10.2 Portrait of Girolamo Cardano, from the title page of his *Libelli duo* (Nurnberg: Apud Jo. Petreium, 1543). By permission of the Osler Library for the History of Science and Medicine, McGill University. Biblioteca Osleriana 2228.

appears with powerful men, love may be just an exercise of power and a display of vanity. Since Cardano believes "there is nothing pleasant in love, no matter how great it is, apart from the feeling of being loved," he rhetorically asks princes, "how can you feel that you are loved if all your friends and lovers find themselves between two most vehement passions, between the fear for your power and the hope to gain some of your riches?"[14] Even the love that parents have toward their children is not natural but the result of education and social constraint.[15]

Against this rather bleak background, Cardano's view of male intimacy and same-sex love is even bleaker. In this case, too, Neoplatonic imagery and patterns of thought do not come to a possible rescue (as was partially the case with Marsilio Ficino).[16] As a general rule, Cardano states that "friendship with boys, youths, and women is unstable and more often than not improper."[17] But "love for young boys is miserable and foolish."[18] As such love "erases any trace of wisdom from the mind," it "partakes of infamy, nor does it draw or drive man to true virtues, as is the case with love for women." On the contrary, love for young boys is often connected with "avarice, filth and many other vices." What is more, adds Cardano, love for boys induces emboldened shamelessness, for, as a result of its characteristic intemperance, suitors become thoughtless and reckless. The lover of boys is "immoderate" because, contravening the laws of nature, he inevitably becomes extreme, and for this reason he is always "unrestrained." The fearlessness induced by male same-sex love does not make such lovers praiseworthy. Famous as they may have become, the classical lovers Harmodius and Aristogeiton, Menalippus and Caritone, accomplished their heroic deeds impelled by insane passion (*infamis amor*), not virtuous ideals. Their battles against tyrants in the name of freedom resulted from a much more dangerous and irrational tyranny, that of the senses and lust. Needless to say, such lack of limits inevitably ends in real madness. After all, Cardano argues, "who could doubt that to love so transient a beauty, without his love being requited, in such a disgraceful practice and with such an unhappy end, is not a sign of folly?"[19]

But it is not merely a matter of perceived immorality and filthiness. A crime is being perpetrated at the boys' expense for, by preventing the boys from procreating, these lovers act unlawfully and unjustly. Furthermore, the difference in age and power creates an asymmetrical relationship that is detrimental to the boy's education and development.

> What kind of progress can a little boy (*puerulus*) make when he is surrounded by such models, whether it is the active one of the father, whom by nature and education he wishes to imitate, or the passive one of his own age? Not to mention the licentiousness and all the other bad habits that he sees among them.

The irrational nature of the love for boys is itself that love's worst penalty ("if lovers of boys had self-control, they would not need law or punishments to be restrained, for that very love is their greatest torment").[20]

Cardano also addresses the topic of male same-sex love from a medical point of view, giving physiognomic directions for the detection of its devotees by analyzing the external features of the body. Interestingly, their *facies* includes various facial patterns corresponding to depraved patterns of behavior. The "obsequious" type "hangs on to young boys" and his traits are "close to a womanly grace," while his "lines between the eye-brows [i.e. lines that are crucial for the correct interpretation of character] are longer, oblique and beautiful." The "mentally deranged" type, who "rejoices at frequenting the company of boys, women and mean inexperienced people," has quite specific and detailed physical characteristics:

> pointed head, nose that bends from the forehead abruptly, almost not defined at all, broad and short, eyes fiery and shining, thick eyelids, ruddy facial color, sharp voice, breast and belly smooth, hairy in the lower parts, legs so plump that they seem hardly to stand apart from each other, toes of the feet crooked, gait quick and uneven. The main lines of the forehead are fragmented, some are small, irregular, oblique, interrupted, misshapen and for the most part situated above the left eye.

A historical paradigm of that type is Sallust's portrait of Catiline: "pale color, foul eyes, a gait that is now quick, now slow."[21] A third, "lascivious" type is characterized by a hairy body, especially in the area of the thighs, "in the same manner as birds." (And birds, according to a very old physiognomic tradition, are notoriously lustful.) The physical portrait is unmistakable:

> the voice is effeminate, thin, broken and uneven, the legs touch each other, the calves are fattier, the complexion is white with spots that look like lentils, the appearance is flattering, unmanly, the rotula of the knee flat, the gait bends to the right during walking, the care of the body is excessive, something which does not become manly dignity, the movements of the hands are turned upwards and careless, and in walking the knees are bent in a characteristically uneven way.

When the lascivious type manifests itself in children and boys, "the appearance is lewd, the habits are licentious, any sense of shame is thrown away, and they show excessive familiarity with strangers." Lascivious men "abandon themselves to filthy and depraved forms of copulation, regardless of whether they are devoted to unnatural lewdness, or pedication (*pedico*), or fellation by others (*irrumator*), or cock-sucking (*phoenicissa*), male prostitution (*sphintria*), or masturbation (*mastuprator*), or fellating others (*fellator*)." Some characteristic marks identify them, such as "loathsome signs impressed in the forehead" and "moles on the top of the nose or in the lower eyelid of the left eye."[22]

Analogous to the physiognomic portrait is the astrological profile. One of Cardano's *Centum geniturae*, discussed in Chapter 9 of this volume, focuses on the nativity of an "effeminate man." Discussing another nativity, Cardano observes that Venus's presence in the first house determines the birth of "beautiful people, favored by pleasantry of speech," but also "entangles them in a good number of vices, making them cinaedi, pedicators, or adulterers; however, together with these vices, it also lavishes on them a certain divine nature."[23] In his own astrological self-portrait, Cardano insists on his horoscope's conventional masculinity, yet confesses addiction to shameful lust (*turpi libidini deditum*) and thoughts about sex (*Venereorum assidua cogitatio*): "I have been always tormented by incessant thinking over sexual matters."[24] The astrological determinant of what Cardano calls his *libidinosa cognitio* is

> Venus in aspect to Saturn and Mercury, and Mars in aspect to both the Sun and the Moon. That I am not to be reprehended with respect to the natural actions [i.e. of sex] is indicated unequivocally by the position according to the nature of the Sun and the Moon, that is to say, the one in a masculine sign, and the other in a feminine one.[25]

Cardano seeks to show that, despite his astral inclinations toward irregular erotic thoughts, the stars have nonetheless demonstrably determined that these are "natural," directed toward the opposite sex.[26]

Cardano's condemnation of every form of same-sex love, homoeroticism, or Socratic love could not be any louder and clearer. He does not spare any form of male friendship and intimacy. And yet, for all his jeremiads he was continually the target of innuendo and accusation. At least, this is what Cardano himself tells us. As he recalls in his autobiography, bad rumors always circulated about the number of boys he used to have in his house. "To those upbraiding me because I brought up so many boys I replied: *My deserts in this are double: I do good, and hear evil of it.*"[27] In *Proxeneta*, when dealing with possible ways of eradicating slanders, Cardano suggests the use of many and powerful friends, an honest lifestyle, and the display of "contrary ways of life." The example given is significant: "if they charge you with being involved with boys (*si de pueris te accusant*), have women in your house."[28] In the same work, Cardano characterizes the accusation of sleeping with boys (*concubitus puerorum*) as an extremely serious charge, as serious as heresy. Both those accusations "do not rely on clear evidence" and "no help comes from the fact that one is innocent." Therefore, "it is better to hope in good luck and not to fall in some suspicion, for things can be so evil and deadly that even the thought of them seems to destroy and pollute a man's life: as if someone could bring himself to believe that he can think erroneously of God."[29] Cardano advises readers who become targets of investigations for sodomy to quash the allegations promptly. When a friend was charged with having sexually corrupted a boy, and asked when he had last gone to bed with a woman, Cardano reports, the man answered in the wrong way by saying that he had stopped doing so four years before. By replying thus he confirmed the suspicions of pederasty.[30] Cardano himself had a similar experience. In *De utilitate* he remembers how, during his years of impotence (from age 21 to 30), he started to avoid intercourse with women to escape embarrassment, but found he thus fueled rumors and suspicions. Hence "the very misfortune I was trying to escape turned into bad repute and an indication of even greater turpitude."[31]

Cardano recounts the circumstances of these rumors in two different versions mixing infamous accusations, portentous events, and paranoid persecutions, one in *De propria vita* and the other in *Paralipomena*. The events happened in the hot summer of 1562, just before Cardano was about to move to Bologna, at a time when "all his affairs and his situation as a whole were confused."[32] In *De propria vita*, the events are staged like a tragicomedy in three acts and with three main villains: Giulio Delfino, in the role of "the Wolf"; Cardano's unnamed competitor at the university of Pavia, as "the Fox"; and Francesco Fioravanti, another professor at the university, as "the Sheep."[33] "In the course of my teaching at Pavia," he writes, "I was used to reading at home. At that time I had in the house a woman who rendered irregular service, the youth Ercole Visconti, two boys, and a manservant, I think. One of the boys was an amanuensis and musician, the other a foot-page." *Paralipomena* provides the latter "boy's" name: Giacomo Antonio Scacabarozzi, age 15. According to Cardano, his ever-plotting academic rivals were planning to murder him after all their previous efforts to get rid of him had failed. The "deadly scheme" was set in motion by a forged letter ostensibly written by Cardano's own son-in-law that questioned Cardano's moral integrity with serious accusations. The physician Fioravanti then wrote a letter complaining that, as Cardano says, "the rumor was being circulated everywhere that I was using my boys for immoral purposes; and that not satisfied with one, I had added another to my household – a state of affairs absolutely unprecedented." The letter finally warned that "houses of certain citizens where these infamies were being committed were to be publicly designated." This time, too, Cardano managed to foil the plot. Nevertheless, having failed to discredit him as "the monstruous spouse of all young boys," the Fox and the Wolf tried again and sought to make him a member of the Pavian *Accademia degli Affidati* (an offer which, in Cardano's eyes, was simply another attempted ambush). But he was again able to survive the alleged assassination attempt.[34]

The third act started again with the Sheep asking Cardano whether he would allow "the two boy musicians" to sing in the celebration of a new mass. This time, he got wind of a poisoning plot with the collaboration of his maidservant, for the two boys were in charge of tasting food and drink before they were served. Cardano found his fears further confirmed two weeks later when the plotters came again to ask permission for the two boys to take part in a comedy.[35] Leaving aside the question of whether the alleged murder attempts were real, we can see that Cardano anxiously focuses on the boys and their potential use as tools of pressure and defamation. In addition to confirming Cardano's paranoid tendencies, the remarkably garbled story manifests the fears of a man constantly threatened with public exposure.

According to the account in *Paralipomena*, a series of extraordinary events also occurred in the house at this time, involving a lost then miraculously found ring and spontaneously igniting flames. Interpreting all these unusual phenomena as bad omens, Cardano decided to spend the following days at home without going out. But then he received news that his little nephew had fallen seriously ill, and he was forced to go to Milan to treat him. This was the beginning of another series of accidents and mishaps: first a bad toothache, then a spread of St Anthony's fire on his face, and finally a fit of gout. No sooner had he thought that his tribulations might have finally satisfied "raging fortune," but his "renown and honor," not to say his "life," were again endangered. "I was looking for a young musician to assuage so many misfortunes," writes Cardano,

> and actually I found a good one. His father permitted him to join my household. The next day, though, the father came back to me to complain about what he had heard, namely, that I had welcomed his son because of sex and, having invented an excuse, he was determined to take him away from me.[36]

As usual Cardano apparently extricated himself from the difficult situation, but the episode is unquestionably another case of shady business involving a young male musician that cast suspicion on Cardano's household.

Cardano often recognizes his own "foolishness" in keeping domestics whom he knew "to be utterly useless," "a cause for shame," or who even tried to kill him for money.[37] Chapter 39 in *Proxeneta* starts with the striking statement that, in order to "keep young boys and adolescents as servants, you must make them submissive to you." The means he suggests to achieve this end are, in the tradition of Socratic love, appealing to their passion for wisdom and the study of music, or, in a less noble way, using "games, hunting, money or girls." More specifically, with respect to young boys, since they tend to run away if they are beaten or seduced, the master has to anticipate their movements and try to keep them in his service by promising gifts and favors. In extreme cases, he can resort to threats or even corporal punishment. But it is always important to exercise caution so as not to damage your reputation.[38] In chapter 73, he explains that to have boys as servants is better than men or women because the former can be easily controlled and manipulated.[39] Furthermore, for those who are old and without children, Cardano recommends adopting a young boy as a son and educating him in all the liberal arts, such as reading, writing, sculpture, painting, singing, playing musical instruments, and so on.[40] The project sounds indeed commendable, but for the fact that, when he tried to carry it out, the outcome was another case of ambiguous attachment, bordering on mistreatment and abandonment. In one of Cardano's most interesting stories about his involvements with boys, he decided to "adopt" a young English boy, named William, before returning to Italy from Dover after his visit to Scotland and England in 1553.[41] Soon Cardano started to neglect him, until he apparently died of hardships and privations. Cardano then wrote a *Dialogus de morte* to assuage his guilt, in which he remembered William as "lucky Wilhelmina," because this is the way he used to call him "jokingly."[42]

Although Anthony Grafton has written that Cardano "did not describe in identifiable detail the sexual inclinations that led him to pedophilia and brought him legal penalties,"[43] Cardano never incurred such legal charges, as far as I can gather from the available documents and testimonies. What we know is that he lived dangerously, surrounded by boys of various ages, fending off rumors of sexual depravity, in an age when even whispers could be grounds for investigative torture in many continental jurisdictions, and prosecution. What we cannot say with certainty is that he was a pedophile. As for the "legal penalties" he incurred, they seem related to specific theological and metaphysical statements and not to same-sex offences. Heresy and homosexuality could somewhat overlap, but the documents concerning Cardano's trial in 1570, especially after the opening of the archives of the Sant'Uffizio in Rome,[44] do not seem even to hint at same-sexual relations involving Cardano. As recent investigations in early-modern legal history have showed, inquisitorial strategy included innuendos and hearsay in tackling sex between males. But historical investigation cannot be founded on such techniques. In any case, pedophilia does not exhaust the whole range of possible forms of male sociability and homoeroticism addressed by Cardano in his oeuvre.

Cardano on music

Together with fishing and chess, singing and playing instruments were Cardano's favorite pastimes.[45] Among his students, some became musicians, like Ercole Visconti, Giovanpaolo Eufomia, Camillo Zanolino.[46] In *De sapientia*, Cardano lists the ability to sing among the good qualities belonging to both the soul and body, and he characterizes such a gift as one of the types of knowledge underlying the *artes delectabiles*.[47] He often hints at the aesthetic pleasure involved in listening to songs and music, while in his autobiography he lists *musicae auditus* among the sources of comfort with which "you would adorn this stage of life," a stage that otherwise would be quite depressing in his view.[48] But music was also an important component of his speculative interests, for it had a remarkable role in his general reorganization of learning, and his contribution to the science of music was significant.[49] In the disciplinary domain of music, Cardano openly addresses issues of male homoeroticism, sex, and the social and legal consequences of incautious behavior.

Music's importance in Cardano's system of knowledge relies on the centrality of order in both his metaphysics and his life. In this respect, he believes that music bears on "divine things." Harmony is the result of a proportion "most simple and varied" among different voices, a mathematical principle that rests upon the cosmological assumption that "all things in the world are connected and tied by the bond of necessity." Music is based on numbers, and numbers, says Cardano, are "the image of the order of the immaterial beings."[50] Indeed, not only is music one of the mathematical disciplines in his view, but in some ways the most exact. In keeping with Pythagorean tradition, Cardano thinks of philosophy as the highest form of music. By bringing the soul into tune with the beauty and goodness of the cosmos, music opens the way to both the discovery of mathematical truth and a morally harmonious way of life. Following Pythagoras and Plato, he assumes that real music comes from the unheard harmonies of the celestial spheres, which "stir up minds without disagreement and are inspired by a certain divine instinct." On the other hand, sounds stir up strong emotions, and those who hear the outward sensible sounds of music (*simulacrum et species musicae*) are influenced in their soul. Leaving aside the "real natures," that is, the heavenly intelligences, who are not moved by the passions, nothing expresses "the image and the likeness" of our passions, both positive and negative, in a more truthful way than "numbers and singing."[51] By insisting on preserving a sharp distinction between theory and practice in music, Cardano confirms the traditional separation between the philosophical and mathematical aspects of music and its eudaimonistic and rhetorical aspects.

But music was not just mathematics for Cardano. If it is true that music originates from the basic ontological principles that govern the genesis and structure of reality, namely, order and the process through which primordial unity gives a harmonious form to the created world, it is also true that music, life, and the senses flow from the same source. Unheard music speaks to the mind; played music (and, even more so, sung music), to the very roots of corporeality. Cardano asks whether musical sounds appeal to human beings because they are embodied numbers or because of something else. Numbers are relevant in any case, he assumes, because in them both the "energy of nature" and the "image of the universe" shine. If this is the case, then the aesthetic pleasure seems to derive from the tie that links the soul with the cosmos. Yet sounds also have an immediate and direct grip over our passions, for "the soul has a special connection with sound." Perception of sound is direct and it reaches the brain almost immediately. The ontological status of sound is therefore Janus-like: it has a privileged relationship with both the body and the mind; it goes directly to the innermost core of the senses with the same swiftness with which it strikes the intellect.[52] Sounds are ambivalent and through them, as both rhetoricians and musicians know very well, the listener's mind can be moved in opposite directions. In Cardano's opinion, music has a special power over "one's own passions," especially because of the ability to bring the past back to memory.[53]

Although music inhabits both the mathematical world of harmony and the bodily world of pleasure for Cardano, his work nonetheless suggest that the senses and the body, rather than the mind, have a closer proximity to music. In *Proxeneta*, music is placed among the disciplines that are involved with the production of pleasure and entertainment.[54] In his self-portrait as a young man, he never tires of characterizing his youth as "given to pleasures, especially to music."[55] While he says that spiritual and pure love (a very rare occurrence in Cardano's world, as we have already noticed), being an image of divine love, inspires the study of music,[56] his usual position is that musical pleasure is vulgar if not cultivated according to the rules of the discipline.[57] Only in this case music may have an important educational role. After all, he reminds the reader, "both Plato and Aristotle prescribe that young boys be instructed in music." And it is one of the activities with which man can interrupt work and spend some hours in a carefree way without idling away his time.[58] Furthermore, sometimes the emotional turmoil caused by music renders men more virtuous, as is the case when they use songs to purify their soul and worship – a use, says Cardano, that may also have medical value.[59] Another benefit resulting from the study of music, whether it is singing or playing instruments, is the attainment of physical abilities such as quickness of movement and timeliness of action.[60]

Unfortunately, Cardano found the music that he practically experienced less a pedagogical and ethical resource than an incentive to moral corruption and escapism. Vocal ensembles, he says, entail not only an "efficacious harmony of singing," but a gathering of "many dissolute habits." It is for this reason, Cardano continues, that

> in our age, one cannot find almost a single musician who does not overflow with all sorts of vices. And therefore not only is this sort of music the greatest hindrance for poor and busy people, but also for all the others. Indeed, of the eminent men of our age I have known – Erasmus, Alciato, Budé, Denores, Vesalius, Gesner – none of them was a musician.

Music, Cardano seems to reason, readily becomes an immoral and disreputable pursuit because it lacks two fundamental requirements of a truly liberal discipline: first, the possibility of enjoying some leisure time (*otium* in the classical sense), the basis for any disinterested activity and growth in knowledge and morality; second, the opportunity to enjoy seclusion. Musicians need to practice and sing together, and the sociable aspect of musical experience, Cardano finds, entails emotional contagion and moral corruption.[61]

His view of polyphonic and instrumental ensembles as microcosms of vanity, competitiveness, and immoral behavior might explain why he always considered music one of the factors that contributed to the ruin of his family and his life. "If I say that music has destroyed my household, I will tell the truth in my own way, for I threw away not a small amount of money and, what is even worse, I corrupted the habits of my children." And the reason, Cardano confirms, is the almost paradoxical fact that music is a vapid and inconsistent pleasure that involves serious training, practice, and commitment. Whereas all other liberal arts are serious work based on disinterested *otium*, music is a luxurious waste of time based on an incredible amount of work and activity. Daily rehearsing is inevitable, which means that the harmony of the household will be disrupted by the guzzling and bustle of shady characters, "drunkards, gluttons, impudent, fickle, impatient, stupid, indolent and tainted by every kind of inordinate desire."[62]

In *Proxeneta*, Cardano provides a list of false pleasures. Frequenting the company of boys and favorites (*societas adolescentium et nepotum*) and excessive application to music (*assiduum musicae studium*) are put together with gambling, usage of prostitutes, gourmandizing, reading popular poetry, staying up all night, fishing, hunting, watching mime shows and sport, interest in alchemy, and tale-telling.[63] Musicians belong to the category of "perverse, stupid, shallow and deceitful characters," who are almost exclusively concerned with what is present or about to happen, and cannot and do not want to see anything else, saying that all depends on either God's will or fortune's arbitrary rule. Social intercourse with them is not only "suspicious," but also "full of danger." A musician of this kind, remembers Cardano, pressed him for advice on preparing poison.[64] Considering why musicians rarely become rich, in his *Problemata* Cardano asks: "Is it because the art is esteemed lightly . . . ? Or is it on account of their youth? Because the period of youth is a little foolish and despised, is every advantage lost for that reason?" Or is it because the performers "are foolish adolescents (*adolescentes stulti*) who have little money and are equipped to go into other activities that are more physical in nature (*in alios usus magis corporeos exponere parati*)?"[65] He does not specify what these other activities are, but it is not difficult to guess what *magis corporei usus* those foolish youths are ready to embark upon.

Nevertheless, Cardano does not conclude that music should be banned from one's house and from the education of one's own children. It can be truly educational according to Aristotle's requirements in his *Poetica*, so as "to strengthen or to change the habits, the passions and the actions."[66] But music played in company (*socialis musica*) is never useful for "poor people, children, boys, and for those in the house who are in charge of the education of the offspring." To initiate children and poor people to music, musical "science" has to be preferred to musical practice, and perfect instruments have to be used.[67] But then, in the same work, Cardano contrarily says that the things that "lessen the burden of poverty are above all those that assuage the asperity of it, like learning, and in particular, learning agreeable matters, such as astrology and music." And people who follow this rule, he confirms, hardly look sad.[68] Cardano, who liked to consider himself poor, clearly saw the addictive and escapist dangers in the practice of music, while admitting also its consolatory and cathartic functions.

As both a practicing doctor and musician, Cardano observed that, aside from epistemological and methodological differences, medicine and music share the same closeness to corporeal life, for they both address the responses of an ensouled body through senses, passions, and temperaments. Music promotes health and wellbeing. Since *dulcedo vocum* produces joy, expands vital powers, and reinforces the original ties (*commercium*) between the soul and body, it is no surprise, writes Cardano, that "the musician Xenophilus lived for one hundred and five years without suffering from any ailment."[69] The fact that the rhythm of life mirrors that of the cosmos makes music a powerful diagnostic tool. "Music supplies physicians with a specific utility for the knowledge of the pulse."[70] But its closeness to life, the senses, and the body is also what make music vulnerable to moral failings. Ethical reservations and social fears represent themselves again when dealing with the "pathogenic" aspects of music with respect to both the body and the mind. Some musical instruments may have unhealthy effects, so that wind instruments are "not honorable and decent," impair the brain, the lungs, and the stomach, and promote hernia.[71] The immediate power that sounds exercise over the passions may cause melancholy and nervous breakdown, Cardano warns: "you must take care not to work with such excessive mental strain that you become insane, so that the remedy becomes a poison; for it is said that when the musician Carpentras labored too strongly in that art (to which the Pope was very devoted), he lost his reason."[72] Moreover, Cardano believes that music, being inherently ambiguous, can either edify or deprave boys. Indeed, when Cardano describes his own moral failings, it is not so much his inability to resist various forms of addiction and gambling that he seems to condemn as his weakness for what we might call the musical lifestyle. Through its association with sensual pleasure, shallow and uninhibited behavior, music reveals its drawbacks as a source of both unproductive pleasure and immoral contagion.

Musicus puer

In *De vinculis in genere*, Giordano Bruno wrote that music has the power to bind the listener in a magical way when played by "a boy or an adolescent, but less so if by a girl or a man."[73] Was the favorable association of music and male youth a commonplace in Renaissance culture? In a way, we might say that music, like male same-sex love, was bound to particular conventions and rituals (for example, the pleasures of pederastic same-sex love as well as the pleasures of music presupposed, as a prerequisite, the involvement of boys). Yet the same conventions and rituals could create situations of perceived moral opprobrium and indecency entailing real or apparent dangers and corrupting influences for the youths involved. Given the characteristics that Cardano attaches to music (sensual allurement, loss of emotional control, waste of time, addictive behavior, and poverty) the correspondences of youthful musical pursuits to intergenerational same-sexual love are not tenuous. It is true that Cardano finds painting and sculpture the most pederastic arts, for these, more than any others, he says, "incline man to the lust for boys (*libido puerorum*)."[74] But it is also undeniable that in his writings the figure of *musicus puer* signals a perilous proximity of music, young males, and sodomy.

Cardano seems to allude to a landscape of male libertinage when he lambasts the lifestyle of musicians and singers. By and large, the *musicus puer* is a recurrent theme in Cardano's treatises on music and ethics. However, not being influenced by any form of Neoplatonic imagery in this province of wisdom, as we have already noticed, Cardano does not provide his *musicus puer* with idealizing angelic traits or mathematical attributes. On the contrary, young musicians are exemplars of foolishness and debauchery. Boys are easily seduced by malicious persons, and fathers or older brothers need to be on the alert that adolescents do not learn music or how to play dice, activities that, for Cardano, represent young people's initiatory rites to debauchery.[75] As we have seen, one of the reasons why, in his opinion, young musicians do not become rich is their *stultitia* and their readiness to be exposed to *alii usus magis corporei*.

Cardano often uses musicians' and singers' social behavior to exemplify amoral, shallow, and sexually uninhibited lifestyles. Their depiction in his manuscript treatise *De musica* is particularly lurid:

> Singers are accused of three things (and not without cause): (1) Their morals are depraved, they are gluttons and disreputable purveyors of every kind of vice. During their leisure time they constantly associate with those who live in debauchery and themselves acquire depraved morals. If easy money is available they squander it profligately on pleasure. When they have no money they are compelled to turn to evil practices. (2) They are accused of acting like fools; also, few have money, for riches follow the prudent. Their foolishness results above all from intemperance, especially drinking wine, and also because their musical tones are carried to the brain with force and weaken it. They associate with the imprudent and occupy themselves with fun and frolics. They also teach, but their pedagogy is senseless. I remember seeing certain singers, even many more foolish than Melitides,[76] who were so tainted with vices that nothing more vile could be imagined. . . . They are accused of acting indecorously while singing, laughing and moving their heads about, so that they seem to be little short of insane. . . . So all these things must be avoided with the greatest care; the art should rather be forgotten than pursued with such detriment to it.[77]

When Cardano listed the six things that caused him most damage in life, he included his passion for music.[78] Casting his own horoscope, he reiterated the usual self-accusation but presumed astrological determinism: "I have always been tormented by thoughts of sexual nature" and "I loved music too much."[79] Music could be extremely dangerous at the time, not just because of the physical ailments caused by singing or the mental ones provoked by the discipline's requirements of intense concentration, but because of the allurements of desire.

The association with young singers and musicians could lead to legal troubles ranging from imprisonment, being sentenced to the triremes, or execution. In *Theonoston* Cardano writes that

> Jacob Bonfadius, a man otherwise not in the last place among the erudite, because of copulation with boys (a most vile and sordid thing), was beheaded in prison and publicly burned. The Frenchman Dominique Phinot, a distinguished musician, was killed in the same way for a very similar folly.[80]

The musician Nicolas Gombert, he reports, "was condemned to the triremes for violation of a boy in the service of the emperor"; but then, thanks to both his courage and good fortune, he managed to rescue himself from the sentence by composing those "swan songs" with which "he earned not only his pardon by the Emperor [Charles V], patron of all illustrious men, but also received a priest's benefice, so that he spent the remainder of his life in tranquility." Cardano does not fail to remark that "Gombert's penalty was not a hard one, for he endured a punishment he deserved."[81]

In a passage in *Proxeneta* all the various elements that we have been examining so far – the unscrupulous and uninhibited behavior of young musicians, the system of family relations, the use of boys for both service and pleasure – coalesce in a portrait of social and family life written with Cardano's usual realism and connoisseurship:

> The boys from Bologna are beautiful, tasteful and for the most part excellent musicians, so much so that they seem to stand out from the rest of the Italian boys. However, they do not gain the same benefits as many other Italian boys of much less merit, like the ones from Milan and Florence, usually get, such as to be appointed heirs by their masters or at least to have some share in their inheritance, or to obtain rich ecclesiastic offices or to be given highly remunerative positions in political administration or in business, or to arrive to a remarkable level of virtue or prestige; and these four benefits are the foundations of a great happiness in this life. Therefore, the first cause is the avarice of their parents and teachers, for they usually rent these boys exactly as if they were houses. As a result, the masters, as if the debt were extinguished, believe that they do not owe anything more and that the boys have no claim on anything else. The second cause is the practice of pleasure. Since they learned from their parents to live in the lap of luxury, they cannot love their masters; indeed, they think their masters should give them more freedom and pleasures of life than the ones provided by their parents. As a consequence, their masters, realizing that they are not loved, but that everything is planned in order to gain profit from them, cannot love the boys.[82] The problem, though, is that all this is just a matter of insane love. The third cause is that, their strength already exhausted because of the musical studies, the boys cannot endure to accomplish anything admirable to the attainment of virtue.

Therefore, they cannot get into the master's good graces and keep their close familiarity with him.

The picture looks dreary for the delightful Bolognese *ragazzi*, but provides a series of strikingly revealing insights into sixteenth-century Italian social life: the opportunistic behavior of young male individuals competing with each other for social recognition and financial security, the elusive nature of the relationships both between parents and sons and between masters and servants. Within such a disillusioned world, music seems to contribute to the boys' moral decadence and to truncating their hopes to rise socially or to reach greater achievements in life.

As was his wont, Cardano was entering dangerous territory in addressing such aspects of social life, but this time his foray did not concern metaphysics or religion. Although he was very vocal in distancing himself from any involvement in the practices of sodomy and pederasty, in claiming the immunity of his indulgence in the pleasures of music from the most sordid aspects of musical culture, and in protesting his innocence and his good faith whenever accused of hosting boys in his house for the sake of sexual pleasure, he did not hesitate to report the connections between music and sodomy. Cardano is the only source that acquaints us with Gombert's legal accidents and Phinot's tragic end. He even reports his own personal experiences in contesting accusations of pederasty, occasioned by the *musici pueri* who were often part of his household. (He never hid the fact that he liked the company of musicians and singers, and he himself liked singing and playing music.)

When so many in Cardano's time were silent about such dangerous matters, why does he speak with such frankness, and divulge his own personal experiences, even when it would have been much wiser, safer, and conventionally polite for him to keep to generalities and be vague about such issues? After all, those accused of sodomy, even with circumstantial evidence, could easily suffer great loss of reputation, undergo terrible investigative tortures in continental Europe, and lose their lives, decapitated or burned at the stake. Cardano's apparent motives are theoretical and practical: in every circumstance, he decided to expose himself to "the false accusations of the envious and the gossip of the mad populace" in order to let truth (*amor veritatis*) and utility (*publica utilitas*) emerge.[83] It might be objected that such reasons are too noble, especially when the search after truth and the moral improvement of mankind are carried on in the domain of human foible. And yet this is precisely the defining characteristic of Cardano's method: reality is complex, and the understanding of it must necessarily include an investigation of its lowest and most hateful aspects. On the other hand, it is not impossible that his statements on pederasty, boys, and his "natural" sexual inclinations could amount to a clever and disingenuous smokescreen.

Cardano's multi-faceted account of music is fascinating. He conflates the several dimensions of music and combines different interpretative layers: the social aspect of music, the domain of musical practice, the physiology and aesthetics of musical perception, its mathematical and metaphysical implications, its rhetorical and psychological components. His bold examination of music as an activity that is both intellectual and social lays bare the existence of social hierarchies, metaphysical priorities, disciplinary boundaries, and gender conditionings. Confronted with the ambiguity of musical experience, he always seems to give his preference to theory rather than practice, music rather than musicians, mathematics rather than rhetoric, solo performance rather than ensembles, playing instruments rather than singing, monophony rather than polyphony, rich rather than poor, adult men rather than boys. In such a context, the portrait of same-sex love offered by Cardano is somber. He portrays male intimacy as suspicious and unnatural. Erotic attraction to boys, besides being a symptom of folly and unrestrained lasciviousness, is abominable and falls into the domain of *kakotropia*.[84] Disciplines such as astrology, medicine, physiognomy, and oneiromancy confirm the negative diagnosis of the ethical investigation. The disparaging view that Cardano has of musicians (not of music) parallels his censure of any form of same-sexual relations. Yet it is nonetheless curious that he maintained such evident appreciation for boys. His sanctions against sex between males evince some restraint, for usage of the most strongly condemnatory vocabulary of *sodomia* is at most rare and perhaps nonexistent in his comments on that topic published in his lifetime.[85]

Acknowledgements

My very special thanks to David Marshall and Kenneth Borris for revising the English of my text. I also would like to thank Monica Azzolini, Colin Homiski, Roberto Poma, and Lucía Díaz Marroquín for their comments.

Notes

1. Cardano makes some remarks on sex between females in his commentary on Ptolemy's *Tetrabiblos*; see Ch. 9, this volume. On the physiological causes of the birth of viragos, see Cardano's *Contradicentium medicorum libri*, in his *Opera omnia* (hereafter abbreviated as *OO*), ed. Charles Spon, 10 vols, Lugduni: Sumptibus Ioannis Antonii Huguetan & Marci Antonii Ravaud, 1663, vol. 6, pp. 651b–652a.

2. See e.g. texts by Caelius Aurelianus, Avicenna, Leone Ebreo, Pietro Aretino (on the husbands of priests in his *Ragionamenti*), and Theodor Zwinger (who catalogues diverse classical exemplars of male same-sex love that Cardano would have encountered in his readings), anthologized in Kenneth Borris (ed.), *Same-Sex Desire in the English Renaissance: A Sourcebook of Texts, 1470–1650*, New York and London: Routledge, 2004.

3. *Encomium Neronis*, *OO*, vol. 1, pp. 214b–216a. See Suetonius, *De vita Caesarum*, 2.68.

4. In *Contradicentium medicorum libri*, Cardano criticizes Galen for not specifying clearly the difference between *pueri* and *adolescentes* in his directions for venesection, and establishes 14 as the division (*OO*, vol. 6, pp. 516b, 567b). On the complexities of *puer* and "boy" in Renaissance usage, see Borris (ed.), *Same-Sex Desire*, pp. 20–1.

5. *Praecepta ad filios*, *OO*, vol. 1, p. 480b. See also *De sapientia*, *OO*, vol. 1, p. 524a; *De utilitate*, *OO*, vol. 2, p. 52b.

6. *De utilitate*, *OO*, vol. 2, p. 79b.

7. *Proxeneta*, *OO*, vol. 1, p. 388b.

8. *De utilitate*, *OO*, vol. 2, p. 4.

9. *De propria vita*, *OO*, vol. 1, p. 6a. On *amor hereos*, cf. John Livingston Lowes, "The Loveres Maladye of Hereos," *Modern Philology*, 11 (1913–14), 491–546; Ioan Peter

Culiano, *Eros and Magic in the Renaissance*, tr. M. Cook, Chicago and London: University of Chicago Press, 1987; Giorgio Agamben, *Stanze: La parola e il fantasma nella cultura occidentale*, Turin: Einaudi, 1977; Michael R. McVaugh, "Introduction," in Arnaldus de Villanova, *Tractatus de amore heroico*, ed. M. R. McVaugh, Barcelona: Publicacions i Edicions de la Universitat de Barcelona, 1985, pp. 11–39; Danielle Jacquart and Claude Thomasset, *Sexualité et savoir médical au Moyen Age*, Paris: PUF, 1985 (esp. ch. 3); M. F. Wack, *Lovesickness in the Middle Ages: The "Viaticum" and its Contemporaries*, Philadelphia: University of Pennsylvania Press, 1990.

10. *De propria vita*, *OO*, vol. 1, p. 10a.
11. *De subtilitate*, *OO*, vol. 3, p. 558b. Cardano refers to Giovanni Pico della Mirandola, *Disputationes adversus astrologiam divinatricem*, ed. Eugenio Garin, Turin: Aragno, 2004, vol. 1, p. 412. I thank Francesco Borghesi for this reference.
12. *De utilitate*, *OO*, vol. 2, p. 77a; *De subtilitate*, *OO*, vol. 3, p. 557.
13. *Proxeneta*, *OO*, vol. 1, p. 364a.
14. *De utilitate*, *OO*, vol. 2, pp. 97a; 146a.
15. *De sapientia*, *OO*, vol. 1, p. 509b; *De summo bono*, *OO*, vol. 1, p. 584b; *De consolatione*, *OO*, vol. 1, pp. 608b–610a. Cardano's notion that parental love of children is not natural was one of his theses condemned by an anonymous censor. See Ugo Baldini, "L'edizione dei documenti relativi a Cardano negli archivi del Sant'Ufficio e dell'Indice: Risultati e problemi," in Marialuisa Baldi and Guido Canziani (eds), *Cardano e la tradizione dei saperi*, Milan: Angeli, 2003, p. 493.
16. Marsilio Ficino coined the successful expression "Platonic love" for the intellectual love between friends. See *Opera*, Basel, 1557, p. 716. Cf. Paul Oskar Kristeller, *The Philosophy of Marsilio Ficino*, Gloucester: Peter Smith, 1964, p. 286; John Charles Nelson, *Renaissance Theory of Love: The Context of Giordano Bruno's "Eroici furori*,*"* New York and London: Columbia University Press, 1958, p. 69; Eugenio Canone, "Il 'senso' nei trattati d'amore: Ficino e la fortuna del modello platonico nel Cinquecento," in Massimo Luigi Bianchi (ed.), *Sensus, sensatio*, Florence: Olschki, 1996, pp. 177–98. On *amor Socraticus* in fifteenth- and sixteenth-century Italy, see E. Meylan, "L'evolution de la notion d'amour platonique," *Humanisme et Renaissance*, 5 (1938), 418–42; Giovanni dall'Orto, "'Socratic Love' as a Disguise for Same-Sex Love in the Italian Renaissance," in Ken Gerard and Gert Hekma (eds), *The Pursuit of Sodomy: Male Homosexuality in Renaissance and Enlightenment Europe*, New York: Harrington Park, 1989, pp. 33–65.
17. *De utilitate*, *OO*, vol. 2, p. 145b. In his commentary on Ptolemy's *Tetrabiblos*, Cardano places sleeping with boys (*concubitus cum pueris*) among the forms of unlawful sex (*illegitima Venus*). *OO*, vol. 5, p. 308a.
18. *Praecepta ad filios*, *OO*, vol. 1, p. 480b.
19. *De utilitate*, *OO*, vol. 2, p. 80a.
20. Ibid.
21. Ibid., p. 172ab. *Fractus incessus* is a sign of an effeminate and unmanly character, reports Quintilian, *Institutiones oratoriae*, 5.9.14.
22. Ibid., p. 178b. Johanne Ramminger, of the *Thesaurus Latinus*, informed me that *phoenicissa* likely means "fellation" (male or female). He observes that the Greek word *phoinikizein* means a "Phoenician" sexual practice, *irrumando*, according to Henri Estienne, *Thesaurus Graecae Linguae*.
23. *Liber de iudiciis geniturarum*, *OO*, vol. 5, p. 434a. The following are other examples of "libidinous" astral configurations: "brachium sinistrum antecedentis gemini, et genum sinistrum sequentis gemini, si cum Venere fuerint, hominem omni libidinis vitio implicant" (p. 437a).
24. *Liber XII. geniturarum*, *OO*, vol. 5, p. 520b.
25. Ibid., pp. 523b–524b.
26. As Germana Ernst advises me. The astral determination of sexual affinities could also undergo phases of major and lesser intensity according to long-term astrological developments. Campanella, for instance, lists specific astral influences among the

reasons behind the perceived increase in effeminacy and pedophilia (*bardascismo*) in his times. See Campanella, *La città del Sole*, ed. L. Firpo, rev. G. Ernst and L. Salvetti Firpo, Roma and Bari: Laterza, 1997, p. 57: "E tutti son maledici li poeti d'ogge per Marte, e per Venere e per la Luna parlano di bardascismo e puttanesmo. E gli uomini si effeminano e si chiamano 'Vossignoria'; e in Africa, dove regna Cancro, oltre l'Amazzoni, ci sono in Fez e Marocco li bordelli degli effeminati publici, e mille sporchezze." Under "Bardassa," the *Dizionario della Crusca* says: "Ragazzo che fa altrui copia di sè medesimo, Bagascione, Cinedo. Forse dall'arabo, uomo tristo, ed anco dal basso greco βαδάς, cinedo." Monica Azzolini informs me that the Iberian conquerors named native American males who lived as women "bardache." See Richard C. Trexler, *Sex and Conquest: Gendered Violence, Political Order, and the European Conquest of the Americas*, Ithaca, NY: Cornell University Press, 1995.

27. *De propria vita*, *OO*, vol. 1, p. 48b; *The Book of my Life*, tr. Jean Stoner, New York: New York Review Books, 2002, p. 230. See also *De morte*, *OO*, vol. 1, p. 675a.
28. *Proxeneta*, *OO*, vol. 1, p. 454a.
29. Ibid., p. 454b. In the German-speaking areas of Europe, "heresy" (*Ketzerei*), "heretic," or "to commit heresy" were frequently associated with male same-sexual contacts in the urban records. See Helmut Puff, *Sodomy in Reformation Germany and Switzerland*, Chicago and London: University of Chicago Press, 2003.
30. *Proxeneta*, *OO*, vol. 1, p. 458b.
31. *De utilitate*, *OO*, vol. 2, p. 77a. Compare pp. 76b, 113b. On Cardano's impotence, see also *De propria vita*, *OO*, vol. 1, p. 51b; *Liber XII. geniturarum*, *OO*, vol. 5, p. 517a.
32. *Paralipomena*, *OO*, vol. 10, p. 459b. Ibid., p. 460b: "nulla aestas fervidior aut aridior memoria nostra alia fuerat."
33. Francesco Fioravanti is not to be confused with the much more famous Leonardo Fioravanti. Paolo Camporesi, *Camminare il mondo: Vita e avventure di Leonardo Fioravanti medico del Cinquecento*, Milan: Garzanti, 1997, p. 61.
34. *De propria vita*, *OO*, vol. 1, pp. 20–1; *Book of my Life*, pp. 96–103.
35. Ibid.
36. *Paralipomena*, *OO*, vol. 10, p. 460b.
37. *De propria vita*, *OO*, vol. 1, pp. 11, 21; *Book of my Life*, pp. 49, 104.
38. *Proxeneta*, *OO*, vol. 1, p. 382b. The whole chapter, together with ch. 73 (pp. 411–14), expounds Cardano's directions to young servants.
39. *Proxeneta*, *OO*, vol. 1, p. 412b.
40. Ibid., pp. 402b–403a.
41. Giovanni Aquilecchia, "L'esperienza anglo-scozzese di Cardano e l'Inquisizione," in Marialuisa Baldi and Guido Canzani (eds), *Girolamo Cardano: Le opere, le fonti, la vita*, Milan: Angeli, 1999, p. 386.
42. *Dialogus de morte*, *OO*, vol. 1, p. 679a: "O beata Guglielmina (nam scio te adolescentem sincerum et optimum saepe ita nominare ioci causa consuesse) qui tui nominis gloriae talem nactus est praeconem, qualem aliquando frustra desiderabunt reges."
43. A. Grafton, *Cardano's Cosmos: The Worlds and Works of a Renaissance Astrologer*, Cambridge, MA, and London: Harvard University Press, 1999, p. 188.
44. See Michaela Valente, "'Correzioni d'autore' e censure dell'opera di Cardano," in Baldi and Canzani (eds), *Cardano e la tradizione dei saperi*, pp. 437–56, and Baldini, "L'edizione dei documenti relativi a Cardano."
45. *De propria vita*, *OO*, vol. 1, pp. 6a, 8a, 12a; *De libris propriis*, ed. Ian Maclean, Milan: Angeli, 2004, p. 240.
46. *De propria vita*, *OO*, vol. 1, p. 26b.
47. *De sapientia*, *OO*, vol. 1, p. 496b: "Sunt et aliqua communia corpori, atque animae: velut artium delectabilium scientia, ut fingendi, pingendi, canendi, scribedi."
48. *De propria vita*, *OO*, vol.1, p. 22b; *Book of my Life*, p. 108.
49. On Cardano as a music theorist, see his *Della natura de' principii et regole musicali*, *OO*, vol. 4, pp. 621–30; *De propria vita*, *OO*, vol. 1, pp. 31a, 39b (*Book of my Life*, pp. 148, 188); *De*

libris propriis, pp. 161, 165, 194, 258, 276. See further *Hieronymus Cardanus (1501–1576): Writings on Music*, ed. and tr. C. A. Miller, [Rome]: American Institute of Musicology, 1973; Ann E. Moyer, *Musica Scientia: Musical Scholarship in the Italian Renaissance*, Ithaca, NY, and London: Cornell University Press, 1992, pp. 158–68; Daniel P. Walker, "Musical Humanism in the 16th and Early 17th Centuries," *Music Review*, 2 (1941), 1–13, 111–21, 220–7, 288–308; 3 (1942), 55–71; Claude V. Palisca, *Humanism in Italian Renaissance Musical Thought*, New Haven and London: Yale University Press, 1985; Christine Suzanne Getz, *Music in the Collective Experience in Sixteenth-Century Milan*, Aldershot: Ashgate, 2005.

50. *Opus novum de proportionibus*, *OO*, vol. 4, pp. 548b, 550b. On music and mathematics, see Fabrizio Della Seta, "*Proportio:* Vicende di un concetto tra Scolastica e Umanesimo," in F. Della Seta and F. Piperno (eds), *In cantu et in sermone: For Nino Pirrotta on his 80th Birthday*, Florence: Olschki, 1989, pp. 75–99.

51. *De utilitate*, *OO*, vol. 2, pp. 116b–117a. See also *De immortalite animorum*, *OO*, vol. 2, pp. 534b–535a.

52. *Liber novum de proportionibus*, *OO*, vol. 4, p. 550b.

53. *Proxeneta*, *OO*, vol. 1, p. 473b. On music and the passions in Cardano, see Ingo Schütze, "Cardano und die Affektenlehre der Musik," *Bruniana et Campanelliana*, 7 (2001), 453–67.

54. *Proxeneta*, *OO*, vol. 1, p. 448b.

55. *De propria vita*, *OO*, vol. 1, p. 52a; *Book of my Life*, p. 245.

56. *De utilitate*, *OO*, vol. 2, p. 79b.

57. Ibid., p. 98a.

58. *De sapientia*, *OO*, vol. 1, p. 506b.

59. *De utilitate*, *OO*, vol. 2, p. 117a. See also *Opus novum de proportionibus*, *OO*, vol. 4, pp. 550a, 552a.

60. *De utilitate*, *OO*, vol. 2, pp. 131a, 132b. See also *Proxeneta*, *OO*, vol. 2, p. 356b.

61. *De utilitate*, *OO*, vol. 2, p. 17ab.

62. Ibid.

63. *Proxeneta*, *OO*, vol. 1, p. 357b.

64. Ibid., p. 412a.

65. *Problemata*, *OO*, vol. 2, p. 661ab; tr. in Miller (ed.), *Writings on Music*, p. 209.

66. *De utilitate*, *OO*, vol. 2, p. 117b. See also *Praecepta ad filios*, *OO*, vol. 1, p. 477b; *Theonoston*, *OO*, vol. 2, p. 343b.

67. *De utilitate*, *OO*, vol. 2, p. 117b.

68. Ibid., p. 125a.

69. *Opus novum de proportionibus*, *OO*, vol. 4, p. 552a.

70. *De utilitate*, *OO*, vol. 2, p. 131a.

71. Ibid., p. 117b.

72. *De sapientia*, *OO*, vol. 1, p. 575a; tr. in Miller (ed.), *Writings on Music*, pp. 207–8.

73. G. Bruno, *Opere magiche*, ed. S. Bassi, E. Scapparone, and N. Tirinnanzi, Milan: Adelphi, 2000, p. 504; Bruno, *Cause, Principle and Unity: Essays on Magic*, ed. Richard J. Blackwell and Robert de Lucca, Cambridge: Cambridge University Press, 1998, p. 169.

74. *De utilitate*, *OO*, vol. 2, p. 132a.

75. *Proxeneta*, *OO*, vol. 1, p. 447b. The gender implications of the musician differ in different cultures. On Islamic society e.g. cf. O. Wright, "Music," in Joseph Schact and C. E. Bosworth (eds), *The Legacy of Islam*, Oxford: Clarendon, 1974, p. 496. I thank Isabelle Dolezalek for this reference.

76. On the saying "Stultior Melitide," see Desiderius Erasmus, *Adagia* (4.4.69), in *Opera omnia*, vol. 2/7, Amsterdam: Elsevier, 1999, pp. 218–20.

77. *De musica*, Vatican MS 5850, tr. in Miller (ed.), *Writings on Music*, pp. 182–3.

78. *Proxeneta*, *OO*, vol. 1, p. 471b.

79. *Liber XII. geniturarum*, *OO*, vol. 5, p. 524b.

80. *Theonoston, OO*, vol. 2, p. 354ab; tr. in Miller (ed.), *Writings on Music*, p. 211. On Phinot, see Clement A. Miller, "Jerome Cardan on Gombart, Phinot, and Carpentras," *Musical Quarterly*, 58 (1972), 416.

81. Ibid. See also *De utilitate, OO*, vol. 2, p. 214b.

82. As Cardano explains in *De utilitate*, "[n]ihil enim infelicius, quam eos, qui te non amant, immodice amare" (*OO*, vol. 2, p. 5).

83. *Liber XII. geniturarum, OO*, vol. 5, pp. 523ab. See also *Commentarius in Ptolomaeum, OO*, vol. 5, p. 308a: "Piget me talia dicere, sed veritas me compellit."

84. *Proxeneta, OO*, vol. 1, pp. 461b–462a.

85. The vocabulary of *sodomia* infrequently appears in Cardano's treatise on metoposcopy first published long after his death. But he could not have authorized its printing in that form. I thank Kenneth Borris for drawing my attention to this point.

11 Mercury falling

Gender flexibility and eroticism in popular alchemy

Allison B. Kavey

Popular alchemical texts printed in England between 1580 and 1680 seek to parse and manipulate the divisions and binaries structuring the natural and social worlds, particularly the fundamental categories of male and female, their relative power, and their relationships to reproduction.[1] These books reflect the emergence of novel early modern ideas about anatomy, bodies, and natural philosophers' relationships to their arts and the world they were trying to change. The books' significance as a site of negotiation for ideas about sex, gender, and sex differences and their place in the changing genre of alchemical writing and practice is epitomized by the image of the chemical marriage and the complicated sexual combinations that romantic image shields. Though becoming increasingly unique within seventeenth-century natural philosophy for championing the sympathetic powers of similarity and the power of metaphor in the face of growing emphases on difference and empiricism, alchemy was not merely a vestige of Renaissance hermeticism, for it prompted the drafting, translation, and printing of thousands of pages during that century alone. Including multiple editions of the same book, more than one hundred English alchemical texts were printed during this period by a large number of printers. No single printer dominated the alchemical book trade in England, though a few repeatedly collaborated.

George Starkey, a seventeenth-century natural philosopher and alchemist who studied the texts of George Ripley, a famous medieval alchemist, and sought to make the stone, introduces the possibility of marriages that contain two same-sex partners in his *Breviary of Alchemy*:

> This is what is intimated in the Vision of Aristaus, who found a People that were Married, yet had no Children, because they married two Males together: such are they who mix *Sol* and *Lune*, both Corporal and fixt together, whom the Spirit will never revive, because there is not conjugal love.[2]

Starkey accomplishes two things in this excerpt: first, he reiterates the alchemical centrality of the metaphoric relation between human and metallic coupling, and second, he establishes that two males can be "married" and function as a pair, though their coupling will not produce offspring. He also raises the question of productivity, noting that two men cannot produce children.

That problem is addressed within alchemical writing through the introduction of spontaneous generation, where under the right conditions male sperm can regenerate itself, by one partner changing sex to act as the female during sections of the recipe that require a metallic womb. The ability to change sex is crucial to maintaining the underlying rules of alchemy, since sodomy would have threatened the natural order that alchemy tried to emulate. George Ripley's introduction to *The Compound of Alchymy* perceives in sodomy a violation of nature that can only be appropriately punished by an eternity in hell: "Sinfull Sodomites for ever were shent, / with *Dathan* and *Abiron* with many moe, / Which sunke for sinne to endless woe."[3]

Historians of early modern alchemy have primarily concentrated on using the laboratory notebooks and manuscripts of practicing adepts to resurrect contemporary laboratory practices,[4] though a few have ventured into the difficult waters associated with sexuality and alchemy. William Newman has investigated the topic of mercury as hermaphrodite, the image of the chemical marriage, and the alchemical role of spontaneous generation in *Promethean Ambitions*, concluding that these ideas placed alchemy alongside other Renaissance natural philosophical preoccupations.[5] Deborah Harkness explores the intersections between alchemy, scrying, and sex in her investigation of John Dee's increasingly desperate search for the philosopher's stone, while Tara Nummedal contends that Anna Zieglerin's position as a female practitioner of this traditionally male art helped to determine her markedly maternal and feminine–sexual metaphors and relationship to alchemy.[6]

Rather than examining the career of a single practitioner or a community of natural philosophers, I will examine the version of alchemical theory and practice forwarded by inexpensive alchemical texts printed in English between 1580 and 1680 and sold for between 6 pence and one shilling by mainstream, successful printers. Given these books' prices and availability and their internal comments to readers who lacked a university education and the resources that typically enabled it, they would have been relatively accessible to a broad range of the reading public. Thirty-one alchemical texts printed in England during this period suited this project's criteria for price and vernacular language.[7] Eighteen of these use some sexual metaphors to explain metallic combinations in alchemy, and nine include same-sex or bisexual combinations of metals in the process of making the philosopher's stone. Some of those texts were related to each other, since George Ripley's medieval *Compound of Alchemy* prompted George Starkey to pen his *A Breviary of Alchemy: or a Commentary upon Sir George Ripley's Recapitulation*, and Starkey also glossed Ripley's *Epistle to King Edward* in his treatise *Sir George Ripley's Epistle to King Edward Unfolded*.

The relationships among these texts point to the importance of historical authority in alchemy, which rooted itself in the classical East and the work of Hermes Trismegistus, who was believed to be a magus of great antiquity during the Renaissance, but whose writings were in fact variously authored in the late Roman Empire. Alchemical discourse thus changed slowly compared to other seventeenth-century intellectual disciplines. Many of the popular texts considered for this project are attributed to real or created medieval authors or, in the case of Starkey's work, provide early modern re-evaluations of actual late medieval and early Renaissance texts.

Alchemical discourse that lends itself to sexual description dismantles a natural world made of binaries in favor of one constructed by systems of sympathy. It consistently presents a world comprised of opposites, then erases their opposition by establishing the shared nature of opposite qualities and creates a new world in which opposites are collapsed into each other, with the result being a whole more perfect and powerful than the sum of its parts. An axiom in the book attributed to Artephius summarizes the centrality of this argument:

> *by the course of nature, he doth not know the making of Mettals that knoweth not the destruction of them.* It behoveth then to joyne together them that are of kindred, for *Natures* doe finde their like *natures*, and being purified, are mixed together, and mortifie themselves.[8]

Here, sympathetic association based upon shared natures determines the correct combinations of metals required to make the stone, but those sympathetic connections are realized through the destruction of the opposing qualities that the ingredients originally bring to the stone. Metallic combinations, particularly those based on opposing qualities, were generally framed within the metaphor of the chemical marriage, which fitted neatly into the more broadly sexual and social world figuratively constructed by alchemical discourse. Paramount in that world was the royal couple, the red king and the white queen, also called the sun and the moon, man and wife, and sulphur and mercury. Their copulation would eventually produce the philosopher's stone, though, as will soon be shown, that conjunction was far from straight or straightforward. Alchemical discourse produces a commentary on fixed sex and sexual affiliation by introducing mercury, which hermaphroditically confounds these divisions as neatly as it confounds the divide between solid and liquid. Examination of binary opposition thus becomes central to the alchemical process; rather than avoiding mercury, or relegating it to the ranks of the freakish and the powerless as if its hermaphroditic nature were monstrous,[9] alchemy assigns it the starring role in the creation of the stone.

Alchemy and alchemical sexes

Early modern alchemical texts attributed to medieval authorities or seeking to decode actual medieval texts rarely contain straightforward instructions for making the philosopher's stone; instead they embed the recipes within a code that refers to the chemical model of the natural world. Readers familiar with that code could change the metaphors into a recipe for the stone, while others would be left confused or impoverished from repeated failures. An introduction to the alchemical code reveals the model of the natural world under discussion in the texts and glosses fundamental alchemical vocabulary. The definitions of the critical terms reflect the structure of the natural world as it was imagined within the alchemical art.

The primary ingredients for the philosopher's stone, focal in the texts reviewed here, are mercury and sulphur. But the texts do not mean the sulphur and mercury that could be purchased at the local apothecary's shop and go to rather extreme lengths to discuss how to prepare common metals for use in the recipe. And an eager alchemist's concoction of mercury and sulphur was destined to fail unless he was familiar with the multiplicity of meanings the two words have in alchemical writing.

The first definition for these two metals comes from the alchemical understanding of metals and their place in the natural world. There were seven metals that corresponded with the seven planets: gold, silver, iron, copper, tin, lead, and mercury. They shared the characteristics of the planets with which they were associated, including the traditional planetary gender and potentialities proposed by astrologers. The heavenly bodies were believed to intervene between the realms of the divine and the natural and stamp the natural world: "each one according to a peculiar understanding, and according to its kind, and in Metals according to their form and gender."[10] These metals also shared some fundamental characteristics with each other, including shininess, solidity (except for mercury), and the ability to be shaped according to human will and intervention. Medieval and Renaissance natural philosophers believed that these shared characteristics meant that all metals were composed of the same ingredients, and that the differences in the metals could be explained by differences in their compositions and in the purity of the original ingredients. So, on Jupiter's place in the metallic hierarchy, the treatise *Of Natural and Supernatural Things* declares,

> Jupiter's Spirit is found not to be wanting in the least, in the generation of Metals, as likewise no one Spirit of all the Metals can be set backwards, because of necessity they accord together from the lowest to the highest degree, and must agree together.[11]

The basic similarities among metals also implied that any metal could be made into any other through combinations of the three principles, mercury, salt, and sulphur, which would push the current metal toward the qualities of the desired one. Accordingly, any metal could become gold if its original ingredients were purified and its excesses of liquidity or solidity corrected. The two qualities that could be found in every metal were sulphur and mercury, or the dry and inflammable principle and the fluid principle, so the process of turning base metals into gold depended upon the purification of those two principles and the correct manipulation of their proportions.

Mercury and sulphur were also under investigation by the "chemical physicians" by the late sixteenth century.[12] The German physician and philosopher Paracelsus proposed a model of the world in which three principles, rather than the Aristotelian four elements, reigned supreme, and were thus the appropriate ingredients for medical remedies, which were administered according to criteria of sympathy. Mercury and sulphur are two of the three principles that comprise the chemical model of the natural world, and when combined with salt, the third principle, they represent the spirit, the soul, and the body in the microcosm. Thus every metal and mineral has aspects of mercury, sulphur, and salt within it, and their varying combinations determine their form, color, and hardness.[13] Finally, all three have metaphorical definitions derived from their connections to classical mythology. Mercury in particular, associated with the planet and god of the same name, is traditionally pictured as an attractive young man whose duty is to serve the higher gods as a messenger. Mercury is also associated with Ganymede, both in classical mythology and in alchemical writing, and this connection with an iconic image of intergenerational male same-sex desire illustrates the complicated role played by mercury in its chemical marriages.

> Then on a copper plate in a flaming fire try this matter [philosopher's mercury], if it will consume in smoke; for you must presume it to be of the nature of the Ganimedes to fly up to Heaven . . . As the Ganimedes went up to Heaven, so thou shalt see this matter exalted . . .[14]

While Ganymedes in the sexual sense were relatively younger males, they were often mentioned alongside the word "whore." Making a whore or a Ganymede into a marriage partner would have been as complicated as the alchemical task of transforming iron into gold.

Alchemy asked a single question, according to its practitioners: how could art intensify and magnify the natural progression of metals toward gold? The answer was originally thought to be grounded in a humoral/Aristotelian model of the world, but for many early modern alchemists that model had to be combined with the chemical/Paracelsian one that subjugated ideas of humors and qualities to the governing structure of the three principles. In order to make this model look as authoritative as the Aristotelian/humoral one, many early modern texts that declared it the structure of the alchemical world were attributed to real or invented medieval authors. Despite this chronological puzzle, the inclusion of the chemical model of the world in the alchemical corpus is critical to thinking about early modern alchemy. These books depended on the presumption of a metaphoric relation between humans and metals in which both are products of the microcosm, their actions reflect divine will, and they act to support the most consistent alchemical analogy, the chemical marriage. In medieval and sixteenth-century alchemical texts, images of coupling and reproduction are crucial to the successful creation of the philosopher's stone.

That tradition begins with Hermes Trismegistus, rumored to have been an ancient magus who learned the secret of the philosopher's stone and recorded it in a scroll found in his tomb. In this aspect, he was, in fact, the product of a late medieval imagination, but his supposed text *The Smaragdine Table* introduced sex and reproduction as fundamental metaphors within alchemical theory and practice. The author used them to illustrate the problem of binary division within nature for an art whose goal was the attainment of perfection through combination and the subversion of imperfect qualities. "His Father is the Sun, his Mother is the Moone, the Winde bore it in her belly, the Earth is his Nurse; the Father of all the Telesme of this world is here, his force and power is perfect if it be turned into Earth."[15] While these are strictly male–female pairings, they nonetheless present multiple parents and imply multiple sexual pairings for the single stone. *The Smaragdine Table* was the foundational text of Renaissance hermetic alchemy, and it illustrates the limitations of binary division and pairings of "opposites," demonstrating the strength to be gained by abandoning opposition in favor of the multiplication of strengths.

The Renaissance effort to decode Trismegistus' work made such multiple pairings part of the alchemical process, since the metals needed to be prepared for their ultimate union in which their individual characteristics, including their sex, would be lost and each ingredient reborn as part of a constructed whole. Various English alchemical texts printed during the sixteenth and seventeenth centuries included both male–male and male–female couplings in their recitation of the steps required to make the stone. Early modern alchemical writing was flexible and varied, and some treatises contain a variety of sexual pairings that are not necessarily consistent throughout the length of the text and certainly not among different texts. When interpreting George Ripley's injunction, "Three of the Wife, and one of the Man thou take," George Starkey concludes "that the Woman is to exceed her Husband in a three-fold proportion. Or Two to One after Reymund: or Four to One according to Alanus; but Three to One is best."[16] This recitation of conflicting alchemical authorities reflects the difficulties facing practitioners who were trying to make sense of the alchemical literary legacy, which is lengthy, chronologically opaque, and often intentionally coded.[17]

Nevertheless, the model of the natural world in these books is relatively consistent, most notably in their concerted attack on the dominant, Aristotelian model of the world. From the fifth century BCE to the middle of the sixteenth century, Western philosophers agreed that the world was composed of four elements, earth, air, water, and fire, and that those elements were related to four qualities, four humors, and the four seasons. This model dictated medical practice, asserting that each person is born with an individual balance of humors, and that disease results from imbalance. It also dictated the terms of natural philosophy, which emphasized the importance of balance in the natural world. But alchemy attacks the oppositions fundamental to this model, destabilizing its claims to difference, by insisting on an underlying similarity among things of the same "nature" (mineral, animal, or vegetable). Alchemy also undermines opposition by assigning things to multiple categories according to their internal principles. Alchemical writers believed that mercury, for example, could have a vegetable, animal, and mineral character, and that all these aspects of its character must be exercised to make the most of its potential.[18]

The world that results from this dismantling of opposition and reassignment to fewer, broader categories is much more tightly interwoven, so that manipulating one factor has profound effects on the existing internal balance. Alchemy can be described as the systematic manipulation of a single mineral, mercury, with the intent of reducing it to its essential nature so as to use it to reduce other minerals to their essential natures in order to speed them on their natural path to perfection. This alchemical model accords the practitioner absolute control over all of the relationships in his crucible, not just the one he has changed. The microcosm is entirely at his fingertips, and his control over the natural world, as long as he practices the art correctly, is complete.[19] This empowerment of the practitioner connects the ongoing literary construction of alchemy with the contemporary rewriting of other disciplines within natural philosophy, particularly medicine, and unites them in their attempts to present a model of the natural world that combined humoral and chemical traditions. The accommodation of same-sex pairings within some alchemical texts suggests that the disruption of easy assumptions about opposition and the assertion of powerful underlying systems of sympathy were meaningful and important parts of this discourse.

Fundamental to Renaissance alchemy was its definition of "nature" because that determined whether two metals could be productively combined. Alchemical texts from the period insist that all metals share a common nature, which includes their tendency to proceed naturally toward perfection. According to *The Secrete Booke of Artephius*, for example, mercury

> brings back the *Bodies* to their first originall, that of *Sulphur* and *Mercury*, that of these, we may afterwards, in a short time, in less than one houre of the day, doe that above the ground which Nature wrought under ground in the mines of the Earth in a thousand yeeres, which is miraculous.[20]

Mercury was deemed capable of reducing other metals to their essential natures, and this step was fundamental to the process of creating the philosopher's stone. *The Practice of Lights* reminds readers of the rationale behind mercury's astonishing power:

> *therefore Water and Earth is the first matter of Mercury, and Mercury is the first matter of all Mettals, and when they be put into that Water, they all melt and dissolve in him as the Ice doth in warm Water,* and why they do so, because they were first Water coupled by cold.[21]

That process required combining things of like natures with each other, to ensure that the end product was not a monster. *The Compound of Alchymy* advises, "Joyne kinde to kinde therefore as reason is."[22] Practitioners were expected to have sufficiently studied the natural processes they were supposed to be imitating so that they would not combine metals in ways that violated the order of nature.

The first step on the ladder to performing transmutation involved understanding mercury and its role in the process. Alchemical treatises offer three possible ways for mercury to reproduce: first, it can switch sexes and couple as both a male and female with sulphur; it can couple with itself and reproduce through spontaneous generation; or it can couple with the products of its own earlier reactions. These writings thereby refer not to the metal mercury, but rather to its central role as one of the three principles in the chemical model of the world and its fundamental position as the fluid principle in all metals. Discussing that "improved mercury," Artephius declares "in this is our *Philosophicall* sublimation, not in the naughty common *Mercury*, which hath no qualities like unto them wherewith our *Mercury* drawn from his *vitriolate* caverns is adorned."[23] Mercury's central position within alchemy is guaranteed not by its own qualities, but by its effect on other metals, which it reduces to their most elemental metallic state: the fluid from which they were formed. That role is gendered female, hence *The Tomb of Semiramus Hermetically Sealed* states,

> The Mercurial Oyl of Salt is exalted to a higher degree of a fiery quality, as it is the foundation of the whole metallick solution (which is to be well observed) without which nothing can be advantageous in the Art, and it acts the part of a Woman in our Work, and is deservedly called the wife of Sol and the Matrix [i.e. womb].[24]

This passage not only genders mercury and restates the centrality of marriage and birth metaphors within alchemical discourse, but also suggests a flexibility of sex on account of mercury's androgynous capabilities. Its identity appears to depend upon its intentionality so that identity is determined by desire, not destiny. This kind of sexual flexibility is somewhat comparable to early seventeenth-century ideas about the effects of same-sexual desire on familial and personal roles. James I, Nora Jones reminds us, included a profusion of terms and family titles in letters to his favorite Ganymede, George Villiers. James conceived of this relationship "as if it were a true marriage in which both partners are wives at the same time that James is father and husband and Villiers is child and wife."[25] Jonathan Goldberg has argued that this kind of confusion implies that same-sex contacts could only be understood as part of a system of dangerous unintelligibility, so that sodomy was sometimes associated with lawlessness, heresy, and even sorcery. In Goldberg's analysis, the dislocation between biological sex and familial roles associated with same-sex relationships appeared to pose too great a risk to the family, the unit which was emerging as the fundamental unit within early modern society.[26] Of course, these perceived dangers were rooted in centuries of "sodomiphobic" Christian tradition. Kings might be able to manipulate family structure at will, but lesser men would be trapped within it or crushed by the consequences of their attempts to modify it to suit their desires. In alchemical discourse, however, mercury's potential to change its sex and gender supports the basic structure of the chemical model of the world, which depends upon all metals being reducible to their shared, fluid essence. Mercury's changeability also reflects its lofty position within the chemical world – like James I, it is able to evade the rules governing other, lesser metals and expose the false binaries that structure the majority of social interactions. The image of the chemical marriage reflects the deconstruction of those binaries, ironically through the manipulation of a highly binary institution.

The chemical marriage

As a structuring metaphor in alchemical discourse, the chemical marriage demonstrated the limitations of binary opposition. Alchemical writers adopted the familiar example of marriage, a uniting of opposites to create a balanced whole, to introduce an unfamiliar model of the world that celebrated the power to be found in reducing things to their shared essences and then building from that essence a quintessential representative of the examined category. In order to accomplish this, alchemical discourse had to deconstruct the apparent oppositions between several integral natural categories, especially male and female, natural and unnatural, productive and unproductive, parent and child, and living and dead. Mercury is essential to undermining at least three of these binaries because of its refusal to remain on only one side of each divide, and its capacity to be on both at the same time. It thoroughly destabilizes the validity of a world model that depends upon adherence to categories defined by opposing characteristics to achieve balance through the creation of pairs.

An alchemical treatise attributed to seventeenth-century English alchemist Nicholas Culpeper says that the true nature of mercury is almost impossible to locate because it takes the characteristics of everything it meets, making it a chameleon as well as a hermaphrodite:

> We are now come to treat of mercury and having looked up and down for him . . . we quickly discovered him, and then we found he was everywhere. Whilst we were admiring at his volatile nature and how versatile he was, and yet we had read long ago in the works of many Astrologers, that Mercury assumed the nature of every planet he was joined with.[27]

A Singular Treatise of Bernard Earl of Trevisan of the Philosopher's Stone describes the highly disparate natures of mercury in a different way, locating them within its internal qualities rather than in external contacts. "But of this Argent-vive, a certain part is fixed and digested, Masculine, hot, dry, and secretly informing: But the other which is Female, is Volatile, crude, cold, and moyst."[28] Since mercury could operate as either a male or a female in sexual combinations and, more importantly, have the characteristics of opposite things at the same time, many Renaissance alchemical texts entitled it "hermaphrodite." In fact, the purpose of preparing common mercury into mercury-vive was to make it more hermaphroditical. It is possible, of course, to read this as the ultimate illustration of oppositional balance, since mercury appears to be constantly in the process of reflecting the power of united opposites. But such a reading would overlook the exact nature of mercury's role in the alchemical process. It is not the end product, but instead the agent that allows other metals to engage with and reveal their true natures.

Mercury's position as "the hermaphrodite" contributes to this explanation of the alchemical model of the world. In early modern England, "hermaphrodite" signified a body with both male and female genitalia, and thus one that refuses to cooperate with the reduction of sex differences and legitimate sexual expression

Of the man and the woman clothed in a gowne of O-range colour vpon a field azure and blew, and of their rowles.

Figure 11.1 Creating the hermaphroditical mercury, from Nicholas Flamel, *Nicholas Flammel, His Exposition of the Hieroglyphicall Figures* (London: T. S. for Thomas Walkley, 1624), p. 82. From the Roy G. Neville Historical Chemical Library, a collection in the Othmer Library, Chemical Heritage Foundation, Philadelphia. Photo by Douglas A. Lockard.

to disparate genitalia and their momentary conjunction. Hermaphrodites were believed to represent both sexes at the same time within a single body, so a partner would not be required to balance their qualities. Medieval and early modern alchemical texts that featured woodcuts and engravings frequently depicted mercury as a male and female squashed together, rather like conjoined twins. This represented its creation, which depended upon the combination of mercury and sulphur to produce a body that had purer versions of each. A text attributed to the medieval French alchemist Nicolas Flamel not only describes the process of creating the hermaphroditical mercury verbally but also depicts it in a small woodcut (Figure 11.1). "I made then to be painted here two bodies, one of a Male, and another of a Female," we are told, "to teach thee, that in this second operation, thou hast truly, but not yet perfectly, two natures conjoined and married together, the Masculine and the Feminine; or rather the Four Elements."[29] The partial conjunction depicted here would be completed by the addition of mercury, which would cause the two bodies to coalesce into a single figure that had all of the female and male qualities. George Starkey describes the completion of the process:

> Our Art therefore is to compound two principles (one in which the salt, and another in which the Mercury of nature doth abound) which are not yet perfect . . . and then by common Mercury to extract not the Pondus, but the celestial virtue out of the compound, which virtue, (being fermental) begets in the common Mercury an offspring more noble than itself, which is our true Hermaphrodite, which will congeal itself and dissolve the bodies.[30]

In an Aristotelian world, that conclusion would have produced an entirely stable chemical hermaphrodite whose balance is internally secured. That hermaphrodite would have lasted forever, but the one required to make the philosopher's stone will not – it is immediately to be put back into reactions. Alchemical production requires combination and destruction. The destruction necessary to make the stone renders an Aristotelian world inappropriate for alchemical theory, since balance in that model of the world would result in stasis. However, in a chemical model of the world, the hermaphrodite's internal balance is turned back on itself, since it first digests the two things that were required to make it, then becomes recombined with mercury to exercise the potentialities of treating something with itself. "It is a content for the Artists to see how the Heterogeneities of Mercury are discovered," observes George Starkey,

> which no other Art save the liquor *Alcahest* can do, and that in a destructive, and not a generative way as this is, for this operation of ours is made between male and female, within their own kind, between which there is a ferment which effecteth that which no other thing in the world could do.[31]

The heterogeneities of mercury abound, and alchemical transmutation depends upon them. The opposing qualities of male and female, cold and hot, dry and wet, continue to exist within the hermaphrodite, and they are brought to bear upon all of the reactions in which their composite figure is involved. They exist, at least after their combination with mercury, as fundamental metallic qualities rather than paired oppositions. Thus when the chemical hermaphrodite interacts with mercury, there is always the potential for a same-sex connection that strengthens, rather than threatens, the process. And while it has no need for external connections to balance its qualities, it seeks them out anyway, since intensification through the combination of similar things, not balance, is the goal of the chemical world.

The importance of destruction through sympathy, and the potential for generation that follows this process, is beautifully presented in *A Treatise of Florian Raudorff*: "this earth is comprised of foure Elements, but are not contrary one to another, for their contrariety is changed or reduced to an agreement unto a uniform Nature."[32] In order to accomplish this perfect reduction into shared essences, a final binary opposition, the one between body and spirit, will be sacrificed, and the potential from its collapse used to build something new that contains all the qualities of metallic nature, and thus can interact with and improve every metal. The creation of the chemical hermaphrodite involves the combination of two metallic "bodies," one male and one female, with the male usually representing the spirit and the female the flesh or the earth. When the two are collapsed into each other, the spirit is released from the heavy body, which destabilizes the latter, leaving it ungrounded and free, like the spirit, to rise in search of something similar to improve it. This reflects the essential similarity between the two. Or as the Raudorff treatise contends, "Thus we have made a spirit out of the body, and a body out of the spirit, one onely Thing."[33] This excerpt asserts the fundamentally destructive nature of alchemy, in which all ingredients and all qualities are reduced to their shared essences and strengthened through systems of sympathy that produce an internally coherent and internally referential philosopher's stone.

It would seem that all of these combinations of like things would make room for same-sex combinations. Alchemical treatises do not entirely ignore this possibility, and frequently they accommodate it by defining the places in which same-sex combinations are not acceptable. In the text attributed to seventeenth-century alchemist Arthur Dee, for example, all same-sex combinations, including alchemical ones, are egregious sins, though the prospect of incest is oddly permissible:

> Let none therefore presume to try the wicked and unnatural conjunction of two males, neither let him conceive any hope of issue from such copulation, but he shall join Gabertius to Beia, and offer the sister to her own brother in firm matrimony, that from thence he may receive Sol's noble Son.[34]

Dee extended the cultural anathema placed upon male same-sex unions to the chemical world, even while he seemingly ignored the cultural taboo applied to incest. His tropes here reflect the familial metaphors (and underscore that they were understood to be metaphors) available to describe sexual relationships, and the cultural currency that this model enjoyed, not just inside the court of James I but among English natural philosophers.

The appropriation of gendered family titles was intended as a metaphoric shorthand for relationships among metals, and it emphasizes the destructive aspects of alchemy. The combination of these very similar metals will result in the death of one – strangely enough, the male:

> Joyn therefore *Gabritius* to his beloved sister *Beya*, which is a tender damsel, and straight-way *Gabritius* will die; that is will lose what he was; and from that place where he appeared to have lost what he was, he shall appear what he was not before.[35]

The combination of these two metals is sufficiently powerful to destroy the nature of one and produce a new metal through the incorporation of its nature with the remaining partner, the sister. This process underlines alchemical dependence on a model of procreative deconstruction accomplished through the combination of two active partners and the reduction of one to its most essential characteristics before a new product can be built of the newly available parts.

Other alchemists were more concerned about a rather different type of violation of nature, one which exceeded even sodomy in its affront to the perceived natural order. This type of warning is recorded in nearly every alchemical treatise, as in Ripley's caution against combining things of *different* kinds. It is reiterated in dire tones in Starkey's *Breviary of Alchemy*: "For likeness of Nature is the Cause of Love, and Oneness of Essence the true ground of Union; among different Substances can only be expected Confusion, if not Destruction."[36] Here destruction is not desirable, since in this case it would be the endpoint of a violation of the natural order, rather than a midpoint in a process of breakdown and resurrection. Furthermore, it is a combination of opposites, which should produce balance but instead produces confusion and leads alchemists to violate nature's order. According to this warning, combining things of like nature, by which is meant metals with similar qualities, will always be productive. This leaves room for productive combinations of all male metals, a possibility that is anticipated by mercury's propensity for combining with itself.

However, such metallic same-sex couplings entail a transition away from traditional ideas about procreation and toward notions of self-reproduction, or even spontaneous generation. Starkey appears to accord all male marriages some legitimacy and even locates them in existing historical tradition, but refuses to grant them the right to reproduce:

> This is that which is intimated in the Vision of Aristaus, who found a People that were Married, yet had no Children, because they married two Males together: Such are those they who mix *Sol* and *Lune*, both corporal and fixt together, whom the Spirit will never revive, because there is not conjugal Love.[37]

Reproduction within all male alchemical couples required practitioners to exercise the androgynous powers available to mercury, which could act the part of a woman and gain the womb to support the role. Here, the metaphoric relationship between metals and humans is put to the test, since by the mid-seventeenth century the medical community had abandoned the humoral belief that women could become men, so that gender affiliation became more fixed. This suggests one reason for removing the chemical marriage, which had played such a central role in alchemical theory, from popular alchemical treatises – it now transgressed against medical and cultural expectations for sex and gender. It also required far too many machinations to produce offspring, though those procedures had long attracted natural philosophers who hoped to extend art sufficiently to produce life in a crucible.

The possibility of spontaneous reproduction did not exist only between alchemical couples of different sexes. The idea of the homunculus, a being that could supposedly be created without sexual contact and using only sperm, had fascinated natural philosophers from the medieval period forward. As William

Newman shows, alchemists were preoccupied with the possibility of creating life, particularly an artificially enhanced life, without the morally damaging and physically messy potentials of heterosexual procreation. What ties alchemy to the creation of the homunculus is the joint desire of both these arts to outdo the powers of nature by creating something greater than other humans or metals. That bond between the two arts is memorialized from the Middle Ages forward by alchemical illustrations featuring the red king and the white queen sealed in a flask, having sex and producing offspring. In alchemy, however, the creation of the homunculus simply serves as a metaphor for the creation of the stone, and it reflects the ways in which mercury was expected to act like a man producing a homunculus in order to improve itself and other metals. Though varying as much as recipes for the stone, directions for making homunculi generally agree that the male sperm must be locked away in an artificial womb and allowed to interact with itself under warm and protected conditions. During this time, it will generate a new life, though the exact process required to accomplish this is rather vague.[38] Alchemical texts make the process of chemical self-reproduction specific. Starkey describes why mercury can generate a new life without the help of another metal: "Know therefore that Mercury hath in itself a Sulphur, which being unactive, our Art is to multiply in it a living active Sulphur, which comes out of the loyns of our Hermaphroditical body."[39] Starkey also indicates the ways in which mercury can take advantage of its hermaphroditical status to both generate and incubate sperm, so that no external container, such as the animal's womb generally used to create homunculi, is required. The process cannot occur without the alchemist's help because he provides the steady heat from the fire and the protected space of the crucible.

The models of self-generation present in alchemy and the creation of the homunculus point to a shared definition of nature in the Starkey text and in the passage discussed above, since all of the ingredients required to make the philosopher's stone share a metallic nature and derive from the components of properly coddled mercury, while all of the ingredients required to make the homunculus share an animal nature and derive from the components of properly incubated sperm. The two processes share the belief that nature trends toward perfection, and that art can speed that movement without violating the natural order. They contend also that art can improve upon nature to create something spectacular, so that the "ferment begets an offspring, more noble than it self a 1000 fold."[40] They both use epithets that reflect more typical forms of combination and procreation, applying the title of "mother" to metals or glass containers, that of "father" to another metal or disembodied sperm, and that of "creator" to a man who has mastered an art.

The natural worlds imagined by creators of the stone and the homunculus are similar, not just in their details, but also in their divergence from a strictly Aristotelian model of the world. Analysis of inexpensive English alchemical texts published between 1585 and 1650 reveals competing worldviews, one of which forwards a world governed by balance achieved through antipathy, whereas the other favors enrichment through the manipulation of systems of sympathy. A text attributed to Flamel uses both systems to discuss alchemical conjugation. He uses the humoral concept of opposites to explain the presence of the male and the female and their associated qualities as the starting point for the process, but then erases their differences through dissolution into shared essential natures:

> in this second operation . . . the foure naturall Enemies, the hote and cold, dry and moist, begin to approach amiably one another and by meanes of the Mediators and Peace-makers, lay downe by little and little, the ancient enmity of the old Chaos.[41]

Alchemical writers used both the Aristotelian and chemical/Paracelsian systems in their texts, and that combination renders their explanatory metaphors, especially sexual coupling and generation, ambiguous. Alchemical language thus invokes an interplay of two different models of the natural world. The sexual combination of a male and a female to produce children is perfectly compatible with the Aristotelian and humoral views of the world; but the Aristotelian model also leaves room for the spontaneous generation of masculine sperm, an inherently independent process that reflects an internal, rather than external, approach to finding balance.[42] The Paracelsian model of the world lacks the obsession with balance that shapes Aristotelian natural philosophy, while sharing the Aristotelian model's belief in the possibility of spontaneous generation, and adds its own preference for change or generation through the combination of similar things. Any attempt to trace the sexuality of the metals expressed by the combination of sulphur and mercury, and the multiplicity of possibilities raised by their potential combination, evinces this confusion of alchemical models. Mercury's relations with sulphur are not all conducive to male–female description. Mercury is the more active partner in this pairing, the traditionally male role, and it acts upon sulphur, which is consistently sexed male. Moreover, the process of dissolution requires the combination of both vulgar and occult sulphur, with the latter disguised in the body of common mercury. In this combination, sulphur and mercury would interact, with the end result being the emergence of occult sulphur (presumably male) and its own interaction with common sulphur (also male).

Such implications appear in Ripley's second gate, or chapter on dissolution:

> One in gender they be, and in number two, Whose father is the Sunne, the Moone the Mother, The Mover is Mercurie, these and no moe, Be our Magnesia, our Adropp, and none other, Things here be, but onely sister and brother, That is to meane agent and patient, Sulphure and Mercury coessential in our intent.[43]

The sun and the moon combine through the agency of mercury to produce the desired result. However, mercury, which is traditionally female, is the more active partner, or "the mover." Sulphur, which is consistently sexed male, is the recipient of mercury's actions, and it acts as the passive "sister" and "patient." This complicates the traditional sexual assignment of both metals by making one male the passive recipient of the other male's attentions, and thus feminizing it. The feminization of sulphur in this reaction is enshrined in *A Treatise Written by Alphonso King of Portugall Concerning the Philosophers Stone*:

> This is the other part of the Earth, Sulphur, Woman, hot, and dry; for when it makes its first change or trucke, that part is wanting which encompassed the humidity; as Penelope made warre in the absence of Ulysses in Italy, so this Widow, so pale and wan, hopes for the returne of her banished Husband.[44]

While sulphur acts as the female in this reaction, feminized sulphur is not perfectly female, for it begins as a male, and lacks mercury's perfect ability to change its sex and gender. We may compare Renaissance medical theory on sexual transformation. All females could theoretically become male, in accord with the one-sex humoral/Galenic model of the body. Some held that males could likewise become female, whereas others maintained that, being more perfect by definition, males could not thus change gender and supposedly degenerate in that sense, even if they were already effeminate. Yet sulphur's chemical feminization does not appear negative, for its combination with mercury makes it more essentially itself, and therefore more masculine than before. Mercury reacts to its partner's newly discovered masculinity, paired with its consistently male body, and abruptly goes back to its original sex and gender so that it can exercise its capacity for getting pregnant and incubating sulphur's semen. George Ripley's text refers to this new sexual role for mercury, as does *The Booke of John Sawtre a Monke*: "the sperme of Sol is to be cast into the matrix of Mercury, by bodily copulation or conjunction, and joining of them together."[45]

The medical belief in the flexibility of biological sex was losing currency in the seventeenth century, partially due to the increase in anatomical knowledge. It was becoming difficult to maintain that male and female genitalia were simply reversed expressions of the same basic organ structure, pushed outside of the body in the case of males by greater natural heat, but retained inside in the case of females. From the late sixteenth century onward, medical authorities increasingly found male and female bodies to be distinctly and inherently different.[46] The fundamental alchemical assertion that only like things could be productively combined, which would have accorded with the perceived homology of male and female genitals when the concepts and metaphoric terminology used in the majority of these treatises were developed, could become culturally transgressive as they were read in the face of new medical ideas about the fundamental difference of male and female bodies. Alchemy would also come to appear increasingly Paracelsian in its presentation of the natural world because the texts' insistence on the productive combination of similar things and their presumption of a natural trend toward perfection were increasingly at odds with contemporary humoral and observational models that emphasized the combination of opposites in order to produce balance.

Some of the sexual assertions in alchemy, however, would have been as transgressive in the fifteenth century as in the seventeenth. The first marriage, when correctly performed, concluded with the female, mercury, ascendant as evidenced by the color of the mixture. "Pythagoras sayth, as long as the obscure blacknesse doth appeare, the woman doth rule, which is the first strength of our stone."[47] In his explication of the meeting of two dragons, an allegory for the initial combination of mercury and sulphur, Flamel observes:

> Hee which is undermost, without wings, he is the fixed, or the male; that which is uppermost, is the volatile, or the female, black and obscure, which goes about to get the domination for many months. The first is called Sulphur, or heat and drynesse, and the latter Argent Vive, or cold and moisture.[48]

With the notable exception of Chaucer's wife of Bath, medieval and early modern women were not expected to dominate marriages, nor in the age of the popular humiliation of the scold and the cuckold, was a female-dominated marriage considered to be "a perfect medicine and mixtion."[49]

But all of these female-dominated unions are temporary, and they reflect a stage in the dissolution of opposition rather than a triumph of one set of qualities over another. Popular English alchemical texts of the late sixteenth through mid-seventeenth centuries erase the differences between male and female by reducing them to their shared natures, so that in the end, sex has no meaning and is entirely interchangeable. The eighth illustration in the text attributed to Flamel features a woman kneeling at the feet of St Paul, who holds a key in one hand and has his other on the woman's shoulder (Figure 11.2).

In this allegory, the woman is the stone in the moment before multiplication, and St Paul the dispenser of knowledge; but gender in the former case, the writer explains, has actually become both interchangeable and optional:

> But why have I made to be painted a *woman*? I could as well have made to be painted a *man*, as a *woman*, or an Angell rather, (for the whole natures are now spirituall and corporall, masculine and feminine:) But I have rather chosen a *woman*, to the end that thou mayest judge, that shee demands rather this [i.e. multiplication], then any other thing, because these are the most naturall and proper desires for a women.[50]

Though the woman in this scene expresses alchemy's reproductive aspect, a man, or even an angel, would have been equally appropriate. As alchemical language is highly metaphorical, so alchemical sex must be read in an early modern context to grasp the nature and applications of these metaphors. Alchemists frequently used male and female labels for metals to encourage readers to think about the qualities generally associated with human males and females, and thus the labels served as a cultural shorthand and means for familiarizing difficult and unfamiliar material. The ways in which male and female disappear within alchemical discourse do not appear to express a social or political argument, but instead a new framework for thinking about change and generation within the natural world. In some cases, we have seen, the sexual politics of perceived sodomy does enter alchemy to some

Figure 11.2 The philosopher's stone before multiplication, from Nicholas Flamel, *Nicholas Flammel, His Exposition of the Hieroglyphicall Figures* (London: T. S. for Thomas Walkley, 1624), p. 96. From the Roy G. Neville Historical Chemical Library, a collection in the Othmer Library, Chemical Heritage Foundation, Philadelphia. Photo by Douglas A. Lockard.

extent, so that its transmutations of gender and gendered couplings seem to have provoked some anxieties, though not in a standardized, consistent way. The politics of alchemy tends rather to be natural philosophical.

Notes

1. This work was supported by the Roy G. Neville Fellowship, which permitted me to work with the rare books in the Roy G. Neville Historical Chemical Library at the Chemical Heritage Foundation in Philadelphia, PA. Eve Kosofsky Sedgwick introduced the concept of structuring binaries as the framework of modern thought in her landmark work, *Epistemology of the Closet*, Berkeley: University of California Press, 1994, ch.1. I would like to extend her work backwards and examine the structuring binaries of the early modern world, and natural philosophy provides an excellent venue for that.
2. George Starkey, *Breviary of Alchemy*, London: William Cooper, 1678, pp. 16–17.
3. George Ripley, *The Compound of Alchymy*, London: Thomas Orwin, 1591, sig. B2r.
4. William R. Newman, *Gehennical Fire: The Lives of George Starkey, an American Alchemist in the Scientific Revolution*, Chicago: University of Chicago Press, 2003;

W. R. Newman and Lawrence M. Principe, *Alchemy Tried in the Fire*, Chicago: University of Chicago Press, 2002; L. M. Principe, *The Aspiring Adept: Robert Boyle and his Alchemical Quest*, Princeton: Princeton University Press, 2000.

5. William R. Newman, *Promethean Ambitions: Alchemy and the Quest to Perfect Nature*, Chicago: University of Chicago Press, 2004, pp. 171–208.
6. Deborah E. Harkness, *John Dee's Conversations with Angels: Cabala, Alchemy, and the End of Nature*, Cambridge: Cambridge University Press, 1999; Tara Nummedal, "Alchemical Reproduction and the Career of Anna Marie Zieglerin," *Ambix*, 48/2 (2001), 56–68.
7. Identified through a search of the English Short Title Catalog. It may not record all English alchemical texts produced during the period. None of these texts lists a price, but by comparing them to texts of similar lengths that do list prices, I concluded that a maximum length of 200 (octavo) or 250 (duodecimo) pages fell within this price range. It necessarily rules out texts that feature multiple elaborate or unique illustrations (either woodcut or copper plate), since these would put the book's price beyond the means of many interested readers. Text length also determined book prices in early modern England, since paper was the most expensive material required to make books. Cheap print, as defined by Margaret Spufford and elaborated by Tessa Watt, generally cost less than 6 pence and was of marginal print quality, printed in octavo or duodecimo, and under 100 pages. Literacy rates were consistently higher in urban areas, where these books were printed and sold, but it is safe to assert that the majority of readers were artisans and merchants, rather than shop boys and apprentices. Tessa Watt, *Cheap Print and Popular Piety, 1550–1640*, Cambridge: Cambridge University Press, 1991; Margaret Spufford, *Small Books and Pleasant Histories: Popular Literature and its Readership in Seventeenth Century England*, Athens, GA: University of Georgia Press, 1982.
8. *The Secret Booke of Artephius*, in *Nicolas Flamel his Exposition of the Hieroglyphicall Figures*, London: printed by T.S. for T. Walkely, 1624, p. 214.
9. Early modern medicine viewed hermaphrodites as either monsters, whose birth signified God's displeasure with the child's parents or their nation, or freakish anomalies whose bodies had somehow exceeded traditional anatomical expectations. The latter explanation became increasingly popular as medical practitioners established strict anatomical delineations between male and female bodies. On hermaphrodites and sexuality, see Emma Donoghue, "Imagined More than Women: Lesbians as Hermaphrodites, 1671–1766," *Women's History Review*, 2/2 (1993), 199–216.
10. *Basilius Valentinus, A Benedictine Monk, of Natural and Supernatural Things. Also of the First Tincture, Root, and Spirit of Metals and Minerals*, tr. D. Cable, London: Moses Pitt, 1670, p. 113.
11. *Ibid*, pp. 126–7.
12. See Allen G. Debus, *The Chemical Philosophy: Paracelsian Science and Medicine in the Sixteenth and Seventeenth Centuries*, New York: Science History Publications, 1977.
13. *Of Natural and Supernatural Things*, p. 113.
14. *A Treatise Written by Alphonso King of Portugall Concerning the Philosopher's Stone*, in *Five Treatises of the Philosophers Stone*, London: Printed by T. Harper, sold by J. Collins, 1652, p. 14.
15. *The Smaragdine Table of Hermes Trismegistus, of Alychmy*, in *Five Treatises of the Philosophers Stone*, London: Printed by T. Harper and sold by J. Collins, 1652, sig. A4v.
16. Starkey, *Breviary of Alchemy*, pp. 12–13.
17. Cf. Lawrence M. Principe, "Robert Boyle's Alchemical Secrecy: Codes, Ciphers, and Concealments," *Ambix*, 39/2 (1992), 63–74.
18. See e.g. *Of Natural and Supernatural Things*, p. 54.
19. William R. Newman argues that alchemy was concerned with the mimicry and ensuing domination of nature and must be analyzed as such, contrary to feminist scholars such as Carolyn Merchant and Evelyn Keller, who have argued that alchemists sought to respect rather than dominate nature. Newman, "Alchemy, Domination, and Gender,"

in Noretta Koertge (ed.), *A House Built on Sand: Exposing Postmodernist Myths about Science*, Oxford: Oxford University Press, 1998, pp. 217–39.

20. *The Booke of Artephius*, in *Nicolas Flamel*, p. 173.
21. *The Practice of Lights*, in *Collectanea Chymica*, London: Printed for William Cooper, 1684, p. 40, italics in the original.
22. Ripley, *Compound of Alchymy*, sig. C3r.
23. *Booke of Artephius*, in *Nicolas Flamel*, pp.185–6.
24. *Semiramus Hermetically Sealed*, in *Collectanea Chymica*, London: Printed for W. Cooper, 1684, pp. 24–5.
25. Nora Johnson, "Ganymedes and Kings: Staging Male Homosexual Desire in *The Winter's Tale*," *Shakespearean Studies*, 26 (1998), 187. See also Letter 218 in G. P. V. Akrigg (ed.), *Letters of King James VI and I*, Berkeley: University of California Press, 1984, p. 31: "That we may make at this Christmas a new marriage ever to be kept hereafter; for God so love me, as I desire only to live in this world for your sake, and that I had rather live banished in any part of the earth with you than live a sorrowful widow's life without you. And so god bless you, my sweet child and wife, and grant that ye may ever be a comfort to your dear dad and husband."
26. Jonathan Goldberg, *Sodometries*, Stanford, CA: Stanford University Press, 1992.
27. Nicolas Culpeper, *Mr Culpeper's Treatise of Aurum Potabile and Culpeper's Ghost*, London: G. Eversden, 1650, pp. 150–1.
28. *A Singular Treatise of Bernard Earl of Trevisan of the Philosopher's Stone*, in *Collectanea Chymica*, London: Printed for W. Cooper, 1684, p. 91.
29. *Nicolas Flamel*, p. 82.
30. George Starkey, *Sir George Ripley's Epistle to King Edward Unfolded*, in *Chymical, Medicinal, and Chyrurgical Addresses*, London: Printed by G. Dawson for G. Calvert, 1655, p. 29. Mercury is also described as a hermaphrodite in the collection of treatises entitled *Philosophia Maturata*, London: G. Sawbridge, 1668; *Paracelsus, his Aurora, and Treasure of the Philosophers*, London: G. Calvert, 1659, p. 51; George Starkey, *The Marrow of Alchemy*, London: Printed by R.I. for E. Brewster, 1654, sig. B4r; *The Booke of Jonathan Sawtre*, in *Five Treatises of the Philosopher's Stone*, London: Printed by Thomas Harper for John Collins, 1651, p. 23; and Thomas Willis, *The Search of Causes*, London: Printed by John Legatt, 1616, pp. 65, 68.
31. Starkey, *Ripleys Epistle*, in *Chymical . . . Addresses*, pp. 31–2.
32. *A Treatise of Florianus Raudorff of the Stone*, in *Five Treatises of the Philosophers Stone*, London: Printed by T. Harper and sold for J. Collins, 1652, p. 59.
33. Ibid., p. 56.
34. Eldest son of the famous alchemist and mathematician John Dee, Arthur lived from 1579 to 1651 and studied natural philosophy with other eminent English natural philosophers. Arthur Dee, *Fasciculus Chemicus or Chemical Collections*, London: J. Flesher for R. Mynne, 1650, p. 177.
35. Starkey, *Breviary of Alchemy*, p. 17.
36. Ibid., p. 10.
37. Ibid., p. 17.
38. Newman, *Promethean Ambitions*, pp.171–208.
39. Starkey, *Ripley's Epistle*, in *Chymical . . . Addresses*, p. 37.
40. Ibid., p.36.
41. *Nicolas Flamel*, p. 84.
42. Aristotle, *Generation of Animals*.
43. Ripley, *Compound of Alchymy*, sig. D1r.
44. *Treatise Written by Alphonso*, in *Five Treatises of the Philosophers Stone*, p. 5.
45. This section of the text is both underlined and marked by a marginal x in the copy held by the Neville Collection at the Chemical Heritage Foundation. *Booke of John Sawtre*, in *Five Treatises*, p. 27.

46. Cf. R. Martensen, "The Transformation of Eve: Women's Bodies, Medicine, and Culture in Early Modern England," in Roy Porter and Mikulas Teich (eds), *Sexual Knowledge, Sexual Science: The History of Attitudes toward Sexuality*, Cambridge: Cambridge University Press, 1994, ch. 16.

47. *Booke of John Sawtre*, in *Five Treatises*, p. 34.

48. *Nicolas Flamel*, p. 65.

49. *Booke of John Sawtre*, in *Five Treatises*, p. 34.

50. *Nicolas Flamel*, p. 130.

Part III
Science and sapphisms

12 Intrigues of hermaphrodites and the intercourse of science with erotica

Winfried Schleiner

If we accept the premise that the early modern period experienced the world through literature to a considerable extent, then female same-sex relations must have appeared rather rare to many. Personal or fictional reports of such are few. If we exclude medical and judicial reports as well as fictional treatments that are based on gender error and poems in the Sapphic tradition usually written by male authors (like John Donne's poem "Sappho to Philaenis"), there is not very much in that period – and that may be an overstatement. Of course, we are here in an area of deliberate obfuscation. Thus, when the important Lusitanian physician publishing in Hamburg, Rodrigo a Castro, wrote his book on women's diseases *De universa mulierum medicina* (1603), he included sections on hermaphrodites as well as on different kinds of *masturbatores*, adding to the latter the disposition that, should his book ever be translated into vernacular languages, this note, since it was addressed to the learned, should not be.[1] To my knowledge his book (which went through several editions) was never translated. I will discuss a work that, though published in 1718, appears to include much Renaissance material, although I cannot always prove that now to every one's satisfaction. Entitled *De Hermaphroditis*, it was published by the notorious printer Edmund Curll, sometimes called the "abominable" Curll because he had a record of printing works that were considered in the margin of the acceptable (and of going to jail for it). At least since the Renaissance, one of the meanings of the word "hermaphrodite" in non-scientific language had been "catamite."[2] Though anonymous and no doubt culled together in the spirit of the time from numerous Renaissance works (sometimes with attributions of the sources, sometimes without), this text is attributed to Giles Jacob (1686–1744), whom the *Dictionary of National Biography* calls "a most diligent compiler."

Why should the title be in Latin while the rest of the work is in English? Perhaps Latin added a little spice with the expectation of pornography. In the Folger copy, the work is bound with an English translation of the German physician Heinrich Meibom's (of course originally Latin) *A Treatise of the Use of Flogging in Venereal Affairs*, which Edmund Curll published in the same year. That work debated the question whether it was ethical to have a man flogged if that was the only way to have his otherwise flaccid organ aroused. While it is at least possible that the original intention of the solidly Protestant physician from Lübeck was serious, since he posed the question within the context of marital duty, there is no question that by Curll's time (who included an engraving showing a husband being beaten by a young female servant, while his wife is shown waiting expectantly in bed), this work had dropped to the level of pornography.[3]

De Hermaphroditis, as we shall see, also refers to flogging as a means of sexual arousal. A Latin title with the word *hermaphroditus*, one of the most charged terms of the period, may have raised exactly such venereal expectations. The little work is actually in English and, according to the elaborately descriptive titles of the period, contains the following three parts:

> A Description of the several Sorts of HERMAPHRODITES; and how the Law regards them in respect to Matrimony.
> Intrigues of HERMAPHRODITES and Masculine FEMALES, and of the outward Marks to distinguish them.
> The material Cause and Generation of HERMAPHRODITES; of unnatural BIRTHS, Generation of MONSTERS, extraordinary CONCEPTIONS, etc.

The first and last parts, entirely traditional, do not particularly interest me here. We are told that a variety of persons "of a mix'd Nature" (p. 4), if they enter marriage, must inevitably be "exposed to the World, as Prodigies and Monsters," no doubt a reference to Ambroise Paré's famous work *Des monstres et prodiges*, and indeed Paré is referred to a little later as source of the famous sex-change episode of Marie Germain leaping over a ditch and turning into a man. Also Columbus (or Realdo Colombo, c.1515–59), who memorably if somewhat grotesquely claimed to have "discovered" the clitoris, is one of the anonymous author's authorities. The most recent important source used is the seventeenth-century French writer Nicolas Venette (c.1631–98), from whose *Tableau de l'amour conjugal ou De la génération de l'homme* the compiler borrows his distinction of five kinds of "hermaphrodites."[4]

A century earlier, in his book on women's diseases already referred to, Rodrigo a Castro listed four kinds, saying that other medical authorities distinguish only three. Most notably for the subject at hand, Castro did not consider as a separate category women with a "monsterously" enlarged clitoris. In his seventeenth-century magisterial work on medical ethics, Paolo Zacchia distinguished four kinds in his section on "De Hermaphroditis," a subsection of "De Monstris."[5] Perhaps the growing number of categories of hermaphrodites is indicative of an older notion of scientific progress that privileged more minute subdivision. The English author does not refer to the debate between Jacques Duval and Jean Riolan about the sexual identity of a person on trial for sodomy in 1601 that has dominated modern accounts of historians of gender.[6]

The author or compiler of our English *De Hermaphroditis* reveals himself to be a traditionalist or Galenist, as in the following definition:

> for the Definition of the Word Sex, it is no other than a Distinction of Male and Female, in which this is most observable, that for the Parts of the Body,

there is but little difference between them; but the Females are colder than the Males, and abound with more superfluous Moisture; wherefore their spermatick Parts are more vigorous than those of Men. (p. 3)

Here is the Galenic homology, what recently has been called the "one-sex model," and the notion that women also have "spermatick parts" or sperm.[7] We will see that, as he will tell his narrative, the author/compiler will forget that last part of the theory.

Throughout, the little treatise gestures to an intent that is scientific. The preface denies charges that its purpose is prurient: "My Design in the following Sheets is merely as an innocent Entertainment for all curious Persons" (p. ii). At the time when the rich and well-traveled had collections of "curiosities," the adjective "curious" could denote something close to scientific interest, and the entire structure of the work, presenting categories first and stories next, operates by the principle of deduction. Indeed the writer of the preface, possibly the printer/publisher, is conscious of some scientific or pre-scientific demands. Just as Montaigne, as he was writing his essay "Des cannibales," felt the need to point to a conversation with a Native American (although one may wonder in what language they communicated), our prefacer feels the urge to produce evidence: "It might be expected by some faithless Persons, that I should produce an HERMAPHRODITE to publick view, as an incontestable Justification of there being Humane Creatures of this kind" (p. iii). He denies the request, possibly half-seriously, by saying that he has no authority to take up any woman's petticoat and that so monstrous a sight "might endanger the Welfare of some pregnant Female," a reference not only to the common belief that the fetus is influenced by what the mother sees but also to the fact that the work, in spite its title, is written in English and thus will have women readers.

Of particular interest (because anything but merely traditional material of a diligent compiler) is the middle part of the treatise, the three narratives called "Intrigues of Hermaphrodites and Masculine Females." All three are situated in Italy and the first is introduced by the assertion, "When I was formerly in Italy, there happen'd a notable Adventure . . ." (p. 19). Part one of the narratives (about two "hermaphrodites," Diana and Isabella) specifies the women's origin as Urbino. This might lead one to conjecture that the compiler found versions of these stories in some Italian source or that he heard them *in situ*. Unquestionably that is what he would like the reader to believe, for (as was just mentioned) he links at least the first of the stories to a trip he took to that country. But the very same story is set in the house of a minister *and his wife*, one of several indications that the location is assumed or fictional.

Although aware of the large theoretical and terminological issues looming, I find myself unable to dispense with the word "homophobia" and take some comfort from Claude J. Summers's essay on anxieties of anachronism.[8] For placing these stories in Italy is more than adding a little spice or perhaps "exoticism" to them, but it is an instance of what I have called in a different context "xeno-homophobia," borrowing the word from Rebecca E. Zorach, who employs it in a provocative article to describe possibilities of homophobic invective used against the last Valois king (Henri III) at the end of the sixteenth century.[9] My argument was that the Protestant Henri Estienne, the famous philologist and astute observer of changes in the spoken French of his time, was influenced in his observations by his deep-rooted antipathy against the Italian language and Italians, because Italy was the country of the Pope or Antichrist. Although Estienne may not have invented the self-serving system in which Frenchmen were good and solid lovers of women and the Italian Papists sodomites, it was most likely through him that literate Englishmen (I pointed to John Selden) learned the system, which they then transposed, converting it to suit their needs: now the English were solidly good and manly, while the French and Italians were effeminate and, in imitation of their leader on the Tiber, sodomites.[10] This is the larger context for the displacement of these stories of "hermaphrodites," which have some clear signs of being home-spun, to Italy.

Is the married condition of the clergyman in Italy merely a slip, an oversight of the author, or is it part of the story? It is clearly the latter. After performing the marriage of a young couple, the clergyman offers the bride and bridegroom as well as the one female guest, Diana, shelter for the night, as it is too late to return to Urbino. Since he has only three bedrooms (and the newly-weds claim one), the minister's wife and Diana are put together in one room and bed. (Thus sharing a bed was, of course, custom in the period.) At night Diana starts to make advances to the good-looking minister's wife. When she finally throws herself on the woman, the aggressed woman shrieks and calls for help. The parson rescues his wife from Diana, "seiz'd *Diana*, and upon Examination, finding her a Hermaphrodite, having the Members of both Sexes," ties her up for the night and in the morning "turn'd *Diana* out of Door with the Indignity she deserv'd" (51).

With this result of the "examination," the assumption is that Diana is one of the five types of hermaphrodites previously listed, although it is not clear exactly which one. The first has entire male genitals in addition to "a pretty deep slit . . . which is of no use in generation"; the second has male genitals in addition to rudimentary female characteristics; the third has a slit through which he urinates, but has no periods; the fourth are women with a clitoris extraordinarily big and long; and the fifth has "privy parts confus'd" but neither the use of one nor the other sex (p. 8). But whether it is type one, two, three, or five, in any case we would have what Valerie Traub discerns in sixteenth- and seventeenth-century medical representations of tribades: an anatomical essentialism in the consideration of gender and sexual affiliation, for the configuration of the genitals supposedly determines sexual behavior.[11]

The same set of convictions is made a little more explicit in the case of Diana's friend Isabella, who attracts the attention of a foreign count, who (after a lavish meal) tries to have intercourse with her.

> Finding an Uneasiness in his amorous Struggles, he put down his Hand to discover what it was, and feeling something like the Testicles of a Man, he rose from her in the greatest Confusion, and calling for his Servant for a

Candle, in his passion, he pull'd out a sharp Pen-knife and cut off the external Members of *Isabella*, highly resenting the Affront, and very much displeas'd with himself, that he should embrace a Monster. (p. 54)

We are told that Isabella "made a hideous outcry," which disturbed the neighborhood, and that the Count sent for a surgeon, who managed to stop the flow of blood. He kept her for the night and in the morning sent her to her female companion. The narrator adds sarcastically that the two women from then on and for a considerable time "liv'd together as Man and Wife (being now better qualified for it)" (p. 55) until they had a quarrel and separated, and that "*Diana* reviving her former Diversions, met at last with the same Fate as *Isabella*, her masculine Instrument likewise sever'd from her Privities, after which, both liv'd to be harmless old Women" (p. 55).

Obviously these women are not simply "lesbians" in the modern sense, who are not usually thought of as definable by their genital physique.[12] Nor are they most likely conceived as tribades: that is, women whose clitoris appears enlarged beyond all credible dimensions in early modern medical accounts, and for whom some anatomists recommended genital amputation (Figure 12.1).

Valerie Traub has devoted an eloquent chapter to that kind of "hermaphrodite" whom we will meet in other parts of *De Hermaphroditis*. Instead, Diana and Isabella illustrate the kind of hermaphrodite that partakes of male and female genital

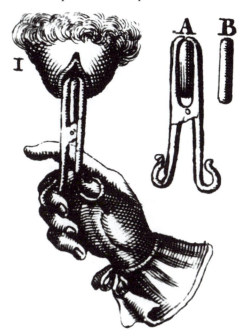

Figure 12.1 Procedure for clitoridectomy, from Johannes Schultes, *Armamentarium chirurgicum* (Leiden: Apud C. Boutesteyn, J. Luchtmans, 1693), p. 176. By permission of the Osler Library for the History of Science and Medicine, McGill University.

characteristics at the same time. Although such permutations of course exist, they are so rare that concern with them in the early modern period seems whipped up to almost pathological dimensions. I hesitate to call this concern a result of male fears (as much of early modern comment on tribadism undoubtedly is) that women might pleasure one another and dispense with male company. More likely, the narratives of this particular section are shaped to emphasize what is conceived as the monstrous or what in the modern vocabulary of Kristeva may be called more precisely the "abject." If male fears are evident, then only in the sense that the narrator plays up concerns that women might hide monstrous characteristics. Men beware women!

Another narrative is also set in Italy, this time specified as the "papal dominions." As mentioned before, there is in the period a tradition for Protestant Englishmen of associating the Pope with "unnatural" sexual practices. It is the story of an Italian lady called Margureta (sic) and a French woman called Barbarissa. "These two Females were in their Statures very near equal to the largest siz'd Male. . . . In short, they resembled Men in all respects, but their dresses, their Gates and Voices, and indeed they were suspected to be Hermaphrodites" (p. 19). Their "intrigues" are told from the perspective of the voyeur, since their servant, interested in discovering those behaviors, drills a hole in the wall across from their bed in order to observe them. Of course the voyeuristic perspective (intercourse seen through a hole or chink in the wall) has a firm position in erotica: from Ariosto's notorious canto 28, where a noble lady is observed through a crevice in the wall as she tries to satisfy herself with a dwarf, to the even closer parallel of an anecdote told by Brantôme in *Les vies des dames galantes* (written c.1585, but not published until 1665–6), in which a boy sees "two great ladies, with petticoats all tucked up and drawers down, lying on top of the other and kissing like doves, rubbing and frigging one another."[13] But the French story of female–female interaction does not present clitoral hypertrophy.

After some foreplay, the two women draw up their petticoats and "employ'd their Hands with each other, in the same force of Inclination, as a juvenile Gallant would make his Approaches" (p. 21). Then one of the ladies throws herself on the bed "displaying herself commodiously," while the other one "covers" her companion. The narrator informs us that unfortunately the voyeur is unable to discern any particulars, but then links this "case" with physical attributes typically associated with tribadism in early modernity:

> They had not continu'd their Sportings long before *Margureta*, which officiated now instead of the Man, arose from *Barbarissa*, and turning towards the Window with her Cloaths up in her Arms, *Nicolini* [the voyeur] immediately discover'd something hang down from her Body of a reddish Colour, and which was very unusual. (p. 21)

In addition to a dangling signifier (of tribadism), this quotation contains a dangling modification. In the first and discursive section, the compiler had echoed first the special permutation of the one-sex system or theory of complementarity ("The

Clitoris in Women suffers erection and falling in the same manner as the *Penis* in Men," p. 16) and had then rehearsed the contemporary view of a clitoris so enlarged that it hindered heterosexual intercourse: "Sometimes the *Clitoris* will grow out of the Body two or three Inches . . . and by this means a man will be hinder'd from knowing his Wife." At the same time this physical condition was seen as lending itself to tribadism. In the narrative, the two women are then described as reversing roles: after merely looking at pictures of a "variety of Postures," possibly a version of Giulio Romano's *Modi*, fails to arouse Barbarissa, Margureta seizes some birchen rods and flogs her. The flogging has the desired response, visible in Margureta. The narrator summarizes:

> The Story sufficiently shews the unnatural Intrigues of some Masculine Females, where by the falling down and largeness of the *Clitoris*, they have been taken for Men . . . and are capable of every Action belonging to a Man, but that of Ejaculation. (pp. 23–4)

Like the story of the Italian clergyman's wife, this one seems like a pseudo-foreign or pseudo-Italian story and thus another instance of xeno-homophobia. It broadcasts in a pornographic vein notions of a vastly enlarged clitoris that had long been current in Europe and tries to anchor female same-sex desire and sexual activity in physiological particularity, what Valerie Traub has called "anatomical essentialism."[14] The male perspective of the narration reveals considerable anxiety that these women may find pleasure without the company of men.

This fear, even here somewhat qualified in the comment about missing ejaculation, is finally neutralized in the third narrative. Set in Ferrara, this is again a story about a young French woman and an Italian lady, both described as unusually beautiful. The writer presenting this "case," as he calls it, spends several pages describing how these young women were in love with male admirers, but were frustrated or disappointed, in one case by parents disallowing marriage, in the other by a jealous and treacherous suitor murdering her lover. The two women, in different ways disappointed by men, resolve never "to fix their Affections upon any Man living":

> Living in Luxury, in the prime of their Years, in a hot Climate, they at length were naturally inclin'd to the most abominable Pollution: They provided artificial *Penis's* of the largest Dimensions, and with Ribbons they fasten'd the Root of the Instrument, in the same Situation as Nature has plac'd the Substance in Man. (p. 41)

The work of the dildo is supplemented by a hand-held device that supplies moisture, "which, with the rubbing, occasion'd such a tickling, as to force a discharge of Matter and facilitate Pleasure" (p. 42).

A young man called Philetus, "a very comely person, but a little effeminate" (p. 42), falls in love with Theodora and after learning the women's secret from a confidant, cross-dresses, since he knows that they will allow only women into their company. Before the love-making starts, Philetus (to pass as a woman of their company) takes a dildo, withdraws and pretends that he is strapping it on.

> He approach'd his Charmer with a Lover's vigour, and *Theodora* was still a Stranger to the Intrigue, 'till the moment of Ejaculation, which was not usual with the same Instrument with her Embraces with *Amaryllis*: When this happen'd she was prodigiously surpriz'd . . . . *Theodora* considering what had happen'd, and experiencing a material Difference between Art and Nature, agreed, on his humble Request, to Marry him. (pp. 44–5)

Again we notice that these women are not "lesbians" in any modern sense. The narrator dwells on their misfortunes and frustrations as lovers of males to such an extent that the story is front-heavy: that section is several times as long as the account of the women's "intrigues" as same-sexual lovers. There is not the least male anxiety about being neglected, left out, or found insufficient. On the contrary, the story is informed by an easy and unreflected confidence in male and heterosexual supremacy. Whatever the women do among themselves is entirely imitative of male behavior, and the compiler, seemingly a Galenist, even seems to forget that according to Galenic tradition women also are supposed to emit semen. As in Amazon plays of the period, where in the end martial women usually abandon their ways and bow to men's rule, and the esthetic pleasure of closure is multiplied if several women are doing the same, so here, after Theodora has recanted, she serves as a model also to Amaryllis: "After these Adventures were over, *Amaryllis* likewise submitted to Matrimony with a Gentleman of *Ferara*; and they both enjoy'd the greatest Happiness, making no difficulty to forget all Sorrows past" (p. 45).

If these women are not lesbians in any modern sense, they may come closer to being that than the tribades, who (according to Valerie Traub and as borne out by these stories) definitely are not. Nor are the "monstrous" hermaphrodites with their mixed or supernumerary genitalia, who are, like the tribades, defined by their anatomy. Although our author locates all of them in a foreign country, foreign travel accounts hardly seem relevant to the stories themselves, and Valerie Traub is again on the mark when she says of the English tribade that she "is not a creature of exotic origins imported to Europe by travel writers, but rather is the discursive effect of travel writers' transposition of ancient and medieval categories of intelligibility onto foreign 'matter'."[15] Indeed the material transposed to "other" lands is only thinly disguised as foreign, and the transposition (whether expressly to the "papal dominions" or not) is motivated, as I tried to suggest, by a Post-Reformation tradition of associating the Pope with what good Englishmen considered reprehensible sexual practices. While keeping the homeland comfortably heterosexual, such transposed stories, clearly on the margin of the deliberately sensationalizing or pornographic, are examples of xeno-homophobia. Perhaps it is a sign of their partaking of the pornographic that, behind a façade of shock and daring, and occasionally gesturing to scientific interests, they are utterly conventional in their outcomes.

Notes

1. Rodrigo a Castro, *De universa mulierium medicina*, part 2, book 1, ch. 15, Hamburg, 1603.
2. For French, see Agrippa d'Aubigné, "Les Princes," l. 667: "les hermaphrodites, monstres effeminez." *Les Tragiques*, ed. Jacques Bailbé, Paris: Flammarion, 1968, p.111. For English, see *OED*.
3. For a reproduction of the illustration mentioned, see my *Medical Ethics in the Renaissance*, Washington, DC: Georgetown University Press, 1995.
4. The 1st edn of Venette's *Tableau*, which was many times republished, seems to be of Amsterdam, 1687. I have used the 7th edn, Cologne, 1696, which enumerates the five kinds of hermaphrodites on pp. 608–12: (1) those who have male parts but also a *fente*/cleft/vulva useless for generation; (2) same as above, but their cleft is less deep and presses their male parts to the sides; (3) those with no male parts but a *fente* through which they urinate; they have no period flow (at about age 15 to 18, their male parts appear and they are clearly men); (4) women with an enlarged clitoris (Venette calls them "tribades" or "ribaudes"); (5) those who have "les parties naturelles confuses," like the woman from Bohemia who asked Colombo to cut her penis and enlarge her vulva (they have no periods).
5. Zacchia, *Quaestiones medico-legales*, Rome, 1634, pp. 491–500. See Ch. 4 below.
6. See Donald Beecher, "Concerning Sex Changes: The Cultural Significance of a Renaissance Medical Polemic," *Sixteenth Century Journal*, 26 (2005), 991–1016.
7. On the controverted issue, see my "Early Modern Controversies about the One-Sex Model," *Renaissance Quarterly*, 53 (2000), 180–91.
8. Claude J. Summers, "Homosexuality and Renaissance Literature: Or, the Anxieties of Anachronism," *South Central Review*, 9 (1992), 2–3.
9. Zorach, "The Matter of France: Sodomy and the Scandal of Style in Sixteenth-Century France," *Journal of Medieval and Early Modern Studies*, 28/3 (1998), 583. My essay, "Linguistic 'Xeno-Homophobia' in Sixteenth-Century France: The Case of Henri Estienne," *Sixteenth Century Journal*, 34 (2003), 747–60.
10. See my "Linguistic 'Xeno-Homophobia'."
11. Valerie Traub, *The Renaissance of Lesbianism in Early Modern England*, Cambridge: Cambridge University Press, 2002, p. 208: "the early modern mapping of the tribade's body produces and is produced by an anatomical essentialism – the riveting of body part to behavior – that continues to underpin modern discourses of sexuality. Such essentialism is the result not of empirical fact, but of a strategy to organize and make intelligible the plurality of corporeal structures and behaviors within the conceptual confines of Renaissance cosmological and earthly hierarchies."
12. Just as it has been claimed by Foucault and others that the modern "homosexual" did not exist before the nineteenth century, so it can be said that the modern lesbian is recent. Cf. e.g. Traub's view: "*Lesbians* today are not assumed to be marked by an anatomical deviation. . . . Their erotic practices are not assumed primarily to take the form of vaginal penetration." Ibid., p. 220.
13. Reprinted in Kenneth Borris (ed.), *Same-Sex Desire in the English Renaissance: A Sourcebook of Texts, 1470–1650*, New York and London: Routledge, 2004, p. 304.
14. Traub, *Renaissance of Lesbianism*, pp. 208, 220 and throughout.
15. Ibid., p. 217.

13 Erotics versus sexualities

Current science and reading early modern female same-sex relations

Harriette Andreadis

The erotic is a resource within each of us that lies in a deeply female and spiritual plane, firmly rooted in the power of our unexpressed or unrecognized feeling. . . .

Of course, women so empowered are dangerous. So we are taught to separate the erotic from most vital areas of our lives other than sex.

When I speak of the erotic, then, I speak of it as an assertion of the lifeforce of women; of that creative energy empowered, the knowledge and use of which we are now reclaiming in our language, our history, our dancing, our loving, our work, our lives.

During World War II, we bought sealed plastic packets of white, uncolored margarine, with a tiny, intense pellet of yellow coloring perched like a topaz just inside the clear skin of the bag. We would leave the margarine out for a while to soften, and then we would pinch the little pellet to break it inside the bag, releasing the rich yellowness into the soft pale mass of margarine. Then taking it carefully between our fingers, we would knead it gently back and forth, over and over, until the color had spread throughout the whole pound bag of margarine, thoroughly coloring it.

I find the erotic such a kernel within myself. When released from its intense and constrained pellet, it flows through and colors my life with a kind of energy that heightens and sensitizes and strengthens all my experience.

(Audre Lorde, "Uses of the Erotic: The Erotic as Power"[1])

[Karl] Abraham [in his 1920 paper on the female castration complex] did not at all recognize how the groom's desire to prove his masculinity with his penis might be misconnecting with the bride's wish to fulfill her femininity in a relationship of tender mutuality, where all her organs of erotic desire – her skin, her clitoris, her nipples, her hair, her eyes – are enlivened and brought into play.

(Louise J. Kaplan, *Female Perversions*[2])

A recent call for proposals for a seminar entitled "Talking about Sex" notes that "Research on sex in Renaissance literature has constantly come up against the question of terminology and methodology: how do we describe the sorts of sexuality we see in these texts? What counts as sex?"[3] That these issues still remain unsettled can be seen as a testament to the rigidity of our post-Freudian binary sex/gender system and its polarized – and polarizing – perspectives. This chapter offers a different standpoint from which we might examine the questions that continue to vex and to perplex current scholarship and suggests fresh avenues for future research and analysis in light of some current scientific understandings and modern psychodynamic paradigms.

First, we might ask why differences in our definitions of "sexual" and "erotic" might matter to how we read literature, particularly premodern literatures? I begin by exploring some of the ways in which acknowledging a difference between the "sexual" and the "erotic" can be useful in helping us make some important conceptual distinctions. As has become ever more apparent in our attempts to recover the historical trajectory of sexual identity formations, definitions of "sex" and the behaviors that construct "sexuality" are culturally and geographically, as well as historically, variable in ways that demand our attention and careful analysis. As we explore the historical nuances and understandings of, for instance, early modern sexual life, a distinction between the "erotic" and the "sexual" can provide a way to think about cultural self-understandings that make their way into literary artifacts but that may not have analogues in modern and postmodern (i.e. twentieth- and twenty-first century) articulations of sexuality.

A brief review of how we use these terms serves to illuminate some of our assumptions and predisposing intellectual perspectives. Contemporary, that is, modern, dictionary definitions of the "erotic" tend to emphasize its congruence with sexuality ever more emphatically as we move from the late nineteenth century into the present, so that most recent dictionaries often simply equate the "erotic" with the "sexual." This has not always been – and sometimes still is not – the case. While an online version of *The American Heritage Dictionary* defines "erotic" as "Tending to arouse sexual desire" or as "Dominated by sexual love or desire" and *Roget's Thesaurus* (1995) relates the "erotic" to "Feeling or devoted to sexual love or desire: amative, amorous, concupiscent, lascivious, lecherous, lewd, libidinous, lustful, lusty, passionate, prurient, sexy,"[4] the thesauri that accompany popular word processing programs tend to include a less sexual and more anodyne range of definitional choices; for example, Microsoft Word, the most extensively used program, includes as synonyms "amorous" and "amative," "romantic" and "amatory."[5]

The *Oxford English Dictionary*, on the other hand, defines "erotic" as follows for the period between the mid-seventeenth and the mid-nineteenth centuries:

> *adj.* Of or pertaining to the passion of love; concerned with or treating of love; amatory.
>
> 1651 CHARLETON *Ephes. & Cimm. Matrons* ii. Pref., That Erotic passion is allowed by all learned men to be a species of Melancholy. *a*1789 BURNEY *Hist. Mus.* (ed. 2) I. v. 61 These modes had other..[sic] dependent on them, such as the Erotic or amorous. 1823 tr. *Sismondi's Lit. Eur.* (1846) I. xvi. 448 The lyric and erotic poets of his country. 1850 SIR J. STEPHEN *Eccl. Biog.* I. 158 Arising from these erotic dreams, he suspended at her shrine his secular weapons. 1865 HOOK *Lives Abps.* III. i. ß9. 101 The common language of civility, as addressed to a lady, was erotic.[6]

The *OED* also provides this gloss for "erotica," beginning in 1854:

> Matters of love; erotic literature or art (freq. as a heading in catalogues).
>
> 1854 (*title*) Erotica. The Elegies of Propertius. 1913 H. JACKSON *Eighteen Nineties* v. 122 The romance, in its unexpurgated form, suggests deep knowledge of that literature generally classed under *facetiae* and *erotica* by the booksellers. 1956 K. CLARK Nude viii. 323 Supplied the Court with presentable *erotica* . . . 1967 G. STEINER *Lang. & Silence* 91 Above the pulp-line . . . lies the world of erotica, of sexual writing with literary pretensions or genuine claims.[7]

The dates associated with these *OED* entries suggest a morphing – and narrowing – of the meaning of "erotic" as we move through the early modern period and into the present. "Erotic" in the sense that appears to have come into use early in the seventeenth century seems more capacious, more inclusive of emotion, passion, love, and feeling, as well as specifically sexual feeling, than do later definitions and uses. This is supported by the *OED*'s entries, beginning in c.1386, for Eros: "Love, the god of love, or a representation of him: = CUPID." A secondary meaning, with a first entry in 1922, reads: "*spec.* in Freudian Psychology: the urge towards self-preservation and sexual pleasure. Also, *in recent Christian writings*, earthly or sexual love, contrasted with AGAPE" (emphasis mine).

What seems clear is that "erotic" historically has *included* "sexual" as part of a more comprehensive set of meanings that encompass a range of emotional and bodily sensations; but increasingly in the modern era, post-Freud, the "erotic" has been defined by and has been regarded as synonymous with "sexuality," which was earlier only one of its referents. Even the antithesis between Eros and Agape has been narrowed in modern times to an opposition between "sex" and "love," whereas its proper classical referents are "sexual *love*" (which entails a full range of emotion) and "altruistic love." This difference between "sexual *love*" and "altruistic love," a distinction only rarely recognized in our own times, is significant for the ways in which we read literary texts, attempt to come to terms with premodern sexual self-understandings, and – not coincidentally – live our lives.

The problems inherent in our postmodern conflation of the erotic with the sexual (particularly in the postmodern cathexis on the sexual as a catch-all for any erotic feeling), and in our muddling of categories formerly thought distinct, are illustrated by efforts to describe what appear to us to be "lesbian" or otherwise "homosexual" behaviors in early modernity. These may rather have been, or in all probability were, behaviors the actors had no means of naming or of identifying except as part of marginalized (and usually vilified) categories with which the individuals in question could not associate themselves without losing social status or respectability. A woman wishing to retain her status as a member of the gentry or "middling sort" in early modern England would have found herself a pariah were she to associate her desires with tribadism and its attendant mythologies of the hypertrophied clitoris.[8] How can we then describe former behaviors that appear to partake of modern sexual identities when they may not or, at the very least, cannot be confirmed to have culminated in genital activity, and when the individuals involved did not recognize them (and certainly did not speak of them) as in any way disrupting the boundaries of customary social intercourse? What language(s) do we have available to us that can open up this (for us) liminal space outside the boundaries of modern sexual identities? What language(s) can provide insight into early modern self-understandings as they relate to amorous relations?

The complexities of the erotic in the work of the seventeenth-century poet Katherine Philips (1632–64) exemplify our present interpretive dilemma. I have made this distinction between sexuality and eroticism: "Philips used the conventions of her time to express in her own poetry a desexualized – though passionate and eroticized – version of platonic love in the love of same-sex friendship."[9] This distinction elicited responses from several readers: Elizabeth Wahl called it a "well-intentioned but utterly confusing description of Philips's poetry," while another, anonymous, reader has called it "mystifying."[10] Ironically – and like others who have objected to my distinction – Wahl herself uses it when she writes that "Philips breaks down the boundary separating the emotional from the physical, the transcendent from the corporeal, and the erotic from the sexual."[11] Perhaps this suggests that the original distinction between the erotic and the sexual has not been entirely lost and is itself seductive, even when we refuse it.

I recently added to my earlier comments on Philips in order to remedy their perceived ambiguity: "I wish to draw here the fine distinction between a generalized erotic and emotional passion – what Ruth Perry has called 'libidinous energy'[12] – and the narrowly focused genital, particularly male genital, definition of sexuality that was pervasive in early modern England."[13] This refinement of the original distinction is not likely to have solved the larger problem of how we recognize, describe, and find a language for the range of intense affect that is not invariably sexualized in the modern sense (that is, does not invariably find its way to genital expression), but is particularly part of female sexual experience and of the intense affectional relations of women with each other throughout history, especially in early modernity.

A review of a recent yet now obscure moment in the social history of the United States might help to bring this problem into sharper focus. Audre Lorde's "Uses of the Erotic: The Erotic as Power," a paper originally presented at the Fourth Berkshire Conference on the History of Women in 1978,[14] as the second wave of the women's movement was cresting at the end of its second decade, marked a time of strength, passion, and optimism in which Lorde expressed what many feminists were experiencing. Those who remembered with her those packets of margarine, and the deeply sensuous experience of kneading a small topaz-like kernel until it colored the soft mass contained by the voluptuous skin of plastic, could identify immediately with her description of the erotic as a bodily passion and energy that might influence the most innocent, and apparently non-sexual, gesture we might make. Lorde was *desexualizing* the erotic to call attention to its many other aspects. For those women in or near her generation, there was nothing at all ambiguous in the distinction she made. Particularly for those who, like her, were self-identified as lesbians, she described entirely too well the experience of being closeted in the 1950s and 1960s, when energies and libidinous desires were channeled throughout every aspect of life rather than being focused on achieving genital satisfaction. During this moment in the women's movement in the United States, attraction to other women was often an emotional and erotic matter in which friendship came first; sexuality seemed merely the fulfillment of a more diffuse (but nonetheless compelling and energizing) complex of feelings. Lorde's emphasis on the power and expressiveness of the erotic in women's daily lives was experienced by many as liberating, as well as powerfully explanatory.

This social microclimate changed shortly afterwards, during the 1980s and 1990s, with the openness that followed the GLBT rights movements and the more general receptiveness of society to sexual variety, especially the accelerated and increasingly aggressive marketing of sexuality by the media and by capitalist enterprise.[15] Simultaneously, mass access to contraceptives, to abortion, and to other reproductive and sexual technologies made it possible to control the consequences of sexual activity and hence obliterated barriers to sex, especially for women, and accelerated the sexualization of *all* relationships.[16] The consequences of these cultural changes are evident in the more recent cultural productions of younger women (for example, the very public performance art of drag kings, the popularity of accessible venues for s/m activity, publications like *On Our Backs*) and in the writings of authors such as Pat Califia. Arguably, these are signs of healthfully unrepressed libidos; but they may also have constrained in many women the ability to recognize other constructions – and other uses – of libidinous energies.

A clash of these two perspectives – the tendency to sexualize romantic relations versus the earlier position that saw them as erotically diffuse – can be seen in the academic opposition between Kate Stimpson on the one hand, insisting on an exclusively sexual definition of "lesbian," and Adrienne Rich, from another perspective, defining "lesbians" as all "women-loving women."[17] These are the extreme poles of a discussion that many feminists have charted in detail; still, it has proved impossible to delineate a space that partakes of each yet is distinct from both, a space that might accommodate both perspectives without falling prey to confusing self-contradictions. The powerfully influential, inclusive views of Rich in the 1970s – who was, not coincidentally, a close friend of Lorde's, and clearly was using Lorde's view of the erotic as a way to understand lesbian relations – gave way in the 1990s to the younger successors to Stimpson's perspective on the exclusivity of a sexual definition of "lesbian." The evolution to accommodate this new perspective created what we might describe as a subcultural paradigm shift.[18] In many respects this shift may be seen to echo the similar but more pervasive one said to have taken place in England in the mid-seventeenth century when, according to one historiographical view, modern sexual identities were being polarized and stabilized as a system of binary sexualities was being crystallized by powerful patriarchal interests.[19] We can perhaps look to this shift in sexual paradigms in our own times for instructive suggestions in reading the past. Most usefully, it can offer a model for how eroticized but non-sexualized relations between women – à la Rich and Lorde – might have been experienced.

Sue Lanser and George Haggerty address these issues in their efforts to redefine our perspective on the early modern period to include representations of affectional preference when we review earlier literary cultures for examples of same-sex relations relevant to same-sex historiography.[20] They aim to broaden how we define same-sex relations in an effort to avoid an exclusive or definitive focus on genital expression. Very properly, they recognize the need to consider a fuller range of affect in our definitions but do not really succeed in evading the difficulties of attempting to define "lesbian" for the earlier periods. Thus far, the project of defining "lesbian" before c.1800 has proved to have insurmountable pitfalls, not least because of the dearth of concrete evidence about how female same-sex erotic activities might have been enacted in daily lives. This lack of evidence and the other hazards of historical research in this area are unlikely to be remedied unless we choose to sidestep the impasse and instead introduce a distinction between erotics and sexuality that will allow us to broaden our understanding about what constitutes romantic relations between women. In doing so, we can include a range of affective relations that would not have been understood as tribadic but that did in fact engage the full spectrum of emotion and behaviors we think of as "lesbian." This critical move can help us preserve historical specificity because we thus avoid conflating sexual and affectional definitions of "lesbian."

While there was an identified sexual category of women called tribades, women who did not want to be reduced to a (denigrated) sexuality would not have been likely to include themselves in that category. Like his contemporaries writing in English, Helkiah Crooke repeats the commentaries of his Greek and Latin predecessors in his 1615 anatomical handbook. Next to the marginal gloss "*Tribades odiosæ feminæ*" ("Tribades, hateful women"), he remarks:

> although for the most part it [the clitoris] hath but a small production hidden under the *Nymphes* and hard to be felt but with curiosity, yet sometimes it groweth to such a length that it hangeth without the cleft like a mans member, especially when it is fretted with the touch of the cloathes, and so strutteth and groweth to a riginitie as doth the yarde of a man. And this part it is which those wicked women doe abuse called *Tribades* (often mentioned by many authours, and in some states worthily punished) to their mutuall and unnaturall lustes.[21]

Evident in Crooke's description are both the contemporary obsession with the homologies between the clitoris and the "yarde"[22] and contempt for female same-sex eroticism, the two no doubt interconnected. In a culture in which sexual expression was defined as a genital activity involving a penis or phallic substitute, or even the genital "rubbing" of tribadism, women whose primary affectional relations were with other women would not have been likely to experience themselves as tribades or necessarily associate their feelings with (genital) sex, whatever their physical contact might entail.

A number of critics, including Sue Lanser and Valerie Traub, have chosen to retain "lesbian" as the descriptor for what might look to us in a postmodern age like "lesbianism."[23] However, there already was a specific identity category for female same-sex genital activity in early modern Europe (tribadism), and as far as we know "lesbian" was not used in England until much later, well into the nineteenth century.[24] Historical, cultural, and geographic fidelity would seem to demand that we employ contemporaneous language whenever it is available.[25] Further, we should attempt, insofar as is possible, to align what we believe we read in early modern texts with careful reconstructions of the ways in which individuals might have understood themselves. While we can recognize that this is in reality a probably unattainable goal, our project is likely to be successful to the degree to which we attempt to maintain this historical integrity.

Paradoxically, postmodern advances in scientific and psychological understanding have created paradigms that may well prove fruitful in our pursuit of better reconstructions of historical models. I explore some of these in the remainder of this chapter, underlining how these paradigms clarify premodern historical moments in light of the distinction between eroticism and sexuality.

Very recent explorations in empirical science and in psychodynamic theory confirm the almost infinitely variable – and surprisingly malleable – nature of human sexual response and the vast number of ways it can be evoked, manipulated, defined, and constructed. Research into physiological and particularly neurological phenomena has just begun to illuminate the mysteries surrounding both normal and unusual brain function. And the complexities of brain function, particularly as these concern its malleability, have profound consequences for our study of sexualities. Phenomena whose presence might previously have been attributed to ESP, to extraordinary artistic or mathematical talents, or even to divine intervention, have now been clearly shown to be manifestations either of the pathological functioning of neurological pathways in the brain or of enhanced functioning of specialized neurological pathways. Prominent examples that, among others, have received considerable attention are phantom limbs in amputees and the heightened sensory sensitivities of synesthetics, both of which are now known to result from complex rewirings, genetic codings, or unusual patternings of brain pathways.[26] Applications of these discoveries have led to experiments that successfully assist amputees in ridding themselves of painful phantom limbs and that have helped synesthetic individuals to understand their unusual perceptual abilities as variant neurological skills. These newly understood phenomena have also yielded practical treatments for the sexual rehabilitation of paraplegic individuals (such as the late Christopher Reeve), the relief of symptoms of obsessive-compulsive disorder, the rehabilitation of various disabilities associated with stroke, and the "normal" sexual functioning of post-operative transsexuals.[27] Most striking is the recognition that ensues from our new understandings of these phenomena and that has led to the opening up of the new field of research in neuroplasticity: the brain can be rewired and sometimes rewires itself; in other words, neurological function is neither static nor impervious to external manipulation.

Because neurological pathways can be rerouted to accommodate loss of function in original, congenital pathways, sexual stimulation need not be genital in order for pleasure to be experienced or for orgasm to be achieved. We now know that if the circuitry of the brain is appropriately rerouted and trained, a paraplegic individual, for example, can achieve the ultimate in sexual pleasure by having her/his ear rubbed or neck massaged; this scientific knowledge has helped newly to enrich the lives of disabled persons and perhaps offers us new ways of understanding the nature of human erotic and sexual experience.

Transsexual performance artist Sandy Stone[28] illustrates erotic malleability to large audiences in one of her performance pieces, in which she introduces her performance with a discussion about sexual technology, about Donna Haraway's human cyborgs, and about the new sexual possibilities that are now available. Her performance approaches its conclusion when she asks the audience to join her with noisemakers as she masturbates to orgasm by rubbing her palm. After the hilarity and general chaos have subsided, she explains that sometimes she actually does have an orgasm during the performance . . . and that sometimes she doesn't; she does not of course reveal which of these was true for the performance in which the audience has just participated. Stone's witty performance shows how sexuality resides almost entirely in the brain and, consequently, that any part of the body – the palm in her just-completed staging – can be taught sexual response.

The fluid and obviously constructed nature of sexual functioning, and the ways in which it is inextricably meshed with non-genital (i.e. what we might call erotic) bodily sensation, are not, of course, news to any attentive reader of Shakespeare, who furnishes an instructive example because of his extensive corpus. The palm throughout his work is an especially frequently cited locus of erotic feeling. Palms, "moist palms" in particular, are often signals of impending sexual arousal. Perhaps the best-known examples occur in *The Winter's Tale* ("paddling palms and pinching fingers," 1.2.117; "Still virginalling / Upon his palm," 1.2.127–8) and in *Othello* ("Didst thou not see her paddle with the palm of his hand?," 2.1.245–6; "This hand is moist, my lady," 3.4.34). But we also see variously nuanced examples in *Venus and Adonis* ("she seizeth on his sweating palm," 1.25), in *Romeo and Juliet* ("And palm to palm is holy palmers' kiss," 1.5.97), in *Love's Labours Lost* ("by this virgin palm now kissing thine," 5.2.88), and in *Coriolanus* ("the virginal palms of your daughters," 5.2.43).[29] Stephen Booth has remarked that "Shakespeare seems to have regarded palm tickling as a telling sign of lasciviousness,"[30] but the pervasiveness of this trope and others that signal eroticism in similar non-genital ways suggests that such locutions were part of the ordinary rhetorical fabric of early modern culture.[31] No doubt the palm in particular was recognized as a seat of eroticism long before our genitally focused culture discovered its significance through medical experimentation. But most important for the way we read early modern texts is that their rhetorical use of the palm and other locutions that eroticize various parts of the body, or that metaphorize its erogenous zones, provide a striking insight into the ways in which sexuality often failed to be genitalized in early modern culture.

If sex is in the brain/mind and if early modern culture recognized, as it appears to have done, that the body has many erogenous zones, then we must look also for non-genital expressions of desire as markers of same-sex eroticism. The variable nature of sexuality and of erotic desire can no longer be ignored once we extrapolate from recent scientific understandings of bodily sensation and incorporate into our thinking the fact that constructions of same-sex relations between women – like all bodily relations between individuals – are profoundly mutable. Once we have set aside the constructed identity of the tribade, with its clear genital reference, we are confronted by the infinite varieties of, for example, "friendship" between equals or affective relations that cross classes (as do those between patron and poet or aristocrat and gentry). Such non-genitally defined, but frequently intense or impassioned relations seem at once to embody and to contain the erotic desires of women – certainly desires of the heart, but also desires of skin, of nipples, of hair, of eyes, and yes, perhaps even of clitoris – for each other. It is important to read these relations in their own terms, as *erotic* (keeping in mind the broad spectrum of that word's signification), but also as not necessarily inflected by a genitally defined sexuality such as we, and also early modern persons, might conceptualize it. Our understanding of the historical variability of the meanings of eroticism and sexuality can thus be sharpened by recent neurological insights into erotic malleability.

Another instance of how we might reread early modern cultural constructs presents itself in the vernacular anatomies and medical texts that circulated sexual information throughout literate English culture.[32] Rather than reading these texts as primarily providing information about what was known about female sexuality and about attitudes towards it, we can begin to understand them as instruments of social control. Their increasingly negative descriptions of tribadism, as in Crooke, and their association of tribades with female lasciviousness in general and sometimes in particular with Sappho, the ancient Greek poet, appear to have had a dual purpose. They are an admonition against increasingly widely recognized female same-sex behaviors and a harsh warning against female literary creativity insofar as it is associated with female lust.

Thomas Bartholin's 1653 revision, expansion, and translation into English of his father's 1633 Latin anatomy of the human body is typical. The entry "Of the Clitoris" includes engravings of that part, with explicit comparisons to the penis, or "yard," and the following description:

> The Greeks call it *clitoris*, others name it *Tentigo*, others the womans Yard or Prick: both because it resembles a Mans Yard, in Situation, Substance, Composition, Repletion, with Spirits and Erection. And Also because it hath somewhat like the Nut and Fore-skin of a Mans Yard, and in some Women it grows as big as the Yard of a man: so that some women abuse the same, and make use thereof in place of a mans Yard, exercising carnal Copulation one with another, and they are termed *Confricatrices* Rubsters. Which lascivious Practice is said to have been invented by Philaenis and Sappho, the Greek Poetress, is reported to have practised the same. And of these I conceive the Apostle Paul speaks in the I. of *Romans* 26. And therefore this part is called *Contemptus virorum* the Contempt of Mankind.[33]

The specific behaviors of tribadism described here appear to include penetration (i.e. "carnal copulation") along with rubbing. Bartholin also introduces the colloquial "Rubsters" as a literal translation of *Confricatrices*, along with *fricatrices*, a synonym for tribades that appears to have been common.[34] He condemns female same-sex activity as an assumption of male prerogatives and goes on to point out that an unusually large clitoris is "praeternatural and monstrous," and that "the more this part encreases, the more does it hinder a man in his business,"[35] or thwart male privilege.

This description of the clitoris, including the incorporation of Sappho as icon of tribadism, subsequently furnished a model for the semi-pornographic medical treatises that were to follow in the eighteenth century.[36] For our period, however, Bartholin's androcentrism, prurience, and anxiety about female sexual self-sufficiency not only provide information about female sexuality, but in unequivocally condemning that sexuality seek to ensure – as did Crooke's description earlier in the century – that female readers will reject any but authorized male–female sexual relations. Bartholin and other anatomists writing in English who reproduced this material contributed to an increasingly circumscribed and narrowed understanding of sexuality in the mid-seventeenth century and beyond. This narrowed understanding in turn began to make liminal the more complex eroticisms of bodily experience, a situation we have seen adumbrated in the evolving definition of the erotic.

Without resorting to the by now well-recognized excesses of Freudian readings, paradigms from feminist psychodynamic theory can be integrated into these insights to provide some useful working hypotheses for reading early modern literary texts. In *Female Perversions*, Louise Kaplan offers an overarching paradigm that might be used to elucidate early modern female sexualities when she describes sexual "perversions" as the use of the "soul-crippling . . . social gender stereotypes to mask cross-gender wishes and desires," and notes that "perversions are certainly about the social constraints placed on human desire."[37] From this perspective, "A female's *forbidden* masculine wishes have the same disastrous impact on her life as the analogous feminine wishes have on the life of a male."[38] While this paradigm assumes the existence of an unconscious and of individual subjectivities, we can still usefully employ its deconstruction of the effects of socially constructed gender role stereotypes on the individual as a way to examine the lives and literary productions of early modern women.

So, for example, we can recognize in the case of the poet Katherine Philips a woman who strove almost compulsively, and with great success, to persuade her contemporaries of her modest, chaste, and very feminine demeanor (in other words, of her conformity to the prescribed gender role stereotype of her time), while courting with impassioned fervor, and in poetry that unveils a sometimes distinctly male-identified eroticism, women with whom she sought intimate (of whatever sort) relations.[39] In this way, Kaplan's paradigm of female "perversion" can illuminate the important role played by Philips's feminine public persona in disguising and diverting attention from her "perverse" desires. I believe that this same "perverse strategy" is variously at work in the writing and lives of a number of well-known women in early modern England who were attempting to retain some semblance of social propriety while at the same time experiencing and perhaps enacting "perverse" desires. Margaret Cavendish, Duchess of Newcastle

(1623–73), and Aphra Behn (1640–89) offer particularly rich instances of women who both in their lives and in their writings enacted or portrayed "perverse" and often transgressive desires that make obvious the crippling constraints imposed by stereotypical gender dynamics. From this perspective, further study of Anne Finch (1661–1720), Anne Killigrew (1660–85), and Mary Leapor (1722–46), among others, may yield additional insights into the workings of early modern socio-sexual dynamics.

We have at once to understand the possibilities of human sexual response within the broadly inclusive parameters of a diffuse eroticism and the pervasive social constraints (including gender constructions) within which this eroticism must be contained. That early modern negotiations of erotic relations were different from our own is certain. But our recent knowledge of the neurological and psychodynamic underpinnings of sexual behavior, and our ability to incorporate them alongside an understanding of the fluidity of eroticisms that may or may not include what we commonly understand as genital sexuality, may offer tools that we can use for more precise historical reconstructions than we have so far been able to accomplish.

"You're certainly a lot less fun since the operation."

Figure 13.1 "You're certainly a lot less fun since the operation," by Gahan Wilson. © The New Yorker Collection 2002 Gahan Wilson from cartoonbank.com. All Rights Reserved.

Notes

1. Audre Lorde, "Uses of the Erotic: The Erotic as Power," in her *Sister Outsider: Essays and Speeches*, Trumansburg, NY: Crossing Press, 1984, pp. 53–9.
2. Louise J. Kaplan, *Female Perversions: The Temptations of Emma Bovary*, New York: Doubleday, 1991, p. 170.
3. Stephen Guy-Bray, *Bulletin of the Shakespeare Association of America* (June 2006), 4.
4. Both *American Heritage* and *Roget's* are available at www.bartleby.com. How the electronic availability of linguistic material may narrow or shape language use is being investigated by language specialists.
5. See as well the popular program WordPerfect, which includes "amorous" and "passionate," but also "sexual," "carnal," "concupiscent," "lecherous," "lustful," "aphrodisiac," "seductive," "titillating," "immodest," "indecent," and "suggestive."
6. The *OED* also lists one early modern example of the obsolete "erotical," "of the nature of, or pertaining to, sexual love." Other examples, including the variants "erotically" and "eroticism," are all from the nineteenth century.
7. See *OED* for further cognates of "erotic." Most, such as "eroticism," "erotism," and "erotize," apparently arose in the later nineteenth or early twentieth centuries and reflect medical and psychological developments. However, *OED* examples do not reliably date word origins.
8. See Harriette Andreadis, *Sappho in Early Modern England: Female Same-Sex Literary Erotics, 1550–1713*, Chicago and London: University of Chicago Press, 2001, pp. 1–24, for a slightly different but more extensively developed argument about sexual self-understandings during the early modern period. Valerie Traub has explored in detail the possible early modern associations between tribadism and the hypertrophied clitoris in "The Psychomorphology of the Clitoris," *GLQ*, 2 (1995), 81–113.
9. Harriette Andreadis, "The Sapphic-Platonics of Katherine Philips, 1632–1664," *Signs*, 15 (1989), 34–60, esp. 39.
10. Susan Elizabeth Wahl, *Invisible Relations: Representations of Female Intimacy in the Age of Enlightenment*, Stanford, CA, and London: Stanford University Press, 1999, p. 303 n. 53. Wahl also raises the related issue of the presumably confused conflation of "erotic" and "platonic." I read "platonic" to mean "not culminating in genital activity"; that is, as possibly "erotic" but not necessarily "sexual."
11. Ibid., pp. 151–2.
12. Ruth Perry, *The Celebrated Mary Astell*, Chicago and London: University of Chicago Press, 1986, p. 141, uses this phrase to describe Mary Astell's expression of her feelings toward other women but to deny Astell's sexual interest in them.
13. Andreadis, *Sappho in Early Modern England*, p. 58. The genital definition of sexuality persists into the present and underlies the question still asked of lesbians, "What do you *do*?," a question whose subtext is "What *can* you do (without a penis)?"
14. At Mount Holyoke College on 25 Aug. Originally published as a pamphlet by Out & Out Books (Crossing Press).
15. I am acutely aware of the limitations of these generalizations, but I also want to call attention to what I believe are powerful cultural trends that are by no means monolithic or singular in the ways they develop and proceed.
16. By now, well into the first decade of the twenty-first century, with the rise of fundamentalism and its right-wing apologists in the United States, we are seeing the gradual reintroduction of the barriers to sex, even to the extent of making access to contraceptives more difficult, so that a culture of sexualized freedoms now coexists side by side with an increasingly vehement, sometimes paranoid, and active culture of repression.
17. See Catharine Stimpson, "Zero Degree Deviancy: The Lesbian Novel in English," in Elizabeth Abel (ed.), *Writing and Sexual Difference*, Chicago: University of Chicago Press,

1982, pp. 243–59; and Adrienne Rich, "Compulsory Heterosexuality and Lesbian Existence," *Signs*, 5 (1980), 631–60.

18. Cf. Thomas Kuhn, *The Structure of Scientific Revolutions*, Chicago and London: University of Chicago Press, 1970, on how paradigms that can no longer accommodate discordant information or facts are replaced with new ones that can account for that initially alien information.

19. Cf. Andreadis, *Sappho in Early Modern England*, pp. 14–15, 95–6.

20. Lanser and Haggerty emphasized this as a crucial issue for future scholarship at the 1998 meeting of the Group for Early Modern Cultural Studies in Newport, RI. See also Susan S. Lanser, "Befriending the Body: Female Intimacies as Class Acts," *Eighteenth-Century Studies*, 32/2 (1998), 179–87; and George E. Haggerty, *Unnatural Affections: Women and Fiction in the Later 18th Century*, Bloomington and London: Indiana University Press, 1998.

21. Helkiah Crooke, *Microcosmographia: A Description of the Body of Man*, London: Thomas and Richard Cotes, 1631, sig. Y5v. 1st edn 1615.

22. See Ian Maclean, *The Renaissance Notion of Woman: A Study in the Fortunes of Scholasticism and Medical Science in European Intellectual Life*, Cambridge and New York: Cambridge University Press, 1980, pp. 28–46; and Thomas Laqueur, "Orgasm, Generation, and the Politics of Reproductive Biology," in Catherine Gallagher and Laqueur (eds), *The Making of the Modern Body*, Berkeley and London: University of California Press, 1987, pp. 1–41.

23. See Lanser, "Befriending the Body," and Valerie Traub, *The Renaissance of Lesbianism in Early Modern England*, Cambridge: Cambridge University Press, 2002. This is similar to, though not quite the same as, the "lesbian-like" descriptor used by Judith Bennett, "'Lesbian-Like' and the Social History of Lesbianisms," *Journal of the History of Sexuality*, 9 (2000), 1–24; and by Martha Vicinus, "Lesbian History: All Theory and No Facts or All Facts and No Theory?," *Radical History Review*, 60 (1994), 57–75. On female same-sex nomenclature, see Andreadis, *Sappho in Early Modern England*, pp. 3–5 and 49–51, and Terry Castle, *The Apparitional Lesbian: Female Homosexuality and Modern Culture*, New York: Columbia University Press, 1993, p. 9. "Sapphist" apparently became a more popular, and perhaps favored, term later on in the late eighteenth and nineteenth centuries.

24. Kenneth Borris (ed.), *Same-Sex Desire in the English Renaissance: A Sourcebook of Texts, 1470–1650*, New York and London: Routledge, 2004, provides evidence that "lesbian" in our modern sense was used on the Continent during the Renaissance. An excerpt from Brantôme's *Les vies des dames galantes* suggests that this usage was familiar to readers. However, a close reading of the passage indicates that, while "tribade" was the word used to describe women engaged exclusively in same-sex sexual activity, "lesbian" may have indicated women who were interested in sexual activity with men as well (p.18 and pp. 298–305, esp. 305).

25. In framing my argument this way, I follow (though I do not necessarily or always subscribe to) the perspective of the social sciences that individuals cannot be described in ways they do not themselves employ for purposes of self-identity.

26. See V. S. Ramachandran and Sandra Blakeslee, *Phantoms in the Brain*, New York: Quill, 1999.

27. Jeffrey M. Schwartz and Sharon Begley, *The Mind and the Brain: Neuroplasticity and the Power of Mental Force*, New York: Regan Books, 2002, describe the extensive, and fascinating, history of animal experiments that led to Schwartz's own work with obsessive-compulsive disorder patients and stroke victims.

28. Sandy Stone is on the faculty at the University of Texas at Austin. This account describes her performance, "Your Words, my Silent Mouth," in conjunction with "Silence and Expression: Histories of Permission and Censorship," a conference sponsored by the Center for Humanities Research at Texas A&M University, 30 March–2 April 2000.

29. Citations from Shakespeare refer to Stephen Greenblatt *et al.* (eds), *The Norton Shakespeare*, New York: Norton, 1997.

30. Stephen Booth, *Shakespeare's Sonnets*, New Haven and London: Yale University Press, 1977, pp. 438–9.

31. Other familiar examples that appear throughout early modern drama and poetry are elaborate erotic tropes that use the lute or the virginals to metaphorize erotic play.

32. See Andreadis, *Sappho in Early Modern England*, pp. 39–53, for a detailed account of the changes that took place as these texts were translated from Latin into English.

33. Thomas Bartholin, *Bartholinus Anatomy*, London: Nicholas Culpepper & Abdiah Cole, 1663, sig. Z2r–v. 1st edn 1653.

34. Neither I nor others have been able to find additional printed occurrences of "rubsters"; but its failure to appear in printed texts should not be surprising since it is likely to have been a mostly verbal usage or street slang.

35. Bartholin, *Bartholinus Anatomy*, sig. Aa1.

36. These later materials are surveyed by Peter Wagner, "The Discourse on Sex – or Sex as Discourse: Eighteenth-Century Medical and Paramedical Erotica," in G. S. Rousseau and Roy Porter (eds), *Sexual Underworlds of the Enlightenment*, Chapel Hill, NC: University of North Carolina Press, 1988, pp. 46–68.

37. See Kaplan's definition of "perversion" as a psychological strategy that demands a performance: "the perverse strategy *is* to divert attention away from the underlying or latent motives, fantasies, wishes, and desires" (*Female Perversions*, p. 10). For Kaplan, the pervert strives to achieve an exaggerated gender stereotype, so that "perversions . . . are as much pathologies of gender role identity as they are pathologies of sexuality" (ibid., p. 14).

38. Ibid., p. 182.

39. See Andreadis, *Sappho in Early Modern England*, pp. 55–75.

Index